Collected Classics

Volume 2

Level 5

Pearson Education Limited
Edinburgh Gate, Harlow,
Essex CM20 2JE, England
and Associated Companies throughout the world.

ISBN 0 582 343658

This collection of classics first published 2000

Typeset by Refine Catch, Suffolk
Set in 11/14pt Bembo
Printed in Spain by Mateu Cromo, S. A. Pinto (Madrid)

Published by Pearson Education Limited in association with
Penguin Books Ltd, both companies being subsidiaries of Pearson Plc

Contents

Pride and Prejudice

JANE AUSTEN

Level 5

Retold by Evelyn Attwood
Series Editors: Andy Hopkins and Jocelyn Potter

Contents

Introduction

Jane Austen was born in Steventon, Hampshire, in the south of England, in 1775. She was the seventh of eight children of George Austen, the minister of Steventon Church, and his wife Cassandra Leigh, whose father was also a church minister. Jane spent the first 25 years of her life at home in Steventon, where she learnt French, Italian, music and needlework. She was taught by her father, who encouraged her to read widely. The family also enjoyed performing plays, and it seems that Jane took part in these. She began writing at the age of fourteen as entertainment for her family.

When George Austen left his post in 1801, the family moved to Bath, a city which often features in Jane Austen's stories. When he died four years later, Jane moved back to Hampshire with her mother and sister and lived there until her death at the age of forty-one. The last few years of her life were affected by the development of the disease from which she died, and the suffering it caused her.

Jane Austen's life was an uneventful one, although some of her relatives led more exciting lives. She never married; she received proposals of marriage, though, and accepted one of them before changing her mind the next day. She was very close to her family, and in particular to her sister Cassandra, who also remained single. It seems that this quiet, ordered existence was necessary to Jane in order that she could write. She wrote very little while living in Bath, which was a relatively unsettled period in her life.

The restricted life that Jane Austen led had a strong influence on the subject matter of her stories, all of which deal with the everyday lives and concerns of middle-class people living in the countryside and towns of England. These people are anxious, above all, about their own and others' social position, about affairs of the heart and marriage. Austen's particular skill is the careful and humorous way in which she explores every detail of their lives. A strong sense of morality underlies her work, which makes it even more powerful. This moral sense is shown through Austen's description of her characters' behaviour; the writer's beliefs are not stated openly.

Austen's early writing often made gentle fun of popular fiction of the time. *Love and Friendship*, her first book (completed in 1790), was not very kind to those writers who scorned emotional self-control. *Northanger Abbey* was written at the same time, but only appeared after her death. The main character in this book reads a great deal, and as a result confuses literature with real life. *Sense and Sensibility* was begun in 1797 but did not appear in print until 1811. This book, *Pride and Prejudice* (1813), *Emma* (1816) and *Persuasion* (1817) are Austen's best-known works; they all deal in sharply and humorously observed detail with the manners and morals of one small social group. A more deeply serious work is *Mansfield Park* (1814); this has never been as popular with the reading public as the others, but to many it is the height of her achievement. Austen's novels were fairly popular in her lifetime, but it was only after her death that they achieved great success and that she was really given the respect she deserved.

Pride and Prejudice was originally written under the title *First Impressions*. Austen then rewrote the book as *Pride and Prejudice*, which appeared in 1813 and became probably the most popular of her works. Austen herself loved the book, calling it "my own darling child", and she was very fond of Elizabeth Bennet, the story's main character.

It was very important at that time for young women of a certain class to marry well, since they had no money or property of their own and were completely dependent on their fathers first and then on their husbands. The story shows how various characters choose their marriage partners, and the mistakes they make along the way. The underlying message is that it is not enough to marry for money alone; this will lead to unhappiness. Correct and polite behaviour is another important subject, but Austen shows that an honest and honourable nature is more important than social rules which are followed only on the surface.

Mrs Bennet's chief anxiety is her urgent need to find good husbands for all five of her daughters. So when a rich, unmarried young man rents a large house in the neighbourhood, her excitement reaches new heights; she is determined that Mr Bingley should marry one of the girls. He does in fact seem to be attracted to her oldest daughter, the calm and lovely Jane, but their relationship is not in fact an easy one. Mr Bingley has a rich friend named Darcy who begins to admire Jane's lively and amusing sister Elizabeth. On first sight, though, Elizabeth finds Mr Darcy much too proud and scornful of the company in which he finds himself, and she wants nothing to do with him. Gradually these four young people get to know each other, and themselves, much better, and they are often surprised by the discoveries they make.

Chapter 1   The Bennets

It is, of course, generally accepted that a wealthy single man must be in search of a wife. As soon as such a man moves into a neighbourhood, each of the families that live there will, without any inquiry as to his own feelings on the subject, immediately consider him the rightful property of one of their daughters.

'My dear Mr Bennet,' said Mrs Bennet to her husband one day, 'have you heard that Netherfield Park has been rented at last?'

Mr Bennet replied that he had not.

'But it has,' she repeated. 'Mrs Long has just been here, and she told me all about it.'

Mr Bennet made no answer.

'Do you not want to know who has taken it?' cried his wife impatiently.

'You want to tell me, and I have no objection to hearing it.'

This was quite enough encouragement.

'Well, my dear, Mrs Long says that Netherfield has been taken by a rich young man from the north of England, that he came down on Monday to see the place and was so pleased with it that he agreed to take possession immediately, and that some of his servants are to be in the house by the end of the week.'

'What is his name?'

'Bingley.'

'Is he married or single?'

'Oh, single, my dear! An unmarried man of large fortune – four or five thousand pounds a year. What a fine thing for our girls!'

'And why is that? What difference does it make to them?'

'My dear Mr Bennet,' replied his wife, 'how can you be so

annoying? You must know that I am thinking of his marrying one of them.'

'Is that his intention in settling here?'

'Intention? Nonsense, how can you talk like that! But it is likely that he may fall in love with one of them, and therefore you must visit him as soon as he comes.'

'I see no reason for that. You and the girls may go, or, even better, you may send them by themselves, because as you are as good-looking as any of them, Mr Bingley might like you the best of the party.'

'My dear, you praise me too highly. I certainly *have* had my share of beauty, but when a woman has five grown-up daughters, she ought to give up thinking of her own appearance. But you must go and see Mr Bingley when he comes.'

'I cannot promise to do so.'

'But consider your daughters. You must go, because it will be impossible for us to visit him if you do not.'

'You are too anxious to do what is proper, surely. I dare say Mr Bingley will be very glad to see you, and I will send him a few words by you to inform him of my complete agreement to his marrying whichever of the girls he chooses, though I must throw in a good word for my little Lizzy.'

'I hope you will do no such thing. Lizzy is not a bit better than the others, but you are always showing a preference for her.'

'They have none of them much about them to admire,' he replied. 'They are all silly and empty-headed like other girls, but Lizzy is a little more intelligent than her sisters.'

'Mr Bennet, how can you speak of your own daughters in such a way? You take pleasure in annoying me. You have no pity on my poor nerves.'

'You are mistaken, my dear. I have a high respect for your nerves. They are my old friends. I have been listening to news of them for the last 20 years.'

'Ah! You do not know how I suffer.'

Mr Bennet was such a strange mixture of cleverness, sharp humour, silence and unexpected changes of mind, that the experience of 23 years had not been long enough to make his wife understand his character. Her mind was less difficult to understand. She was a foolish woman. When she was anxious, she imagined herself to be ill. The business of her life was to get her daughters married; its pleasure was visiting and news.

Chapter 2   New Neighbours at Netherfield

Mr Bennet was among the first of those who visited Mr Bingley. He had always intended to do so, though he continued to let his wife believe that he would not go. He finally made his intentions known in the following way.

Watching his second daughter occupied in sewing a coloured band around a hat, he suddenly addressed her with:

'I hope Mr Bingley will like it, Lizzy.'

'We are not in a position to know *what* Mr Bingley likes,' said her mother bitterly, 'if we are not to visit him.'

'But you forget, mother,' said Elizabeth, 'that we shall meet him at the public balls, and that Mrs Long has promised to introduce him.'

'I do not believe Mrs Long will do any such thing. She has two nieces of her own. She is a selfish, insincere woman, and I have no opinion of her.'

'Neither have I,' said Mr Bennet, 'and I am glad to find that you do not depend on her serving you.'

Mrs Bennet would not make any reply, but, unable to control her annoyance, began complaining to one of her daughters.

'Don't keep coughing so, Kitty! Have a little pity on my poor nerves.'

11

'Kitty lacks judgment in her coughs,' said her father. 'She chooses the wrong moment.'

'I do not cough for my own amusement,' replied Kitty. 'When is your next ball to be, Lizzy?'

'In two weeks from tomorrow.'

'So it is,' cried her mother, 'and Mrs Long does not come back until the day before, so it will be impossible for her to introduce him, because she will not know him herself.'

'Then, my dear, you may have the advantage of your friend, and introduce Mr Bingley to *her*.'

'Impossible, Mr Bennet, impossible, when I am not acquainted with him myself. How can you be so annoying!'

'Well, if you will not perform this duty, I will do it myself.'

The girls looked at their father. Mrs Bennet said: 'Nonsense, nonsense! I am sick of Mr Bingley.'

'I am sorry to hear that, but why did you not tell me so before? If I had known it this morning, I certainly would not have gone to see him. It is very unlucky, but as I have actually paid the visit, we cannot escape the acquaintance now.'

The astonishment of the ladies was just what he wished, that of Mrs Bennet being perhaps beyond the rest, though when the first excitement was over, she began to say that it was what she had expected all the time.

'How good it was of you! I was sure you loved your girls too well to neglect such an acquaintance. Well, how pleased I am! And it is such a good joke, too, that you went this morning, and never said a word about it until now.'

'Now, Kitty, you may cough as much as you choose,' said Mr Bennet, as he left the room, having had enough of his wife's talk.

'What an excellent father you have, girls,' she said, when the door was shut. 'I do not know how you will ever repay him for his kindness. At our time of life, it is not so pleasant, I can tell you, to be making new acquaintances every day, but for our dear daughters we would do anything. Lydia, my love, though you are the youngest, I dare say Mr Bingley will dance with you at the next ball.'

'Oh,' said Lydia confidently, 'I am not afraid. Though I am the youngest, I'm the tallest.'

The rest of the evening was spent discussing how soon Mr Bingley would return Mr Bennet's visit, and deciding when they should ask him to dinner.

◆

All that Mrs Bennet, together with her five daughters, could ask on the subject, was not enough to draw from her husband any satisfactory description of Mr Bingley. They were forced at last to accept the second-hand information of their neighbour, Lady Lucas. Her report was highly favourable. He was quite young, very good-looking, extremely agreeable, and, in addition to all this, he planned to be at the next public ball. Nothing could be more exciting!

In a few days Mr Bingley returned Mr Bennet's visit, and sat for about ten minutes with him in the library. He had hoped to see the young ladies, of whose beauty he had heard a great deal, but he saw only the father. The ladies were more fortunate. They had the advantage of observing, from an upstairs window, that he wore a blue coat and rode a black horse.

An invitation to dinner was sent soon after, and Mrs Bennet had already planned the meal that was to show the quality of her housekeeping, when an answer arrived which changed everything. Mr Bingley found it necessary to be in London the following day, and was therefore unable to accept the honour of their invitation. Mrs Bennet was both disappointed and worried. She began to fear that he might always be flying about from one place to another, and never settled in Netherfield as he ought to be. Lady Lucas quietened her fears a little by spreading the word that he had gone to London only to collect a large party for the ball, and a report soon followed that Mr Bingley would bring twelve ladies and seven gentlemen with him. The girls were unhappy at the thought of such a large number of ladies, but were comforted to find, when the party entered the ballroom, that it was in fact made up of only five altogether: Mr Bingley, his two sisters, the husband of the older one, and another young man.

Mr Bingley was good-looking and gentlemanly. His sisters were fine women dressed in the latest fashions. His sister's husband, Mr Hurst, simply looked like the gentleman he was, but Mr Darcy soon drew the attention of everyone by his fine tall form, noble face, and the report, which was passed round the room within five minutes of his entrance, that he had an income of ten thousand pounds a year. He was looked at with admiration for half the evening, until his manners caused a general disgust which ended his popularity.

Mr Bingley had soon made himself acquainted with all the important people in the room. He danced every dance, was angry that the ball closed so early, and talked of giving one himself at Netherfield. What a difference between himself and his friend! Mr Darcy danced only once with Mrs Hurst and once with Miss Bingley, refused to be introduced to any other lady, and spent the rest of the evening walking around the room. Mrs Bennet's dislike of his behaviour was sharpened by his having made one of her daughters appear neglected.

Elizabeth Bennet had been forced, by the small number of gentlemen, to sit out for two dances, and during part of that time Mr Darcy had been standing near enough for her to hear, against her will, a conversation between him and Mr Bingley, who left the dancing for a few minutes to urge his friend to join in.

'Come, Darcy,' he said, 'I hate to see you standing around by yourself like this. You really should be dancing.'

'I certainly shall not. Both your sisters already have partners, and there is not another woman in the room with whom I would care to dance.'

'I would not like to be so difficult to please as you are,' cried Bingley. 'I have never met with so many pleasant girls in my life.'

'You are dancing with the only good-looking one,' said Mr Darcy, looking at the oldest Miss Bennet.

'Oh, she is the most beautiful creature that I ever saw! But there is one of her sisters sitting down just behind you, who is very attractive and probably very agreeable. Do let me ask my partner to introduce you.'

'Which do you mean?' Darcy asked. Turning round, he looked for a moment at Elizabeth, until, catching her eye, he looked away and coldly said: 'She is fairly pretty, but not good-looking enough.'

He walked off, and Elizabeth remained with no very friendly feelings towards him. But she told the story with great spirit among her friends, because she had a playful nature and a strong sense of humour.

The evening on the whole passed off pleasantly for all the family. Mrs Bennet had seen her oldest daughter much admired by the Netherfield party. Mr Bingley had danced with her twice, and she had been an object of attention by his sisters. Jane was as much pleased by this as her mother, though in a quieter way. Elizabeth shared Jane's pleasure, as she always did. Lydia and Kitty had never been without partners, and Mary, the least pretty of the family, had heard herself praised to Miss Bingley as a skilled musician.

They returned, therefore, in good spirits to Longbourn, the village in Hertfordshire where they lived, and of which they were the most important family.

◆

Within a short walk of Longbourn there lived a family with whom the Bennets were especially friendly. Sir William Lucas had formerly been in trade in the town of Meryton, where he had made a fairly large fortune and risen to the honour of a title of rank. This honour had, perhaps, been felt too strongly. It had given him a disgust for his business and for his home in a small market town, and, leaving them both, he had moved with his family to a house about a mile from Meryton, which he called Lucas Lodge. But though proud of his rank, he was friendly and ready to help anyone who needed it. Lady Lucas was a very good kind of woman, not too clever to be a valuable neighbour to Mrs Bennet. They had several children. The oldest of them, a sensible young woman of about twenty-seven, was Elizabeth's special friend.

It was a time-honoured tradition for the Misses Lucas and the Misses Bennet to meet and talk after a ball, and so the following morning brought the former to Longbourn for that purpose.

'You began the evening well, Charlotte,' said Mrs Bennet, with forced politeness, to Miss Lucas. 'You were Mr Bingley's first choice.'

'Yes, but he seemed to like his second better.'

'Oh, you mean Jane, I suppose, because he danced with her twice. Certainly that did seem as if he admired her. It *does* seem as if – but it may not lead to anything, you know.'

'But Mr Darcy is not so worth listening to as his friend, is he?' said Charlotte. 'Poor Eliza! To be only just *fairly* pretty!'

'I hope you will not put it into Lizzy's head to be annoyed by his rude treatment. He is such a disagreeable man that it would be quite a misfortune to be liked by him. Mrs Long told me last night that he sat next to her for half an hour without once opening his lips.'

'Are you quite sure, madam? Is there not some mistake?' said Jane. 'I certainly saw Mr Darcy speaking to her.'

'Yes, because she finally asked him how he liked Netherfield, and he could not help answering her, but she said he seemed very angry at being spoken to.'

'Miss Bingley told me,' said Jane, 'that he never speaks much except among people he knows well. With them he is extremely agreeable.'

'I do not believe a word of it, my dear.'

'I do not mind his not talking to Mrs Long,' said Miss Lucas, 'but I wish he had danced with Eliza.'

'Another time, Lizzy,' said her mother, 'I would not dance with him, if I were you.'

'His pride,' said Miss Lucas, 'does not offend me so much as pride often does, because there is an excuse for it. One cannot be surprised that such a fine young man with family and fortune should think highly of himself.'

'That is very true,' replied Eliza, 'and I could easily forgive his pride, if he had not wounded *mine*.'

Chapter 3   Jane Gains an Admirer

The ladies of Longbourn soon visited those of Netherfield. The visit was formally returned. Miss Bennet's pleasing manners continued to win the approval of Mrs Hurst and Miss Bingley, and though the mother was considered to be unbearable, and the younger sisters not worth speaking to, a wish was expressed to be better acquainted with the two oldest. This attention was received by Jane with the greatest pleasure, but Elizabeth saw pride in their treatment of everybody, even her sister, and could not like them. But it was plain that their brother *did* admire Jane, and Elizabeth observed that Jane was giving way to the preference which she had begun to feel for him from the first, and was beginning to be very much in love.

While Elizabeth was watching Mr Bingley's attentions to her sister, she did not realize that she herself was becoming an object of some interest in the eyes of his friend. Mr Darcy had at first hardly admitted her to be pretty; he had seen her without admiration at the ball, and when they next met, he looked at her only to criticize. But he had no sooner decided that no single part of her face was particularly attractive than he began to find that the whole was made uncommonly intelligent by the beautiful expression of her dark eyes. She was completely unconscious of this. To her, he was only the man who had made himself agreeable nowhere, and who had not thought her attractive enough to dance with.

He began to wish to know her better.

One day, a large party was amusing itself at Sir William Lucas's. A number of young ladies, and two or three army officers, were occupied in dancing at one end of the room. Mr Darcy stood near them, and Sir William was trying to make conversation with him. As Elizabeth moved towards them at this moment, Sir William was struck with the idea of doing the polite thing, and called out to her:

'My dear Miss Eliza, why are you not dancing? Mr Darcy, you must allow me to present this young lady to you as a very desirable partner. You cannot refuse to dance, I am sure, when so much beauty is in front of you.' And, taking her hand, he would have given it to Mr Darcy, who, though extremely surprised, was not unwilling to receive it, when she immediately pulled away, and said in some confusion to Sir William:

'Sir, I have not the least intention of dancing. Please do not suppose that I moved this way in order to beg for a partner.'

Mr Darcy, with great politeness, requested to be allowed the honour of her hand, but without success. Elizabeth was determined, and Sir William's attempt at persuasion met with no success.

'You are such an excellent dancer, Miss Eliza, that it is cruel to refuse me the happiness of seeing you, and though this gentleman dislikes the amusement in general, he can have no objection, I am sure, to doing us this honour for one half-hour.'

'Mr Darcy is all politeness,' said Elizabeth smiling. She turned away. Her refusal had not harmed her in the gentleman's opinion, and he thought of her with some admiration.

◆

The village of Longbourn was only one mile from the town of Meryton – a most convenient distance for the young ladies, who usually went there three or four times a week to make a visit to an aunt, Mrs Philips, who was married to a lawyer, and to look at a hat shop just over the way. The two youngest of the family, Catherine and Lydia, were particularly frequent in these attentions. They always managed to learn some news, and at present they were well supplied by the arrival of a regiment in the neighbourhood, which would remain for the whole winter. They could talk of nothing but officers.

After listening one morning to their excited remarks on this subject, Mr Bennet sharply observed:

'From all that I can understand from your manner of talking, you must be two of the silliest girls in the country.'

Kitty was a little ashamed, and did not answer, but Lydia laughed loudly.

'I am astonished, my dear,' said Mrs Bennet, 'that you should be so ready to think your own children silly. As a matter of fact, they are all very clever.'

'This is the only point on which we do not agree.'

Mrs Bennet was prevented from replying by the entrance of a servant with a note for Miss Bennet. It came from Netherfield. Mrs Bennet's eyes brightened with pleasure, and she called out eagerly, while her daughter read:

'Well, Jane, who is it from? What is it about? What does he say? Well, Jane, hurry up and tell us.'

'It is from Miss Bingley,' said Jane, and then read it aloud:

NETHERFIELD PARK
10th October

My dear Jane,

Will you be so kind as to come to dinner today with Louisa and me? We are all alone. Come as soon as you can on receiving this. My brother and the gentlemen are to have dinner with the officers.

Yours ever,
CAROLINE BINGLEY.

'Having dinner out,' said Mrs Bennet, 'that is very unlucky.'

'Can I have the carriage?' asked Jane.

'No, my dear, you had better go on horseback, because it seems likely to rain and then you must stay all night.'

'That would be a good idea,' said Elizabeth, 'if you were sure that they would not offer to send her home.'

'Oh, but the gentlemen will have used Mr Bingley's carriage to go to Meryton.'

'I would much rather go in the carriage,' repeated Jane.

'But, my dear, your father does not have enough horses. They are wanted on the farm.'

Jane was therefore forced to go on horseback, and her mother followed her to the door with many cheerful wishes for bad weather. Her hopes were answered. Jane had not been gone long before it rained hard. Her sisters were anxious for her, but her mother was pleased. The rain continued the whole evening. Jane certainly could not come back.

'This was a good idea of mine!' said Mrs Bennet.

Breakfast was hardly over next morning when a servant from

Netherfield brought a note for Elizabeth from Jane to say that she was unwell.

'Well, my dear,' said Mr Bennet, when Elizabeth had read the note out loud, 'if your daughter should have a dangerous attack of illness – if she should die – it will be a comfort to know that it was all the result of going after Mr Bingley, and following your orders.'

'Oh, I am not afraid of her dying. People do not die of little things like colds. They will take good care of her.'

Elizabeth, feeling really anxious, decided to go to her sister. The carriage was not available, and as she did not ride a horse, walking was her only possible way.

'How can you be so silly,' said her mother, 'in all this mud! You will not be fit to be seen when you get there.'

'I shall be very fit to see Jane, which is all I want.'

'We will go as far as Meryton with you,' offered Lydia and Kitty. Elizabeth accepted their company, and the three young ladies set off together.

At Meryton they parted, and Elizabeth continued her walk alone, crossing field after field impatiently, and finding herself at last within sight of the house, with tired feet, dirty shoes, and a face bright with the warmth of exercise.

Her appearance caused a great deal of surprise. Elizabeth guessed that Mrs Hurst and Miss Bingley were scornful that she should walk 3 miles so early and in such weather. She was received, though, very politely, and in their brother's manner was something better than politeness – kindness and pleasure. Mr Darcy said very little. He was occupied with admiring the brightness that exercise had added to the colour in her face.

Her sister Jane had hardly slept at all, and was feverish. The doctor came, advised her to return to bed, and promised some medicine. The fever increased, and her head ached badly.

Elizabeth stayed with her until three o'clock, and then felt she must go. But Jane showed such disappointment at parting from her that Miss Bingley was forced to invite her to remain at Netherfield for the present, and Elizabeth thankfully accepted this offer. A servant was sent to Longbourn to tell the family of her stay and to bring back a supply of clothes.

◆

At half past six, Elizabeth was called to dinner. Jane was not at all better. Mr Bingley's sisters, on hearing this, repeated three or four times how sorry they were, how unpleasant it was to have a bad cold, and how very much they disliked being ill themselves, and then thought no more of the matter. Their lack of real feeling towards Jane, when she was not actually in their presence, brought back to Elizabeth all her original dislike of them.

Their brother was in fact the only one whose anxiety for Jane seemed sincere. His attentions to Elizabeth herself were most pleasing, and they prevented her from feeling herself such an unwelcome guest as she believed she was considered to be by the others.

When dinner was over, she returned directly to Jane, and Miss Bingley began criticizing her as soon as she was out of the room. How poor her manners were – a mixture of pride and lack of good family. She had no powers of conversation, no style, no taste, no beauty. Mrs Hurst thought the same, and added:

'There is nothing to admire in her except being an excellent walker. I shall never forget her appearance this morning. She really looked almost wild.'

'She certainly did, Louisa. Her hair so untidy!'

'Yes, and her skirt! I hope you saw her skirt, covered in mud.'

'I thought Miss Elizabeth Bennet looked extremely well when she came into the room this morning,' said Mr Bingley. 'Her dirty skirt quite escaped my notice. Her coming shows a concern for her sister that is very pleasing.'

'I am afraid, Mr Darcy,' observed Miss Bingley, in a half-whisper, 'that this adventure has rather lessened your admiration for her fine eyes.'

'Not at all,' he replied. 'They were brightened by the exercise.'

A short pause followed this speech, and Mrs Hurst began again:

'I am extremely fond of Jane Bennet. She is really a very sweet girl. I wish with all my heart that she were well settled. But with such parents, and such low relations, I am afraid there is no chance of it.'

'It must greatly lessen her chance of marrying a man of good position,' replied Mr Darcy.

Mr Bingley made no answer to this speech, but his sisters gave it their full agreement, and continued for some time to make fun of their dear friend's inferior relations.

◆

Elizabeth spent most of the night in her sister's room, and in the morning requested that a note be sent to Longbourn, asking her mother to visit Jane and form her own judgment on her condition. The note was immediately sent, and Mrs Bennet, with her two youngest girls, reached Netherfield soon after breakfast.

If Mrs Bennet had found Jane in any real danger, she would have been very upset, but when she was satisfied that her illness was not serious, she had no wish for her immediate recovery, as her return to health would probably remove her from Netherfield. She would not listen, therefore, to her daughter's proposal of being taken home; nor did the doctor, who arrived at about the same time, think it advisable.

Mrs Bennet repeated her thanks to Mr Bingley for his kindness to Jane, with an apology for troubling him also with Lizzy. Mr Bingley was eager that his two guests should remain, and forced his younger sister to be polite too. She did this duty, even if rather unwillingly, but Mrs Bennet was satisfied, and left soon after that.

The day passed much as the day before had done. Jane was slowly recovering. In the evening, Elizabeth joined the company in the sitting room, and took up some needlework. Mr Darcy was writing a letter.

When that business was over, he asked Miss Bingley and Elizabeth to play some music. Miss Bingley moved eagerly to the piano. After a polite request for Elizabeth to begin the performance, which Elizabeth refused with equal politeness, Miss Bingley seated herself.

Mrs Hurst sang with her sister; and while they were employed in this, Elizabeth could not help noticing how frequently Mr Darcy's eyes fixed themselves on her. She could hardly imagine that she could be an object of admiration to so great a man, but it seemed even stranger that he should look at her so, because she knew he disliked her. She could only suppose that she drew his attention because there was something wrong about her. The supposition did not upset her; she liked him too little to care for his opinion.

Soon after, as Miss Bingley began to play a lively Scottish tune, Mr Darcy, approaching Elizabeth, said to her:

'Do you not feel a great desire, Miss Bennet, to seize such an opportunity for a dance?'

She smiled, but made no answer. He repeated the question, with some surprise at her silence.

'Oh,' she said, 'I heard you before, but I could not decide immediately on what to say in reply. You wanted me, I know, to say "Yes", so that you might have the pleasure of thinking badly of my taste, but I always enjoy defeating such intentions. I have, therefore, made up my mind to tell you that I do not want to dance; and now, think badly of me if you dare.'

'I do not dare.'

Elizabeth, having rather expected to offend him, was astonished at his politeness, but there was a mixture of sweetness and intelligence in her manner that made it difficult for her to offend anybody. Darcy had never been so attracted to any woman as he was to her. He really believed that, if it were not for her inferior relations, he would be in some danger of falling in love.

Miss Bingley saw, or thought she saw, enough to be jealous, and her anxiety for the recovery of her dear friend Jane was increased by her desire to get rid of Elizabeth.

As a result of an agreement between the two sisters, Elizabeth wrote the next morning to her mother to beg her to send the carriage for them during that day. Mrs Bennet sent them a reply that they could not possibly have it before Tuesday. But Elizabeth had decided that she could stay no longer, nor did she very much expect that she would be encouraged to. She urged Jane to borrow Mr Bingley's carriage immediately.

The master of the house heard with real sorrow that they were leaving so soon, and repeatedly tried to persuade the older Miss Bennet that it was not safe for her, but Jane was always able to be decisive when she believed herself to be right.

It was welcome news to Mr Darcy. Elizabeth attracted him more than he wished. He decided to be particularly careful that no sign of admiration should now escape him. He kept steadily to his purpose, and hardly spoke to her through the whole of the day, and although they were at one time left by themselves for half an hour, he kept firmly to his book and would not even look at her.

On the next morning, they left for home. They were not welcomed back very gladly by their mother, but their father was really happy to see them. The evening conversation had lost much of its liveliness, and most of its good sense, during the absence of Jane and Elizabeth.

Chapter 4   Mr Collins

'I hope, my dear,' said Mr Bennet to his wife, as they were at breakfast the next morning, 'that you have ordered a good dinner today, because I have reason to expect an addition to our family party.'

'Whom do you mean, my dear? I know of nobody that is coming, I am sure, unless Charlotte Lucas should happen to call, and I hope my dinners are good enough for *her*.'

'The person of whom I speak is a gentleman and a stranger.'

Mrs Bennet's eyes brightened. 'A gentleman and a stranger! It is Mr Bingley, I am sure! Why, Jane, you never mentioned a word about this! But – good heavens! How unlucky! There is not a bit of fish to be got today! Lydia, my love, ring the bell. I must speak to the cook immediately.'

'It is *not* Mr Bingley,' said her husband. 'It is a person whom I have never seen in the whole of my life.'

This caused general astonishment, and he had the pleasure of being eagerly questioned by his wife and all five of his daughters at once.

After amusing himself for some time by not answering their questions, he explained:

'A short time ago I received a letter. It was from my cousin, Mr Collins, who, when I am dead, may put you all out of this house as soon as he pleases.'

Mr Bennet's property was, unfortunately for his daughters, to pass by law after his death to his nearest male relative, a distant cousin.

'Oh, my dear,' cried his wife, 'I cannot bear to hear that mentioned. Please do not talk of that hateful man.' It was a subject on which she could never see reason.

'But if you will listen to his letter, you may perhaps be a little softened by his manner of expressing himself:

Dear Sir,

The disagreement that existed between yourself and my honoured father always caused me much anxiety, and since his death I have frequently wished for a renewal of friendship between our two branches of the family.

My mind is now made up on the subject. I have recently become a minister of the church and I have been fortunate enough to become the object of attention of the Lady Catherine de Bourgh. By her generosity I have been presented with a valuable position in this area, where I shall try to behave with grateful respect towards her.

As a churchman, I feel it to be my duty to encourage peace among all families within my influence, and for these reasons I consider that my offer of friendship is deserving of praise, and that the fact that I am heir to your property will be kindly forgiven by you.

I am troubled at being the means of harming your daughters, and beg to apologize for it, as well as to inform you of my readiness to do what is in my power to lessen the wrong done to them.

If you have no objection to receiving me into your house, I intend to visit you and your family on Monday next week, at four o'clock, and would be thankful to remain as your guest until the Saturday of the following week.

I remain, dear sir, with respectful greetings to your lady and daughters, your well-wisher and friend,

WILLIAM COLLINS.

'At four o'clock, therefore, we may expect this peace-making gentleman,' said Mr Bennet, as he folded up the letter. 'He seems a most dutiful and polite young man.'

'There is some sense in what he says about trying to lessen the harm done to the girls,' his wife agreed.

'Though it is difficult,' said Jane, 'to guess in what way he intends to do so.'

Elizabeth was chiefly struck with his high degree of respect for Lady Catherine. As for her mother, Mr Collins's letter had taken away much of her unfriendly feeling, and she prepared herself to see him with a calmness that astonished her husband and daughters.

◆

Mr Collins arrived on time, and was received with great politeness by the whole family. Mr Bennet said little, but the ladies were ready enough to talk, and Mr Collins seemed very willing to do so himself. He was a tall, heavy-looking young man of about twenty-five. His manner was serious and his behaviour very formal. He had not been seated long before he began to offer his congratulations to Mrs Bennet on having such a fine family of daughters, and to admire their beauty. He added that he did not doubt that she would in time see them all well settled in marriage. This speech was not much to the taste of some of his hearers, but Mrs Bennet answered most readily:

'You are very kind, sir, I am sure, and I wish with all my heart that it may be so, or they will be poor enough. These matters are settled in such a strange way.'

'I am conscious, madam, of the injustice to your lovely daughters, but they may be sure that I have come prepared to admire them. At present I will say no more, but perhaps, when we are better acquainted . . .'

He was interrupted by the announcement of dinner, and the girls smiled at each other. They were not the only objects of Mr Collins's admiration. The hall, the dining room, and all its furniture, were examined and highly praised, and his approval would have touched Mrs Bennet's heart, if she had not believed that he was viewing it all as his own future property. The dinner, too, in its turn, was much admired, and he begged to know which of his cousins had prepared the excellent meal. But here he was corrected by Mrs Bennet, who informed him rather sharply that they could very well afford to keep a good cook, and that her daughters had nothing to do in the kitchen. He begged pardon for having displeased her. She replied in a softer voice that she was not at all offended, but he continued to apologize for about a quarter of an hour.

After dinner, Mr Bennet thought it was time to have some conversation with his guest. He therefore chose a subject on which he expected Mr Collins would be pleased to speak, and began by observing that he seemed very fortunate in receiving such an excellent living from Lady Catherine. Mr Bennet could not have thought of a better beginning. Mr Collins praised her loudly, expressing himself in an extremely respectful manner. By teatime his host had had enough, and was glad to take the young man into the sitting room and invite him to read to the ladies. Mr Collins readily agreed, and a book was produced, but at the sight of it he quickly stated, begging pardon, that he never read works of fiction. Kitty and Lydia looked at him in surprise. Other books were offered, and he chose a collection of writings on matters of religion. Lydia turned away as he opened the book, and before he had, in a dull voice, read three pages, she interrupted to speak to her mother. Her two oldest sisters urged her to hold her tongue, but Mr Collins, much offended, laid the book down.

◆

Mr Collins was not a sensible man, and neither education nor society had improved him much. He was too conscious of his own importance, and, at the same time, too afraid of giving offence, especially to those above him in rank.

A fortunate chance had brought him to the attention of Lady Catherine de Bourgh, when the position at Hunsford became free. Having now a good house and a large enough income, he intended to marry. In ending the quarrel with the Longbourn family, he was thinking of a wife, as he meant to choose one of the daughters. This was his plan of lessening the wrong done to them by his being the heir to their father's property, and he thought it was an extremely generous one.

His plan did not change on seeing them. Miss Jane Bennet's beautiful face soon attracted him, and for the first evening *she* was his settled choice. But the next morning caused a change, because in a quarter of an hour's private talk with Mrs Bennet before breakfast, he received a warning about the cousin whom he had fixed on. 'As to her *younger* daughters, she could not be sure, she could not answer immediately – but her *oldest* daughter, she must just mention, she felt it her duty to state, was likely to be very soon engaged to be married.'

Mr Collins had only to change from Jane to Elizabeth. It was done in a moment. Elizabeth, next to Jane both in birth and beauty, followed her as his choice as a matter of course.

Mrs Bennet was pleased with this suggestion, and trusted that she might soon have two daughters married. The man whom she could not bear to speak of the day before now stood high in her regard.

Chapter 5   Mr Wickham

Lydia intended to walk to Meryton that morning, and every sister except Mary, who preferred to read, agreed to go with her. Mr Collins was their companion, at the request of Mr Bennet, who was most anxious to get rid of him and have his library to himself because his cousin never stopped talking.

The girls listened politely to his remarks until they entered Meryton. The attention of the younger ones was then no longer to be won by *him*. Their eyes were immediately wandering up the street in search of the officers.

But the attention of every lady was soon caught by a young man whom they had never seen before. He was of a most gentlemanly appearance and was walking with an officer on the other side of the road. All were struck by the stranger's manner. Kitty and Lydia knew the officer, and decided to find out who his friend was. They led the way across the street, under pretence of wanting something in a shop opposite, and had just reached the pathway when the two gentlemen arrived at the same place. Mr Denny, the officer, addressed them directly and introduced his friend, Mr Wickham, who had just joined the army.

The young man appeared very pleasant. He was good-looking and he had a fine figure and very pleasing manners. The whole party was still having a pleasant conversation, when the sound of horses drew their attention, and Darcy and Bingley were seen riding down the street. On recognizing the ladies in the group, the two gentlemen came directly towards them, and began the usual polite greetings. Bingley was the chief speaker, and Miss Jane Bennet the chief object. He was then, he said, on his way to Longbourn to inquire after her health. Mr Darcy followed him, and was beginning to decide to keep his eyes away from Elizabeth, when they suddenly became fixed on the stranger. Elizabeth happened to see the faces of both when they looked at each other, and was astonished at the effect of the meeting. The face of one became white, the other turned red. Mr Wickham, after a few moments, touched his hat in greeting, but Mr Darcy seemed hardly to move a finger in return. What could be the meaning of it? It was impossible to imagine, and it was impossible not to want to know the reason for this behaviour.

In another minute, Mr Bingley, who seemed not to have noticed what had happened, said goodbye to the ladies and rode on with his friend.

As they walked home, Elizabeth described to Jane what she had seen pass between the two gentlemen, but Jane could no more explain such behaviour than her sister.

♦

At Meryton the young people had accepted an invitation from their aunt to supper and cards. The carriage took Mr Collins and his five cousins at a suitable hour to the town, and the girls had the pleasure of hearing, as they entered the sitting room, that Mr Wickham had accepted an invitation from their uncle to be present, and was already in the house.

When this information was given, and they had all taken their seats, Mr Collins was free to look around him and talk. To the girls the time of waiting appeared very long, but it was over at last. The gentlemen joined them, and when Mr Wickham walked into the room, Elizabeth felt that she had not been thinking of him with at all unreasonable admiration.

Mr Wickham was the happy man towards whom almost every lady's eye was turned, and Elizabeth was the happy woman by whom he seated himself at last. With such fine men as Mr Wickham and the officers in competition for the attention of the ladies, Mr Collins seemed to sink into unimportance, but he still had from time to time a kind listener in Mrs Philips.

Elizabeth was very willing to hear Mr Wickham talk, though she could not hope to be told what she chiefly wished to hear – the history of his acquaintance with Mr Darcy. But her interest was most unexpectedly satisfied. Mr Wickham began the subject himself. He asked slowly how long Mr Darcy had been staying in the area.

'About a month,' said Elizabeth, and then, unwilling to let the subject drop, she added: 'He is a man of very large property in Derbyshire, I believe.'

'Yes,' replied Wickham, 'Pemberley, his property there, is a noble one — at least ten thousand a year. You could not have met with a person better able to give you information about it than myself. I have been connected with his family since my birth.'

Elizabeth could not help looking surprised.

'You may well be surprised, Miss Bennet, at such a statement, after seeing the very cold manner of our meeting yesterday. Do you know Mr Darcy well?'

'Quite as well as I ever wish to do,' cried Elizabeth warmly. 'I have spent several days in the same house with him, and I find him very disagreeable.'

'I cannot pretend to be sorry,' said Wickham, after a short pause. 'His behaviour to me has been shameful. I could have forgiven him anything, though, except for his disappointing the hopes of his father and bringing shame on his memory.'

Elizabeth's interest in the subject increased.

'I was educated for the Church,' continued Mr Wickham, 'and Mr Darcy's father left me, on his death, the best living to which he had the power to make an appointment, as soon as it became free. He was my godfather and he was very fond of me. He thought that he had provided for my future, but the living was given to somebody else.'

'Good heavens!' said Elizabeth. 'But surely that was against the law?'

'My godfather's wishes were not expressed clearly. Mr Darcy treated his father's words as a suggestion with certain conditions connected with it, and claimed that I had no right to the living because of some imagined wrongdoings of mine. But the fact is that he hates me.'

'This is quite shameful! He deserves that the truth should be made public.'

'Until I can forget his father, I can never be the means of shaming the son.'

Elizabeth honoured him for such feelings.

'We were born in the same place, and brought up together. My father managed the late Mr Darcy's affairs, and gave all his time to the care of his property.'

'I am surprised that Mr Darcy's pride has not made him fairer to you. I should have thought that he would have been too proud to be dishonest.'

'It is surprising,' replied Wickham, 'because his pride has often caused him to be generous, to give his money freely, to be an excellent host and a kind landowner, and to do good to the poor. He also has brotherly pride. He looks after his sister very well.'

'What sort of a girl is Miss Darcy?'

He shook his head. 'I wish I could call her likeable. But she is too much like her brother – very, very proud.'

'I am astonished at Mr Darcy's friendship with Mr Bingley. How can Mr Bingley, who is so agreeable and friendly to everyone, like such a man? He cannot know what Mr Darcy is.'

'Probably not. But Mr Darcy can please when he wishes. He can be a good companion if he thinks it worth taking the trouble. He is a very different man among those who are his equals in the world.'

Mr Wickham's attention was caught a little later by Mr Collins mentioning the name of Lady Catherine de Bourgh. He asked Elizabeth in a low voice whether her relations were acquainted with the family.

'You know, of course, that Lady Catherine de Bourgh and Lady Anne Darcy were sisters, and therefore she is aunt to the present Mr Darcy. Her daughter, Miss de Bourgh, will have a very large fortune, and it is believed that she and her cousin will unite the two properties by marriage.'

This information made Elizabeth smile, as she thought of Miss Bingley. All that lady's hopes would be disappointed, if he was already promised to another.

Chapter 6   The Ball at Netherfield

Elizabeth repeated to Jane, the next day, what had passed between Mr Wickham and herself. Jane listened with astonishment and concern. She could not believe that Mr Darcy could be so undeserving of Mr Bingley's friendship, but it was not in her nature to question the truthfulness of a young man of such pleasing appearance as Wickham.

'They have both been mistaken, I expect,' she said, 'in some way or other, of which we can form no idea.'

The two young ladies were called from the garden, where this conversation was taking place, by the arrival of some of the persons of whom they had been speaking. Mr Bingley and his sisters came to give their personal invitation for the long-expected ball at Netherfield, which was fixed for the following Tuesday. Miss Bingley and Mrs Hurst appeared very pleased to see their dear friend again, and complained that it was a long time since they had last met. They took very little notice of the rest of the family, avoiding Mrs Bennet as much as possible, saying not much to Elizabeth, and nothing at all to the others.

The thought of the Netherfield ball was exciting to every female of the family. Mrs Bennet considered it to be given as a mark of attention to her oldest daughter, and was particularly pleased at receiving the invitation from Mr Bingley himself, instead of by means of a formal card. Jane pictured to herself a happy evening in the society of her two friends and the attentions of their brother, and Elizabeth thought with pleasure of dancing a great deal with Mr Wickham. The happiness of Kitty and Lydia depended less on any special event or person. All that they wished for was plenty of partners. Even the serious-minded Mary was willing to go.

Elizabeth's spirits were so high that though she did not often speak unnecessarily to Mr Collins, she could not help asking him whether he intended to accept Mr Bingley's invitation. To her surprise, he replied that he would go, and added:

'I shall hope to be honoured in the dance with the hands of all my cousins in the course of the evening, and I take this opportunity of asking for yours, Miss Elizabeth, for the first two dances especially. I trust that my cousin Jane will understand the reasons for this preference, and not think that it is in any way disrespectful to her.'

Elizabeth felt herself completely at a disadvantage. She had fully intended being promised to Wickham for those same dances, and to have Mr Collins instead! Her liveliness had never been expressed at a worse moment. But she could do nothing. Mr Collins's offer was accepted with as much pleasure as she could manage to show. It now first struck her, though, that *she* was chosen from among her sisters as being suitable in his opinion to be his wife at Hunsford Parsonage. The idea was soon strengthened as she observed his increasing politeness to her, and though she herself was more astonished than pleased, it was not long before her mother let her know that the possibility of their marriage was extremely pleasing to *her*. Elizabeth pretended not to understand her, because she knew very well that a serious argument would result from any reply. Mr Collins might never make the offer, and until he did, it was useless to quarrel about him.

If there had not been a ball to get ready for and to talk about, the younger Misses Bennet would have been in a sad state at this time. From the day of the invitation to the day of the ball, continuous rain prevented them from walking to Meryton. No aunt, no officers, no news could be looked for. Even Elizabeth might have found some test of her patience in weather that delayed the development of her acquaintance with Mr Wickham, and nothing less than a dance on Tuesday could have made such a Friday, Saturday, Sunday and Monday bearable to Kitty and Lydia.

♦

On the Tuesday evening, Elizabeth entered the sitting room at Netherfield, and looked without success for Mr Wickham among the group of officers present there. Until then, no doubt about him coming had entered her mind. She had dressed with more care than usual, and readied herself in the highest spirits to complete the winning of his heart. But in a moment the terrible thought came to her that he had been purposely left out of the Bingleys' invitation to the officers, for Mr Darcy's pleasure, and although this was not exactly the case, his friend Mr Denny told them that Wickham had had to go to London on business, and added:

'I do not imagine that he would have gone just now, if he had not wished to avoid a certain gentleman here.'

This information sharpened Elizabeth's feelings of displeasure against Mr Darcy, and although she tried to be cheerful, the first two dances brought a return of unhappiness. Mr Collins, serious and awkward, apologizing instead of paying attention, and often moving wrongly without being conscious of it, brought her all the shame and unhappiness which a disagreeable partner can give.

She danced next with an officer. Then she found herself suddenly addressed by Mr Darcy, who took her so much by surprise in his request for her hand that, without knowing what she did, she accepted him.

Elizabeth took her place in the set, astonished at the honour at which she had arrived in being allowed to stand opposite to Mr Darcy, and seeing in the faces of her neighbours their equal astonishment. They spoke very little until they had finished the dance, when he asked her if she and her sisters did not often walk to Meryton. She answered that this was so, and, unable to stop herself, added, 'When we met you the other day there, we had just been forming a new acquaintance.'

The effect was immediate. The expression on his face became prouder than ever. At last he spoke:

'Mr Wickham is fortunate enough to have such pleasing manners that he can always be sure of *making* friends. It is less certain that he is able to *keep* them.'

'He has been unlucky enough to lose *your* friendship,' replied Elizabeth.

Darcy made no answer, and seemed anxious to change the subject. At that moment Sir William Lucas appeared, and stopped to offer him a mark of attention.

'My dear sir, such very high-class dancing is not often seen. I must hope to have this pleasure often repeated, especially after a certain desirable event,' and he looked towards Jane and Mr Bingley. 'What congratulations will then flow in!'

Sir William's mention of his friend seemed to strike Darcy with some force, and his eyes were directed with a very serious expression towards Bingley and Jane, who were dancing together.

When the dance was over, Miss Bingley came towards Elizabeth, and, with a look of scorn, addressed her as follows:

'So, Miss Eliza, I hear you are quite pleased with George Wickham. But let me warn you not to trust what he says. The story that Mr Darcy has wronged him is completely untrue. He has always been kind to him, though Wickham treated him in a shameful manner. I do not know the details, but I do know that Mr Darcy is not to blame. I pity you, Miss Eliza, but really, considering his family, one could not expect much better.'

'His guilt and his family appear, by your account, to be the same,' said Elizabeth angrily.

'I beg your pardon,' replied Miss Bingley, turning away. 'My words were kindly meant.'

Elizabeth then went in search of her oldest sister, who met her with a smile of such sweet satisfaction that Elizabeth immediately understood her feelings and forgot everything else for the moment in the hope that Jane was on the way to happiness. Jane began to talk about Mr Wickham. 'Mr Bingley does not know the whole of the history, but is sure that his friend has acted rightly and honourably. I am sorry to say that by his account Mr Wickham is not at all a respectable young man.'

'Mr Bingley does not know Mr Wickham himself?'

'No. He never saw him until the other morning at Meryton.'

'This explanation, then, is what he has received from Mr Darcy. I am perfectly satisfied. Mr Bingley has defended his friend, but I shall continue to hold the same opinion.'

She then changed the subject to one more pleasing to them both, and listened with pleasure to the happy hopes which Jane had of Mr Bingley's feelings towards her. When Mr Bingley himself joined them, Elizabeth moved away to Miss Lucas.

Shortly afterwards, Mr Collins came up to them in a state of great excitement. He had discovered that Mr Darcy was a relative of Lady Catherine.

'You are not going to introduce yourself to Mr Darcy?'

'Of course I am.'

Elizabeth tried hard to persuade him against this, warning him that Mr Darcy would consider it as a piece of impoliteness rather than as a mark of respect for his aunt.

'Pardon me for neglecting to take advantage of your advice,' was his reply, 'but in the case before us I consider myself more fitted by education and study to decide on what is right than a young lady like yourself.' And, with that, he left her to approach Mr Darcy, whose astonishment was plain, and who replied with cold politeness.

Elizabeth felt ashamed of her cousin, and turned her attention to the more pleasing subject of Jane's future. Her mother's thoughts were plainly of the same kind, and when they sat down to supper, Elizabeth was deeply annoyed to find that Mrs Bennet was talking loudly to Lady Lucas of nothing else but her expectations that Jane would soon be married to Mr Bingley. Elizabeth tried without success to control her mother's words, because she could see that they were heard by Mr Darcy, who sat opposite them. Nothing she could say had any effect. Elizabeth reddened with shame.

When supper was over, singing was mentioned, and Elizabeth had the added discomfort of seeing Mary getting ready to entertain the company. Mary was the least pretty of the five sisters, so she had tried to make herself more attractive by becoming more able than the others, and was always eager to bring her musical skill to notice. But her powers were by no means fitted for this kind of performance. Her voice was weak, and her manner unnatural. Elizabeth listened with impatience. Mary sang twice, and Elizabeth could see Mr Bingley's sisters exchanging scornful smiles. She looked at her father, who understood and gently stopped his daughter.

The rest of the evening brought Elizabeth little amusement. Mr Collins continued at her side and would not leave her alone. Mr Darcy took no more notice of her, even when he was standing near her.

But Mrs Bennet left Netherfield perfectly satisfied. She was fully confident that she would see Jane married in the course of three or four months. She thought with equal certainty of having another daughter married to Mr Collins. She loved Elizabeth less than her other daughters, and she thought Mr Collins quite good enough for her.

Chapter 7
Mr Collins Makes a Proposal of Marriage

The next day opened a new scene at Longbourn: Mr Collins made a formal proposal of marriage. Having decided to do it without delay, and having no lack of self-confidence, he began in a very orderly manner with all the ceremony which he supposed to be a regular part of the business. On finding Mrs Bennet, Elizabeth and one of the younger girls together soon after breakfast, he addressed the mother in these words:

'May I hope, madam, to speak privately with your lovely daughter Elizabeth?'

Before Elizabeth had time to express her surprise, Mrs Bennet immediately answered:

'Oh, yes, certainly. I am sure that Lizzy can have no objection. Come, Kitty, I want you upstairs.' And picking up her sewing, she was hurrying away, when Elizabeth called out:

'I beg you not to go. Mr Collins must excuse me. He can have nothing to say to me that anybody need not hear. I am going away myself.'

'No, no, nonsense, Lizzy. I desire you to stay where you are.' And when Elizabeth seemed about to escape, she added, 'Lizzy, you must stay and hear Mr Collins.'

Elizabeth could not oppose such a command, and a moment's consideration made her realize that it would be better to get the matter settled, so she sat down again. Mrs Bennet and Kitty walked off, and as soon as they were gone, Mr Collins began:

'Believe me, my dear Miss Elizabeth, your behaviour only adds to your other perfections. You would have been less pleasing in my eyes if there had *not* been this little unwillingness, but allow me to inform you that I have your respected mother's permission for this address. Almost as soon as I entered this house, I made you my choice as the companion of my future life. My reasons for marrying are, first, I think it a right thing for every church minister to set an example by doing so; secondly, I am sure that it will add very greatly to my happiness; and thirdly, Lady Catherine has advised it. As I am heir to this property on the death of your honoured father, I decided to choose my wife from among his daughters. I know very well that you have little fortune, but I shall never blame you for that when we are married.'

It was necessary to stop him now.

'You are in too much of a hurry, sir,' she cried. 'You forget that I have made no answer. Accept my thanks for the honour that you are showing me, but it is impossible for me to do otherwise than to refuse your proposal.'

'I quite understand,' replied Mr Collins, with a wave of the hand, 'that it is usual for young ladies to refuse the man whom they secretly mean to accept, when he asks for the first time.'

'On my honour, sir,' cried Elizabeth, 'I am perfectly serious in my refusal.'

'When I next speak to you on this subject,' continued Mr Collins, 'I shall expect to receive a more favourable answer.'

Elizabeth tried without success to make him believe her. He had too good an opinion of himself and his position, and he pointed out that she was too poor to receive many other offers. To this she could make no reply, and immediately, and in silence, left the room, with the intention of asking for her father's support.

◆

Mrs Bennet had waited in the hall for the end of the conversation. As soon as she saw Elizabeth open the door and, with a quick step, pass her towards the stairway, she entered the breakfast room and congratulated both Mr Collins and herself. Mr Collins received and returned these good wishes, but when he went on to give details of his conversation with Elizabeth, the information astonished Mrs Bennet.

'But you may depend on it, Mr Collins,' she added, 'that Lizzy shall be made to behave reasonably. I will speak to her myself immediately. She is a very foolish girl, and does not know her own interest, but I will *make* her know it. I will go to Mr Bennet, and we shall very soon settle the matter with her, I am sure.'

She would not give him time to reply, but hurried immediately to her husband, and called out as she entered the library: 'Oh, Mr Bennet, you are wanted immediately. You must come and make Lizzy marry Mr Collins, because she swears she will not have him.'

Mr Bennet raised his eyes from his book as she entered, and fixed them on her face with a calm unconcern which was not in the least changed by her information.

'I have not the pleasure of understanding you,' he said, when she had finished her speech. 'What are you talking about?'

'Mr Collins and Lizzy. Lizzy says that she will not have Mr Collins, and if you do not hurry, he will change his mind and not have *her*.'

'And what am I to do about it? It seems a hopeless business.'

'Speak to Lizzy about it yourself. Tell her that she must marry him.'

'Let her be called down. She shall hear my opinion.'

Mrs Bennet rang the bell and Miss Elizabeth was sent for.

'Come here, child,' said her father as she appeared. 'I have sent for you on an affair of importance. I understand that Mr Collins has made you an offer of marriage. Is it true?' Elizabeth replied that it was. 'Very well – and you have refused this offer of marriage?'

'I have, sir.'

'Very well. We now come to the point. Your mother demands

that you accept it. Is it not so, Mrs Bennet?'

'Yes, or I will never see her again.'

'An unhappy choice is before you, Elizabeth. From this day you will be a stranger to one of your parents. Your mother will never see you again if you do *not* marry Mr Collins, and I will never see you again if you *do*.'

Elizabeth could not help smiling at such an ending to such a beginning. Mrs Bennet, on the other hand, was extremely disappointed. She returned to the subject repeatedly, using both persuasion and threats to try and change her daughter's mind. Mr Collins himself remained silent and offended, unable to understand how his cousin could possibly refuse him.

While the family were in this state, Charlotte Lucas came to spend the day with them. Mr Collins's attentions were now turned to her, which Elizabeth found to be a great relief.

Chapter 8   Netherfield Is Empty

After breakfast the next day, the girls walked to Meryton to inquire if Mr Wickham had returned. He joined them as they entered the town, and went with them to their aunt's. He explained to Elizabeth his absence from the ball.

'I found,' he said, 'as the time approached, that I had better not meet Mr Darcy – that to be in his company might be more than I could bear.'

Elizabeth highly approved of his good sense. As Wickham and another officer walked back with them to Longbourn, she was able to introduce him to her father and mother.

Soon after their return, a letter was delivered to Miss Bennet. It came from Netherfield, and was opened immediately. Elizabeth saw her sister's face change as she read it. But she soon controlled herself and, putting the letter away, tried to join in the conversation with her usual cheerfulness. But as soon as the officers had left, a look from Jane invited Elizabeth to follow her upstairs.

When they had reached their own room, Jane, taking out the letter, said, 'This is from Caroline Bingley. What it contains has surprised me a great deal. The whole party have left Netherfield by this time, and are on their way to town, and without any intention of coming back again.'

She then read the letter out loud. It spoke of the writer's sorrow at parting from Jane, and urged her to write frequently. Elizabeth judged this to be insincere. It stated that Mr Bingley had business in town, and would be in no hurry to leave it again.

'It is clear from this that he will come back no more this winter,' said Jane.

'It is clear that Miss Bingley does not intend that he *should*.'

'Why do you think so? It must be his own decision. He is free to act as he wishes. But you do not know everything. I will read you the words that hurt me most. I will have no secrets from you.' The letter then told of the beauty of Mr Darcy's young sister, and of Mr Bingley's admiration for her, and of the family's hopes that they would marry.

'Is it not clear enough? Does it not plainly state that Caroline neither expects nor wishes me to be her sister, and that she believes that her brother does not care for me? She means – most kindly – to warn me. Can there be any other opinion on the subject?'

'Yes, there can. Mine is totally different. Miss Bingley sees that her brother is in love with you, and wants him to marry Miss Darcy. She follows him to town in the hope of keeping him there, and tries to persuade you that he does not care about you.'

Jane shook her head.

'Really, Jane, you ought to believe me. No one who has ever seen you together can doubt his love. But the case is this – we are not rich enough or grand enough for them.'

Elizabeth spoke comfortingly to her sister, and gradually persuaded her that Mr Bingley would return later and answer every wish of her heart. To their mother they decided only to announce that the Netherfield party had left for a short time.

Chapter 9   Mr Collins Makes Another Proposal

The Bennets were invited to dinner with the Lucases, and again, most of the time, Miss Lucas was kind enough to listen to Mr Collins. Elizabeth thanked her warmly, and Charlotte told her friend that she was glad to be of service to her. This was very helpful of her, but the real reason for Charlotte's kindness was something that Elizabeth had no idea of – a desire to attract Mr Collins herself. When they parted later that night, Charlotte would have felt almost certain of success if he had not been planning to leave Longbourn. But Mr Collins, wasting no time, escaped from the Bennets early next morning with great skill. Miss Lucas noticed him from an upper window as he walked towards her parents' house. She came down quickly to the garden, and there, meeting him as if by accident, received his proposal of marriage.

Sir William and Lady Lucas were immediately asked for their agreement, which they willingly gave. Mr Collins's present position made it a good marriage for their daughter, to whom they could give little fortune, and in the future he would be Mr Bennet's heir. Charlotte was fairly well satisfied. Mr Collins was neither sensible nor agreeable, but she, on the other hand, was twenty-seven, and with little chance of other offers.

She decided to give the news to the Bennets herself, and therefore asked Mr Collins to say nothing when he returned to Longbourn, which he was leaving the next day.

When Elizabeth was privately informed by Charlotte, her astonishment was so great that she could not help crying out:

'Engaged to be married to Mr Collins! My dear Charlotte, impossible!'

'I see what you are feeling,' replied Charlotte. 'You must be surprised, very much surprised, as Mr Collins was so recently wanting to marry you. But I do not expect very much from marriage, you know. I shall be satisfied with having a comfortable home.'

Elizabeth answered quietly and, after an awkward pause, they returned to the rest of the family. Charlotte did not stay much longer, and Elizabeth was left to think over what she had heard. The strangeness of Mr Collins's making two offers of marriage within three days was nothing in comparison with his being now accepted. She would never have expected Charlotte to give up her finer feelings to gain no more than comfort. She felt that her friend had shamed herself, and she did not believe it possible for her to be happy in the life she had chosen.

As for Mrs Bennet, she was astonished and shocked by the news. A week passed before she could see Elizabeth without scolding her, and a month before she could speak to Sir William or Lady Lucas without being rude. Lady Lucas was not without pleasure in being able to talk to Mrs Bennet about the comfort of having a daughter well married, and she visited Longbourn rather oftener than usual, to say how happy she was. Between Elizabeth and Charlotte there was an awkwardness that kept them silent on the subject. Elizabeth felt that there could never be any real confidence between them again, and she turned with greater fondness to her sister Jane, for whose happiness she became daily more anxious.

Chapter 10   Jane Goes to London

Neither Jane nor Elizabeth was comfortable on the subject of Mr Bingley's continued absence. Even Elizabeth began to fear, not that Bingley's feelings had changed, but that his sisters and the amusements of London would be successful in keeping him away. Jane wished to hide her anxiety, and never mentioned it, but an hour rarely passed without some remark from her mother which it needed all Jane's patience to bear in silence.

Mrs Bennet was really in a most pitiable state. She was continually thinking about why Mr Bingley had not returned. Then, too, the sight of Miss Lucas was hateful to her. She regarded her with jealous dislike as the wife of the future owner of Longbourn. Whenever Charlotte came to see them, Mrs Bennet imagined that she was thinking of the time when she would take possession.

Jane had written to Miss Bingley, and in a little while a reply arrived and put an end to doubt. The first sentence announced that they were all settled in London for the winter, and the letter ended with her brother's sadness at not having had time to say goodbye to his friends before leaving.

Hope was over, completely over. Elizabeth's heart was divided between sympathy for her sister and anger against the others. Secretly she blamed Mr Bingley for his weakness in being persuaded by his sisters, and she was angry because she believed that Mr Darcy had helped to influence him.

Jane bore her sorrow with gentle sweetness, and tried to believe that she had only imagined Mr Bingley to be fond of her, and that she had only herself to blame.

◆

On the following Monday, Mrs Bennet had the pleasure of receiving her brother and his wife, who came, as usual, from

London to spend Christmas at Longbourn. Mr Gardiner was a sensible, gentlemanly man, of much finer character than his sister, and Mrs Gardiner, who was several years younger than Mrs Bennet, was a pleasant, intelligent, well-dressed woman, and a great favourite with her nieces.

The first part of Mrs Gardiner's business, on her arrival, was to give her presents and describe the newest fashions. When this was done, she had a less active part to play. It became her turn to listen. Mrs Bennet had many troubles to tell, and much to complain of. Two of her girls had been on the point of marriage, but nothing had happened after all.

'I do not blame Jane,' she continued, 'but Lizzy! Oh, sister! It is very hard to think that she might have been Mr Collins's wife by this time, if it had not been for her own bad character! He made her an offer, here in this room, and she refused him. The result of all this is that Lady Lucas will have a daughter married before I have. It is very bad for my nerves to be annoyed so by my own family. But your coming at this time is the greatest of comforts, and I am glad to hear about the new dresses.'

When Mrs Gardiner was alone with Elizabeth afterwards, she spoke on the subject of Jane.

'Poor Jane! I am sorry for her, because, with her character, she may not recover for some time from such a disappointment. But do you think that she could be persuaded to go back to town with us? A change of scene might be of help to her.'

Elizabeth was extremely pleased with this proposal.

'I hope,' added Mrs Gardiner, 'that no thought of this young man will influence her. We live in such a different part of the town, and mix with such a different class of society, that she is not likely to meet him, unless he really comes to see her.'

Miss Bennet accepted her aunt's invitation with pleasure, and the Gardiners left Longbourn after a week's stay. Before she went, though, Mrs Gardiner, who guessed from Elizabeth's behaviour her feelings for Wickham, gave her a word of advice.

'Seriously, I would advise you to be careful. I have nothing to say against *him*. He is a most interesting young man, and if he had the fortune that he ought to have, I should think that you could not do better. But as it is – you have sense, and we all expect you to use it. You must not disappoint your father.'

◆

January and February were dull months. Elizabeth missed Jane sadly. Charlotte was married and had left for Hunsford. There was little except the walks to Meryton, sometimes muddy and sometimes cold, to help pass the time.

Elizabeth wrote and received many letters. She exchanged news with Charlotte as regularly as ever, but their friendship could never be as close as it had been before. From London Jane wrote that she had neither seen nor heard anything of Miss Bingley. But she accounted for this by supposing that her last letter to her friend had by some accident been lost.

'My aunt,' she continued, 'is going tomorrow into that part of the town, and I shall take the opportunity of visiting Caroline.'

She wrote again after she had made the visit. 'I did not think that Caroline was in good spirits,' were her words, 'but she was glad to see me and cross that I had given her no notice of my coming to London. I was right, therefore. My last letter had never reached her. I inquired after her brother, of course. He is so busy in society that they hardly ever see him. My visit was not long, as Caroline and Mrs Hurst were going out.'

Elizabeth shook her head over this letter.

Four weeks passed, and Jane saw nothing of Mr Bingley. She could no longer be blind to Miss Bingley's inattention. At last the visitor did appear, but the shortness of her stay and the change in her manner no longer made it possible for Jane to deceive herself. It was plain that she received no pleasure from coming. She made a slight, formal apology for not visiting her before, said not a word about wishing to see her again, and was in every way so unfriendly that Jane decided not to continue the acquaintance.

To Mrs Gardiner, Elizabeth wrote of her own affairs. Wickham's attentions to her were over, and he was now the admirer of Miss Mary King, a young lady whose grandfather had just died and left her ten thousand pounds. Elizabeth's heart had been only slightly touched, and her pride was satisfied with believing that *she* would have been his only choice, if fortune had permitted.

Chapter 11   Elizabeth Visits Hunsford

In March, Elizabeth was visiting Hunsford, at Charlotte's invitation. She had not at first thought very seriously of going there, but she found that her friend was depending on the arrangement. Absence had increased her desire to see Charlotte again, and lessened her disgust for Mr Collins. The journey would also give her a moment with Jane as she would spend the night in London. She would travel with Sir William Lucas and his second daughter Maria.

It was only 24 miles to London, and they began early so that they could arrive before midday. As they drove to Mr Gardiner's door, Jane was at a sitting room window watching for their arrival. When they entered the hall, she was there to welcome them, and Elizabeth, looking closely at her face, was pleased to see it as healthy and beautiful as ever. On the stairs was a crowd of little girls and boys, whose eagerness for their cousin's appearance would not allow them to wait in the sitting room, and whose shyness, as they had not seen her for a year, prevented them from coming down any further.

All was joy and kindness. The day passed away most pleasantly, the afternoon in shopping, and the evening at one of the theatres.

During the performance, Elizabeth managed to sit by her aunt. Their first subject was her sister, and she was more troubled than surprised to hear that, though Jane struggled to be cheerful, there were times when she was very sad. It was reasonable, though, to hope that this would not continue for too long.

Before they were separated by the end of the play, Elizabeth had the unexpected happiness of an invitation to go with her uncle and aunt on a tour which they planned to take in the summer.

'We have not quite decided how far it will take us,' said Mrs Gardiner, 'but perhaps to the Lakes.'

No plan could have been more welcome to Elizabeth, and her acceptance of the invitation was immediate and grateful.

♦

Every object in the next day's journey was new and interesting to Elizabeth. When they left the main road for the smaller road to Hunsford, every eye was in search of the Parsonage. At last it appeared. Mr Collins and Charlotte were at the door, and the carriage stopped at the small gate among the smiles and greetings of the whole party. Mrs Collins welcomed her friend with the greatest pleasure, and Elizabeth was more and more pleased that she had come, as she found herself so warmly received.

She could not help thinking, as Mr Collins proudly showed her his house and furniture, that he wished to make her feel what she had lost by refusing him. She was not able to please him, though, by any sign of unhappiness; instead she looked with surprise at her friend, who could appear so cheerful with such a companion. After admiring the house, they were invited by their host to take a walk in the garden. One of his chief pleasures was to work in the garden, and Elizabeth smiled to herself as she heard Charlotte talk of the healthiness of the exercise, and say that she encouraged it as much as possible.

The house itself, though small, was neat and convenient, and when Mr Collins could be forgotten, there was a great feeling of comfort everywhere – and by Charlotte's enjoyment, which was quite plain, Elizabeth supposed he must often be forgotten.

It was mentioned at dinner that Lady Catherine was still in the country. Mr Collins poured out his praises of her kind attentions to himself and Charlotte, and expressed the expectation that she would honour Elizabeth with her notice.

The evening was spent chiefly in talking over the news from home, and when it had passed, Elizabeth, in the quietness of her own room, had to think over Charlotte's degree of satisfaction, to understand her skill in guiding her husband, and her self-control in managing to deal with him, and to admit that it was well done.

At around the middle of the next day, as she was in her room getting ready for a walk, a sudden noise below showed the whole house to be in a state of excitement, and, after listening for a moment, Elizabeth heard somebody running upstairs in a violent hurry, and calling loudly to her. She opened the door, and met Maria, who cried to her to come down that moment.

Elizabeth asked questions without success. Maria would tell her nothing more, and they ran down to the dining room in search of the cause of her excitement. It was two ladies stopping in a carriage at the garden gate.

'And is this all?' cried Elizabeth. 'I expected at least that the pigs had got into the garden, and here is nothing but Lady Catherine and her daughter!'

'My dear!' said Maria, quite shocked at the mistake. 'It is not Lady Catherine. The old lady is Mrs Jenkinson, who lives with them. The other is Miss de Bourgh. Only look at her. Who would have thought she could be so thin and small!'

'I like her appearance,' said Elizabeth, who was struck with other ideas. 'She looks weak and disagreeable. Yes, she will suit him very well. She will make him a very fitting wife.'

Chapter 12   Lady Catherine de Bourgh

The purpose of the ladies' visit had been to ask the whole party to dinner at Rosings, where Lady Catherine lived, and Mr Collins's proud excitement at this invitation was complete. Hardly anything else was talked of the whole day. Mr Collins carefully explained what they should expect, so that the sight of such rooms, so many servants, and so excellent a dinner would not completely astonish them. While they were dressing, he came two or three times to their doors to urge them to be quick, as Lady Catherine very much objected to being kept waiting for dinner. Such accounts quite frightened Maria Lucas, who had been little used to society, but Elizabeth's courage did not fail her. She had heard nothing of Lady Catherine that filled her with respect for cleverness or goodness, and she thought that she could meet the grandness of money and rank without fear.

Elizabeth found herself quite equal to the occasion when she was introduced to Lady Catherine, and was able to look at the three ladies in front of her calmly. Lady Catherine was a tall, large woman, with strongly marked features. Her behaviour was not friendly, and her manner of receiving them did not allow her visitors to forget their inferior rank. Whatever she said was spoken in a commanding voice that expressed her belief in her own importance. Miss de Bourgh looked pale and weak, and spoke only in a low voice to Mrs Jenkinson.

The dinner was extremely fine, and all was as Mr Collins had promised. His loud praises of everything were continually repeated by Sir William. Lady Catherine smiled at them, and seemed pleased by their extreme admiration.

When the ladies returned to the sitting room, there was little to be done except listen to Lady Catherine talk, which she did without stopping, giving her opinion loudly on every subject in a manner that showed that she was not used to having her judgment opposed. She asked Elizabeth many things about her family: their number, their education, whether any of them was likely to be married, and what her mother's name had been before marriage. Elizabeth felt all the impoliteness of these questions, but answered them calmly. Lady Catherine then asked:

'Do you play and sing, Miss Bennet?'

'A little.'

'Oh, then – some time or other we shall be happy to hear you. Our piano is a very good one – probably much better than – do your sisters play and sing?'

'One of them does.'

'Why did you not all learn? You ought all to have learned. Do you draw?'

'No, not at all.'

'What, none of you?'

'Not one.'

'That is very strange. But I suppose you had no opportunity. Are any of your younger sisters out in society,★ Miss Bennet?'

'Yes, all of them.'

'All! What, all five at the same time? Very strange! And you only the second. What is your age?'

'With three younger sisters grown up,' replied Elizabeth smiling, 'you can hardly expect me to speak on that subject.'

Lady Catherine seemed quite astonished at not receiving a direct answer, and Elizabeth thought that perhaps she was the first person who had dared to speak to her in that way.

★out in society: considered old enough to attend dinner parties, balls and other social events.

'You cannot be more than twenty, I am sure – therefore you need not hide your age.'

'I am not yet twenty-one.'

When the gentlemen joined them, the card tables were placed. At one table Lady Catherine played with Sir William and with Mr and Mrs Collins; at the other, Miss de Bourgh with Mrs Jenkinson and the two girls. Lady Catherine continued to talk, pointing out the mistakes made by others. Mr Collins agreed with everything she said, thanking her for every game he won, and apologizing if he thought he had won too many. Hardly a word was spoken at the other table, and Elizabeth found the game extremely boring.

Chapter 13   Visitors to Rosings

In a quiet way, with walks and occasional visits to Rosings, the first two weeks of Elizabeth's stay soon passed. Sir William Lucas had returned home, but the next week brought an addition to the family at Rosings. Mr Darcy was expected, and when he came, he brought with him Colonel Fitzwilliam, his cousin.

The day after their arrival, they came to the Parsonage. Colonel Fitzwilliam was about thirty, not very good-looking, but in person and manners most truly a gentleman. Mr Darcy looked just as he had always done, was polite but spoke little. Elizabeth only lowered her head in greeting without saying a word.

Colonel Fitzwilliam entered into conversation directly, with the confidence of a man of good family. After a long silence, Mr Darcy inquired after the health of Elizabeth's family. She answered him in the usual way and, after a moment's pause, added: 'My oldest sister has been in town during the last three months. Have you not seen her?'

She thought that he looked a little confused as he answered

that he had not been so fortunate as to meet Miss Bennet.

It was some days before the next invitation came from Rosings. While there were visitors in the house, the company from the Parsonage were not necessary. When the invitation did arrive, and they joined the party in Lady Catherine's sitting room, Lady Catherine received them politely, but it was clear that they were not as welcome as they had been when she could get nobody else.

Colonel Fitzwilliam seemed really glad to see them. Anything was a welcome relief at Rosings, and Mrs Collins's pretty friend had attracted him. He now seated himself by her, and talked so agreeably that Elizabeth had never been half so well entertained in that room before. Their conversation was so full of spirit that it drew the attention of Lady Catherine herself. As for Mr Darcy, his eyes had been soon and repeatedly turned towards them with a look of interest. At last Lady Catherine called out:

'What are you saying, Fitzwilliam? What is it you are talking of? What are you telling Miss Bennet?'

'We are speaking of music, madam,' he said.

'Of music! Then please speak out loud. I must have my share in the conversation, if you are speaking of music. There are few people in England, I suppose, who have a better natural taste in music than myself. I would have been an excellent performer.'

She then inquired after the playing of Darcy's sister, Georgiana, and he spoke in brotherly praise of her skill.

'She must practise continually,' Lady Catherine went on. 'I have told Miss Bennet several times that she will never play really well unless she practises more, and though Mrs Collins has no instrument, she is very welcome to come to Rosings every day and play the piano in Mrs Jenkinson's room. She would be in nobody's way, you know, in that part of the house.'

Mr Darcy looked a little ashamed of his aunt's lack of good manners, and said nothing.

When coffee was over, Colonel Fitzwilliam reminded Elizabeth that she had promised to play to him, and she sat down immediately at the piano. He pulled a chair up near her. Lady Catherine listened to half a song and then talked to her other nephew, until Darcy walked away from her, and, moving towards the piano, positioned himself so that he had a view of the performer's face. Elizabeth saw what he was doing, and at the first convenient pause turned to him with a smile and said:

'You mean to frighten me, Mr Darcy, by coming with all this ceremony to hear me. But I will not be afraid, though your sister *does* play so well.'

'I shall not say that you are mistaken,' he replied, 'because you could not really suppose me to have any intention of frightening you.'

Elizabeth laughed, and said to Colonel Fitzwilliam: 'Your cousin will teach you not to believe a word I say. It makes me want to behave badly towards him.'

'Then let me hear why you are angry with him,' said Colonel Fitzwilliam.

'You shall hear – but be ready for something very terrible. The first time I ever saw him was at a ball – and what do you think he did at this ball? He danced only four dances, though there were very few gentlemen and, to my certain knowledge, more than one young lady was sitting down for lack of a partner.'

'I had not at that time the honour of knowing any lady there, except from my own party.'

'True, but can nobody ever be introduced in a ballroom?'

'Perhaps,' said Darcy, 'I would have behaved better if I had asked for an introduction, but I am not someone who can easily make friends with strangers.'

'Shall we ask your cousin the reason for this?' said Elizabeth, addressing Colonel Fitzwilliam.

'I can answer your question,' said Fitzwilliam. 'It is because he will not give himself the trouble.'

'I have certainly not the ability that some people possess,' said Darcy, 'of holding a conversation easily with those whom I have never seen before.'

Here they were interrupted by Lady Catherine, who called out to know what they were talking about. Elizabeth immediately began to play again. Lady Catherine came nearer, and, after listening for a few minutes, said to Darcy:

'She uses her fingers well, though her taste is not equal to Anne's. Anne would have been a truly great performer if her health had allowed her to learn.'

Elizabeth looked at Darcy to see whether he agreed with this praise of his cousin, but neither at that moment nor at any other could she see any sign of love. Lady Catherine continued her remarks on Elizabeth's performance until her carriage was ready to take them all home.

◆

Elizabeth was sitting by herself the next morning writing to Jane, while Mrs Collins and Maria were gone on business into the village, when she was interrupted by a ring at the front door, the signal of a visitor. When the door of the room was opened, to her great surprise Mr Darcy, and Mr Darcy alone, entered.

He seemed astonished, too, to find her alone, and apologized for the interruption by letting her know that he had expected all the ladies to be at home.

They then sat down, and when her inquiries after Rosings were made, seemed in danger of sinking into total silence. It was necessary, therefore, to speak of something, so, wanting to know what he would say on the subject of their leaving Netherfield so quickly, she remarked:

'How very suddenly you all left Netherfield last November,

Mr Darcy! Mr Bingley and his sisters were well, I hope, when you left London?'

'Perfectly so, thank you.'

After a short pause, she added:

'I understand that Mr Bingley has not much idea of ever returning to Netherfield again?'

'It is probable that he may spend very little of his time there in future.'

'If he means to be very little at Netherfield, it would be better for the neighbourhood that he should give up the place completely, for then we might possibly get a settled family there.'

'I should not be surprised,' said Darcy, 'if he were to give it up, if he found another property that suited him.'

Elizabeth made no answer. She was afraid of talking longer of his friend, and, having nothing else to say, was now determined to leave the trouble of finding a subject to him.

He understood, and very soon began with, 'Mr Collins appears to be very fortunate in his choice of a wife. It must be very pleasant for her to be settled within such an easy distance of her own family and friends.'

'An easy distance, do you call it? It is nearly 50 miles. I should never have said that Mrs Collins was settled near her family.'

'It is a proof of your own close ties to your home. Anything beyond the very neighbourhood of Longbourn, I suppose, would appear far.'

Then he moved his chair a little towards her, and said, '*You* cannot have a right to such very strong local feeling. *You* cannot always have been at Longbourn.'

Elizabeth looked surprised. The gentleman experienced some change of feeling. He moved his chair back again, took a newspaper from the table, and said in a colder voice:

'Are you pleased with Kent?'

A short conversation on the subject of the country followed. It was soon brought to an end by the entrance of Charlotte and her sister, who had just returned from their walk.

'What can be the meaning of this?' said Charlotte, as soon as Darcy was gone. 'My dear Eliza, he must be in love with you, or he would never have visited us in this familiar way.'

But when Elizabeth told of his silence, it did not seem very likely to be the case, and they could only suppose his visit to result from the difficulty of finding anything to do at that time of year. Gentlemen cannot always stay indoors, and the nearness of the Parsonage encouraged the two cousins, from this period, to walk there almost every day, sometimes separately and sometimes together. It was plain that Colonel Fitzwilliam came because he found pleasure in their society, but Mr Darcy could not come for that reason, because he frequently sat there for ten minutes at a time without opening his lips. Mrs Collins did not know how to explain it. He certainly looked at Elizabeth a great deal, and she once or twice suggested to her friend the possibility that he was interested in her, but Elizabeth always laughed at the idea.

Chapter 14   Mr Darcy

During Elizabeth's daily walk within the park of Rosings, which the people at the Parsonage were permitted to visit, she more than once unexpectedly met Mr Darcy. To prevent it ever happening again, she took care on the first occasion to inform him that it was her favourite part. It was very strange, therefore, that it happened a second time. But it did, and even a third. He actually thought it necessary to turn back and walk with her. He never said a great deal, and she did not give herself the trouble of talking or listening much.

One day she was reading Jane's last letter again as she walked, when, instead of being again surprised by Mr Darcy, she looked up and saw that Colonel Fitzwilliam was coming to meet her. They walked together towards the Parsonage.

'Is it settled that you leave Kent on Saturday?' she asked.

'Yes – if Darcy does not put it off again. But he arranges our business just as he pleases. I share with him the responsibility of looking after Miss Darcy.'

'Do you really? And does she give you much trouble? Young ladies of her age are sometimes difficult to manage.'

As she spoke, she saw him looking at her very seriously, and his manner made her believe that she had somehow or other got fairly near the truth. She replied immediately:

'You need not be frightened. I have never heard any harm of her. She is a great favourite of some ladies of my acquaintance, Mrs Hurst and Miss Bingley. I think that you know them.'

'I know them a little. Their brother is a great friend of Darcy's.'

'Oh, yes,' said Elizabeth sharply, 'Mr Darcy is uncommonly kind to Mr Bingley, and takes great care of him.'

'Care of him! Yes, I really believe Darcy *does* take care of him. From something that he told me, I have reason to think that Bingley must have cause to be very grateful to him.'

'What do you mean?'

'It is a matter which Darcy, of course, could not wish to be generally known, because if it were to reach the lady's family it would be an unpleasant thing.'

'You may depend on my not mentioning it.'

'What he told me was this: that he congratulated himself on having saved a friend from the inconveniences of a most unwise marriage, but without mentioning names or any other details.'

'Did Mr Darcy give you his reasons for his involvement?'

'I understood that there were some very strong objections to the lady.'

Elizabeth walked on, her heart swelling with anger. She could not trust herself further with the subject, and therefore, quickly changing the conversation, talked about different matters until they reached the Parsonage. There, shut in her own room as soon as their visitor had left them, she could think without interruption of all that she had heard. She had never doubted that Mr Darcy had been involved in the action taken to separate Mr Bingley and Jane, but she had always blamed Miss Bingley as the chief person responsible. But now she knew. *He* was the cause – his pride was the cause – of all that Jane had suffered. He had ruined every hope of happiness for the most loving, most generous heart in the world.

'There were some very strong objections to the lady,' were Colonel Fitzwilliam's words, and these strong objections probably included her having one uncle who was a country lawyer and another who was in business in London.

'To Jane herself,' she whispered, 'there could be no possible objection – she is all beauty and goodness! Her understanding is excellent, her mind improved, and her manners excellent. Neither could my father be to blame, since he has abilities that Mr Darcy himself could not fail to respect.' But when she thought of her mother her confidence *did* weaken a little.

The excitement and tears which the subject caused brought on a headache, and it became so much worse towards the evening that, added to her unwillingness to see Mr Darcy, it made her decide not to go with her cousins to Rosings, where they were invited to take tea. Mrs Collins, seeing that she was really unwell, did not urge her to go, and prevented her husband as much as possible from urging her, but Mr Collins could not hide his fear that Lady Catherine might be rather displeased by her staying at home.

◆

When they had gone, Elizabeth, as if intending to sharpen her anger as much as possible against Mr Darcy, chose for her employment the examination of all the letters which Jane had written to her since her arrival in Kent. They contained no actual complaint, but in all, and in almost every line of each, there was a lack of the cheerfulness that had always been natural to her. Mr Darcy's shameful pride in what he had been able to cause gave Elizabeth a keener sense of her sister's sufferings.

At this point she was suddenly interrupted by the sound of the doorbell and, to her complete astonishment, she saw Mr Darcy walk into the room. In a hurried manner he immediately began an inquiry after her health. She answered him with cold politeness. He sat down for a few moments, and then, getting up, walked around the room. Elizabeth was surprised, but did not say a word. After a silence of several minutes, he came towards her in a troubled manner, and began to speak:

'I have struggled without success. My feelings will not be controlled. You must allow me to tell you how warmly I admire and love you.'

Elizabeth's astonishment was beyond expression. She looked away, red in the face, and was silent. He considered this enough encouragement, and the expression of all that he felt for her immediately followed.

He spoke well, but there were other feelings to be described besides those of his heart, and his words were more concerned with pride than love. His sense of her inferiority, his feeling that he was lowering himself, the family considerations that had caused his judgment to oppose his preference, all were expressed with a force that was unlikely to make his proposal acceptable.

In spite of her deeply rooted dislike, she could not fail to realize what an honour it was to receive such a man's attention, and though her intentions did not change for one moment, she was at first sorry for the pain that he would receive, until, insulted by his language as he continued, she lost all pity in anger. She tried to control herself, so she could answer him patiently when he had finished. He ended by expressing the hope that he would now be rewarded by her acceptance of his hand in marriage. As he said this, she could clearly see that he had no doubt of a favourable answer. Such confidence could only increase her annoyance, and when he had ended, the colour in her face deepened and she said:

'If I could feel grateful, as I believe one should in such a situation, I would now thank you. But I cannot – I have never desired your good opinion, and you have certainly given it most unwillingly. The reasons which, you tell me, have long prevented the expression of your feelings, can have little difficulty in bringing them under control.'

Mr Darcy, whose eyes were fixed on her face, seemed to hear her words with no less anger than surprise. He became pale, and the confusion in his mind was plain in every feature. Finally, in a voice of forced calmness, he said:

'And this is all the reply which I am to have the honour of expecting! I might, perhaps, wish to be informed why, with so little attempt at politeness, I am refused.'

'I might as well inquire,' she replied, 'why, with so clear an intention of insulting me, you chose to tell me that you liked me against your will. Was that not some excuse for impoliteness, if I was impolite? But I have other reasons. Do you think that any consideration would lead me to accept the man who has been the means of ruining, perhaps for ever, the happiness of my most dearly loved sister?'

As she spoke these words, Mr Darcy's face changed colour, but he listened without interrupting her while she continued:

'Nothing can excuse the unjust and ungenerous part that you played there. You cannot state that you have not been the chief, if not the only means of dividing the pair of them.'

She paused, and saw that he was listening in a manner that proved him to be unmoved.

'Is it not true that you have done it?' she repeated.

He then replied with calmness: 'Yes, it is true that I did everything in my power to separate my friend from your sister, and that I am glad of my success. I have been kinder towards him than towards myself.'

Elizabeth appeared not to notice this polite remark, but its meaning did not escape her, nor was it likely to soften her feelings.

'But it is not only this affair,' she continued, 'on which my dislike is based. Long before, your character was made plain in the story which I received many months ago from Mr Wickham.'

'You take an eager interest in that gentleman's concerns,' said Darcy, in a more troubled voice, and with deeper colour in his face.

'No one who knows his misfortunes can help feeling an interest in him.'

'His misfortunes!' repeated Darcy scornfully. 'Yes, his misfortunes have been great.'

'And you are responsible,' cried Elizabeth with energy. '*You* have reduced him to his present state.'

'And this,' cried Darcy, as he walked with quick steps across the room, 'is your opinion of me. I thank you for explaining it so fully. But perhaps,' he added, stopping in his walk, and turning towards her, 'these offences might have been forgiven if your pride had not been hurt by my honest explanation of the reasons that made me wait so long. I am not ashamed of the feelings that I expressed. They were natural and fair. Could you expect me to be happy about the inferiority of your relations?'

Elizabeth felt herself becoming more angry every moment, but she tried to speak calmly as she said:

'You could not have made me the offer of your hand in any

possible way that would have led me to accept it.'

Again his astonishment was clear. She went on:

'From the very beginning, your manners struck me as showing the greatest pride in yourself and scorn for the feelings of others, and I had not known you a month before I felt that you were the last man in the world whom I could ever be persuaded to marry.'

'You have said quite enough, madam. Forgive me for having wasted so much of your time, and accept my best wishes for your health and happiness.'

And with these words he quickly left the room.

The disorder of Elizabeth's mind was now painfully great, and from actual weakness she sat down and cried for half an hour. Her astonishment increased every moment. That she should receive an offer of marriage from Mr Darcy! That he should be so much in love with her that he wished to marry her in spite of all the objections that had made him prevent his friend's marrying her sister, and which must appear equally strong in his own case! And his shameful pride! His shameless admission of what he had done with regard to Jane! His unfeeling manner, his cruelty towards Mr Wickham!

She continued with these unhappy thoughts until the sound of the others returning from Rosings made her hurry away to her own room.

Chapter 15   Elizabeth Receives a Letter

Elizabeth woke the next morning to the same thoughts. It was impossible to fix her mind on anything else, so she decided soon after breakfast to give herself air and exercise. She was going directly towards her favourite part of the park, when she remembered that Mr Darcy sometimes came there, and she turned up the narrow road outside Rosings.

After a little time she caught sight of a gentleman within the park. She had turned away, but when she heard a voice calling her, though it was Mr Darcy's, she moved towards the gate. He, too, had reached it by this time. Holding out a letter, he said, with a look of proud calm, 'Will you do me the honour of reading this?' Then he turned and was soon out of sight.

Elizabeth opened the letter and saw two sheets, completely covered in handwriting. The letter had been written at Rosings, at eight o'clock in the morning, and read as follows:

Do not be troubled, madam, on receiving this letter. I write without any intention of upsetting you, or wounding my own self-respect, by mentioning unnecessarily what passed between us last night. But my character demands this to be written and read. You must, therefore, pardon the freedom with which I ask your attention. You will, I know, give it unwillingly, but I must request it as a matter of justice.

Last night, you charged me with two offences of a very different kind. The first was that I had separated Mr Bingley from your sister, and the other that I had ruined the hopes of Mr Wickham. I must now explain these matters.

I had not been in Hertfordshire for long before I saw that Bingley preferred your oldest sister to any other young woman there. I did not take this seriously, because I had often seen him in love before. But at the ball at Netherfield, while I had the honour of dancing with you, I first realized, through Sir William Lucas's accidental information, that Bingley's attentions to your sister had caused a general expectation that they would be married. From that moment I watched my friend carefully, and saw that his attraction to Miss Bennet was beyond what I had ever seen in him before. I also watched your sister. Her look and manner were open, cheerful and pleasing as ever, but I saw no sign of strong feeling. If *you* have not been mistaken here, I must have been deceived. Your greater knowledge of your sister makes it probable that you were right.

My objections to the marriage were not only those which I mentioned last night in my own case. There were others. The inferiority of your mother's family, though a problem, was nothing compared with the total lack of good manners so frequently shown by herself, by your three younger sisters, and occasionally even by your father. Pardon me – it pains me to offend you. Let it be of comfort to you that the behaviour of yourself and your older sister has been so honourably free from such faults.

The anxiety of Bingley's sisters had been excited as much as my own. The action that followed is known to you. But I do not suppose that the marriage would have been prevented if I had not persuaded Bingley that your sister did not care for him. He believed me when I told him that he had deceived himself.

I cannot blame myself for having done this. There is only one point on which I feel some discomfort, and that is that I purposely deceived him by hiding from him the fact of your sister's being in town.

With regard to that other charge, of having done harm to Mr Wickham, I can only defend myself by telling the whole story. Mr Wickham was the son of my father's manager, a respectable man. My father had the son well educated, and, hoping that the church would be his profession, intended to provide for him in it. I, as a young man of about the same age, very soon realized that he had a bad character, a fact which he carefully hid from my father. Before he died, my father asked me to encourage his development, and, if he joined the church, to let him have a valuable family living. Shortly afterwards, Mr Wickham wrote to say that he had decided against becoming a minister. He wished instead to study law, and demanded money to help him. I willingly gave him this, knowing that he was not fit for the church, and he then in return gave up all claim to any appointment in it. Later, the position became free, and, having neglected his studies of the law and lived a life of laziness, he demanded it, and I refused.

Last summer he again most painfully forced himself on my notice. I must now mention a family matter that I would myself wish to forget, and which only present necessity causes me to make known to you. I feel quite confident of your ability to keep my secret.

My sister, who is ten years younger than I am, had just left school, and was placed in the care of a lady in Ramsgate. My trust in this woman was not well judged. She allowed Wickham, whom she knew, to make love to my sister, who agreed to run away with him. I went down to see her just before the intended flight. Georgiana was ashamed, and told me everything. You may imagine what I felt, and how I acted.

Wickham's chief object was, without doubt, my sister's fortune, which is thirty thousand pounds, but I cannot help supposing that he also hoped to annoy me.

Colonel Fitzwilliam will bear witness to the truth of everything that I have written here. I shall try to find some opportunity of putting this letter into your hands during the morning.

Sincerely,

FITZWILLIAM DARCY.

As Elizabeth eagerly read the letter, she experienced every kind of feeling. She began with a strong prejudice against whatever it might contain, and wished to disbelieve completely all the explanations that it put forward. She repeatedly told herself: 'This must be false! This cannot be!' When she had gone through the whole document, she put it away, promising herself

70

that she would never look at it again.

But she could not do that. In half a minute the letter was unfolded again. She read and reread, with the closest attention, the details about Wickham. Of the two men concerned, one was free from blame, the other worthless. But how to decide between them? She tried to remember some example of goodness on Wickham's side. She could find none. He had pleased her by his appearance, his voice and his manner, but she knew nothing about his real character. The story of his intentions regarding Miss Darcy received some support from her conversation with Colonel Fitzwilliam only the morning before, and, according to Darcy, the Colonel would support every detail of this story.

She perfectly remembered everything that had passed in conversation between Wickham and herself during their first evening at Mr Philips's. Many of his expressions were still fresh in her memory. She was now struck with the bad taste of such remarks made to a stranger, and was surprised that it had escaped her notice before. She saw the lack of good breeding in the way in which he had put himself forward. She remembered that he had claimed to have no fear of seeing Mr Darcy, but he had avoided the Netherfield ball the very next week. She remembered also that until the Netherfield family had left the area, he had told his story to no one but herself, but after their removal he had discussed it freely, although he had told her that respect for the father would always prevent him from making public the injustice that was done to him by the son.

She became completely ashamed of herself. She felt that she had been blind, prejudiced, unreasonable.

She read again the part of the letter about Jane and was forced to admit to herself the justice of Darcy's description of her sister. She knew that Jane's feelings, though strong, were usually well hidden.

When she came to the part in which her family were

mentioned, in words so wounding to her pride but still so just in the blame that they expressed, her sense of shame was severe. The praise of herself and her sister was not unfelt, but it could not comfort her, and when she considered that Jane's disappointment had, in fact, been the work of her nearest relations, she felt in lower spirits than she had ever been before.

She soon began to know much of the letter by heart. She studied every sentence, and her feelings towards its writer were at times widely different. When she remembered the manner in which he had addressed her, she was still full of anger, but when she considered how unfairly she had misjudged him, her anger was turned against herself, and his disappointed feelings became the object of pity. She could feel grateful for his attachment and could respect his general character, but she could not approve of him, or be sorry about her refusal, or feel the slightest desire ever to see him again. In her own past behaviour, there was a continual cause for annoyance, and in the faults of her family, a subject of even heavier sorrow. They would never be put right. Her father, happy to laugh at them, would never trouble himself to control the wild foolishness of his youngest daughters, and her mother, with manners so far from perfect herself, was completely unconscious of the evil. Elizabeth had frequently united with Jane in an attempt to control the silliness of Kitty and Lydia, but while they were encouraged by their mother's fond carelessness, what chance could there be of improvement? Kitty, weak-spirited, nervous, and completely under Lydia's influence, had always been offended by their advice, and Lydia, careless and determined to have her own way, would hardly give them a hearing. They were foolish, lazy and empty-headed. While there was an officer in Meryton, they would be trying to attract him, and while Meryton was within walking distance of Longbourn, they would be going there for ever.

Anxiety for Jane was another cause of concern, and Mr

Darcy's explanation, by bringing back all her former good opinion of Bingley, increased the sense of what Jane had lost.

It may easily be believed that the events of the last two days had such an effect on Elizabeth's naturally happy spirits that she found it almost impossible to appear even reasonably cheerful. It was with a ready heart that she watched her visit to Hunsford come to an end in the next week. Mr Darcy had, she knew, left shortly after handing her the letter.

At last the boxes were packed, and the goodbyes over, not without a long speech from Mr Collins. The carriage drove off towards London, where Jane was to join the party for home.

'Oh!' cried Maria, after a few minutes' silence. 'It seems only a day or two since we first came! But so many things have happened!'

'A great many,' said her companion sadly.

'We had dinner nine times at Rosings, besides drinking tea there twice! How much I shall have to tell!'

Elizabeth privately added, 'And how much I shall have to hide!'

Chapter 16   Elizabeth and Jane Return Home

It was the second week in May when Jane, Elizabeth and Maria set out from London together for Hertfordshire, and as they came near the small hotel where Mr Bennet's carriage would meet them, they saw both Kitty and Lydia looking out of an upstairs room. These two girls had been in the place for more than an hour, happily employed in visiting a hat shop opposite and arranging a meal.

After welcoming their sisters, they proudly pointed to a table laid out with cold meat, crying, 'Isn't this nice? Isn't it a pleasant surprise?'

'And we want all of you to be our guests,' added Lydia, 'but you must lend us the money, because we have just spent ours at the shop over there.' Then, showing the things that she had bought: 'Look here, I have bought this hat. I don't think that it is very pretty, but I thought I might as well buy it as not. I shall pull it to pieces as soon as I get home, and remake it.'

And when her sisters criticized it as ugly, she added, 'It will not much matter what one wears this summer, as the regiment is leaving Meryton in two weeks' time.'

'Are they, really?' cried Elizabeth, with the greatest satisfaction.

'They are going to be camped near Brighton, and I do so want our father to take us all there for the summer! Mother would like to go, too, of all things!'

'Yes,' thought Elizabeth, '*that* would be pleasant. Oh, heavens! Brighton and a whole campful of soldiers, to us, who have been troubled enough already by one small regiment and the monthly dances at Meryton!'

'Now I have some news,' said Lydia, as they sat down at the table. 'It is excellent news about a person whom we all like.'

Jane and Elizabeth looked at each other, and the waiter was told that he need not stay. Lydia laughed, and said:

'Why must you always be so formal and correct? You thought that the waiter must not hear, as if he cared! But he is an ugly man! I am glad that he has gone. Well, but now for my news. It is about dear Wickham. There is no danger of his marrying Mary King. She has gone away. Wickham is safe.'

'And Mary King is safe!' added Elizabeth. 'Safe from a marriage which would be unwise in regard to fortune.'

As soon as everyone had eaten, and the older ones had paid, the carriage was ordered and the whole party, with their boxes, needlework bags and packages, and the unwelcome addition of all Kitty's and Lydia's shopping, were seated in it.

'How nicely we are packed in!' cried Lydia. 'Now let us be quite comfortable, and talk and laugh all the way home. And in the first place, let us hear what has happened to you all since you went away. Have you seen any pleasant men? I was in great hopes that one of you would have got a husband before you came back. Jane is almost twenty-three! How ashamed I should be of not being married before that age! Oh, how I should like to be married before any of you!'

In this noisy manner, with the help of Kitty, Lydia tried to amuse her companions all the way to Longbourn. Elizabeth listened as little as she could, but there was no escaping the frequent mention of Wickham's name.

Their welcome home was most kind. Mrs Bennet was glad to see Jane as beautiful as ever, and more than once Mr Bennet said to Elizabeth: 'I am glad that you have come back, Lizzy.'

Their party was large, as almost all the Lucases came to meet Maria and hear the news. Lady Lucas was inquiring of Maria, across the table, after the health and housekeeping affairs of her oldest daughter. Mrs Bennet was doubly engaged, on the one hand collecting an account of the present London fashions from Jane, who sat some way below her, and, on the other, repeating them all to the younger Miss Lucases. Lydia, in a voice rather louder than anyone else's, was describing the various pleasures of the morning to anybody who would listen to her.

'Oh, Mary,' she said, 'I wish you had gone with us! We had such fun! We talked and laughed so loudly that anybody might have heard us 10 miles away!'

To this, Mary replied, 'Do not think, my dear sister, that I scorn such pleasures. But I admit that they have no attraction for me. I would much prefer a book.'

But Lydia heard not a word of this answer. She rarely listened to anybody for more than half a minute, and never attended to Mary at all.

In the afternoon, Lydia was anxious for the other girls to walk to Meryton, but Elizabeth steadily opposed the suggestion. It should not be said that the Misses Bennet could not be at home half a day before they were in search of the officers. She did not want to see Wickham again, and was determined to avoid doing so for as long as possible.

◆

Elizabeth's impatience to inform Jane of what had happened could no longer be controlled, and at last, having decided to keep back every detail with which her sister was concerned, and having warned her to be surprised, she described to her the next morning most of the scene between Mr Darcy and herself. She then spoke of the letter, repeating all that it contained which mentioned George Wickham. What a blow this was for poor Jane, who would willingly have gone through the world without believing that so much evil existed in the whole human race, as was collected here in one person.

'I do not know when I have been more shocked,' she said. 'Wickham so very bad! It is almost beyond belief. And poor Mr Darcy! Dear Lizzy, only consider what he must have suffered! Such a disappointment, and with the knowledge of your bad opinion too! And having to tell such a thing about his sister!'

'There is one point on which I want your advice. I want to be told whether I ought or ought not to make known the truth about Wickham's character to our friends in general.'

Miss Bennet thought a little, and then replied, 'Surely there can be no reason for shaming him so terribly. What is your own opinion?'

'That it ought not to be attempted. Mr Darcy has not given me permission to make his information public. At present I will say nothing about it.'

'You are quite right. It might ruin him for ever, if his past became known. He is now, perhaps, sorry for what he has done, and anxious to improve.'

The confusion in Elizabeth's mind was relieved by this conversation. She had got rid of two of the secrets which had weighed on her for two weeks, and was certain of a willing listener in Jane whenever she might want to talk again of either. But she dared not tell the other half of Mr Darcy's letter, nor explain to her sister how sincerely she had been valued by his friend. Here was knowledge which no one could share.

She now had time to observe the real state of her sister's spirits. Jane was not happy. She still had very warm feelings for Bingley.

'Well, Lizzy,' said Mrs Bennet one day, 'what is your opinion now of this sad business of Jane's?'

'I do not think that Mr Bingley will ever live at Netherfield again.'

'Oh, well! It is just as he chooses. Well, my comfort is, I am sure that Jane will die of a broken heart, and then he will be sorry for what he has done.'

But as Elizabeth could not receive comfort from any such expectations, she did not answer.

'Well, Lizzy,' her mother continued, soon afterwards, 'and so the Collinses live very comfortably, do they? Charlotte is an excellent manager, I expect. If she is half as sharp as her mother, she is saving enough. And I suppose they often talk of having Longbourn when your father is dead. They look on it quite as their own, I dare say. I would be ashamed of owning somewhere that was left me on such unjust conditions.'

Chapter 17   The Regiment Leaves Meryton

The second week of their return was the last of the regiment's stay in Meryton, and all the young ladies in the neighbourhood were in the lowest of spirits. Only the older Misses Bennet were still able to eat, drink and sleep, and to continue the usual course of their lives. Very frequently they were charged with heartlessness by Kitty and Lydia, whose own unhappiness was extreme.

'Heavens! What will become of us?' they would often cry in bitterness. 'How can you be smiling so, Lizzy?' Their fond mother shared all their unhappiness. She remembered what she had suffered on a similar occasion in her youth.

'I am sure,' she said, 'that I cried for two days when Colonel Millar's regiment went away. I thought that my heart would break.'

'I am sure that *mine* will break,' said Lydia.

'If only we could go to Brighton,' said Mrs Bennet.

'Oh, yes! But Father is so disagreeable.'

Such were the complaints continually repeated at Longbourn House. Elizabeth tried to be amused by them, but all sense of pleasure was lost in shame. She felt once more the justice of Mr Darcy's criticisms, and she had never been so ready to pardon his part in the affairs of his friend.

But the darkness of Lydia's future was lightened shortly afterwards. She received an invitation from Mrs Forster, the wife of the colonel of the regiment, to go with her to Brighton. This friend was a young woman, and very recently married.

The joy of Lydia on this occasion, the pleasure of Mrs Bennet, and the jealous anger of Kitty, are hardly to be described. Without any concern for her sister's feelings, Lydia flew about the house in restless excitement, calling for everybody's congratulations, and laughing and talking with more violence than ever, while the luckless Kitty continued to complain.

'I cannot see why Mrs Forster did not ask me as well as Lydia,' she said, 'I have just as much right to be asked as she has, and more, too, because I am two years older.'

Elizabeth tried to make her more reasonable, and Jane urged her to bear her disappointment quietly, but without success. As for Elizabeth herself, she considered this invitation as the deathblow to any possibility of common sense in Lydia, and, though such an act would make her hated if it became known, she could not help secretly advising her father not to let her go. She suggested to him the probability of Lydia's being even more foolish with such a companion at Brighton, where the opportunities for silliness must be greater than at home.

'If you knew,' said Elizabeth, 'of the very great disadvantage which has already come from the public notice of Lydia's uncontrolled behaviour, I am sure that you would judge it unwise to let her go.'

'Already come!' repeated Mr Bennet. 'What! Has she frightened away some of your lovers? Poor little Lizzy! But do not be disheartened. Young men who cannot bear to be connected with a little silliness are not worth worrying over.'

But Elizabeth, excusing herself for speaking so plainly to her father, continued in her attempt to persuade him of the growing lack of self-control that both his younger daughters showed in public, and the danger of their characters becoming fixed. He saw that her whole heart was in the subject and, taking her hand warmly, said in reply:

'Do not make yourself anxious, my love. Wherever you and Jane are known, you must be respected and valued, and you will not appear to less advantage because you have a pair of – or I may say, three – very silly sisters. We shall have no peace at home if Lydia does not go to Brighton. Let her go, then. Colonel Forster is a sensible man, and will keep her from any real harm, and she is luckily too poor to attract any fortune-hunters. At Brighton she will be of less importance than here. Let us hope, therefore, that it may teach her a little about life.'

With this answer Elizabeth was forced to be satisfied.

♦

Elizabeth now saw Wickham for the last time. Having met him frequently since her return, she had become fairly well used to the situation. Her interest in him had quite gone, and in his present behaviour to herself she had a fresh cause for displeasure. The readiness that he soon showed in renewing his attentions to her, now that Miss King had gone, proved that he judged her to be foolish enough to be pleased by notice from him at any time that he chose to give it.

On the very last day of the regiment's stay he had dinner, with some other officers at Longbourn. Elizabeth was so unwilling to part from him in a friendly way that she mentioned the fact that Colonel Fitzwilliam and Mr Darcy had both spent three weeks at Rosings, and asked him whether he was acquainted with the former.

He looked surprised, displeased, anxious; but, controlling himself, soon replied that he had formerly seen him often, and asked how she liked him. She answered warmly in his favour, and went on to say that from knowing Mr Darcy better, he, too, was better understood and liked.

Wickham's anxiety now appeared in a reddened face and a troubled look. He did not dare to say much more, but in spite of an appearance of cheerfulness, it was clear that he would now be glad to leave the area.

When the party ended, Lydia returned with Mrs Forster to Meryton, from which place they would set out early the next morning. The separation between her and her family was noisy rather than painful. Kitty was the only one to cry, and her tears were from jealousy and from pity for herself. In the loud happiness of Lydia herself in saying goodbye, the more gentle last words of her sisters were spoken without being heard.

Chapter 18   Pemberley

Mr Bennet's marriage had been the result of a lack of good judgment. Attracted by youth and beauty, and that appearance of good temper which they usually give, he had married a woman whose weak understanding and narrow mind had very soon put an end to real love for her. Respect and confidence had gone for ever, and his hopes of happiness at home were ended. But he was fond of the country and of books, and his wife's foolishness and lack of knowledge gave him amusement.

Elizabeth had never been blind to the unfitting nature of her father's behaviour as a husband. It had always upset her, but, respecting his abilities and grateful for his caring treatment of herself, she had tried to forget what she could not fail to notice. But she had never felt so strongly as now the disadvantages that must be experienced by the children of so unsuitable a marriage.

When Lydia went away, she promised to write very often and in great detail to her mother and Kitty, but her letters were always long expected and very short. Those to her mother contained little but unimportant news, and those to Kitty, though longer, contained too many secrets to be read to the family.

Life in Meryton was undoubtedly duller after the regiment had left. Elizabeth began to look forward to her northern tour with her aunt and uncle, the date of which was approaching. Her disappointment was therefore great when she learnt that business prevented her uncle from being away from London as long as he had hoped. They were forced to give up the visit to the Lakes, and to choose a shorter tour; according to the present plan, they were to go no further north than Derbyshire, where Mrs Gardiner hoped to revisit the town in which she had spent the earlier part of her life. There were many ideas connected in Elizabeth's mind with the mention of Derbyshire. It was impossible for her to see or hear the word without thinking of Pemberley and its owner.

♦

At last the period of waiting was over, and Mr and Mrs Gardiner, with their four children, appeared at Longbourn. The children, two girls of six and eight years old, and two younger boys, would be left in the special care of their cousin Jane, who was the favourite, and whose steady good sense and sweetness of temper exactly suited her for looking after them in every way – teaching them, playing with them, and loving them.

The Gardiners stayed at Longbourn for only one night, and set out the next morning with Elizabeth on their travels. One enjoyment was certain – that of pleasure in each other's company.

Their journey took them to many interesting and well-known places – Oxford, Blenheim, Warwick, Kenilworth, and others. At last, after having seen all the chief sights of the area, they continued on their way to the little town of Lambton in Derbyshire, the scene of Mrs Gardiner's former home, and Elizabeth found that Pemberley was only 5 miles away from Lambton. In talking over their plans, Mrs Gardiner expressed a wish to see the place again. Mr Gardiner expressed his willingness, and their niece was asked for her approval.

Elizabeth was in an awkward situation. She felt that she had no business at Pemberley, and she pretended, therefore, that she was tired of seeing great houses. Mrs Gardiner thought this stupid, and Elizabeth did not know what to do. The possibility of meeting Mr Darcy was frightening. She trembled at the very idea. Fortunately, she was able to find out from a servant at the hotel where they were staying that Pemberley's owner was absent, so when the subject was mentioned again the next morning, she readily agreed, because her unwillingness had turned to interest.

As they drove along, Elizabeth's mind was too full for conversation, but she saw and admired every notable view. The park was very large, and they passed through a beautiful wood stretching over a wide area. Pemberley House was a large, fine-looking stone building, on ground slightly higher than the park; in front, a stream had been widened without making it appear at all artificial. Elizabeth had never seen a place for which nature had done so much, or where natural beauty had been so little spoilt by awkward taste. Her aunt and uncle were equally warm in their admiration, and at that moment she felt that there were in fact advantages to being the lady of Pemberley!

On arriving at the house, they were admitted to the hall. The housekeeper was a respectable-looking woman, who showed them round the chief rooms. From every window there were beauties to be seen. The rooms themselves were of good height and fine shape, and with furniture in excellent taste.

'I might have been the lady of this place,' she thought. 'Instead of viewing it as a stranger, I might have been welcoming my aunt and uncle as my guests. But no,' she remembered, 'I would not have been allowed to invite my relations.'

This was a lucky thought – it saved her from feeling sorry for herself.

She wished very much to inquire of the housekeeper whether her master was really absent. At last the question was asked by her uncle, and she turned away anxiously when the reply came, 'We expect him tomorrow, with a large party of friends.'

Her aunt now called her to look at a picture, and asked her with a smile how she liked it. It was of Wickham. The housekeeper mentioned his name, and added, 'He has now gone into the army, but I am afraid that he has turned out very wild.'

Mrs Gardiner looked at her niece with a smile, but Elizabeth could not return it.

They then looked at pictures of Mr Darcy and his sister.

'And is Miss Darcy as good-looking as her brother?' said Mr Gardiner.

'Oh, yes,' replied the housekeeper, 'the best-looking young lady that ever was seen, and so skilled! She plays and sings the whole day long. In the next room there is a new instrument that has just arrived for her – a present from my master. She is coming here tomorrow with him.'

'Does your master spend much time at Pemberley?'

'Not as much as I would wish, sir. Miss Darcy is always here for the summer months.'

'Except,' thought Elizabeth, 'when she goes to Ramsgate.'

'If your master married, you might see more of him.'

'Yes, sir, but I do not know who is good enough for him.'

Mr and Mrs Gardiner smiled.

'I say no more than the truth. I have never had an angry word from him in my life, and I have known him ever since he was four years old.'

Elizabeth's keenest attention was excited. This was praise of the strongest kind, and most opposite to her ideas.

'He is the best master that ever lived. Some people call him proud, but I never saw anything of it.'

Mr Gardiner was highly amused as she continued to describe the good qualities of her master. He judged that her extreme praise of him was the result of family prejudice.

'This fine account of him,' whispered Mrs Gardiner to her niece, 'does not agree with his behaviour to our poor friend.'

Elizabeth said rather quietly that they might have been deceived.

'That is not very likely. Our information was *too* direct.'

They were then shown into a very pretty little sitting room with new furniture, and were told that it was done just to give pleasure to Miss Darcy, who had become fond of the room when last at Pemberley.

'It is always the way with him,' the housekeeper explained. 'Whatever can give his sister pleasure is sure to be done.'

'He is a good brother,' said Elizabeth.

There was certainly at this moment in her mind a more gentle feeling towards him than she had ever had when she was closely acquainted with him. Every idea brought forward by the housekeeper was favourable to his character, and as she looked once again at his picture, she felt more grateful to him for his good opinion of her than she had ever done before.

◆

The house had now been examined, and they went outside in the charge of the gardener to admire the grounds. As they walked towards the river, Elizabeth turned back to look again, and as she did so, the owner of the building suddenly came forward from the road that led behind it.

They were within 20 yards of each other, and his appearance was so sudden that it was impossible to avoid him. Their eyes met immediately. He stopped, and then for a moment seemed unable to move from surprise. Quickly recovering his self-control, though, he walked towards the party and spoke to Elizabeth, if not with perfect calm, at least with perfect politeness.

She had immediately turned away, but when he approached she received his greetings with a confusion that it was impossible to control. Mr and Mrs Gardiner stood a little way off while he was talking to their niece, who, shocked by their meeting, hardly dared lift her eyes to his face and did not know what answer she returned to his polite inquiries after her family. She was full of surprise at the change in his manner since they last parted, and found that every sentence that he spoke was increasing her confusion. As the realization of the awkwardness of her being found there returned to her mind, the few minutes in which they were together were some of the most uncomfortable in her life. He did not seem less shocked. When he spoke, his voice had none of its usual calmness, and he repeated some of his questions more than once.

At last, every idea seemed to fail him and, after standing for a few minutes without saying a word, he suddenly went away. The others then joined her. Elizabeth was filled with shame and annoyance. Her coming there was the most unfortunate, most unwise thing in the world! How shameful it must appear to a man who thought so highly of himself! It might seem as if she had purposely put herself in his way again. Oh! Why had she come? Or why did he come a day before he was expected? And his behaviour, so noticeably changed — what could it mean? It was astonishing that he should ever speak to her — but to speak with such politeness, to inquire after her family! Never in her life had she seen him so gentle. She did not know what to think.

They now entered a beautiful walk by the water, but it was some time before Elizabeth could give it any attention, although she replied without thinking to the remarks of her companions. She greatly wished to know what was passing in Mr Darcy's mind, and whether, in spite of everything, she was still dear to him.

After wandering on for some time quite slowly, because Mrs Gardiner was not a great walker and was becoming tired, they were again surprised by the sight of Mr Darcy approaching them. Elizabeth saw that he had lost none of his recent politeness, and to show that she too could be polite, she began to admire the place. But she had not got beyond the word "beautiful", when some unlucky thought reminded her that praise of Pemberley might be misunderstood. The colour in her face deepened, and she said no more.

As she paused, he asked her if she would do him the honour of introducing him to her friends. This was quite unexpected. 'What will be his surprise,' she thought, 'when he knows who they are? He thinks that they are people of social position.'

The introduction, though, was made immediately, and as she named them as family relations of hers, she took a secret look at him to see how he bore it. It was plain that he was surprised, but instead of going away, he turned back with them and entered into conversation with Mr Gardiner. Elizabeth could not help being pleased. It was comforting that he should know that she had some relations of whom there was no need to be ashamed. She listened carefully, and felt happiness in every expression, every sentence of her uncle that showed his intelligence, his taste, or his good manners.

The conversation soon turned to fishing, and she heard Mr Darcy, with the greatest politeness, invite him to fish there as often as he chose. Mrs Gardiner, who was walking arm in arm with Elizabeth, gave her a look of surprise. Elizabeth said nothing, but she was extremely pleased. The mark of attention must be all for herself.

A little later, Mrs Gardiner, tired by the exercise of the morning, found Elizabeth's arm not strong enough to support her, and therefore preferred her husband's. Mr Darcy took her place by her niece. After a short silence, the lady spoke first. She wished him to know that she had been informed of his absence before she came to the place. He admitted that he had put forward his arrival because of some business. 'The rest of my party,' he continued, 'will be here tomorrow, and among them are some with whom you are acquainted – Mr Bingley and his sisters.'

Elizabeth answered only by a slight lowering of her head.

After a pause, he added: 'There is also a person who especially wishes to be known to you. Will you allow me, or do I ask too much, to introduce my sister to you?'

The surprise of such a request was great – too great for her to remember later in what manner she agreed. They now walked on in silence. Elizabeth was not comfortable – that was impossible – but she was pleased by his attention.

When Mr and Mrs Gardiner came up to them at the house, they were all urged to go inside and take some tea, but this was politely refused. Mr Darcy handed the ladies into the carriage, and when it drove off, Elizabeth saw him walking slowly towards the house.

Her uncle and aunt now began to speak very favourably of his effect on them. They were cross with her, saying, 'Why did you tell us he was so disagreeable?'

Elizabeth excused herself as well as she could.

She then felt it her duty to tell them, in as careful a manner as she could, that she believed herself to have been mistaken in thinking that he had been at fault in his treatment of Wickham. Mrs Gardiner was surprised, but as they were now approaching the scenes of her youth, all her interest was soon taken up by the pleasures of her memories, and the meeting after many years of old friends, so Elizabeth was set free from awkward questions, and could be left with her own thoughts.

Chapter 19   The Bingleys

Mr Darcy brought his sister to visit Elizabeth a few hours after her arrival the next day. The Gardiners were surprised again, and a new idea on the subject began to enter their heads.

Elizabeth saw with astonishment that the young lady with

whom she was now made acquainted was not extremely proud, as had been reported, but only extremely shy. The expression on her face showed sense and natural good temper, and her manners were perfectly gentle.

They had not been together long before Bingley also came to call on Elizabeth. His manner was unchanged, and he looked and spoke with friendly confidence. To Mr and Mrs Gardiner, who knew what he meant to Jane, he was hardly a less interesting person than to herself. The whole party excited their attention. They were taken up in observing Mr Darcy and their niece. They remained a little in doubt about the lady's feelings, but it was clear that the gentleman was overflowing with admiration.

Elizabeth, on her side, had much to do. She wished to be agreeable to her visitors. She was watching Bingley with Miss Darcy, who had been put forward as a competitor to Jane. She saw nothing in the behaviour of either that gave support to the words of Miss Bingley. In a voice of real sadness, Bingley observed to her, at a moment when the others were talking together, that they had not met for eight months, not since 26 November, when they were all dancing together at Netherfield. Elizabeth was pleased that his memory was so exact. He later took an opportunity to ask her privately whether *all* her sisters were at Longbourn. There was not much in the question, but his look and manner gave it meaning.

It was not often that she could turn her eyes on Mr Darcy himself, but when she did manage to look in his direction, she saw him doing his best to gain the good opinion of her relations, and when the visit came to an end, the wish was expressed of seeing them all at dinner at Pemberley two days later.

♦

It had been agreed between the aunt and the niece that such a striking piece of politeness as Miss Darcy's, in coming to see them on the very day of her arrival, ought to be returned, though it could not be equalled. It was therefore decided to call on her at Pemberley the following morning. Elizabeth was pleased, though when she asked herself the reason, she had very little to say in reply.

When they reached the house, they were received by Miss Darcy, who was sitting with Mrs Hurst and Miss Bingley and the lady with whom she lived in London. Georgiana's welcome was very shy, and might have given a false idea of pride, but Mrs Gardiner and her niece understood her difficulty and pitied her.

Mrs Hurst and Miss Bingley greeted them in few words, and when they were seated an awkward pause followed. It was broken by Miss Darcy's companion, a woman of good breeding, who carried on a conversation with Mrs Gardiner with some help from Elizabeth. Miss Darcy looked as if she wished for courage enough to join in.

Elizabeth soon saw that she was closely watched by Miss Bingley. After a quarter of an hour, Miss Bingley inquired coldly after the health of her family, and Elizabeth replied just as coldly.

Some servants then entered with cold meat, cake, and a variety of all the finest fruits in season, and soon after that Mr Darcy, who had been fishing with Mr Gardiner, made his appearance.

Elizabeth decided to appear perfectly calm and relaxed, especially when she realized that the suspicions of the whole party were causing close observation of every word, expression and movement from Darcy or herself. In no face was this so clearly expressed as in Miss Bingley's, in spite of the smiles that spread over it when she addressed one of them. Jealousy had not yet made her give up hope, and she still planned to win Mr Darcy. But a little later, in an unwise moment of anger, she said with scornful politeness:

'I believe, Miss Eliza, that the regiment has left Meryton. They must be a great loss to *your* family.'

Elizabeth answered calmly, and while she spoke, she noticed that the colour in Darcy's face had deepened, and that his sister was full of confusion. Miss Bingley little knew what pain she was giving her friend. She had only intended to anger Elizabeth, and make her show some feeling that might harm her in Darcy's opinion. Elizabeth's self-control soon lessened his discomfort, and as Miss Bingley, annoyed and disappointed, dared not move any closer to the subject of Wickham, Georgiana, too, recovered in time.

Their visit did not continue for long after this, and when Mr Darcy returned from walking them to their carriage, Miss Bingley was busy criticizing Elizabeth's appearance, behaviour and dress.

'How very ugly Eliza Bennet looks this morning!' she cried. 'I have never in my life seen anyone so much changed as she is since the winter. She has become so brown and rough-looking. I must admit, though, that I could never see any beauty in her. Her features are not at all attractive, and as for her eyes, they have a sharp look to them.'

As Miss Bingley believed that Mr Darcy admired Elizabeth, this was not the best way of persuading him that he should prefer her, but angry people are not always wise. He looked annoyed, but remained silent, and from a determination to make him speak, she continued:

'I remember, when we first knew her in Hertfordshire, how you yourself said one night, after they had been having dinner at Netherfield, "She, a beauty! I should as soon call her mother a person of high intelligence!" But I believe you thought her rather pretty afterwards.'

'Yes,' replied Darcy, who could no longer control himself. 'For many months I have considered her to be one of the best-looking women of my acquaintance.'

In the carriage, as they returned to their hotel, Mrs Gardiner and Elizabeth talked of all that had happened during their visit, except what particularly interested them both and the person who had attracted their attention most. They spoke of his sister, his friends, his house, his fruit, of everything except himself! But Elizabeth was anxious to know what Mrs Gardiner thought of him, and Mrs Gardiner would have been extremely pleased if her niece had introduced the subject!

Chapter 20   Lydia and Wickham

Elizabeth had been a good deal disappointed in not hearing from Jane on their arrival at Lambton, and this disappointment was renewed on both mornings that had now been spent there, but on the third her anxiety was relieved by receiving two letters together, of which the earlier one had been sent elsewhere because the address was not clearly written.

Her aunt and uncle set out on a walk, leaving her to enjoy them in quiet. The earlier one had been written five days before, and began with an account of their little parties and social events and unimportant local news, but the second half, which was dated a day later, gave more important information. It said:

Since writing yesterday, dearest Lizzy, something of a most unexpected and serious nature has happened. What I have to say concerns poor Lydia. An urgent message from Colonel Forster came at twelve last night, just as we had all gone to bed, to inform us that she had gone off to Scotland with one of his officers – to tell the truth, with Wickham! Imagine our surprise. But to Kitty it does not seem completely unexpected. I am very, very sorry. Such an unwise marriage on both sides! They went off on Saturday night at about twelve, but were not missed until yesterday morning. I must end this letter, because I cannot spend long away from my poor mother, who is sadly troubled. I am afraid that you will not be able to read this letter, for I hardly know what I have written.

Without allowing herself time for consideration, Elizabeth immediately seized the other letter and, opening it with the greatest impatience, read as follows:

By this time, my dearest sister, you will have received my hurried letter. I hope this will be clearer, but my head is so confused that I cannot be certain of it. Dearest Lizzy, I have bad news for you, and it cannot be delayed. Although a marriage between Mr Wickham and our poor Lydia would be very unwise, we are now anxious to be sure that the ceremony has actually been performed. Though Lydia left a short note for Mrs Forster giving her the idea that they were going to Gretna Green,* something that Denny said showed his belief that Wickham never intended to go there, or to marry Lydia at all. This was repeated to Colonel Forster, who immediately became anxious and set out in search of them. He managed to follow their course, but only as far as London, where they have disappeared. After making every possible inquiry, he kindly came on to Longbourn and told us the bad news.

Our anxiety, my dear Lizzy, is very great. My mother and father believe the worst has happened, but I cannot think so badly of Wickham. Perhaps they have some reason for being married privately in town. My poor mother is really ill, and as for my father, I never in my life saw him so troubled. Poor Kitty has to bear our parents' anger for having hidden the nature of their friendship, but as it was a matter of confidence, one cannot be

*Gretna Green: a place in Scotland where young people could marry quickly and without their parent's permission.

surprised that she did so. I am truly glad, dearest Lizzy, that you have been saved from some of these scenes, but now that the first shock is over, shall I admit that I greatly wish for your return? But I am not so unkind as to urge it, if it is inconvenient. My father is going to London immediately to try to discover Lydia, but the extreme state of his feelings will not allow him to act in the wisest way. At a time like this, my uncle's advice and help would be everything in the world.

'Oh, where, where is my uncle?' cried Elizabeth, jumping from her seat as she finished the letter, in eagerness to follow him without loss of time. But as she reached the door, it was opened by a servant, and Mr Darcy appeared. Her pale face and hurried manner struck him immediately, and before he could recover from his surprise, she quickly said, 'I beg your pardon, but I must leave you. I must find Mr Gardiner this moment on business that cannot be delayed.'

'Oh, heavens! What is the matter?' he cried, with more feeling than politeness. Then, calming himself, he added, 'I will not keep you a minute, but let me, or let the servant, go after Mr Gardiner. You are not well enough. You cannot go yourself.'

Elizabeth paused, but her knees trembled under her and, calling back the servant, she gave him the message. When he had left the room, she sat down, unable to support herself, and looked so ill and unhappy that it was impossible for Darcy to leave her, or to prevent himself from saying, in a voice of gentleness and sympathy, 'Let me call a woman for you. Is there nothing you could take to give yourself some relief? Shall I get you a glass of wine? You are very ill.'

'No, I thank you,' she replied, trying to recover herself. 'I am quite well. I am only anxious about some terrible news from home.'

She burst into tears as she mentioned it, and for a few minutes could not speak another word. Finally she went on, 'My youngest sister has left all her friends – has run away – has thrown herself into the power of – of Mr Wickham. She has no money, nothing that he could want – she is ruined for ever.'

Darcy stood still with astonishment.

'When I consider,' Elizabeth added, 'that I might have prevented it! I, who knew what he really was. But it is too late!'

Darcy quietly expressed his sympathy, and Elizabeth, in answer to his inquiries, told him what details she knew. He hardly seemed to hear her, and was walking up and down in deep thought, with a serious and troubled expression on his face. Elizabeth immediately understood. Her power over him was sinking under such a proof of family weakness, such a certainty of the deepest dishonour. She could neither blame him, nor feel any surprise, but the situation was exactly of a kind to make her understand her own wishes, and she had never so honestly felt that she could have loved him as now, when all love must be without hope.

But her own troubles were soon swallowed up in the memory of Lydia and, covering her face with her hands, she was soon lost to everything else. After a pause of several minutes, she was brought back to the present situation by the voice of her companion, who said, 'This unfortunate affair will, I fear, prevent my sister's having the pleasure of seeing you at Pemberley today.'

'Oh, yes! Please be kind enough to apologize for us to Miss Darcy. Say that urgent business calls us home. Hide the truth as long as possible.'

He agreed to do so and, with only one serious parting look, went away. As he left the room, Elizabeth felt how improbable it was that they should ever see each other again in such a friendly way. Looking back over the whole of their acquaintance, so full of differences and variety, she felt saddened at the awkward change in her feelings, which would now have encouraged its continuance, and would formerly have been glad at its ending.

If grateful feelings and respect form part of love, Elizabeth's change of feelings will be considered neither improbable nor faulty. The fact is certain that she saw him go with sadness and found additional pain in this early example of what Lydia's behaviour must produce. She had no hope of Wickham meaning to marry her sister. She had never noticed, while the regiment was in Meryton, that Lydia had any special liking for him, but she was sure that Lydia only needed encouragement to form a strong relationship with anybody. Sometimes one officer, sometimes another had been her favourite. Though she did not suppose Lydia to be purposely running away without the intention of marriage, she believed that she would easily be tricked by a deceitful man.

Mr and Mrs Gardiner had hurried back, worried, and Elizabeth told them the cause of her message. Although Lydia had never been a favourite with them, they could not help being deeply shocked. After they had expressed their feelings of sympathy, Mr Gardiner promised every help that it was in his power to give, and everything concerning their journey was speedily arranged.

'But what is to be done about Pemberley?' cried Mrs Gardiner.

'I told Mr Darcy that we should not be able to go there tonight. That is all settled.'

'What is all settled?' repeated Mrs Gardiner to herself, as she ran to her room to get herself ready for travelling. 'And do they know each other so well that she can tell him the real truth? How I wish that I knew!'

Packing had to be done, and notes had to be written to all their friends in Lambton, with excuses for their leaving so suddenly. An hour, though, was enough to complete everything, and at the end of that hour Elizabeth found herself seated in the carriage, on the road to Longbourn.

Chapter 21   Mr Gardiner Goes to London

They travelled as quickly as possible, and, having slept one night on the way, reached Longbourn by dinnertime the next day.

The little Gardiners, attracted by the sight of the carriage, were standing on the steps of the house, and the joyful surprise that lit up their faces was the travellers' first welcome.

Elizabeth jumped out, gave each of them a quick kiss, and hurried into the hall, where Jane, who came running downstairs from her mother's room, met her immediately.

As Elizabeth greeted her warmly, tears filled the eyes of both sisters. The younger, though, did not lose a moment before asking whether anything had been heard of the missing pair.

'Not yet,' replied Jane.

'Is our father in town?'

'Yes, he went on Tuesday.'

'And have you heard from him often?'

'Only once, to say that he had arrived and to give me his address. He only added that he would not write again until he had something important to mention.'

'And our mother – how is she?'

'Fairly well, though her nerves are troubling her a great deal, and she is still in bed. Mary and Kitty, thank heaven, are quite well.'

'But you – how are you?' cried Elizabeth. 'You look pale. How much you must have suffered!'

Her sister told her that she was perfectly well, and their conversation, which had been continued while Mr and Mrs Gardiner were with their children, was now ended by the approach of the whole party.

Mrs Bennet, to whose room they all went, received them exactly as might be expected, with tears and expressions of sadness, angry words against Wickham, and complaints of her own sufferings. She blamed everybody but the person who, by bringing up her daughter so carelessly, was chiefly responsible for her faults.

'If I had been able,' she said, 'to go to Brighton with all my family, *this* would never have happened – but poor dear Lydia had no one to look after her. Poor dear child! And now here's Mr Bennet gone away, and I know he'll fight Wickham, and then he'll be killed, and what will become of us all? The Collinses will turn us out before he is cold in his grave and if you are not kind to us, brother, I do not know what we shall do.'

They all comforted her against such terrible ideas, and Mr Gardiner told her that he would go directly to London and give Mr Bennet every help in his search.

'Oh, my dear brother,' replied Mrs Bennet, 'that is exactly what I could most wish for. And now do, when you get to town, find them, wherever they may be, and if they are not already married, *make* them marry. And as for clothes for the wedding, do not let them wait for that, but tell Lydia that she shall have as much money as she chooses to buy them, after they are married. And above all things, keep Mr Bennet from fighting. Tell him what a terrible state I am in – that I am frightened to death, and have such tremblings all over me, and such pains in my head, and such beatings of my heart that I can get no rest by night or by day. And tell my dear Lydia not to give any orders about her clothes until she has seen me, because she does not know the best shops. Oh, brother, how kind you are! I know that you will manage everything.'

Mr Gardiner could not avoid advising her not to be extreme, in her hopes as well as her fears, and the conversation continued in this manner until dinner was on the table and they left her to the attentions of the housekeeper.

Although Mr and Mrs Gardiner were sure that there was no real necessity for her to stay in bed, they did not attempt to oppose her desire, because they knew that she had not enough good sense to keep quiet while the servants were around.

They were joined by Mary and Kitty, who had been too busy in their separate rooms to make their appearance before. The one came from her books, the other from the business of dressing herself. They were both fairly calm, and no change was noticeable in either, except that the loss of her favourite sister, or the anger which she herself had had to bear in the matter, had made Kitty more complaining than usual.

In the afternoon, the two older Misses Bennet were able to have half an hour by themselves in serious talk. Elizabeth learnt that Wickham's bad character had begun to be known. Colonel Forster believed him to be a careless and wasteful spender, and it was now said that he had left Meryton greatly in debt.

'Oh, Jane, if we had been less secretive, if we had told what we knew of him, this could not have happened.'

'We acted with the best intentions.'

Jane then showed Elizabeth Lydia's letter to Mrs Forster, which the Colonel had brought with him. This is what it contained:

My dear Harriet,

You will laugh when you know where I have gone, and I cannot help laughing myself at your surprise tomorrow morning, as soon as I am missed. I am going to Gretna Green, and if you cannot guess with whom, I shall think you very stupid, because there is only one man in the world that I love, and he is perfect. I could never be happy without him, so I think it will do no harm to run away with him. You need not tell them at Longbourn if you do not want to, because it will make the surprise much greater when I write to them and sign my name Lydia Wickham. What a good joke it will be! Please make my excuses to Pratt for not keeping my promise to dance with him tonight. I shall send for my clothes when I get to Longbourn, but I wish you would tell the servant to mend a great hole in my blue dress before it is packed. Goodbye. Give my love to Colonel Forster. I hope that you will drink to our good journey.

Your loving friend,

LYDIA BENNET.

'Oh, thoughtless, thoughtless Lydia!' cried Elizabeth when she had finished reading. 'What a letter this is to be written at such a moment! But at least it shows that she was serious in the object of her journey. My poor father! How he must have felt!'

'I never saw anyone so shocked. He could not speak a word for fully ten minutes. Our mother was taken ill immediately, and the whole house was in confusion.'

'Oh, Jane,' cried Elizabeth, 'was there one servant belonging to us who did not know the whole story before the end of the day?'

'I do not know. I hope so. But it is very difficult to be careful at such a time.'

'You do not look well. You have had every care and anxiety to bear by yourself.'

'Mary and Kitty have been very kind, and would have shared every duty, I am sure, but Kitty is thin and delicate, and Mary studies so much that she should not be interrupted during her hours of rest. Our Aunt Philips came to us after our father had gone away, and was of great use and comfort, and Lady Lucas has been very kind, and walked over here to offer her sympathy and help.'

'It would have been better if she had stayed at home,' cried Elizabeth. 'Perhaps she meant well, but in a time of such a misfortune as this, one cannot see too little of one's neighbours.'

Chapter 22   Mr Bennet Returns

All Meryton now seemed eager to speak badly of the man who, only three months before, had been considered to be the perfect gentleman. He was said to be in debt to every shopkeeper in the place, and to have made love to most of their daughters. Everybody spoke of him as the worst young man in the world, and everybody began to find out that they had always distrusted the appearance of his goodness.

Mrs Philips visited the Bennets frequently with the intention, she said, of cheering them up, but as she never came without reporting some fresh example of his wrongdoings, she rarely went away without leaving them in lower spirits than she had found them.

Every day at Longbourn was now a day of anxiety, but the most anxious part of each was when the post was expected. Still no news of any importance came from London, but a letter arrived for their father from a different direction, from Mr Collins. As Jane had been told by Mr Bennet to open everything that came for him in his absence, she read it, and Elizabeth, who knew how strange Mr Collins's letters always were, looked over her shoulder and read it too.

My dear Sir,

I feel it is my duty, as a relative of yours, and because of my situation in life, to sympathize with you in your present misfortune, which must be of the bitterest kind, since it stems from a cause that no time can remove. The death of your daughter would have been a relief in comparison with this. It is all the worse, because I understand there is reason to suppose that this behaviour of your daughter was caused by a lack of rules at home, though at the same time I suspect that her character must be naturally bad. In any case, you are greatly to be pitied, in which opinion I am joined not only by my wife, but also by Lady Catherine and her daughter. They agree with me that this foolish act will harm the fortunes of all your other daughters, for who will connect themselves with such a family? This consideration leads me to think with increased satisfaction of a certain event of last November, for if it had been otherwise, I should have shared all your sorrow and shame. Let me advise you, my dear sir, to throw off your ungrateful child for ever, and leave her to the fruits of her wrongdoings.

I am, dear sir, etc.

At last, after the failure of all attempts to find his daughter, Mr Bennet agreed to Mr Gardiner's request that he should return to his family and leave it to him to do whatever seemed advisable. When Mrs Bennet was told of this, she did not express as much satisfaction as her children expected.

'What! Is he coming home, and without poor Lydia? Who is to fight Wickham and make him marry her, if he comes away?'

As Mrs Gardiner began to wish to be at home, she and her children left in the carriage that would bring Mr Bennet back to Longbourn. She went away still as confused as ever about Elizabeth and her Derbyshire friend.

When Mr Bennet arrived, he had all the appearance of his usual calmness. He said as little as ever, and made no mention of the business that had taken him away, and it was some time before his daughters had the courage to speak of it.

It was not until the afternoon, when he joined them at tea, that Elizabeth dared to introduce the subject, and in answer to her expressions of sympathy, he said, 'Say nothing of that. It is right that I should suffer. It has been my own doing, and I ought to feel it.'

Then he continued, 'Lizzy, I have no bad feelings towards you for being right in your advice to me last May.'

They were interrupted by Jane, who came to collect her mother's tea.

'This is a ceremony,' he cried, 'which does me good! Another day I will behave as your mother does. I will sit in the library, and give as much trouble as I can – or perhaps I can delay it until Kitty runs away.'

'I am not going to run away, Father,' said Kitty. 'If I should ever go to Brighton, I would behave better than Lydia.'

'*You* go to Brighton! I will not trust you anywhere near it, not for fifty pounds! No, Kitty, I have at least learnt to be careful, and you will feel the effects of it. No officer is ever to enter this house again, or even to pass through the village. Balls are completely forbidden, unless you dance with one of your sisters. And you are never to go out of doors until you can prove that you have spent ten minutes of every day in a sensible manner.'

Kitty, who took all these threats seriously, began to cry.

'Well, well,' he said, 'do not make yourself unhappy. If you are a good girl for the next ten years, I will take you to the theatre at the end of them.'

Chapter 23   Lydia and Wickham Are Found

Two days after Mr Bennet's return, as Jane and Elizabeth were walking in the garden behind the house, they saw the housekeeper coming towards them.

'I beg your pardon, madam, for interrupting you,' she said to Jane, 'but I was hoping that you might have had good news from town, and I dared to come and ask.'

'What do you mean? We have heard nothing from town.'

'Dear madam,' cried the housekeeper, 'don't you know that an urgent letter came from Mr Gardiner half an hour ago?'

The girls ran away, too eager to reach the house to have time for speech. They ran through the hall into the breakfast room, and from there to the library. Their father was in neither. They were on the point of looking for him upstairs with their mother, when they were met by a manservant, who said:

'If you are looking for my master, madam, he is walking towards the little wood.'

They immediately left the house again, and ran across the grass after their father. Jane, who was not so light as Elizabeth, soon slowed down, while her sister, out of breath, reached him and eagerly cried out:

'Oh, Father, what news? Good or bad?'

'What good is to be expected?' he said, taking the letter from his pocket. 'But perhaps you would like to read it.'

Elizabeth impatiently caught it from his hand. Jane now came up and joined them.

'Read it out loud,' said their father.

Elizabeth read:

GRACECHURCH STREET
Monday, August 2nd

My dear brother,

At last I am able to send you some news. I have discovered my niece and the young man. They are not married, and I do not believe that they ever intended to be, but if you are willing to keep the promises that I have been forced to make in your name, I hope it will not be long before they are. All that is necessary is that you should settle on your daughter, by law, her equal share of the five thousand pounds that will come to your children after the death of yourself and my sister, and, in addition, that you should enter into an agreement to allow her, during your life, one hundred pounds a year. Mr Wickham's condition as regards money is not so hopeless as was believed, and I am happy to say that there will be a little of his own money left, even when his debts have been paid. There is not the smallest necessity for you to come to town, as I will give your lawyer all details about making the agreement. Send back your answer as soon as you can. We have judged it best that my niece should be married from this house, and I hope you will approve.

Yours, etc.

EDWARD GARDINER.

'And have you answered the letter?'

'I dislike it very much,' he replied, 'but it must be done.'

He turned back with them, and walked towards the house.

'And may I ask something?' said Elizabeth. 'The conditions must, I suppose, be agreed to?'

'Agreed to? I am only ashamed of his asking so little.'

'And they *must* marry! Even though he is *such* a man!'

'Yes, yes, there is nothing else to be done. But there are two things that I very much want to know – one is, how much money your uncle has paid out to arrange this, and the other, how I am ever going to pay him back.'

'Money! My uncle!' cried Jane. 'What do you mean, sir?'

'I mean that no man in his right mind would marry Lydia for so little as one hundred pounds a year.'

'That is very true,' said Elizabeth, 'though I had not thought of it before. His debts will be paid, and something will still remain! Oh, it must be my uncle's doing. Generous, good man! A small sum could not do all this.'

'No,' said her father, 'Wickham's a fool if he takes her with a penny less than ten thousand pounds.'

'Ten thousand pounds! How is half such a sum to be repaid?'

Mr Bennet made no answer, and each of them, deep in thought, continued to walk in silence until they reached the house. Their father then went to the library to write.

'And they are really to be married!' cried Elizabeth, as soon as she and Jane were by themselves. 'How strange this is! Although their chance of happiness is small, and his character is worthless, we are forced to be glad! Oh, Lydia!'

The girls now remembered that their mother probably knew nothing of what had happened. They went, therefore, and asked their father's permission to tell her. Without raising his head from his writing, he replied coldly:

'Just as you please.'

'May we take my uncle's letter to read to her?'

'Take whatever you like, and get away.'

After a slight warning of good news, the letter was read to Mrs Bennet. Their mother could hardly control herself. Her joy burst out after the first few sentences. She had no fears for her daughter's happiness, nor shame from any memory of her misbehaviour.

'This is so exciting!' she cried. 'She will be married at sixteen! How I wish to see her and dear Wickham too! But the clothes, the wedding clothes! I will write to my sister Gardiner about them directly. Ring the bell, Kitty, for the servant. I will dress in a moment. I will go to Meryton as soon as I am dressed, and tell the good, good news to my sister Philips. And as I am coming back, I can call on Lady Lucas and Mrs Long.'

She then began to tell the news to the servant, who expressed her joy. Elizabeth received her congratulations with the rest, and then, sick of this foolishness, went to her own room so that she could think in peace.

Chapter 24   Mr Bennet Agrees to Their Marriage

Mr Bennet had often wished, before this period in his life, that instead of spending his whole income, he had saved a yearly sum to provide for his children – and his wife, if she lived longer than he did. He now wished this more than ever. If he had done his duty in that matter, Lydia need not have depended on her uncle for whatever respectability could now be bought for her.

When Mr Bennet first married, saving was considered to be perfectly useless, for of course they would have a son. The son would, as heir, be willing at the age of twenty-one to make more suitable arrangements for the property, so that the wife and other children would be provided for. Five daughters, one after another, entered the world, but the son still did not come. They had, at last, given up hope, but it was then too late to begin saving. Mrs Bennet was naturally careless about money, and only her husband's love of independence prevented them from spending more than their income.

Five thousand pounds had been settled by marriage agreement on Mrs Bennet and her children, but the share that the children would receive depended on the wishes of the parents. This was one point, with regard to Lydia at least, which could now be settled, and Mr Bennet immediately accepted the proposal of his wife's brother. He had never supposed that the affair could have been arranged with so little inconvenience to himself. He would hardly be ten pounds poorer after hundred was paid each year to the young pair, because the cost of keeping Lydia at home – her pocket money, and the continual presents in money which passed to her through her mother's hands – amounted to very little less than that sum.

He wrote, therefore, to give his agreement and thanks to Mr Gardiner, but was too angry with Lydia to send any message to her.

It was two weeks since Mrs Bennet had last been downstairs, but on this happy day she again took her seat at the head of the table, and in extremely high spirits. No feeling of shame caused her joy to be lessened. Her thoughts ran completely on clothes, carriages, servants, and a large enough house for Lydia. Her husband allowed her to talk on without interruption while the servants remained. But when they had gone, he said to her, 'Mrs Bennet, before you take any or all of these houses for your daughter, understand that she shall never have admittance into this one, at least.'

A long argument followed this statement, but Mr Bennet was firm. It soon led to another, and Mrs Bennet found, with astonishment and shock, that her husband would not give one penny to buy clothes for her daughter. He declared that she should receive no sign of love whatever from him on the occasion. Mrs Bennet was more troubled by the shame of Lydia's lack of new clothes than the shame of the conditions which had made her marriage necessary.

Elizabeth was now deeply sorry that she had, in her unhappiness at the moment, made known to Mr Darcy her fears for her sister, since now Lydia's marriage would hide her earlier fault from all those who were not closely connected with the affair. She knew that she could trust him to keep the secret, but at the same time she was ashamed and full of sorrow that he, of all people, should know of her family's shame.

She felt sure that his wish to gain her respect would be destroyed by such a blow as this. She became desirous of his good opinion, when she could no longer hope to have the advantage of it. She wanted to hear of him, when there seemed the least chance of receiving information. She was quite sure now that she could have been happy with him, when it was no longer likely that they would meet.

What a victory for him, as she often thought, if he could only know that the proposals which she had so proudly scorned only four months ago would now have been gladly and gratefully received!

She began to realize that he was exactly the man who, in character and ability, would most suit her. It was a union that would have been to the advantage of both. By her confidence and liveliness, his mind might have been softened and his manners improved, and from his judgment, information and knowledge of the world, she would have received advantages of greater importance.

♦

The day of their sister's wedding arrived, and Jane and Elizabeth had urged their father so seriously but so gently to receive her and her husband at Longbourn after the event that he was at last persuaded to act as they wished. It would only be for a short time, as a move had been arranged for Wickham to another regiment stationed in the north of England, where he could make a fresh start in life.

The carriage was sent to meet them, and they were to return in it by dinnertime. Their arrival was expected by the two older Misses Bennet with a mixture of discomfort and anxiety.

They came. The family were waiting in the breakfast room to receive them. Smiles covered the face of Mrs Bennet as the carriage drove up to the door. Her husband looked serious, and her daughters anxious and nervous.

Lydia's voice was heard in the hall. The door was thrown open, and she ran into the room. Her mother stepped forward, kissed her, and welcomed her with joy, giving her hand with a warm smile to Wickham, who followed his lady.

Their welcome by Mr Bennet, to whom they then turned, was colder. His face became even more serious, and he hardly moved his lips. The easy confidence of the young pair was enough to anger him. Elizabeth was disgusted, and even Jane was shocked. Lydia was still Lydia, uncontrolled, unashamed, wild, noisy, fearless. She turned from one sister to another, demanding their congratulations, while Wickham was all smiles and easy politeness. Neither Lydia nor her mother could talk fast enough.

'To think that it has been three months,' cried Lydia, 'since I went away! I am sure that I had no idea of being married before I came back, though I thought it would be very good fun if I was.'

Her father lifted his eyes, and Elizabeth looked expressively at her, but she continued brightly, 'Oh, mother, do the people at Meryton know I am married today? I was afraid they might not, so as we came through I let my hand rest on the window frame of the carriage, so that they could see the ring.'

As they passed through the hall to the dining room, Lydia, with anxious importance, walked up to her mother's right hand, and said to her oldest sister, 'Ah, Jane, I take your place now, and you must go lower, because I am a married woman.'

'Well, mother,' she said, after the meal, 'what do you think of my husband? Is he not a fine-looking man? I am sure that my sisters must all be jealous of me. I only hope that they may have half my good luck. They must all go to Brighton. That is the place to get husbands. Or you must all come and see us in the north. I expect that there will be some dances, and I will take care to get good partners for my sisters. And then, when you go away, you may leave one or two of them behind, and I am sure that I shall get husbands for them before the winter is over.'

'I thank you for your advice,' said Elizabeth, 'but I do not especially like your way of getting husbands.'

Wickham's love for Lydia was just what Elizabeth had expected it to be – not equal to Lydia's for him. She guessed that their running away together had been caused by the strength of *her* love rather than by his, and that escape from his debts had been the main reason for his leaving Brighton, though he was not the kind of young man to refuse the opportunity of having a companion.

Lydia was extremely fond of him. He was her dear Wickham on every occasion. No one could be compared with him. He did everything best in the world.

One morning soon after their arrival, as she was sitting with her two oldest sisters, she said to Elizabeth:

'Lizzy, I never gave you an account of my wedding. You were not present when I told the others. Are you not interested in hearing how it was managed?'

'No, really,' replied Elizabeth, 'I think there cannot be too little said on the subject.'

'Oh! How strange you are! But I must tell you how it happened. Well, the day came, and I was so excited! I was so afraid, you know, that something would happen to delay it. And there was my aunt, all the time that I was dressing, talking away just as if she were a minister in church. But I did not hear a word of it, because I was thinking about whether my dear Wickham would be married in his blue coat. Well, and just as the carriage came to the door, my uncle was called away on business. I was so frightened that I did not know what to do, because my uncle was to act in place of my father at the ceremony, and give me in marriage, and if we were late we could not be married all day. But I remembered afterwards that it need not have been delayed, because Mr Darcy might have taken his place.'

'Mr Darcy!' repeated Elizabeth in astonishment.

'Oh, yes! He came there with Wickham, you know. But heavens! I quite forgot! I promised not to mention it. It was a secret.'

'In that case,' said Elizabeth, although she was burning with a desire to know more, 'we will ask you no questions.'

'Thank you,' said Lydia, 'because if you did, I should certainly tell you all, and then Wickham would be so angry.'

With such encouragement, Elizabeth was forced to help her sister keep her secret by leaving the room.

But it was impossible not to ask for information on this matter. Mr Darcy had been at her sister's wedding! What could be the reason? Seizing a sheet of paper, she wrote a short letter to her aunt to request an explanation, if it could be given without breaking confidence. 'And if it cannot,' she added at the end of the letter, 'and if you do not tell me in an honourable manner, my dear aunt, I shall certainly be forced to use some trick to find out!'

◆

Elizabeth had the satisfaction of receiving an immediate answer to her letter. As soon as she was in possession of it, she hurried off to the little wood, where she was least likely to be interrupted.

GRACECHURCH STREET
September 6th

My dear niece,

I have just received your letter and must admit to being surprised by your request. Don't think me angry, though, because I only mean that I had not imagined such inquiries to be necessary on *your* side. Your uncle is as much surprised as I am, and nothing but the belief of your involvement in the affair would have allowed him to act as he has done. But if you really know nothing of the matter, I must give you an explanation.

On the same day as my return from Longbourn, your uncle had a most unexpected visit from Mr Darcy, who talked with him in private for several hours. He came to tell Mr Gardiner that he had found out where your sister and Mr Wickham were, and that he had talked to them. From what I can understand, he left Derbyshire only one day after ourselves, and came to town with the intention of hunting for them. He generously gave as a reason for this that he felt himself responsible for the whole situation, because he had not made public in Meryton last year his knowledge of Wickham's worthlessness. He blamed his own pride for this.

It seems that there is a lady who was formerly a private teacher to Miss Darcy and who was dismissed for some good reason that he did not mention. She had then rented a house in London and supported herself by letting rooms. Knowing that she had been friendly with Mr Wickham, Darcy went to her, and succeeded with some difficulty in getting his address. He first tried to persuade Lydia to leave her shameful situation and return to her friends, but he found her determined to remain where she was. She was sure that Wickham would marry her sometime or other, and it did not much matter when. The gentleman himself, it appeared, had no such intention. He still hoped to make his fortune by a good marriage in some other place. But an agreement was at last reached which was satisfactory to both sides.

Our visitor, Darcy, refused every attempt by Mr Gardiner to share these responsibilities. Nothing was done that he did not do himself, though I am sure that your uncle would most willingly have settled the whole matter. They argued over it together for a long time, but at last your uncle was forced to agree. Wickham's debts will be paid, another thousand pounds will be settled on her, and a good position in the army will be obtained for him.

There may be some truth in the reasons given by Mr Darcy for acting so generously, but in spite of all this fine talk, my dear Lizzy, you may be sure that your uncle would never have agreed if we had not believed him to have *another interest* in the affair. Will you be very angry if I take this opportunity of saying how much I like him? His behaviour, his understanding and opinions all please me, and he only lacks a little liveliness, and *that*, if he marries the *right* person, his wife may teach him. I thought him very secretive. He hardly ever mentioned your name. But secrecy seems to be the fashion. Please forgive me if I have said too much, or at least do not punish me so far as to forbid me to visit you at P.

But I must write no more. The children have been wanting me for the last half-hour.

Your loving aunt,

M. GARDINER.

The information in this letter unsettled Elizabeth's spirits. Darcy had done all this for a woman whom he must scorn and the man whom he most wished to avoid! Her heart *did* whisper that he had done it for *her*. Oh, how sorry she was for every unkind feeling that she had ever encouraged towards him! For herself, she felt ashamed and small, but she was proud of him – proud that in a cause of honour he could defeat his own nature. She read over her aunt's praise of him again and again. It was hardly enough, but it pleased her.

Chapter 25   Return to Netherfield

The day soon arrived when the young pair had to leave, and Mrs Bennet was forced to bear the separation.

'Write to me often, my dear Lydia,' she cried.

'As often as I can, but married women never have much time for writing. My sisters may write to *me*. They will have nothing else to do.'

Mr Wickham's goodbyes were much warmer than his wife's. He smiled a lot and said many pretty things.

As soon as he was out of the house, Mr Bennet said bitterly: 'He is as fine a young man as ever I saw. He smiles sweetly, and makes love to us all. I am extremely proud of him. Even Sir William Lucas could not produce a better husband for his daughter.'

The loss of Lydia made Mrs Bennet very dull for several days, but her spiritless condition was relieved soon afterwards by a piece of news which then began to be passed round. The housekeeper at Netherfield had received orders to prepare for the arrival of her master. Mrs Bennet was quite unsettled. She looked at Jane, and smiled and shook her head.

Jane had not been able to hear of his arrival without trembling a little, and Elizabeth could easily see that it had had an effect on her spirits. Elizabeth herself was confused by the visit. Had he come with his friend's permission, or was he brave enough to act without it?

'I am beginning to be sorry that he is coming at all,' said Jane to Elizabeth a few days later. 'It would be nothing, I could see him with complete lack of interest, but I can hardly bear to hear it continually talked about. My mother means well, but she does not know how I suffer from what she says.'

Mr Bingley arrived. On the third morning after his coming, Mrs Bennet saw him from her dressing-room window as he rode towards the house.

Her daughters were eagerly called on to share her joy. Jane firmly stayed at her place at the table, but Elizabeth, to satisfy her mother, went to the window.

She looked, saw Mr Darcy with him, and sat down again by her sister.

'There is a gentleman with Mr Bingley, Mama,' said Kitty. 'It looks like that tall, proud man, who used to be with him before – I've forgotten his name.'

'Oh, heavens! Mr Darcy! Well, I must say that I hate the sight of him.'

Both Elizabeth and Jane were uncomfortable, but the former

had a cause for discomfort which could not be guessed by Jane, to whom she had never yet had the courage to show Mrs Gardiner's letter, or to tell of her own change of feeling. Her astonishment at his coming and wishing to see her again was almost as great as she had experienced when she had first observed his changed behaviour in Derbyshire. Her face, which had become pale for half a minute, now found its colour again with an additional warmth, and a smile of pleasure added brightness to her eyes, as she thought that his love and wishes must still be unchanged – but she could not be sure.

She sat busily at work, trying not to appear excited. Jane looked a little paler than usual. When the gentlemen appeared, she received them fairly calmly. Elizabeth said as little as politeness would allow, and sat again at her work. She had dared to take only one look at Darcy. He looked serious as usual.

Bingley, she saw, was both pleased and confused. He was received by Mrs Bennet with an amount of attention which made her two oldest daughters feel ashamed, especially when it was compared with the cold and ceremonious politeness of her behaviour to his friend. Elizabeth especially, who knew what her mother owed to Mr Darcy.

Darcy said hardly anything to her. He was not seated by her, so perhaps that was the reason for his silence. When sometimes, unable to prevent it, she raised her eyes to his face, she found him looking at Jane quite as often as at herself. She was disappointed, and angry with herself for being so.

At this time Mrs Bennet was talking to Bingley happily about Lydia's marriage, and receiving his congratulations.

'It is a satisfying thing, to be sure, to have a daughter married,' Mrs Bennet continued, 'but at the same time it is very hard to have her taken away from me. Her husband has been moved to another regiment, you know. Thank heavens he has *some* friends, though not, perhaps, as many as he deserves.'

Elizabeth, who knew that this was directed against Mr Darcy, thought that she could now feel no greater shame. But her discomfort soon received relief from seeing how much the beauty of her sister was bringing back the admiration of her former lover, who seemed to be giving her more and more of his attention.

When the gentlemen rose to go, they were invited to eat at Longbourn in a few days' time.

◆

As soon as they had gone, Elizabeth walked in the garden to recover her spirits. Mr Darcy's behaviour astonished and confused her. She could explain it in no way that gave her pleasure.

'Why did he come at all, if it was only to be silent and serious? If he fears me, why come here? If he no longer cares for me, why be silent? Annoying man! I will think no more about him.'

Her sister approached, and joined her with a cheerful smile.

'Now,' she said, 'that this first meeting is over, I feel perfectly relaxed. I am glad that he will eat here on Tuesday. It will then be publicly seen that we meet only as ordinary and uninterested acquaintances.'

'Very uninterested!' said Elizabeth laughingly. 'I think that you are in very great danger of making him as much in love with you as ever.'

They did not see the gentlemen again until Tuesday, when there was a large party at Longbourn. As the two men entered the dining room, Elizabeth eagerly watched to see whether Bingley would take the place which, at all their former parties, had belonged to him, by her sister. Her careful mother, having the same idea, did not invite him to sit by herself. He seemed to pause, but Jane looked round and smiled. It was decided. He placed himself beside her.

117

Elizabeth, with a feeling of victory, looked towards his friend. He bore it well, and she would have imagined that Bingley had received his permission to be happy, if she had not seen his eyes turned towards Mr Darcy with an expression of anxiety.

His behaviour towards her sister during dinner showed such admiration that Elizabeth believed that, if left completely to himself, Jane's happiness, and his own, would be speedily gained.

Mr Darcy was on one side of her mother. She knew how little such a situation could give pleasure to either. She was not near enough to hear any of their conversation, but she could see how rarely they spoke to each other, and how formal and cold their manner was whenever they did.

She hoped that the evening would provide some opportunity of bringing herself and Mr Darcy together. Anxious and uncomfortable, the period which passed in the sitting room before the gentlemen came in was tiring and dull.

The gentlemen came, and she thought that he looked as if he would have answered her hopes, but oh! the ladies had crowded so closely round the table, where Jane was making tea and Elizabeth pouring out the coffee, that there was not a single space near her where a chair could be placed. He walked away to another part of the room.

She was a little cheered, though, by his bringing back his coffee cup himself, and she seized the opportunity to inquire after his sister. He replied, and then stood beside her for some minutes in silence.

When the tea things had been removed, and the card tables placed, they were seated far from each other, at different games, and she lost every expectation of pleasure. Mrs Bennet was in high spirits when the guests had gone.

'Well, girls,' she said, as soon as they were left to themselves, 'I think everything passed off uncommonly well. The dinner was as well cooked as any I ever saw. The meat was cooked to perfection. The soup was 50 times better than that we had at the Lucases' last week. And, my dear Jane, what do you think Mrs Long said? "Ah, Mrs Bennet, we shall have her at Netherfield at last!" I do think that Mrs Long is as good a woman as ever lived – and her nieces are very well-behaved girls, and not at all good-looking. I like them very much.'

◆

A few days later, Mr Bingley called again, and alone. His friend had left that morning for London, but would return in ten days' time. He sat with them for over an hour, and was in noticeably good spirits. Mrs Bennet invited him to dinner with them, but unfortunately he had another engagement. He eagerly accepted an invitation, though, for the following day.

He came, and so early that none of the ladies was dressed. Mrs Bennet ran into her daughter's room with her hair half-finished, crying out:

'My dear Jane, hurry down. He has come. Hurry, hurry.'

'We shall be down as soon as we can,' said Jane, 'but I dare say that Kitty will be ready before either of us.'

'Oh, never mind about Kitty! What has she to do with it? Come, be quick!'

The same anxiety to get Jane and Mr Bingley by themselves was plain again in the evening. After tea, Mr Bennet went to the library, as was his custom, and Mary went upstairs to her piano. Two of the five being removed, Mrs Bennet sat making signals with her eyes at Elizabeth and Kitty for some time, without having any effect on them. Elizabeth did not take any notice, and when at last Kitty did, she said in surprise, 'What is the matter, Mother? Is something wrong? What should I do?'

'Nothing, child, nothing.'

Five minutes later, she suddenly got up, and saying to Kitty, 'Come here, my love, I want to speak to you,' took her out of the room. A look from Jane begged Elizabeth to remain, but when, some moments later, the door half opened and her mother called out that she wanted her, she was forced to go.

Her mother announced her intention of sitting upstairs, and as soon as she was out of sight, Elizabeth returned to the sitting room.

Bingley was everything a gentleman should be for the rest of the evening. He bore all Mrs Bennet's silly remarks with the greatest patience. After this day, Jane said no more about being uninterested. Elizabeth believed that all must speedily be brought to a successful ending, unless Mr Darcy returned too soon. She felt, though, that all this must be happening with that gentleman's approval.

Bingley spent the next morning shooting with Mr Bennet, and returned with him to dinner. After the meal Elizabeth had a letter to write and, believing that the others were all going to sit down together to cards, she went to her own room.

But on returning to the sitting room, she found that her mother had again been arranging matters. Her sister and Bingley were standing together by the fireplace as if in serious conversation, and the faces of both, as they quickly turned and moved away from each other, told everything. Not a word was said by either, and Elizabeth in her confusion was just going away again, when Bingley suddenly whispered a few words to her sister, and ran out of the room.

Jane could have no secrets from Elizabeth, and immediately admitted that she was the happiest being in the world. Elizabeth's congratulations were given with sincerity and pleasure. Jane then ran to her mother.

In a few minutes Elizabeth was joined by Mr Bingley, whose conversation with Mr Bennet had been short and successful. He claimed her good wishes and love as a sister, and they shook hands with great pleasure.

It was an evening of excitement for them all. Jane's happiness made her look more beautiful than ever. Kitty smiled, and hoped that her turn was coming soon. Mrs Bennet could not express her feelings often enough, and when Mr Bennet joined them at supper, his voice and manner plainly showed how happy he was.

Not a word passed his lips about it until his visitor had gone. He then turned to his daughter and said:

'Jane, I congratulate you. You will be a very happy woman.'

Jane went to him, kissed him, and thanked him for his goodness.

'You are a good girl,' he replied, 'and I have no doubt that you will suit each other. You are each so ready to give way to the other that nothing will ever be decided on; so trusting that every servant will cheat you, and so generous that you will always spend more than your income.'

'Spend more than their income!' cried his wife. 'My dear Mr Bennet, what are you talking of? He has four or five thousand pounds a year, and very likely more.' Then, addressing her daughter, 'Oh, my dear, dear Jane, I am so happy! I am sure that I shall not get a moment's sleep tonight. I knew that you could not be so beautiful for nothing. Oh, he is the best-looking young man that ever was seen!'

Wickham, Lydia, were all forgotten. Jane was at that moment her favourite child, and she cared for no other.

Bingley, from this time, was of course a daily visitor at Longbourn. The situation could not remain a secret for long. Mrs Bennet whispered it to Mrs Philips, who passed on the news without permission to all her neighbours. The Bennets were spoken of as the luckiest family in the world, though only a few weeks before, when Lydia had run away, they had been generally believed to be the most unfortunate.

Chapter 26 Lady Catherine Visits Longbourn

One morning, about a week later, a carriage suddenly appeared outside the house. It was too early for visitors, and neither the carriage nor the uniform of the servant was familiar. The two lovers immediately escaped to the garden, leaving the rest of the ladies to guess who the stranger could be, until the door was thrown open and Lady Catherine de Bourgh entered.

She walked in, looking more disagreeable than usual, made no other reply to Elizabeth's greeting than a slight movement of the head, and sat down without a word.

After sitting for a moment in silence, she said, very stiffly, to Elizabeth:

'I hope you are well, Miss Bennet. That lady, I suppose, is your mother?'

Elizabeth replied shortly that she was.

'And *that*, I suppose, is one of your sisters?'

'Yes, madam,' replied Mrs Bennet, to whom Elizabeth had mentioned the visitor's name, and who was feeling highly honoured by her coming.

'You have a very small park here,' observed Lady Catherine, after a short silence, 'and this must be a most inconvenient sitting room for the evening in summer. The windows appear to be facing west.'

Mrs Bennet informed her that they never sat there after dinner, and then added:

'May I ask whether you left Mr and Mrs Collins well?'

'Yes, very well.'

Elizabeth now expected that she would produce a letter for her from Charlotte, because it seemed the only likely reason for her visit. But no letter appeared, and she could not understand the visit at all.

Mrs Bennet, with great politeness, begged Lady Catherine to

have something to eat or drink, but this was decidedly, and not very politely, refused. Then, rising, Lady Catherine said to Elizabeth: 'Miss Bennet, I should be glad to take a walk in your garden, if you will give me your company.'

Elizabeth obeyed. As they passed through the hall, Lady Catherine opened the doors of the other rooms, and announced that they were a reasonably good size.

They walked in silence towards the little wood. Elizabeth was determined to make no effort at conversation with a woman who was now more than usually rude and disagreeable.

As soon as they entered the wood, Lady Catherine began in the following manner:

'You can have no difficulty, Miss Bennet, in understanding the reason of my visit. Your own heart, your own conscience must tell you why I have come.'

Elizabeth looked at her in astonishment.

'Miss Bennet,' she continued in an angry voice, 'you ought to know that I will not be treated without proper regard for my position. A report of a most upsetting nature reached me two days ago. I was told that you, Miss Elizabeth Bennet, would in all probability be soon united to my nephew, my own nephew. Though I *know* that it must be a shameful lie, I immediately decided to come here so that I could make my feelings known to you.'

'If you believed it impossible,' said Elizabeth, her face turning red with astonishment and scorn, 'I am surprised that you took the trouble of coming so far.'

'This is not to be borne. Miss Bennet, I will be satisfied. Has he, has my nephew, made you an offer of marriage?'

'You have said that it is impossible.'

'Miss Bennet, do you know who I am? Let me be rightly understood. Mr Darcy is engaged to my daughter. Now, what have you to say?'

'Only this – that if it is so, you can have no reason to suppose that he will make an offer to me.'

Lady Catherine paused for a moment, and then replied:

'The arrangement between them is of a special kind. From their childhood they have been intended for each other. It was the favourite wish of his mother, as well as of myself. Have you no respect for the wishes of his relations?'

'But what is that to me? If Mr Darcy wishes, may he not make another choice? And if I am that choice, why may I not accept him?'

'I will not be interrupted! Hear me in silence. I see there is a seat over there. Let us sit down. My daughter and my nephew are made for each other. Their birth and their fortunes are noble. And what will divide them? The plans of a young woman without rank or money?'

'Your nephew is a gentleman, and I am a gentleman's daughter.'

'But what is your mother? Who are your uncles and aunts? Do you imagine that I am without knowledge of their condition?'

'If your nephew does not object to them,' replied Elizabeth, 'it can be nothing to you.'

'Tell me, are you engaged to him?'

Elizabeth could only say: 'I am not.' Lady Catherine seemed pleased.

'And will you promise never to become engaged to my nephew?'

'I will make no promise of any kind.'

'Miss Bennet, I am shocked. The facts concerning your youngest sister are fully known to me. Is such a girl to be my nephew's sister? Is *her* husband, the son of his father's servant, to be his brother?'

'You can now have nothing further to say to me,' Elizabeth

answered with bitterness. 'You have insulted me in every possible way. I must beg to return to the house.'

She rose as she spoke. Lady Catherine also rose, highly angered. She talked on, making many threats, until they were at the door of her carriage, when, suddenly turning round, she added:

'I leave you without a goodbye, Miss Bennet. I send no greetings to your mother. You do not deserve such attention. I am most seriously displeased.'

Elizabeth made no answer, but walked quietly into the house. Her mother met her impatiently. 'Had she anything special to say, Lizzy?'

Elizabeth was forced to tell a small lie here, for to admit the truth about their conversation was impossible.

◆

This astonishing visit upset Elizabeth for some time. She could not imagine what could be the origin of the report that she was engaged, unless talk had followed the news about Jane and Bingley. She could not help feeling some discomfort about the result of Lady Catherine's words, because she did not know the degree of her influence over her nephew. If he had been holding back before, his aunt's arguments might settle every doubt.

'If, therefore, an excuse for not returning should come to his friend within a few days,' she thought, 'I shall lose all hope in the strength of his love.'

The next morning, as she was going downstairs, she was met by her father, who came out of his library with a letter in his hand.

'Lizzy,' he said, 'I was going to look for you. Come into my room.'

She followed him in, and they both sat down. He then said:

'I have received a letter this morning concerning yourself that

125

astonishes me. I did not know that I had *two* daughters about to be married. Let me congratulate you.'

She now reddened in the immediate belief that it was a letter from the nephew instead of the aunt. He continued:

'You look self-conscious, but I am sure that you cannot guess the name of your admirer. This letter is from Mr Collins.'

'From Mr Collins! And what can he have to say?'

'He begins with congratulations about Jane. He then goes on: "Your daughter Elizabeth, it is supposed, will also not long bear the name of Bennet, and her future partner has every kind of good fortune, in property, relations and influence. Yet in spite of all these, let me warn my cousin Elizabeth and yourself of the risks that she runs in accepting this gentleman's proposals." Have you any idea, Lizzy, who this gentleman is? But now it comes out. "His aunt, Lady Catherine de Bourgh, does not look on the relationship with a friendly eye." *Mr Darcy*, you see, is the man! Now, Lizzy, I think that I *have* surprised you! Could he have chosen a more unlikely man? Mr Darcy, who probably never looked at you in his life!'

Elizabeth tried to join in her father's amusement, but could only force one unwilling smile. His joking had never been so little pleasing to her.

'Are you not amused?'

'Oh, yes! Please read on.'

'He continues: "I thought it my duty to give information of this immediately to my cousin, so that she and her noble admirer may not act without careful thought." After that he adds, "I am truly happy that my cousin Lydia's sad business has been so well hidden. But I must not neglect the duties of my position, and must state my astonishment on hearing that you received the young pair into your house. You ought certainly to forgive them, but never to admit them to your sight or allow their names to be mentioned." *That* is his idea of forgiveness! But Lizzy, you look as if you did not enjoy it. You are not going to pretend to be insulted, I hope, by stupid talk. For what do we live, if not to amuse our neighbours, and laugh at them in our turn?'

'I am extremely amused!' said Elizabeth. 'But it is so strange!'

'Yes, if they had fixed on any other man, it would have been nothing. But *his* complete lack of interest in you, and *your* sharp dislike of him, make it so particularly entertaining! And Lizzy, what did Lady Catherine say about this report? Did she call to refuse her agreement?'

To this question his daughter replied only with a laugh, and as it had been asked without the least suspicion, she was not put into an awkward position by his repeating it. Elizabeth had never found it more difficult to make her feelings appear what they were not. It was necessary to laugh, when she would rather have cried. Her father had most cruelly wounded her by what he said of Mr Darcy's lack of interest, and she feared that perhaps instead of his noticing too *little*, she might have imagined too *much*.

Chapter 27   Elizabeth and Mr Darcy

Instead of receiving any such letter of excuse from his friend, as Elizabeth half expected Mr Bingley to do, he was able to bring Darcy with him to Longbourn before many days had passed. The gentlemen arrived early, and Bingley suggested that they all go for a walk. Mrs Bennet was not in the habit of walking, and Mary could never give up the time, but the remaining five set out together. Bingley and Jane, though, soon allowed the others to get ahead of them, and Elizabeth, Kitty and Darcy were left to entertain each other.

Kitty wanted to call on the Lucases, and when she left the other two, Elizabeth went on bravely with Darcy alone. She had secretly been making a difficult decision, and perhaps he had been doing the same. Now was the moment to put hers into action, so she said:

'Mr Darcy, I am a very selfish creature, and, in order to give relief to my own feelings, do not care how much I may be wounding yours. I can no longer help thanking you for your deep kindness to my poor sister.'

'I am sorry,' replied Darcy, in a voice full of surprise and feeling, 'that you have ever been informed of what may, by mistake, have given you discomfort of mind.'

'Do not blame my aunt. Lydia's thoughtlessness first caused the truth to be known, and I could not rest until I knew the details. Let me thank you again, in the name of all my family.'

'If you *will* thank me,' he replied, 'let it be for yourself alone. Your family owe me nothing. Much as I respect them, I believe that I thought only of you.'

Elizabeth was too confused to say a word. After a short pause, her companion added: 'You are too generous to keep me in uncertainty. If your feelings are still what they were last April, tell me so at once. My love and wishes are unchanged, but one word from you will silence me on this subject for ever.'

Elizabeth now forced herself to speak, and made him understand that her feelings had changed so completely since that period that she was grateful and pleased to hear his present words. The happiness that this reply produced was greater than he had probably ever experienced before, and he expressed himself on the occasion as warmly as a man who is violently in love can be expected to do.

They walked on without knowing in what direction. There was too much to be thought, and felt, and said, for attention to anything else. She soon learnt that they owed their present good understanding to the efforts of his aunt, who *did* call on him to describe her conversation with Elizabeth, but with the opposite effect to that which she intended.

'It taught me to hope,' he said, 'as I had hardly allowed myself to hope before. I knew enough of your character to be certain that if you had been completely decided against me, you would have admitted it to Lady Catherine openly.'

Elizabeth laughed as she replied, 'Yes, you knew enough of my readiness to speak plainly to believe that I was able to do that. After criticizing you so shamefully to your face, I could have no fear of criticizing you to your relations.'

'What did you say of me that I did not deserve? For though your charges were mistaken, my behaviour to you then was unpardonable. I have been selfish all my life. Unfortunately, I was spoiled by my parents, who, though good themselves, encouraged me to be proud and to think with scorn of the rest of the world. That is how I was, and how I might still be if I had not met you, dearest Elizabeth! You taught me a lesson, a hard one, but most advantageous. You showed me how small were all my claims to please a woman who deserved to be pleased.'

'I am almost afraid to ask what you thought of me when we met at Pemberley. Did you blame me for coming?'

'No, no, I felt nothing but surprise.'

'I admit that I did not expect to be so well received.'

'My aim then,' replied Darcy, 'was to show you, by every attention, that I had no bad feelings for you, and I hoped to obtain your forgiveness, and lessen your bad opinion of me, by letting you see that I was trying to cure my faults.'

After walking several miles in an unhurried manner, they examined their watches and found that it was time to be at home.

Wherever were Mr Bingley and Jane! This thought introduced a discussion of their affairs. Darcy was very happy that they had become engaged.

'I must ask you whether you were surprised,' said Elizabeth.

'Not at all. When I went away, I felt it would happen.'

'That is to say, you had given your permission.' And though he refused to say so, she found that it was very much the case.

'I told him, before I left, that I thought that I had given him mistaken advice, and that I had been at fault in supposing your sister did not care for him.'

'Did you speak from what you had seen yourself, or only from my information last spring?'

'From the former. I watched your sister closely during the two visits which I recently made here, and I felt sure of her love for Bingley.'

Elizabeth would have liked to remark that Mr Bingley was a most satisfactory friend, so easily guided, but she controlled herself. She remembered that Darcy still had to learn to be laughed at, and it was rather early to begin.

They continued in conversation until they reached the house, and parted in the hall.

♦

'My dear Lizzy, where have you been walking to?' was the question which Elizabeth received from Jane as soon as she entered the room, and from all the others when they sat down to table. She had only to say that they had wandered about until they had lost their way. Her face turned slightly red as she spoke, but nobody suspected the truth.

The evening passed quietly. It was not in Darcy's nature to express happiness through high spirits, and Elizabeth was thinking of what her family would feel when everything was known.

At night, she opened her heart to Jane.

'You are joking, Lizzy. Engaged to Mr Darcy! No, no, you shall not deceive me. I know that it is impossible.'

'But, it's true, I am serious. I speak nothing but the truth.'

'Oh, Lizzy, I know how much you dislike him.'

'*That* is all forgotten. Perhaps I did not always love him as well as I do now.'

'But are you certain – forgive the question – are you quite certain that you can be happy with him?'

'There can be no doubt of that. But are you pleased, Jane?'

'Very, very much. Nothing could give Bingley or myself greater pleasure. Oh, Lizzy, are you sure that you feel what you ought to feel?'

'I am only afraid you will think that I feel *more* than I ought, when I tell you all.'

'What do you mean?'

'Well, I must admit that I love him better than I do Bingley. I am afraid that you will be angry.'

'My dearest sister, be serious. Will you tell me how long you have loved him?'

'I believe that I must date it from my first seeing his beautiful grounds at Pemberley.'

Another request that she should be serious produced the desired effect, and she soon made Jane believe in her sincerity. Elizabeth told the reasons for her former secrecy: her unsettled feelings, and her unwillingness to mention Bingley, which she could hardly have avoided doing if she had spoken of the meeting in Derbyshire. Half the night was spent in conversation.

'Oh, heavens!' cried Mrs Bennet, as she stood at the window the next morning. 'That disagreeable Mr Darcy is coming here again with our dear Bingley! What can he mean by being so annoying? Lizzy, you must walk out with him again, so that he will not be in Bingley's way.'

Elizabeth could hardly help laughing at so convenient a proposal, but she was really annoyed that her mother should be speaking of him in such a manner.

As soon as they entered, Bingley looked at her so expressively, and shook hands with such warmth, that she was in no doubt of his knowledge, and he soon afterwards said, 'Mrs Bennet, have you no more country roads round about here, in which Lizzy may lose her way again today?'

'I advise Mr Darcy and Lizzy and Kitty,' said Mrs Bennet, 'to walk to Oakham Mount this morning. It is a nice long walk, and Mr Darcy has never seen the view.'

'I am sure that it would be too much for Kitty,' said Bingley.

Kitty admitted that she would rather stay at home. As Elizabeth went upstairs, her mother followed her, saying:

'I am sorry, Lizzy, that you should be forced to have that disagreeable man all to yourself, but it is all for Jane, you know. There is no need to talk to him, except just now and then, so do not put yourself to inconvenience.'

During the walk, it was decided that Mr Bennet's agreement to the marriage should be asked during the evening. Elizabeth kept for herself the duty of asking her mother's.

In the evening, soon after Mr Bennet had gone to his library, Mr Darcy followed him. Elizabeth's anxiety was extreme. She did not fear her father's opposition, but that *she* should be making him unhappy by her choice was a troubling thought. She was a little relieved by Darcy's smile on his return, when he whispered to her, 'Go to your father.' She went directly.

Her father was walking about the room, looking serious. 'Lizzy,' he said, 'what are you doing? Are you out of your mind, to be accepting this man? Have you not always hated him?'

How deeply she then wished that her former opinions had been more reasonable, and her expression of them less extreme! It would have saved her explanations that it was very awkward to give. She told him, in some confusion, of the strength of her feelings for Mr Darcy.

'That is to say, you are determined to have him. He is rich, to be sure, and you may have more fine clothes and fine carriages than Jane. But will they make you happy? We all know him to be a proud, unpleasant man.'

'I do, I do like him,' she replied, with tears in her eyes. 'And what you say of him is untrue. You do not know what he really is.'

'Lizzy,' said her father, 'I have agreed. But let me advise you to think better of it. I know your nature, Lizzy. I know that you could not be happy unless you truly respected your husband. My child, do not let me have the unhappiness of seeing you unable to think well of your partner in life.'

At last, by repeating that Mr Darcy was really the object of her choice, by explaining the gradual change in her feelings, and her proof of the unchanging nature of his, and describing with energy all his good qualities, she did persuade her father to believe her, and make him satisfied with her choice. To complete his favourable opinion, she then told him what Mr Darcy had done for Lydia.

'Well, my dear,' he said, when she had finished speaking, 'if this is the case, he deserves you. I could not have parted with you, my Lizzy, to anyone who did not.'

He then reminded her of her confusion a few days before when he was reading Mr Collins's letter and, after laughing at her, allowed her to go, saying as she left the room, 'If any young men come for Mary or Kitty, send them in. I am not busy.'

Elizabeth's mind was now relieved of a very heavy weight, and after half an hour's quiet thought in her own room, she was able to join the others in fairly settled spirits.

When her mother went up to her dressing room at night, she followed her and made the important announcement. Its effect was most astonishing. When she heard it, Mrs Bennet sat quite still, unable to say a word. Only after many, many minutes could she understand what she had heard. She began at last to recover, to move about in her chair, get up, sit down again, and every now and then let out a small laugh.

'Oh, heavens! Lord save me! Only think! Mr Darcy! Who would have thought it! Oh, my sweetest Lizzy, how rich and great you will be! What jewels, what carriages you will have! Jane's is nothing to it – nothing at all. Such a pleasant man! So good-looking! So tall! Oh, my dear Lizzy! Do apologize for my having disliked him so much before. Dear, dear Lizzy. A house in town! Three daughters married! Ten thousand a year! Oh, heavens! What will happen to me? I shall go out of my mind.'

This was an unpleasing example of what her mother's behaviour might be like in the presence of Mr Darcy, but the next day passed off better than Elizabeth expected. Luckily Mrs Bennet was so filled with respect for her intended son-in-law that she did not dare to speak to him, except to offer him some mark of attention.

Elizabeth had the satisfaction of seeing her father making every effort to know him better, and Mr Bennet soon informed her that Mr Darcy was rising in his opinion every hour.

Chapter 28   The End

It was a happy day for all her feelings as a mother, when Mrs Bennet saw her two most deserving daughters married. It may be guessed that she afterwards visited Mrs Bingley, and talked of Mrs Darcy, with excited pride. I wish I could say that the satisfaction of her dreams for them made her a sensible woman for the rest of her life, though perhaps it was lucky for her husband's amusement that she still often had an attack of nerves, and was never anything but silly.

Mr Bennet missed his second daughter very much. His love for her caused him to travel from home more often than anything else could do. He enjoyed going to Pemberley, especially when he was least expected.

Mr Bingley and Jane remained at Netherfield for only a year. The nearness of her mother was not desirable even to his kindly nature or her loving heart. He then bought a property in Derbyshire, and Jane and Elizabeth, in addition to every other happiness, lived within 30 miles of each other.

Kitty, to her very great advantage, spent most of her time with her two older sisters. In society that was so much better than what she had generally known, her improvement was great. She was not of so uncontrollable a nature as Lydia, and when she was removed from the influence of her example became less complaining and less silly. Although Lydia frequently invited her to come and stay with her, with promises of dances and young men, her father would never allow her to go.

Mary was the only daughter who remained at home, and she was necessarily interrupted in her studies and her efforts at making music by the fact that Mrs Bennet was quite unable to sit alone. Mary was forced to mix more with the world, and as her more beautiful sisters were no longer there to be compared with her, she was not unwilling to do so.

As for Lydia and Wickham, their characters remained unchanged. He bore with calmness the knowledge that Elizabeth must now have learnt every detail about his past, and both he and Lydia were not without hope that Darcy could still be persuaded to make his fortune. Elizabeth did frequently send some relief from her own private money, and because of his love for Elizabeth, Darcy helped Wickham to get a better position in the army. Although her husband could never be received at Pemberley, Lydia was sometimes a visitor there, and they both of them frequently stayed so long with the Bingleys that even Bingley's good temper failed him.

Miss Bingley was much annoyed by Darcy's marriage, but as she wanted to continue to visit Pemberley, she was forced to be polite to Elizabeth.

Pemberley was now Georgiana's home, and the sisterly love that grew between her and Elizabeth was exactly what Darcy had hoped to see. Georgiana had the highest opinion in the world of Elizabeth, though at first she often listened with astonishment to her lively, joking way of talking to the brother for whom she, as a much younger sister, felt so much respect.

Lady Catherine was extremely angry at the marriage of her nephew, and expressed her feelings in a letter so insulting to Elizabeth that for a time all friendly connections were ended. The Collinses removed to Lucas Lodge until the storm had blown over, which it did at last, when Elizabeth persuaded her husband to offer to end the quarrel.

With the Gardiners they had always the warmest relationship. Darcy, as well as Elizabeth, really loved them, and they both felt most grateful towards the persons who, by bringing her to Derbyshire, had been the means of uniting them.

ACTIVITIES

Chapters 1–4

Before you read

1 Think about the title of the book. What are the possible causes and effects of:

   a pride? **b** prejudice?

2 Find these words in your dictionary. They're all in the story.

   carriage   lodge   parsonage   regiment

   Match these groups of people with the four new words.

   Which group might you find in each place?

   _____ **a** soldiers, captain, commander

   _____ **b** passengers, travellers, driver

   _____ **c** husband, wife, children

   _____ **d** priest, Christian minister, church secretary

3 Check the meaning of these words in your dictionary.

   agreeable   engaged   inferior   lively   noble

   Complete each sentence with one of the new adjectives.

   a Mr. Gordon was an .... host. He was pleasant to everybody.

   b The boys and girls were exhausted after the .... dance.

   c His work is always .... to mine.

   d The .... couple went to the jewellerís to look at rings.

   e People throughout the country respected the king because he had a .... character.

4 Find these three verbs in your dictionary:

   acquaint   astonish   neglect

   Add *-ment*, *-ance* or *-ful* to the new words to complete the conversations. Look at your dictionary for help.

   a A: I've lost my job.

      B: Why? What happened?

      A: My boss said I was .... of my duties.

b A: Mr. Brown, please meet an .... of mine.
   This is Miss Ward.

   B: Nice to meet you, Miss Ward.

c A: What happened?

   B: To my ...., a man jumped off that bridge.

After you read

5 Name:

  a Mr Bennet's daughters (in order of age).

  b Mr Bennet's heir.

  c Mr Bingley's proud friend.

  d Elizabeth's best friend.

  e the nearest town to Longbourn.

6 Who is the speaker? What are they talking about?

  a 'What a fine thing for our girls!'

  b '. . . I could easily forgive *his* pride, if he had not wounded mine.'

  c '. . . you must be two of the silliest girls in the country.'

  d 'They were brightened by the exercise.'

  5 'I am conscious, madam, of the injustice to your lovely daughters . . .'

7 Discuss how men and women of this period and class seemed to spend their time. What forms of social behaviour were important?

Chapters 5–10

Before you read

8 How successful do you think a marriage between Mr Collins and Elizabeth Bennet would be? Why?

9 Find these words in your dictionary:

  g*odfather   heir   relief   scorn*

  a Which word means a person who might give advice?

  b Which word means a person who might expect to receive some money?

  c Describe three pairs of people who might *scorn* each other.

  d We may feel *relief* when a difficult situation ends. Think of one or two examples of situations like this.

After you read

10 How does:

    a Mr Wickham describe Mr Darcy?

    b Mr Bingley describe Mr Wickham?

    c Mrs Bennet view a possible marriage between Elizabeth and her cousin?

    d Mr Bennet view the same possibility?

    e Jane view Mr Bingley's departure from Netherfield?

    f Charlotte Lucas view her own marriage?

    g Mrs Gardiner feel about a possible marriage between her niece and Mr Wickham?

    h Elizabeth feel about Mr Wickham's relationship with Mary King?

11 Play the parts of Elizabeth and Mr Wickham at Mrs Philips's house. Discuss your feelings about Mr Darcy.

12 Play the parts of Elizabeth and Mr Collins on the occasion of Mr Collins's proposal of marriage.

Chapters 11–16

Before you read

13 What hope is there now for a relationship between:

    a Jane and Mr Bingley?

    b Elizabeth and Mr Wickham?

14 Check the meaning of these words in your dictionary:

    colonel   prejudice

    a In what ways do you think *prejudices* can hurt people in a school or in a neighbourhood?

    b Do people in your country respect people with titles like *colonel*? Why not?

After you read

15 Who:

    a travels with Elizabeth to visit Mr and Mrs Collins?

    b 'looks weak and disagreeable'?

    c asks Elizabeth her age?

    d is invited to use the housekeeper's piano at Rosings?

    e has 'saved a friend from the inconvenience of a most unwise marriage'?

    f 'is all beauty and goodness'?

    g is in love in spite of his best attempts to be sensible?

    h did Mr Wickham almost persuade to run away with him?

16 Discuss the reasons why Mr Darcy would prefer not to be in love with Elizabeth. How much sympathy do you have with his anxieties?

17 Imagine that you are Elizabeth. Tell your sister Jane, at your next meeting, about Mr Darcy's proposal and the range of emotions you felt at that time.

Chapters 17–22

Before you read

18 Explain why Elizabeth now feels she has been 'blind, prejudiced, unreasonable'.

After you read

19 Why:

    a is Lydia so happy to receive an invitation to Brighton?

    b is Wickham glad to leave Meryton?

    c did Mr Bennet marry his wife?

    d is Elizabeth worried about visiting Pemberley?

    e is Elizabeth interested in listening to the housekeeper at Pemberley?

    f are the Gardiners so surprised when Mr Darcy is polite to them?

    g is 26 November fixed in Mr Bingley's memory?

    h is Miss Bingley so rude to Elizabeth?

    i is Elizabeth so upset by Jane's letters?

    j   do Lydia's father and uncle travel to London?

    k   is Mr Collins's advice strange for a religious man?

    l   is Mr Bennet so severe to Kitty?

20 Do you agree with Elizabeth that 'in a time of such a misfortune as this, one cannot see too little of one's neighbours'?

21 Imagine you are one of these characters. Give your views on the causes and effects of Lydia's behaviour.

    a Mrs Bennet

    b Mr Bennet

    c Mr Darcy

    d Mr Collins

    e Jane Bennet

    f Elizabeth Bennet

Chapters 23–28

Before you read

22 How do you think the story will end for each of the main characters?

After you read

23 Answer questions about this part of the book.

    a Who marries whom?

    b Whose fortune makes one of the weddings possible?

    c Who is unhappy about one or more of the marriages?

24 'For what do we live, if not to amuse our neighbours and laugh at them in our turn?' What does Mr Bennet's remark tell us about his own character and attitudes? Do you agree with him?

25 Discuss how much you admire:

    a Mr Bennet, as a father.

    b Mrs Bennet, as a mother.

    c Mr Darcy, as a brother.

    d Jane Bennet, as a sister.

    e Mr Collins, as a church minister.

Writing

26 What part do pride and prejudice play in the development of the story?

27 Write both the letter in which Lady Catherine expresses to Mr Darcy her feelings about his proposed marriage, and her nephew's response to it.

28 Compare the marriages of two of the Bennet sisters. How suited are the women to their partners? Which marriage is likely to be more successful?

29 Which character do you find the most unpleasant? Explain why.

30 Explain why you would or would not have enjoyed the kind of lifestyle led by the Bennets, Bingleys and Darcys.

31 What do you think are the reasons for the book's continuing popularity?

Answers for the Activities in this book are published in our free resource packs for teachers, the Penguin Readers Factsheets, or available on a separate sheet. Please write to your local Pearson Education office or to: Marketing Department, Penguin Longman Publishing, 5 Bentinck Street, London W1M 5RN.

Wuthering Heights

EMILY BRONTË

Level 5

Retold by Evelyn Attwood
Series Editors: Andy Hopkins and Jocelyn Potter

Contents

Introduction

Emily Jane Brontë was born in Yorkshire, England, in 1818, the fifth of six children in a family of writers. Their father, Patrick, was an Irishman who became the minister of a church in Haworth in 1820. Their mother, Maria Branwell, died in 1821, and her older sister came to look after the household. Mr Brontë himself educated Branwell, the one boy in the family, at home. But their aunt was not able to deal with the girls' education and in 1824 Maria and Elizabeth were sent away to a religious school in Cowan Bridge, where Charlotte and Emily joined them later. Conditions at the school were difficult and Maria and Elizabeth were taken ill and sent home. Maria died in May 1825 and Elizabeth in June of the same year. Charlotte and Emily were then taken away from the school.

For the next five years the four remaining children stayed at home. Branwell received lessons from his father and the girls, Charlotte, Emily and Anne, educated themselves as well as they could. The children all read widely. They saw little of other families and to make their dull life in the small village where they lived more interesting, they began to invent stories. Many of those stories still exist today.

In 1831 Charlotte went away to school again, returning a year later to teach her sisters. She went back to the school as a teacher in 1835 and took Emily with her, but she found teaching difficult both at the school and in the two positions as governess that followed. During this period she had two offers of marriage, which she refused. She was keen to open a school of her own, and in 1842 she went to Belgium with Emily to improve her French. When their aunt died, the girls returned home. Charlotte then went back to Brussels by herself but was lonely, became ill and left again for Haworth. Her brother Branwell had failed at every job he tried and increasingly turned to alcohol and drugs. To add to her unhappiness, Charlotte's attempts to open a school in Haworth failed.

In 1846, Charlotte persuaded her sisters Emily and Anne to allow their poems to appear in a book with her own poems. The book, which they paid for themselves, was not a financial success, but they all continued to write. Charlotte's story *Jane Eyre* came out first, in 1847, and was an immediate popular success. Later the same year Anne's *Agnes Grey* and Emily's *Wuthering Heights* appeared.

Branwell died in September 1848. At his funeral Emily caught a fever and became very ill. She died in December. Anne died in May of the following year, at Scarborough, where she had hoped the sea air would help to improve her health. In spite of these terrible events, Charlotte struggled on with her writing and managed to complete two more books. She married in 1854, but died a year later. Her husband continued to look after Mr Brontë, who lived longer than all his children and died at the age of eighty-four.

Wuthering Heights is Emily Brontë's only full-length story. It is set on the wild and lonely Yorkshire moors that Emily knew and loved more than any of her sisters. The book is an imaginative and moving story, but was not well received when it first appeared. It was criticized as being cruel and miserable. The rough, hard emotions that fire the book are completely different from the gentle touch and polite subject matter of most stories written at the time. It was considered especially shocking that such scenes had been written by a woman. Only later was the book recognized as one of the most powerful and important works of fiction of the nineteenth century.

Wuthering Heights is the name of an old house, set high up on the wind-swept Yorkshire moors. At the end of the eighteenth century it is home to the Earnshaw family. Another family, the Lintons, live in the valley at the more comfortable Thrushcross Grange. Mr Earnshaw, father of Catherine and Hindley, goes to Liverpool one day on business and brings home with him a child who has been living on the streets in the worst part of the city. Mr Earnshaw takes the child as his son, giving him the name of Heathcliff. Nothing is the same again. A chain of events begins which splits both families apart. Heathcliff's influence on the family, and particularly his emotional relationship with Catherine, the strong-willed daughter of the household, drive this beautiful and powerful story.

Told by Mr Lockwood, tenant of Thrushcross Grange

Chapter 1   A Rough Welcome

I have just returned from a visit to my landlord, the only neighbour I shall have for many miles. In all England, I don't believe I could have fixed on a country house more distant from society.

Mr Heathcliff and I are a suitable pair to share this loneliness. As I rode up, his black eyes stared at me in a most unfriendly manner from under his dark forehead.

'Mr Heathcliff?' I said.

He nodded.

'I am Mr Lockwood, your new tenant at Thrushcross Grange, sir. I felt I should call on you as soon as possible after my arrival.'

He made no offer to shake hands. His hands remained in his pocket.

'Walk in!' He spoke with closed teeth, and continued to lean over the gate. When he saw my horse's chest pushing against it, he did take out his hand to unchain it, and then walked in front of me up the stone path, calling, as we entered the yard: 'Joseph, take Mr Lockwood's horse, and bring up some wine.'

'There must be only one servant,' I thought. 'That must be why the grass is growing up between the stones, and the plants are growing wild.'

Joseph seemed an unpleasant old man. 'The Lord help us!' he murmured in a disapproving voice, as he took my horse.

ᒐᒐ ⋅ Wuthering Heights is the name of Mr Heathcliff's house. 'Wuthering' is a local word, used to describe the wildness of the

151

weather in this part of Yorkshire in time of storm. One may guess the power of the north wind by the way the few poorly grown trees at the end of the house lean towards the ground, and by a row of bushes all stretching their branches in one direction, as if begging for the warmth of the sun.

Before I entered the house, I paused to admire some unusual decorative stonework over the front. Above it I saw the date '1500' and the name 'Hareton Earnshaw'. I would have asked for a few details about the place, but the owner appeared impatient.

One step brought us into the family sitting room. On the wall at one end there was row after row of large metal dishes, with silver pots and drinking cups right up to the roof. There was no ceiling. Above the fireplace were several evil-looking guns. The floor was of smooth white stone. The chairs were high-backed and painted green. In a corner lay a large dog and her young ones. Other, smaller dogs sat in other corners.

The room and furniture would have been nothing out of the ordinary if they had belonged to a simple Yorkshire farmer, but Mr Heathcliff seems out of place in his home and way of living. He is a dark-skinned gypsy in appearance, but in manners and dress a gentleman: that is, as much a gentleman as many country landowners – rather careless of his dress, perhaps, but upright and good-looking. His expression is rather severe and unsmiling.

I took a seat by the fire and filled up a few minutes of silence by trying to make friends with the largest dog.

'You'd better leave her alone,' said Heathcliff roughly, pushing the animal away with his foot, as she showed me all her teeth. Then, crossing to a side door, he shouted again, 'Joseph!'

Joseph murmured in the room below, but gave no sign of returning, so his master went down after him, leaving me face to face with the dogs, who watched all my movements. I sat still, but could not help showing my dislike of the animals, and soon the biggest jumped at my knees. I knocked her back, and got the table between us. This excited the others, who ran to join in. I was surrounded, and had to call for help.

Mr Heathcliff and his man were slow to answer. Luckily, a big strong woman with red cheeks rushed in from the kitchen and drove off the attack with a cooking pan. Heathcliff entered shortly after that.

'What the devil is the matter?' he asked.

I gave him my opinion of his dogs.

'They won't attack people who touch nothing,' he remarked, putting a bottle in front of me, and moving the table back into position. 'The dogs are right to be watchful. Take a glass of wine.'

'No, thank you.'

'Not bitten, are you?'

'If I had been, I would have left my mark on the biter!'

Heathcliff laughed.

'Come, come,' he said, 'you are upset, Mr Lockwood. Here, take a little wine. Guests are so rare in this house that I and my dogs, I'm prepared to admit, hardly know how to receive them. Your health, sir!'

I smiled, beginning to see that it was foolish to be annoyed by a lot of badly behaved dogs, and unprepared to provide my host with further amusement by losing my temper.

He probably realized the foolishness of offending a good tenant. He began to talk with greater politeness, and on a subject that he supposed might interest me. I found him very intelligent, and before I went home I was ready to offer another visit tomorrow. He showed no further wish for my company, but I shall go in spite of this.

Chapter 2   Even Less Welcome

Yesterday afternoon was misty and cold. I nearly decided to spend it by my sitting room fire, but when I came up from dinner the servant was still trying to light it. I took my hat and, after a four-mile walk, arrived at Heathcliff's garden gate just in time to escape the first light feathers of a snowfall.

On that cold hill-top the earth was frozen hard and the air made me shiver. I knocked on the front door, and the dogs began to make a noise.

I knocked a second time. The head of the unfriendly Joseph appeared out of a round window of the storehouse.

'What do you want?' he shouted. 'The master's down at the farm.'

'Is there nobody to open the door?' I called.

'There's only the mistress, and she won't open, even if you shout until night-time.'

'Why? Can't you tell her who I am?'

'It's not my business.' His head disappeared.

The snow began to fall thickly. I was about to knock a third time, when a young man without a coat and carrying a spade came from the yard behind the house.

He called to me to follow him and, after marching through a wash-house and an area containing a coalhouse and a pump, we at last arrived in the large, warm cheerful room in which I was received before.

A fire was burning and near the table, which was laid for an evening meal, I was pleased to see the 'mistress'.

I greeted her and waited, thinking she would ask me to take a seat. She looked at me, leaning back in her chair, and remained silent and still.

'It's rough weather,' I remarked. 'I had hard work, Mrs Heathcliff, to make your servant hear me.'

She never opened her mouth, but kept her eyes on me in an extremely unpleasant manner.

'Sit down,' said the young man roughly. 'He'll be in soon.'

I obeyed.

One of the dogs now came up in a more friendly manner than before.

'A beautiful animal,' I began again. 'Do you intend to keep the little ones, Mrs Heathcliff?'

'They are not mine,' said the mistress of the house, more rudely than Heathcliff himself.

I repeated my remark on the wildness of the weather.

'You shouldn't have come out,' said the lady, rising and reaching two painted tea boxes from the shelf above the fireplace.

Her position until she stood up had been sheltered from the light. Now I had a clear view of her whole face and figure. She seemed little more than a girl, with an admirable form and the most delicate little face that I had ever had the pleasure of seeing.

The boxes were almost out of her reach. I made a movement to help her. She turned on me.

'I don't want your help,' she said sharply.

I quickly begged her pardon.

'Were you asked to tea?' she demanded, standing with a spoonful of tea held over the pot.

'No,' I said, half smiling. 'You are the proper person to ask me.'

She threw the tea back, spoon and all, and returned to her chair. Her lower lip was pushed out, like a child's, ready to cry.

The young man was looking down on me fiercely.

I began to doubt that he was a servant. Both his dress and his speech were rough, his hair was uncut, and his hands were as brown as a farm worker's; but his manner was free, almost proud, and he showed no sign of serving the lady of the house.

Five minutes later, Heathcliff arrived.

'I am surprised that you chose the thick of a snowstorm to

walk out in,' he said, shaking the white powder from his clothes. 'Do you know you run the risk of being lost? Even people familiar with these moors often lose their way on an evening like this.'

'Perhaps I can get a guide from among your boys? Could you do without one for a few hours?'

'No, I could not.'

'Are you going to make the tea?' asked the young man, looking at the lady.

'Is *he* to have any?' she asked, turning to Heathcliff.

'Get it ready, will you?' was the answer, so fiercely spoken that I moved in surprise.

When the preparations were completed, he invited me to join them: 'Now, sir, bring your chair forward.'

We all pulled out chairs round the table, and the meal began without further conversation.

I could not believe that they sat together every day in such an unfriendly silence. If I had caused the cloud, I thought, it was my duty to try to drive it away.

'Many could not imagine living in happiness so far from society,' I began, 'but you, Mr Heathcliff, with your wife—'

'My wife is no longer alive, sir.'

I realized that I had made a mistake. I looked at the young man.

'Mrs Heathcliff is my son's wife.' As he spoke, Heathcliff turned a strange look of hate in her direction.

'And this young man . . .'

'Is not my son. My son is dead.'

The youth became red in the face.

'My name is Hareton Earnshaw,' he said roughly, 'and I advise you to respect it!'

He fixed his eye on me in a threatening manner. I began to feel very much out of place in this strange family circle, and I decided to be more careful about risking my presence under its roof a third time.

When the business of eating was over, I went to the window. Dark night was coming on, and the sky and hills were hidden from sight by the wild movement of the snow in the wind.

'I don't think it will be possible for me to get home now without a guide,' I said.

'Hareton, drive those sheep into shelter,' said Heathcliff.

'What must I do?' I continued.

There was no reply and, looking round, I saw only Joseph bringing in the dogs' food and Mrs Heathcliff leaning over the fire.

'Mrs Heathcliff,' I said anxiously, 'you must excuse me for troubling you. Do point out some landmarks by which I may know my way home.'

'Take the road you came by,' she answered, settling herself in a chair with a book and a candle. 'I can't show you the way. They wouldn't let me go beyond the garden wall.'

'Are there no boys at the farm?'

'No. There are only Heathcliff, Earnshaw, Zillah, Joseph and myself.'

'I hope this will be a lesson to you, to make no more foolish journeys on these hills,' cried the voice of Heathcliff from the kitchen. 'As for staying here, I don't keep rooms for visitors.'

'I can sleep on a chair in this room.'

'No! A stranger is a stranger, whether rich or poor. It will not suit me to have anyone wandering round this place when I am not on guard.'

With this insult, my patience was at an end. I pushed past him into the yard. It was so dark that I could not see the way out.

Joseph was milking the cows by the light of a lamp. I seized it and, calling that I would send it back the next day, rushed to the nearest gate.

'Master, master, he's stealing the lamp!' shouted the old man. 'Hold him, dogs, hold him!'

Two hairy animals jumped at my throat, bringing me to the ground and putting out the light, while rude laughter from Heathcliff and Hareton increased the force of my anger and shame. There I was forced to lie until they called the dogs off.

The violence of my anger caused my nose to bleed. Heathcliff continued to laugh, and I continued to shout angrily. At last Zillah, the big woman servant, came out to see what was happening.

'Are we going to murder people right on our doorstep? Look at that poor young gentleman – he can hardly breathe! Come in, and I'll cure that.'

With these words, she suddenly threw some icy water down my neck and pulled me into the kitchen.

I felt sick and faint. Heathcliff told Zillah to give me something strong to drink. I then allowed her to lead me to bed.

Chapter 3   An Uncomfortable Night

On the way upstairs, Zillah advised me to make no noise, as the master had some strange idea about the room she was taking me to, and would never allow anyone to sleep there.

I locked my door and looked around. The only furniture in the room was a chair, a long heavy chest for clothes, and a large wooden box, with square windows cut in the top. I looked inside this piece of furniture, and found it was a strange, ancient kind of bed, forming a little room of its own, the broad edge of which conveniently served as a table. I slid back the doors, got in with my light, and pulled them together again.

The shelf, on which I placed my candle, had a few old books piled up in one corner, and was covered with handwriting. This writing was just a name repeated many times – 'Catherine Earnshaw', sometimes changed to 'Catherine Heathcliff', and then again to 'Catherine Linton'.

I leaned my head against the window and continued to read the names again and again until my eyes closed. I had not rested five minutes, though, before I discovered that my candle had fallen on one of the books, and there was a smell of burning leather. I sat up and examined the book. It had the name 'Catherine Earnshaw' on the first page, and a date about a quarter of a century old. I shut it, and took up another book, and another, until I had examined them all.

The books had been well used, though not always for the usual purpose. Every bit of empty space was filled with childish writing, parts of which took the form of a record of daily happenings. At the top of one page I was highly amused to find an excellent drawing of Joseph. I felt an immediate interest in the unknown Catherine, and I began to read out the faint words:

A terrible Sunday. I wish my father were alive again. Hindley is hateful. His treatment of Heathcliff is terrible.

All day it has been pouring with rain. We could not go to church. While Hindley and his wife sat downstairs by a comfortable fire, we were commanded to take our prayer books and go up to the top of the house to listen to Joseph praying. We stayed there for three hours, but my brother still thought we came down too soon.

'Remember that you have a master here,' he said. 'I'll kill the first person that makes me angry. Oh, boy? Was that you? Frances, pull his hair as you go by.'

Frances did so, then went and sat with her husband. We hid ourselves in a corner but were soon driven out by Joseph, who said we were wicked to start playing on a Sunday. I wrote in this book for twenty minutes, but my companion is impatient and suggests that we should have a run on the moors. We cannot be wetter or colder in the rain than we are here.

I suppose that they did this, as the next sentence began a new subject:

I never thought that Hindley would ever make me cry so! My head aches terribly! Poor Heathcliff! Hindley calls him a gypsy, and won't let him sit with us or eat with us any more. My brother says that Heathcliff and I must not play together, and threatens to turn him out of the house if we disobey his orders. He has been blaming our father for treating Heathcliff too kindly, and swears he will reduce him to his right place.

My head began to fall over the yellowed page. My eye wandered on, but I soon sank back in bed and fell asleep.

Oh, the effects of bad tea and bad temper! What else could have caused me to pass such an uncomfortable night?

One horrible dream followed another . . . Joseph was guiding me home. He led me instead to the church I had passed on my way to the Heights. The priest's talk was divided into 490 parts. I became tired and restless: my head began to drop. In a voice of thunder he called on all his listeners to punish me for my wickedness. All the churchgoers rushed at me with uplifted sticks, and I, having no weapon, began struggling with my nearest attacker, Joseph.. The church was full of the sound of blows . . .

The blows sounded so loud that I awoke.

What had caused the noise? A branch of a tree touching my window.

I turned in my bed, and slept again. This time, I remembered where I was lying, and I heard the sound of the wind and the branch on the window. It annoyed me so much that I was determined to silence it. I got up and tried to open the window, but without success.

'I must stop it, in spite of that!' I murmured, breaking the glass with my hand and stretching it out to seize the annoying branch.

Instead, my fingers closed on the fingers of a small ice-cold hand!

Great fear came over me. I tried to pull back my arm, but the hand held on, and a sad voice cried: 'Let me in! Let me in!'

'Who are you?' I asked, while struggling to free myself.

'Catherine Linton,' it replied. (Why did I think of 'Linton'? I had read 'Earnshaw' twenty times, compared with 'Linton'.) 'I've come home. I'd lost my way on the moor.'

As it spoke, I saw, faintly, a child's face looking through the window.

'Let me in!' came the cry once more, while the hand continued to hold on to mine, almost maddening me with fear.

'How can I?' I said at last. 'Let me go, if you want me to let you in!'

The fingers loosened. I drew mine hurriedly through the hole, piled the books up against it, and closed my ears against the voice.

I seemed to keep them closed for over a quarter of an hour, but the moment I listened again, the sad cry was repeated.

Fear made me cruel.

'Go away!' I shouted. 'I'll never let you in, not if you beg for twenty years.'

'It is twenty years,' said the voice. 'Twenty years! I've been wandering for twenty years!'

The pile of books on my shelf moved as if they were being pushed forward. I tried to jump up, but could not, so I shouted aloud in fear.

Rapid footsteps hurried towards my door. Somebody pushed it open with a violent hand, and a light appeared. I sat up shivering.

In a half-whisper, clearly not expecting an answer, a voice said: 'Is anyone here?'

I pushed open the doors of my resting place. I shall not soon forget the effect that my action produced.

Heathcliff stood near the entrance, in his shirt and trousers, with a candle in his hand and his face as white as the wall behind him. My first movement affected him like an electric shock. The light fell from his hand.

'It's only your guest, sir,' I called out. 'I had the misfortune to cry out in my sleep, owing to a frightful dream.'

Heathcliff murmured a curse. He set the candle on a chair.

'And who showed you up to this room?' he asked.

'It was your servant, Zillah,' I replied. 'I suppose she wanted proof that there is a ghost. Well, there is!'

'What do you mean?' asked Heathcliff. 'Nothing could excuse the horrible noise you made, unless you were having your throat cut!'

'If that little ghost had got in at the window, she would probably have finished me!' I replied. 'As for Catherine Linton, or Earnshaw, or whatever she was called, she told me she had been walking the earth for twenty years now.'

I had hardly spoken these words, when I remembered the joining of Heathcliff's name with Catherine in the writing in the book.

'What do you mean by talking in this way to *me*?' thundered Heathcliff. 'How *dare* you, under my roof?'

I began to dress. Heathcliff sat down on the bed. I guessed by his irregular breathing that he was struggling against some powerful feeling.

'Mr Lockwood,' he said at last, 'you may go to my room. Your childish shouting has finished my chances of sleep for the night.'

'And mine too,' I replied. 'I'll walk in the yard until daylight, and then I'll be off.'

I left the room and then, not knowing the way, turned back to ask and saw, without intending to, the strange behaviour of my host.

He had got on to the bed and pulled open the window, bursting, as he did so, into a fit of uncontrollable weeping.

'Come in! Come in!' he cried. 'Cathy, do come! Oh, do, once more! Oh, my heart's dearest! Hear me this time, Catherine, at last!'

The spirit made no reply, but the snow and wind blew wildly in.

There was such suffering in this wild speech that I began to pity him. I went quietly down to the back kitchen, where I found the remains of a fire. Only half warm, I stretched myself on a wooden seat until morning, when I left as early as possible.

The air was clear, and cold as ice. Before I reached the bottom of the garden, my host came after me, and offered to go with me across the moor. I was glad that he did, as the whole hillside was one white ocean of snow, and the path was completely hidden.

We exchanged little conversation, and parted company at the entrance to Thrushcross Park. After losing myself among the trees, and sinking up to my neck in snow, I reached the Grange some time later, to a warm welcome from Mrs Dean, my housekeeper, who was beginning to believe that I had died on the moor.

Chapter 4   My Neighbours

By this time I was half frozen. I dragged myself upstairs, put on dry clothes, and sat in my sitting room, almost too weak to enjoy the cheerful fire and the hot coffee that the servant had prepared.

I had chosen this place, I remembered, for its loneliness. But how little we human beings know our own minds! Did I really want to live here?

163

By evening, I was already tired of my own company. I requested Mrs Dean, when she brought the supper, to sit down while I ate.

'You have lived here for some time,' I began.

'Eighteen years, sir. I came when the mistress was married, to help her. After she died, the master kept me as his housekeeper.'

'I'll turn the talk on my landlord's family,' I thought, 'and the pretty girl – I should like to know her history.'

With this intention, I asked why Heathcliff let Thrushcross Grange and preferred to live in a place so much less grand.

'Isn't he rich enough to keep the property in good order?' I inquired.

'Rich, sir!' she replied. 'Yes, he's rich enough to live in a finer house than this. But he's very careful with his money.'

'He had a son, it seems?'

'Yes, he had one. He is dead.'

'And the young lady, Mrs Heathcliff – where did she come from.'

'She is the daughter of my master, sir, who is now dead. Catherine Linton was her name before she married. I was her nurse, poor thing!'

'What! Catherine Linton!' I exclaimed. But a moment's thought told me that it was not my ghostly Catherine. 'And who is that Earnshaw, Hareton Earnshaw, who lives with Mr Heathcliff? Are they relations?'

'No. He is Mrs Linton's nephew, and the young lady's cousin. Hareton is the last of the Earnshaws, a very old family who owned Wuthering Heights, and Catherine is the only one left of the Lintons, whose family home was Thrushcross Grange. Have you been to the Wuthering Heights, sir? I should like to hear how she is.'

'Mrs Heathcliff? She looked very well, and very pretty, but not, I think, very happy.'

'Oh, well, I'm not surprised. And how did you like the master?'

'A rough man, Mrs Dean. Do you know anything of his history?'

'Everything, sir, except where he was born, and who his parents were, and how he first got his money. And Hareton has lost his rights! The unfortunate boy does not guess how he has been cheated of his property!'

'Well, Mrs Dean, I shall not rest if I go to bed. Be so good as to stay and tell me something about my neighbours.'

'Oh, certainly, sir! I'll just fetch a little sewing, and then I'll sit as long as you please.'

She hurried off, and I moved nearer to the fire. My head felt hot, and the rest of me felt cold. I was excited by the events of the last two days, and I began to fear that the effect on my health might be serious.

My fears proved to be true. The next weeks were spent in bed, and during my illness Mrs Dean often came to sit and keep me company.

While she sat, she told me, little by little, the story that follows.

PART 2   THE FIRST CATHERINE (1771–1784)

Told by Mrs Ellen (Nelly) Dean, housekeeper at Thrushcross Grange and formerly servant at Wuthering Heights

Chapter 5   The Unwanted Stranger

Wuthering Heights was built by the Earnshaws about 300 years ago, and until recently it remained the family home. Before I came to live at the Grange, I was almost always at the Heights, because when I was a baby my mother was nurse to Hindley Earnshaw, who was Hareton's father. As a child I often played with the children, Hindley and Catherine. I did little jobs, too, and helped on the farm when I was asked to.

One fine summer morning, Mr Earnshaw, the old master, came downstairs dressed for a journey. After he had told Joseph what had to be done during the day, he turned to his children and asked what he should bring them from the port of Liverpool. But, he said, it must be something small, as he intended to walk there and back, which was sixty miles each way. Hindley asked for a drum, and Cathy chose a whip; although she was hardly six years old, she could ride any horse on the farm. He then kissed his children goodbye and set out.

It seemed a long time to us all, the three days of his absence. Mrs Earnshaw expected him by supper time on the third evening, and she delayed the meal hour after hour but there was no sign of his coming. It became dark, and she would have sent the children to bed, but they begged sadly to stay up.

Just about eleven o'clock, the door opened and the master stepped in. He threw himself into a chair laughing and then he opened his big coat, which he held wrapped up in his arms.

'See here, wife! You must take this as a gift of God, though it's as dark as if it came from the devil.'

We crowded round, and over Catherine's head I had a view of a dirty, black-haired child in torn clothes. It was big enough both to walk and talk; in fact its face looked older than Catherine's. But when it was placed on its feet, it only stared around and repeated some sounds that nobody could understand. I was frightened, and Mrs Earnshaw was ready to throw it out of doors.

The master had seen it dying of hunger, and homeless, and unable to speak any English, in the streets of Liverpool. No one knew to whom it belonged. He was determined not to leave it so, his time and money being limited, he thought it better to take it straight home with him. I was told to wash it, give it clean clothes, and let it sleep with the children.

Hindley and Cathy were happy to look and listen, until they both began searching their father's pockets for the presents he had promised them. Hindley was a boy of fourteen, but when he took out what had been a drum, now broken to bits, he wept aloud; and Cathy, when she learned that the master had lost her whip in looking after the stranger, showed her temper by making ugly faces at the little thing, and received a blow from her father. They refused to have the child in their room, and so I put it outside on the stairs, hoping it might be gone in the morning. It crept to Mr Earnshaw's door, and there he found it. As a punishment for my unkindness I was sent out of the house.

On returning a few days later, I found they had called the child Heathcliff. It was the name of a son of the Earnshaws who had died in childhood, and it has served him ever since as both first and last name.

Miss Cathy and he were now very friendly, but Hindley hated him and the mistress never said a word when she saw him badly treated. He seemed a patient, unsmiling child used, perhaps, to unkindness, who would suffer Hindley's blows without complaint. When Mr Earnshaw discovered his son hitting the poor, fatherless child, as he called him, he was furious. He became strangely fond of Heathcliff, far more than of Catherine, who was too strong-willed and naughty to be a favourite.

From the beginning Heathcliff caused bad feeling, and by the time Mrs Earnshaw died two years later, the young master had learned to think of his father as hard and unkind, and of Heathcliff as the thief of his father's love.

I often asked myself what my master saw to admire so much in the unpleasant boy, who never, as far as I can remember, showed any signs of being grateful for the fond treatment he received.

I remember Mr Earnshaw once bought a pair of horses for the boys. Heathcliff took the finer one, but it soon hurt its foot. When he discovered this, he said to Hindley: 'You must exchange horses with me, or I'll tell your father of the three beatings you've given me this week.'

Hindley threatened him with an iron weight.

'Throw it,' said Heathcliff, 'and I'll tell how you said that you would turn me out of doors as soon as he died, and we'll see whether he won't turn you out immediately.'

Hindley threw it, hitting him on the chest, and knocking him over. He was up again at once, breathless and pale, and if I hadn't prevented it, he would have gone to the master and got full revenge.

'Take my horse, you dirty gypsy,' said young Hindley, 'and I pray he may break your neck!'

Heathcliff had gone to take possession of the animal, when Hindley finished his speech by knocking him over. I was surprised to see how calmly the child picked himself up. I persuaded him to let me lay the blame for the marks left by Hindley's blows on the horse, and he did not mind what story was told, since he had got what he wanted.

Chapter 6   Hindley Becomes Master

In the course of time, Mr Earnshaw's health began to fail. His strength left him suddenly, and he became easily annoyed. He got it into his head that because he liked Heathcliff, everyone hated the boy and wished to do him harm. It was a disadvantage to young Heathcliff, because as we didn't wish to upset the master, we all, except his son, gave in to him, and this was an encouragement to the boy's pride and black temper. Hindley's expressions of scorn moved his father to fury: Mr Earnshaw would seize his stick to strike him, and shake with anger at his own helplessness.

At last a friend of our employer, who earned some money by teaching the young Lintons and Earnshaws, advised that Hindley should be sent away to college, and Mr Earnshaw agreed, though with a heavy heart.

I hoped we would have peace now, and so we might have, except that Miss Cathy and Joseph were just as bad. Night after night the old servant had a string of complaints against Heathcliff and Cathy. As for Cathy, certainly she had ways such as I never saw in a child before. She put us out of patience fifty times and more in a day. From the hour she came downstairs until the hour she went to bed, we hadn't a minute's rest from her naughtiness. Her spirits were always high, her tongue was always going – singing, laughing, interrupting everybody. She was a wild, wicked young thing, but she had the prettiest eye and sweetest smile and lightest foot in our part of the country, and after all, I think she meant no harm. She was much too fond of Heathcliff. The greatest punishment we could invent for her was to keep her separated from him.

The hour came at last that ended Mr Earnshaw's troubles on earth. He died quietly in his chair one October evening.

Mr Hindley came home for the funeral and, a thing that set the neighbours whispering, he brought a wife. What she was, and where she was born, he never informed us. Probably she had neither money nor name, or he would never have kept his marriage secret from his father.

She was rather thin, but young and fresh, and her eyes were bright as diamonds. I did notice, it's true, that going upstairs made her breathe rather fast, and that she coughed rather badly sometimes.

Young Earnshaw had changed during the three years of his absence. He spoke and dressed quite differently. His wife expressed pleasure at having Cathy as a sister, kissed her, and gave her quantities of presents. Her love for her new sister didn't last

169

very long, though, and a few words from her, mentioning a dislike for Heathcliff, were enough to stir up in her husband all his former hate for the boy. He drove him from their company to the servants, stopped his education, and made him work as hard as any other boy on the farm.

Heathcliff bore his treatment fairly well at first, because Cathy taught him all she learned and worked or played with him in the fields. They were both growing up quite wild and without manners, since the young master did not care how they behaved as long as they kept away from him.

One of their chief amusements was to run away to the moors in the morning and remain there all day. The punishment that followed was only something to be laughed at: they forgot everything the minute they were together again.

◆

One Sunday, it chanced that Catherine and Heathcliff were sent from the sitting room for making a noise. When I went to call them to supper, I couldn't find them anywhere. At last Hindley in a fury told us to lock the doors, and swore that nobody should let them in that night.

Everyone else went to bed, but I, too anxious to lie down, opened my window and put out my head to listen. After a time, I heard faint footsteps coming up the road. There was Heathcliff by himself.

'Where is Miss Catherine?' I cried. 'No accident, I hope?'

'At Thrushcross Grange,' he answered. 'Let me take off my wet clothes, and I'll tell you all about it.'

I urged him to take care not to wake the master. As he was undressing, he continued, 'Cathy and I escaped from the house to have an hour or two of freedom and, catching sight of the Grange lights, we thought we would just go and see how the Lintons passed their Sunday evenings. We ran from the top of the Heights to the Park without stopping — Catherine was completely beaten in the race, because she had no shoes on. You'll have to look for her shoes out there tomorrow. We crept through a broken fence and stood on a flowerbed under a window. By pulling ourselves up, we were able to see — ah! it was beautiful! — a lovely room, with chairs covered in red, and tables too, and a red floor, and a pure white ceiling bordered with gold, and little glass balls hanging in silver chains from the centre and shining with soft little lights. Edgar and his sister were there. Shouldn't they have been happy? And guess what they were doing! Isabella — I believe she is eleven — lay shouting at one end of the room. Edgar stood by the fire weeping, and in the middle of a table sat a little dog, which they had nearly pulled in two. That was their pleasure! We laughed at the spoilt things. Would you find me wishing to have what Catherine wanted? I'd not exchange my condition here for Edgar Linton's at Thrushcross Grange, not for a thousand lives!'

'Speak more quietly!' I interrupted. 'Still you haven't told me how Catherine was left behind.'

'I told you we laughed,' he answered. 'The Lintons heard us, and began to cry for their mother and father. We made horrible noises to frighten them even more, and then we dropped down from the edge of the window, because someone was coming outside. I had Cathy by the hand, and was urging her on, when suddenly she fell. They had let the watch-dog loose, and he had seized her leg. She didn't cry — no, she would not have done that. I got a stone and pushed it between the animal's jaws, but he held on. A servant came out. He got the dog off, and lifted Cathy up. She was sick, not from fear, I'm certain, but from pain.

'"What have you caught, Robert?" called Mr Linton.

'"A little girl, sir," he replied, "and there's a boy who looks like a thief," he added, catching hold of me. "Mr Linton, sir, keep your gun ready."

'He pulled me under the light, and Mrs Linton put her

glasses on and raised her hands in fear. The children crept nearer, and Isabella cried, "Lock him up, Papa. He's exactly like the son of the gypsy who stole my pet bird." Cathy now recovered from her faint. She heard the last speech and laughed. Edgar recognised her. They see us in church, you know.

'"That's Miss Earnshaw," he whispered to his mother.

'"Miss Earnshaw? Nonsense! Miss Earnshaw running about the country like a gypsy! But yes, surely it is – and her foot is bleeding."

'"What carelessness of her brother!" exclaimed Mr Linton, "to let her grow up like this! And where did she pick up this companion? A wicked boy, and quite unfit for a respectable house. Did you hear the language he was using?"

'I began cursing again, and so the servant was ordered to send me away. The curtain at the window was still partly open, and I stood to watch, because if Catherine had wished to return and they did not let her leave, I intended breaking the glass. She sat quietly on a comfortable chair. A servant brought a bowl of warm water and washed her feet. Mr Linton gave her a hot drink, and Isabella put a plateful of cakes on her knee. Afterwards, they dried and combed her beautiful hair and put her near the fire, and I left her cheerfully bringing a little life to the dull blue eyes of the Lintons. I saw they were full of stupid admiration. She is so completely superior to them, and to everybody else on earth – isn't she?'

'There will be trouble when Mr Hindley knows, Heathcliff,' I said.

My words came truer than I wished. Hindley was furious. The next day Mr Linton paid us a visit and talked to the young master about his responsibilities to his sister. As a result, Heathcliff was told that the next time he spoke to Catherine, he would be sent away.

Chapter 7   Catherine's Homecoming

Catherine stayed at Thrushcross Grange for five weeks, until Christmas. By that time her ankle was cured and her manners much improved. She had learned to enjoy fine clothes and admiration, so that instead of a wild, hatless, unmannered little thing jumping into the house and rushing up to us, a well-dressed little person, very careful of her appearance, climbed down from her horse. Hindley exclaimed with pleasure, 'Well, Cathy, you are quite a beauty! You look like a lady now.'

The dogs came running up to welcome her, but she hardly dared touch them for fear that they would spoil her beautiful dress. She kissed me carefully: I had flour on my clothes from making the Christmas cake. Then she looked round for Heathcliff.

He was hard to find at first. Since Cathy had been away, the treatment of him had been ten times worse than before. There was no one except me even to tell him to wash himself. His clothes had seen long service in mud and dust, his thick hair was uncombed, his face and hands needed soap and water. He had good reason to hide.

'Heathcliff, you may come forward,' cried Mr Hindley, enjoying his shame. 'You may come and wish Miss Catherine welcome, like all the other servants.'

Cathy flew to kiss her friend seven or eight times on his cheek, and then stopped, and stepping back, burst into a laugh, exclaiming, 'Why, how very dark and unpleasant you look! But that's because I'm used to Edgar and Isabella Linton.'

'Shake hands, Heathcliff,' ordered Hindley.

Shame and pride kept the boy immovable.

'I shall not,' he said at last. 'I shall not stand to be laughed at.'

He would have moved away from them, but Miss Cathy seized him.

'I didn't mean to laugh at you,' she said. 'It was only that you looked so strange. You're so dirty!'

She looked anxiously at her dress, fearing that he had marked it.

'You needn't have touched me,' he answered, following her eye. 'I shall be as dirty as I please.'

He rushed from the room, followed by the laughter of my master and mistress. Cathy was upset and could not understand his bad temper.

It was the evening before Christmas Day. Joseph had gone to pray. I sat alone in the kitchen, remembering my old master and his kindness to me. From these thoughts I passed to his fondness for Heathcliff and his fear that the boy would suffer after his death.

Catherine was in the sitting room with her brother and his wife, looking at the presents they had bought for her to give to the Lintons. I found Heathcliff in one of the farm buildings.

'Hurry, Heathcliff,' I said. 'Let me make you tidy before Miss Cathy comes out, and then you can sit together by the fire in the kitchen and have a long talk before bedtime.'

He went on with his work and never turned his head.

Cathy sat up late, preparing for her new friends, who were going to visit her the next day. She came into the kitchen once to speak to her old friend, but he was not there.

Chapter 8   An Unhappy Christmas

The next day Heathcliff rose early and took his bad temper on to the moors, not reappearing until the family had left for church.

By this time he seemed to be in a better state of mind. He stood near me for a time, and then finding his courage, said, 'Nelly, make me tidy. I'm going to be good.'

'It's time that you behaved,' I said. 'You have hurt Catherine's feelings. You are too proud. If you're ashamed, you must ask pardon. And though I have dinner to get ready, I'll make time to arrange you so that Edgar Linton shall look like a baby beside you. You are younger, but you're taller and twice as broad across the shoulders. You could knock him down in a second.'

Heathcliff's face brightened for a moment, then it darkened again.

'But Nelly, it wouldn't make him less good-looking. I wish I had light hair and a fair skin, and was as well dressed and rich as he!'

'And cried for his mother and sat at home all day if there is a little rain!' I added. 'Oh, Heathcliff, you are showing a poor spirit! Now, look in the glass and tell me if you don't find yourself rather good-looking too, now you're washed and combed and have finished with your bad temper. For all we know, your father was a king in some faraway country, and your mother a queen, and you were seized as a child by wicked sailors, and brought to England!'

So I continued to talk, and Heathcliff was beginning to look quite pleasant, when suddenly our conversation was interrupted by the sound of wheels moving up the road and entering the yard.

From the window we saw the two Lintons, covered with furs, climbing down from their horses. Catherine took each of the children by the hand and brought them into the house.

I urged my companion to go and show his good temper, but unfortunately for him, when he opened the door leading from the kitchen on one side, Hindley opened it on the other. They met, and the master, annoyed at seeing him clean and cheerful, or perhaps remembering Mr Linton's words, pushed him back sharply and ordered Joseph to send him upstairs until dinner was over.

'Away, you gypsy!' he cried. 'What! Are you trying to make

yourself look like your superiors! Wait till I get hold of that fine hair – see if I won't pull it a little longer!'

'It's long enough already,' remarked Edgar Linton from the doorway. 'It's like horse hair.'

Heathcliff's violent nature was not prepared to accept this insult. He seized a dish of hot apple pie and threw it right in the speaker's face. Edgar began to cry, and Isabella and Catherine hurried in. Mr Hindley dragged Heathcliff outside, while I got a kitchen cloth and rather unkindly rubbed Edgar's nose and mouth clean. Cathy stood by, confused and turning red with embarrassment.

'You shouldn't have spoken to him!' she said to Edgar. 'Now he'll be beaten, and I hate that! I can't eat my dinner.'

'I didn't speak to him,' wept the youth. 'I promised my mother I wouldn't say a word to him.'

'Well, don't cry,' said Catherine scornfully. 'You're not dead. My brother is coming. Be quiet!'

At the sight of all the food on the table, the little visitors recovered their good spirits. They were hungry after their journey, and no real harm had been done. I waited at the table behind the mistress's chair. Cathy lifted a mouthful, and then set it down again. Her cheeks were hot and the tears poured over them. She quickly dropped her fork and bent beneath the tablecloth to hide her feelings. She was unhappy all day.

In the evening we had a dance. Cathy begged that Heathcliff, who had been locked up by the master, might be freed, as Isabella had nobody to dance with; but Mr Hindley would not listen, and I had to fill the place. Our pleasure in the exercise was increased by the arrival of a band of fifteen musicians, and some singers too. Young Mrs Earnshaw loved the music, so they gave us plenty.

Catherine loved it too, but she said it sounded sweetest at the top of the stairs, and she went up in the dark. I followed. They shut the door below, never noticing our absence. She did not stop at the head of the stairs, but went on up the ladder to the top of the house, where Heathcliff was locked in, and spoke to him through the door.

When the singers had finished, I went to warn her. Instead of finding her outside, I heard her voice from inside. The naughty little thing had crept out through one small window in the roof, and along the outside and in through the window of Heathcliff's prison, and it was with the greatest difficulty that I could persuade her to come out again. When she did come, Heathcliff came with her.

I told them that I didn't mean to encourage their tricks, but as Heathcliff had not eaten at all since yesterday's dinner I would shut my eyes for once to his deceiving Mr Hindley. He went down, and I set him in a chair by the fire in the kitchen.

He was sick, and could eat little. He sat with his head in his hands. When I inquired what he was thinking about, he answered: 'I'm trying to decide how I shall take my revenge on Hindley. I don't care how long I wait, if only I can do it in the end.'

Chapter 9   'No Company At All'

On the morning of a bright day in the following June, 1778, Hareton, the last of the ancient family of Earnshaw, was born. He was a fine boy. The doctor said, though, that his mother had had a sickness of the lungs for many months and would not live long. Mr Hindley refused to believe it, but one night, while she was leaning on his shoulder, a fit of coughing seized her. He raised her in his arms; she put hers around his neck, her face changed, and she was dead.

The child, Hareton, was left completely in my charge. His father, so long as he saw him healthy and never heard him cry, was happy. He had room in his heart for only his wife and himself, and he could not bear the loss. He neither wept nor prayed; he cursed God and man, and gave himself up to wild living. The servants all left: Joseph and I were the only two who would stay. Cathy's teacher stopped visiting us, and nobody respectable came near us except Edgar Linton, who came to see Cathy.

At fifteen she was the queen of our part of the country: a proud, strong-willed girl, but completely dependable and loyal. Heathcliff still had his place in her heart and Linton, with all his superiority, found it difficult to awaken equally strong feelings.

Catherine did not show her rough side in the Lintons' company, but had the good sense to be ashamed of being rude where she was received with such unfailing good manners. The old lady and gentleman were deceived by her pretty ways, and became fond of her, and she gained the admiration of Isabella and the heart and soul of her brother.

One afternoon, Mr Hindley had gone out, so Heathcliff had given himself a holiday. He had reached about the age of sixteen and had by that time lost the advantage of his early education. His childhood sense of superiority, developed by the love that old Mr Earnshaw felt for him, had disappeared. He had struggled for a long time to keep up with Catherine in her studies but had given up. Then his appearance began to show his state of mind. His walk lacked confidence, he looked unpleasant and rarely spoke, and he took pleasure in stirring up the dislike of those whom he met.

Catherine and he were still loyal companions when his work was done, and on this occasion he came into the house in search of her. I was helping her to arrange her dress, as she thought she had the whole place to herself and had let Edgar Linton know of her brother's absence.

'Why have you got that silk dress on?' asked Heathcliff. 'Nobody is coming here, I hope?'

'Not that I know of,' replied Catherine rather awkwardly, 'but you should be in the fields now, Heathcliff.'

'Hindley doesn't often free us of his presence,' remarked the boy. 'I'll not work any more today. I'll stay with you.'

He moved towards the fire. Catherine looked at him uncertainly.

'Isabella and Edgar Linton talked of calling this afternoon,' she said, after a short silence. 'As it's raining, I don't really expect them, but they may come.'

'Order Ellen to say that you are out, Cathy,' he went on. 'Don't turn me out for those miserable, silly friends of yours.'

'And should I always be sitting with you?' she demanded. 'What good do I get? You might be a baby, unable to talk, for anything you say to amuse me!'

'You never told me before that I talked too little, or that you disliked my company, Cathy!' exclaimed Heathcliff, greatly upset.

'It's no company at all, when people know nothing, and say nothing,' she complained.

Her companion rose, but he had no time to express his feelings further, because a horse's feet were heard on the stone path outside, and after a gentle knock young Linton entered, his fair, good-looking face shining with pleasure. No doubt Cathy noticed the difference between her friends, as the one came in and the other left.

'I've not come too soon, have I?' said Edgar, giving me a look.

'No,' answered Catherine. 'What are you doing here, Nelly?'

'My work, miss,' I replied. Mr Hindley had given me orders to be present at any private visits young Linton chose to pay.

She stepped up behind me and whispered: 'Take yourself and your work off!'

'It's a good opportunity, now that the master is away,' I answered loudly. 'He hates me to do this tidying when he is in the room. I'm sure Mr Edgar will excuse me.'

179

She, thinking that Edgar could not see her, pulled the cloth from my hand and hit me very sharply on the arm. She hurt me, and besides, I enjoyed punishing her pride, so I got up and cried out: 'Oh, Miss Cathy, that's a nasty trick! You've no right to hit me.'

'I didn't touch you, you lying thing!' she exclaimed, her fingers ready to repeat the act, and her ears red with fury.

'What's this, then?' I replied, showing the mark on my arm.

She struck the ground with her foot; then, driven by the naughty spirit within her, hit me on the cheek, a blow that filled both my eyes with tears.

'Catherine! Catherine!' exclaimed Edgar, deeply upset by the double fault of lying and violence.

Little Hareton, who followed me everywhere and was sitting near me on the floor, began crying and talking of 'wicked Aunt Cathy', which turned her fury against him. She seized his shoulders and shook him until he became pale and Edgar, without thinking, took hold of her hands to free him. In a moment one hand was pulled from his, and the surprised young man felt it on his own ear in a way that could not be mistaken for a joke.

The insulted visitor moved to the place where he had put down his hat, pale and with a trembling lip.

'Where are you going?' demanded Catherine, moving to the door.

'Can I stay after you have struck me?' asked Edgar.

Catherine was silent.

'You've made me afraid and ashamed of you,' he continued. 'I'll not come here again.'

Catherine's tears began to fall.

'And you told an untruth,' he said.

'Well, go, if you please! Get away! And now I'll cry – I'll cry until I'm sick!'

She dropped down on her knees by a chair.

Edgar walked out into the yard, and then he looked back through the window. He possessed the power to go away as much as a cat possesses the power to leave a mouse half killed, or a bird half eaten. He turned and hurried into the house again and shut the door.

When I went in later to inform them that Earnshaw had come home furiously drunk, I saw that the quarrel had simply brought them closer and helped them to put off the appearance of friendship and admit to being lovers.

Chapter 10   Cathy's Choice

My warning of Mr Hindley's arrival drove Edgar to his horse and Catherine to her room. I hurried to hide Hareton, and to take the shot out of the master's gun for fear that in his excited condition he would do harm.

Earnshaw entered, murmuring terrible curses, and caught me just as I was putting his son out of sight. He picked up the boy, who was shouting and kicking, as the child had an equal terror of his fondness and of his fury. The drunken father carried him upstairs, and paused unsteadily, looking down, as I begged him to take care. Still struggling in his father's arms, Hareton managed to free himself and fell.

At that exact moment Heathcliff arrived below and, by a natural movement, caught the child and set him on his feet. His face became dark with anger when he looked up and realized that he had missed an excellent opportunity for revenge.

Earnshaw came slowly down, a little ashamed.

'It's your fault,' he said to me. 'You should have kept him out of sight. Is he hurt?'

'Hurt!' I cried angrily. 'I am surprised that his mother

doesn't rise from her grave to see how you treat him!'

He took a bottle of wine and poured some into a glass, impatiently ordering us to go.

I carried the child into the kitchen, and sat down to calm him. Heathcliff, as I thought, walked out into the yard. I found out afterwards that he only got as far as the other side of the high-backed kitchen seat, behind which he sat unseen.

I was nursing Hareton on my knee, when Cathy put her head in at the door and whispered: 'Are you alone, Nelly?'

'Yes, miss.'

'Where's Heathcliff?'

'Doing his work outside.'

He did not call out that this was not so. Perhaps he was half asleep.

A long pause followed. A tear fell from Catherine's cheek.

'Oh!' she cried at last. 'I'm very unhappy!'

'That's a pity,' I replied. 'You're hard to please: so many friends and so few cares, and you can't make yourself happy.'

'Nelly, will you keep a secret?' She knelt down beside me. 'I want to know what I should do. Today Edgar Linton has asked me to marry him. I accepted him. Say whether I was wrong.'

'Do you love him?'

'Who can help it? Of course I do.'

'Why do you love him, Miss Cathy?'

'Well, because he's very good-looking, and pleasant to be with.'

'That's bad.'

'He'll be rich, and I shall like to be the greatest woman in the area.'

'Then why are you unhappy? Your brother will be pleased. The old lady and gentleman won't object, I think. You will escape from a disorderly, comfortless home into a wealthy, respectable one. Where is the difficulty?'

'Here – and here!' replied Catherine, putting one hand on her forehead and the other on her breast. 'In whichever place the soul lives. In my soul and in my heart, I'm certain I'm wrong.'

She seated herself by me. Her face became sadder; her hands trembled.

'I have no right to marry Edgar Linton, and if that wicked brother of mine had not brought Heathcliff to such a low state, I wouldn't have thought of it. It would degrade me to marry Heathcliff now, so he shall never know how I love him – and that, not because he's good-looking, Nelly, but because he's more myself than I am.'

I heard a slight movement before the speech ended. I turned my head and saw Heathcliff rise from a seat and creep out. He had listened until he heard Catherine say it would degrade her to marry him.

I urged my companion to speak lower.

'Why?' she asked, looking round nervously.

'Joseph is here,' I answered, 'and I think that Heathcliff is about at this moment.'

'Oh, he couldn't have heard me!' she said. 'Give me Hareton while you get the supper, and let me have it with you. I will feel much more comfortable if I can persuade myself that Heathcliff has no idea of my feelings. He hasn't, has he? He doesn't know what being in love is?'

'I see no reason why he shouldn't know as well as you,' I answered, 'and if you are his choice, he is the most unfortunate being that ever was born! As soon as you become Mrs Linton, he loses friend and love and all! Have you considered how you'll bear the separation, and how he'll bear to be left quite friendless in the world?'

'He left friendless! We separated! Not as long as I live! Edgar must get rid of his dislike of him. Nelly, did it never strike you that if Heathcliff and I married, we would have nothing, but if I marry Edgar I can help Heathcliff to rise in life, and place him out of my brother's power?'

'With your husband's money? That's the worst reason you've given for being the wife of young Linton.'

'It's not! It's the best! This is for one who . . . I can't express it; but surely you and everybody have an idea that there is or should be an existence of yours beyond you? My great miseries in this world have been Heathcliff's miseries: my life is his. If everything else were destroyed, and he remained, I should still continue to be; and if everything else remained, and he were gone, the universe would seem a stranger. My love for Edgar is like the leaves in the woods: time will change it, as the winter changes the trees. My love for Heathcliff is like the unchanging rocks beneath: a cause of little conscious pleasure, but necessary to my being. Nelly, I am Heathcliff! He's always in my mind, as part of me.'

'If I can make any sense of your nonsense, miss, it only causes me to believe that either you know nothing of the duties that you take on yourself in marrying, or else you are a wicked girl.'

The entrance of Joseph put an end to our talk.

Hours passed by, and there was no sign of Heathcliff. Catherine became worried, especially when I told her that he had really heard a large part of what she had said.

'Where do you think he is? What did I say? I've forgotten. Was he upset by my bad temper this afternoon? I do wish he'd come.'

It was a very dark evening for summer, and at about midnight, while we were still sitting up, a storm came over the Heights. There was a violent wind, as well as thunder and lightning, and either one or the other split a tree and knocked down a part of the east chimney.

Catherine remained out by the gate, waiting for Heathcliff, listening and calling, careless of the weather, until she was wet to the skin. She refused to take off her wet things, and in the morning I found her still seated near the fireplace. She was shivering uncontrollably, and Hindley ordered me to get her to bed.

I shall never forget the scene when we reached her room. It frightened me. I thought she was going mad, and I begged Joseph to run for the doctor. It was the beginning of high fever. The doctor declared her to be dangerously ill, told me to feed her on liquids and to take care that she did not throw herself from the window. He then left, as he had enough to do in the area, where the houses were often widely separated.

I was not a gentle nurse and Joseph and the master were no better. Cathy was as tiring and as difficult to manage as any sick person can be. Old Mrs Linton paid us several visits and, when Catherine was recovering, took her to Thrushcross Grange. The poor lady had reason to be sorry for her kindness. She and her husband both caught the fever and died within a few days of each other.

Our young lady returned to us prouder and more violent in temper than ever. Heathcliff had never been heard of since the thunderstorm, and one day I had the misfortune to lay the blame for his disappearance on her, where in fact it belonged. For several months she would not speak to me, except as a servant. She considered herself to be a woman now, and our mistress, and thought her recent illness gave her a special claim to attention. The doctor had said that she could not bear people going much against her wishes, and ought to have her own way, so no one dared disobey her. Her brother was worried by the threat of some kind of fit that often attacked her during her fury; he allowed her whatever she pleased, in order to avoid awakening her fierce temper.

Three years after his father's death, Edgar Linton led her to church and married her, believing himself the happiest man alive.

Chapter 11 The Return

Much against my wishes, I was persuaded to leave Wuthering Heights and go with Cathy to her new home. Little Hareton was nearly five years old and I had just begun to teach him his letters. We parted sadly.

When she was at Thrushcross Grange, Catherine behaved much better than I had dared to expect. She seemed almost too fond of Edgar, and even to his sister she showed plenty of love. I noticed that Mr Edgar had a fear of causing her the least displeasure. In order not to cause grief to a kind master I learned to be more careful with my tongue, and for the space of half a year the gunpowder lay harmless as sand because no fire came near to explode it. Catherine had days of low spirits now and then, which her husband respected as the result of her former illness, but I believe they were really in possession of deep and growing happiness.

It ended.

On a golden evening in September I was coming from the garden with a basket of apples that I had been collecting. It was half dark, and the moon looked over the high wall of the yard, making strange shadows in the corners of the building.

My eyes were on the moon, when I heard a voice behind me say: 'Nelly, is that you?'

It was a deep voice, and foreign in sound, but something in the manner of pronouncing my name made it familiar. Somebody moved near the door of the house, and as I came nearer I saw more clearly a tall man dressed in dark clothes.

'Who can it be?' I thought.

A beam of light fell on his face. The cheeks were pale, and half covered with black hair; the forehead was heavy, the eyes deep-set and strange. I recognized the eyes.

'What!' I cried. 'You've come back? Is it really you?'

'Yes, it's Heathcliff,' he replied, looking from me up at the windows. 'Are they at home? Where is she? Speak! I want to have one word with her – with your mistress. Go, and say that some person from Gimmerton village desires to see her.'

'How will she take it? How changed you are! Have you been a soldier?'

'Go and carry my message,' he interrupted. 'I'm in a state of misery until you do!'

When I got to the sitting room, Mr and Mrs Linton were sitting together at a window looking out at the trees. Everything looked peaceful, and I could not persuade myself to speak.

I was actually going away leaving the words unsaid, when a sense of my own foolishness forced me to return and give the message.

'Close the curtains, Nelly, and bring up tea. I'll be back again soon.'

She left the room, and Edgar inquired carelessly who it was.

'Someone that mistress does not expect. That Heathcliff, sir, who used to live at Mr Earnshaw's.'

'What! The gypsy – the farm boy?'

'Take care! You must not call him by those names, master. She was nearly heartbroken when he ran off.'

Shortly after, Catherine flew upstairs, wild and breathless.

'Oh, Edgar, Edgar,' she exclaimed, throwing her arms round his neck, 'Heathcliff's come back!'

'Well, well,' cried her husband, sounding displeased, 'there's no need to be so excited, surely!'

'I know you didn't like him,' she answered, controlling her pleasure a little, 'but, for me, you must be friends now. Shall I tell him to come up?'

'Here?' he said. 'Wouldn't the kitchen be a more suitable place?'

Mrs Linton looked at him. 'No,' she replied, half angry, half amused, 'I can't sit in the kitchen.'

She was about to run off again, but Edgar stopped her.

'You ask him to step up,' he said, addressing me. 'Catherine, the whole household need not witness the sight of your welcoming a runaway servant as a brother.'

Heathcliff followed me up without further speech, and I brought him into the presence of the master and mistress, whose red cheeks showed signs of heated argument. The lady ran forward, took his hands, and led him to Linton; then she seized Linton's fingers and pressed them into his.

Now clearly shown up by the fire and candlelight, the change in Heathcliff surprised me more than ever. He had grown into a tall, active, well-formed man, beside whom my master seemed only a youth. His upright appearance suggested that he had been in the army. His face was older in expression and firmer in shape; it looked intelligent, and had lost all former marks of degradation. A fierceness lay hidden in the eyes, but his manner was serious, even gentlemanly, and quite without roughness. My master's surprise equalled or went beyond mine, and for a minute he was puzzled as to how to receive the farm boy, as he called him.

'Sit down, sir,' he said at last. 'It is Mrs Linton's wish that you should be welcomed here, and of course I am happy to give her pleasure.'

'And I also,' answered Heathcliff. 'I shall be pleased to stay an hour or two.'

He took a seat opposite Catherine, who kept her eyes fixed on him. He did not raise his eyes to her often, but each time they expressed more confidently the pure pleasure he felt in her presence.

'I shall think it a dream tomorrow,' cried Catherine. 'But, cruel Heathcliff, you don't deserve this welcome. To be absent and silent for three years, and never think of me!'

'A little more than you have thought of me,' he replied.

'I heard of your marriage, Cathy, not long ago, and I planned to have just one quick look at you, take my revenge on Hindley, and then put an end to my own life. Your welcome has put such ideas out of my head. I've fought through a bitter life since I last heard your voice, and you must forgive me, because I struggled only for you!'

'Catherine, unless we are to have cold tea, please come to the table,' interrupted Linton, trying to speak in his ordinary voice but pale with annoyance.

Catherine took up her post, and Miss Isabella came in. The meal was over in a few minutes. Catherine's cup was never filled: she could neither eat nor drink. Edgar hardly swallowed a mouthful.

Their guest did not stay more than an hour longer. I asked, as he left, if he was going to Gimmerton.

'No, to Wuthering Heights,' he answered. 'I called this morning, expecting you would still be there, Nelly, and could give me news of Catherine. There were some persons there sitting at cards, whom I joined and, finding I have plenty of money now, Hindley invited me to repeat my visit. I shall try to stay there, so I can be within walking distance of Catherine. Hindley is greedy, and I shall pay him well.'

Mr Earnshaw invited him! I had a feeling in my heart that Heathcliff should have remained away.

Chapter 12   Miss Isabella

Heathcliff – Mr Heathcliff, I should say in future – used his freedom to visit Thrushcross Grange only occasionally at first. Catherine also judged it wise not to show too much pleasure in receiving him. My master's anxiety died down and, for a time, turned in another direction.

The new cause of trouble came from an unexpected misfortune. Isabella Linton suddenly developed strong feelings for the visitor. She was now a young lady of eighteen, childish in her manners though possessing a quick understanding and a quick temper, too, if annoyed. Her brother loved her dearly and, besides the shame of a marriage with a man of unknown origin, he had the sense to see that Heathcliff's nature was unchangeable, even if his outer appearance had improved.

We had all noticed for some time that Miss Linton was pale and unhappy and hard to please, and we had excused her in some degree because her health was weak. One day, when she had been particularly difficult, Mrs Linton threatened to send for the doctor. Isabella at once exclaimed that her health was perfect, and that it was only Cathy's unkindness that made her unhappy.

'How can you say I am unkind?' cried the mistress, surprised. 'When have I been unkind? Tell me.'

'Yesterday,' replied Isabella, weeping.

'Yesterday? On what occasion?'

'In our walk on the moor. You told me to wander where I pleased, while you went on with Mr Heathcliff.'

'And that's your idea of unkindness?' said Catherine laughing.

'You wished me away, because I wanted to be with . . .'

'Well?' said Catherine, seeing her pause.

'With him, and I won't always be sent off! You are a selfish thing, Cathy, and want no one to be loved but yourself.'

'I hope I have misunderstood you, Isabella?'

'No, you have not. I love him more than you ever loved Edgar; and he might love me, if you would let him!'

'I wouldn't like to be you at all, then!' declared Catherine. 'It's only because you haven't the least idea of his real nature that you can allow such a dream to enter your head. Don't imagine that he's got a heart of gold: he's a fierce, pitiless, cruel man. I know he couldn't love a Linton, but he might be ready to marry you for your money. There's my picture of him, and I'm his friend.'

'For shame! For shame!' cried Isabella. 'You're worse than twenty enemies, you poisonous friend!'

'Put him out of your thoughts, Miss Isabella,' I said. 'Mrs Linton spoke strongly, but I can't say that she's wrong. She has greater knowledge of his heart than anyone else. Honest people don't hide what they have done. How has he been living? How has he got rich? Why is he staying at Wuthering Heights, with a man whom he hates? They say Mr Hindley is worse since he came. They sit up all night playing cards and drinking, and Hindley has been borrowing money to pay his debts.'

'You're as bad as the rest, Ellen,' she replied. 'I shan't listen to your stories.'

The next day my master had to go to a neighbouring town on business and Heathcliff, knowing of his absence, called rather earlier than usual. Catherine and Isabella were sitting in the library, unfriendly and silent. The younger lady was worried by her own recent foolishness in revealing her secret feelings, and Catherine was really offended and ready to punish her companion. As she saw Heathcliff pass the window, she smiled to herself. Isabella, her head in a book, remained unconscious of the visitor until the door opened and it was too late to escape.

'Come in!' exclaimed the mistress brightly, pulling a chair to the fire. 'You're just the person we would both of us choose for our companion. Heathcliff, I'm proud to show you somebody who is fonder of you than myself. Poor little Isabella is breaking her heart for you! No, no, Isabella, you shan't run off,' she continued, taking a firm hold of the girl's wrist.

Heathcliff showed no sign of interest, and Isabella whispered an urgent request to be set free.

'Certainly not!' cried Mrs Linton. 'I won't be called a selfish thing again. Heathcliff, why don't you look pleased?'

Heathcliff looked hard at Isabella. 'I think you are mistaken,' he said. 'She wishes to be out of my society now, in any case.'

The poor girl could not bear it. Her face became white and then red. Catherine still refused to let her go, until she began to use her nails.

'What did you mean by treating the poor thing in that way, Cathy?' Heathcliff asked, when the door had closed after her. 'You weren't speaking the truth, were you?'

'I promise you I was,' she replied.

'All her brother's possessions will one day be hers, won't they?' he asked, after a short pause.

'Not if I bear a son,' answered his companion. 'Forget this matter. You're too fond of thinking of other people's possessions.'

They did dismiss the subject from conversation, but I saw Heathcliff smile in a most unpleasant way when Mrs Linton was out of the room.

Chapter 13 An Evil Influence

Mr Heathcliff's visits worried me as much as they did my master, and his long stay at the Heights was a mystery with no solution. Sometimes I thought I would go and see how everything was at the farm, but then I remembered Mr Hindley's hopelessly bad habits, and I decided not to re-enter that unhappy house.

One time I passed near the farm on a journey to Gimmerton. It was a bright autumn afternoon, but the sunshine reminded me of summer, and I came to the stone marking the way across the moor. It was a favourite place of mine, a place loved by Hindley and myself twenty years before. Bending down I saw at the bottom of the rock a hole, where we used to keep our little toys, still now full of shells and smooth stones; and then it seemed that I saw my former childhood friend seated on the grass.

The child lifted its face and stared straight into mine. It

disappeared at once, but it was waiting for me when I reached the gate of the Heights, and further thought suggested that this must be Hareton, my Hareton, not changed greatly since I left him ten months before.

'My little dear!' I cried, forgetting my foolish fears. 'Hareton, it's Nelly, your nurse.'

He moved back, and picked up a large stone. He didn't recognize me. I began to speak, but the stone struck my head, and the little boy shouted a string of curses, twisting his baby face into an evil expression that shocked me. Ready to weep, I took an orange from my pocket and offered it. He paused, and then seized it from my hand.

'Who taught you those fine words, my child?' I asked.

He swore at me. I offered another orange, but kept it out of reach.

'Tell me where you get lessons, and you shall have it. Who's your master?'

'My father.'

'And what do you learn from him?'

'Nothing,' he said, 'but to keep out of his way. He can't bear me because I swear at him.'

'And who teaches you to swear?'

'Heathcliff.'

I asked whether he liked Heathcliff.

'Yes.'

I tried to find out the reason. I could only understand the sentences, 'I don't know; he punishes my father for what he does to me – he curses him. He says I must do as I like.'

'And don't you have a teacher to show you how to read and write, then?' I continued.

'No. There was one, but Heathcliff promised to knock his teeth out if he came again.'

I put the orange into his hand and told him to let his father know that a woman called Nelly Dean was waiting to speak to him. He entered the house but, instead of Hindley, Heathcliff appeared at the door, and I turned and ran down the road, as frightened as if I had seen an evil spirit.

Chapter 14   The Quarrel

The next time Heathcliff came, my young lady chanced to be feeding some birds in the courtyard. He was not in the habit of showing her any special attention but this time, as soon as he saw her, he looked carefully up at the front of the house. I remained hidden behind the kitchen window.

He stepped across to Isabella, and said something. She seemed anxious to get away, but to prevent it he laid his hand on her arm. She turned her face away. With another quick look up at the house, and supposing himself to be unseen, he put his arms around her.

'For shame!' I cried.

'Who is it, Nelly?' said Catherine's voice behind me.

'Your worthless friend!' I replied. 'What excuse do you think he will find for making love to Miss Isabella, when he told you he hated her?'

Mrs Linton saw Isabella struggle to free herself and run into the garden. A minute later, Heathcliff opened the door.

'Heathcliff, what are you doing? I said you must let her alone!'

'What is it to you?' he answered roughly. 'I have a right to kiss her, if she chooses. I'm not your husband: you needn't be jealous of me. And, Catherine, I have a few plain words to say to you now. I want you to understand that you have treated me shamefully! Do you hear? And if you think I'll suffer unrevenged, you are mistaken. For now, though, thank you for telling me Isabella's secret. I'll make good use of it.'

'What new side to his character is this?' exclaimed Mrs Linton.

'I have no wish to take revenge on you,' continued Heathcliff less violently. 'You are welcome to play with me until my death for your amusement, only allow me to amuse myself a little in the same way. Having ruined my life, don't expect me to be good!'

'Oh, you want to make people suffer, do you!' cried Catherine. 'You prove it! Edgar has just got back his good temper, and I begin to feel safe and comfortable, so you are determined to start a quarrel. Quarrel with Edgar, if you please, and deceive his sister; you'll have chosen just the best way to revenge yourself on me.'

The conversation ended.

Catherine sat by the fire, disturbed and unhappy. Her temper was getting beyond her control. Heathcliff stood with folded arms, thinking dark thoughts. In this position I left them to look for the master.

'The mistress is in the kitchen, sir,' I said. 'She's very upset by Mr Heathcliff's behaviour.' And I told him as much as I dared of what had happened.

'I won't bear this!' he declared. 'Call me two men from the servants' hall, Ellen.'

He went downstairs and, followed by me, entered the kitchen. Catherine and Heathcliff had returned to their quarrel. On seeing him, they became silent.

'I have been patient with you until now, sir,' said Linton to Heathcliff. 'I have foolishly allowed you here, because Catherine wished to keep up the connection. Your presence is a moral poison that would harm the purest. For that reason, and to prevent further evil, I demand that you leave this house immediately, and for the last time.'

Heathcliff looked scornfully at him.

'Cathy, this lamb of yours threatens like a lion!' he said.

My master signalled to me to fetch the men. Mrs Linton

pulled me back and locked the inner door.

'Fair means!' she said to her husband. 'If you haven't the courage to attack him yourself, say you are sorry, or allow yourself to be beaten.'

Mr Linton tried to seize the key from her, but she threw it into the hottest part of the fire. He was attacked by a nervous trembling and became as pale as death.

'I wish you joy of him, Cathy!' said her friend. 'And that is the weak-kneed thing that you preferred to me! Is he weeping, or is he going to faint with fear?'

He gave the chair on which Linton was leaning a push. My master jumped up and struck him on the throat. It took away Heathcliff's breath for a minute. Linton walked out of the back door into the yard, and from there to the front entrance.

'There, you can't come here again now,' cried Catherine. 'Get away. He'll return with guns. You've played an evil trick on me, Heathcliff!'

'Do you suppose I'm going, with that blow to answer?'

Two of the gardeners, with Linton, had already entered the yard. Heathcliff, on further thought, decided to avoid a struggle against three servants. He broke the lock of the inner door and made his escape.

Mrs Linton, who was by now very much excited, told me to go upstairs with her.

'I'm nearly mad, Nelly,' she exclaimed. 'My head is bursting. Tell Isabella to avoid me. She is the cause of all this, and if anyone makes me angrier at present I shall become wild. And, Nelly, if you see Edgar again tonight, tell him I'm in danger of being seriously ill. I hope I shall be, because I want to frighten him. Besides, he might come and begin a string of complaints. I'm certain I should answer back, and God knows where we should end! You know that I am in no way to blame in this matter. Well, if I can't keep Heathcliff as my friend – if Edgar will be jealous and selfish – I'll try to break their hearts by breaking my own. Nelly, I wish you would look rather more anxious about me.

I thought privately that she could have managed to control herself, and I did not wish to frighten her husband. I therefore said nothing when I saw him coming upstairs.

'I shall not stay, Catherine,' he said, without any anger in his voice. 'I have only one question to ask: will you give up Heathcliff, or will you give me up?'

'Oh, heavens!' interrupted the mistress. 'Let us hear no more of it now! Your cold blood can't be worked into a fever, but mine can!'

'To get rid of me, answer my question,' went on Mr Linton. 'You must answer it, and your violence does not frighten me. You can be as calm as anyone when you please.'

'I demand to be left alone,' exclaimed Catherine furiously. 'Don't you see that I can hardly stand? Leave me!'

She rang the bell until it broke. I had been waiting outside, but I did not hurry to enter. Her fury was enough to make the calmest person lose their temper. There she lay, striking her head against the arm of a chair. Mr Linton stood looking at her, and told me to fetch some water.

She would not drink, so I shook some drops on her face. In a few seconds she stretched herself out stiff, while her cheeks became pale as death. Linton looked worried.

'There is nothing the matter,' I whispered. I didn't want him to give in, though I too was afraid. I told him how she had wished to frighten him by one of her fits. She was well enough to hear and understand me, because she jumped up, her eyes flashing, and rushed from the room. The master directed me to follow, but she locked herself in her bedroom, where she remained for the next three days refusing all offers of food.

As for Mr Linton, he spent his time in the library. He had an hour's private talk with Miss Isabella, in which he warned her

197

that if she were mad enough to encourage Heathcliff, it would end all ties between them as brother and sister.

Chapter 15   Illness

Miss Linton wandered round the park, always silent and almost always in tears. Her brother shut himself up among books that he never opened, in the faint but continuing hope that Catherine would ask his pardon for her behaviour. She went on refusing food, with the idea that her absence from the meal table would bring Edgar to her feet. I went on with my duties as usual, believing that I was the only sensible person in the house.

At last, on the third day, or rather, late in the evening, Mrs Linton, looking pale and tired, unlocked her door, and asked for food and water as she believed she was dying. I brought her tea and bread and butter.

'What is that dull being doing?' she demanded.

'If you mean Mr Linton,' I replied, 'he's fairly well. He is continually among his books.'

I would not have spoken so if I had known her true condition, but I could not get rid of the idea that she was acting a part of her illness.

'Among his books!' she cried. 'And I am near the grave! Oh, does he know how changed I am?' She stared at her face in a mirror hanging on the opposite wall.

'If I were sure it would kill him,' she went on, 'I'd kill myself now.'

She could not bear the thought that I had put into her head, of Edgar's quiet lack of interest. Throwing herself from side to side, she became feverish; then, raising herself up, burning with heat, she demanded that I should open the window. It was the middle of the winter, and I objected. The expression on her face began to worry me terribly. It reminded me of her former illness, and of the doctor's warning that no one should go against her wishes. She had even torn the bedclothes with her teeth.

'Lie down and shut your eyes,' I said. 'A sleep would do you good.'

'Oh, I wish I were a girl again! If only I were in my bed in my old home!' she cried. 'And the wind sounding through the trees near the window! Do let me feel it – it comes straight from the moor!'

To please her, I held the window open for a few seconds. An icy wind rushed through. I closed the window again.

'How long is it since I shut myself up here?' she asked suddenly.

'Four nights and three days,' I replied. 'Long enough to live on cold water and bad temper.'

'It seems a great many hours. I remember being in the sitting room after they had quarrelled, and running upstairs. As soon as I locked the door, complete blackness came over me. I couldn't explain to Edgar how certain I felt of having a fit if he went on annoying me. Open the window wide again,' she commanded. 'You won't give me a chance of life. Very well, I'll do it myself.'

Before I could stop her, she crossed the room unsteadily and threw open the window, careless of the air, which cut like a knife. I begged, and at last tried to force her back to bed, but her feverish strength resisted mine.

I was planning how to reach something to wrap around her, without letting go my hold of her, when Mr Linton entered.

'Oh, sir!' I cried, making signs to him to keep back the exclamation that rose to his lips at the sight that met him. 'My poor mistress is ill, and I can't manage her at all. Please, come and persuade her to go to bed.'

'Catherine ill!' he said, hurrying to us. 'Shut the window, Ellen!'

He was silent, worried by the change in Mrs Linton's appearance. I murmured something about not having known of her condition before, but I felt that I gave my explanations awkwardly. My master looked displeased and took his wife in his arms. At first she made no sign of recognition, but by degrees she fixed her attention on him.

'Ah! You've come, have you, Edgar Linton,' she said in an angry voice. 'You are one of the things that are never found when they are wanted. You'll be sorry when I'm in my grave, where I'm going before spring is over!'

'Catherine! Am I nothing to you any more? Do you love that miserable Heath—'

'If you mention that name, I'll end the matter by a jump from this window! Return to your books. I don't want you now.'

'Her mind wanders, sir,' I said. 'She has been talking nonsense the whole evening. We must be careful not to annoy her.'

'I want no further advice from you,' answered Mr Linton. 'You knew your mistress's nature, and you encouraged me to go against her. And not to give me any idea of how she has been all these three days! It was heartless!'

I began to defend myself, thinking it too bad to be blamed for the faults of another. Then, determined to go for medical help on my own responsibility, I left the room.

In passing through the garden, I saw something white hanging from a hook fixed into the wall. It was Miss Isabella's little dog, tied with a handkerchief and nearly at its last breath. While untying the animal, it seemed to me that I heard the sound of horses' feet moving rapidly at some distance, but I had so many things on my mind that I hardly gave a thought to the strangeness of such a noise at two o'clock in the morning.

Doctor Kenneth, a plain, rough man, was luckily just coming out of his house to see a sick man in the village. He turned back with me.

'Nelly Dean,' he said, 'I can't help thinking there is another cause for this. A healthy girl like Catherine doesn't become ill for nothing. What started it?'

'The master will tell you,' I replied carefully, 'but you know the Earnshaws' violent natures, and Mrs Linton is worse than any of them.'

On examining the case for himself, he spoke to Mr Linton of her return to health, if only we could keep her completely quiet. To me, he said the danger was not so much of death as of lasting damage to the mind.

I did not close my eyes that night, nor did Mr Linton: in fact, we never went to bed, and the servants were all up long before the usual hour. Everybody was active except Miss Isabella, and we all began to notice how deeply she slept. Her brother, too, asked if she had got up, and seemed hurt by her lack of anxiety for Catherine.

One of the servants, a thoughtless girl, came crying up the stairs: 'Oh! Oh! What will we have next? Master, master, our young lady—'

'Less noise!' I exclaimed quickly.

'Speak quietly, Mary. What's the matter?' said Mr Linton.

'She's gone! She's gone! Heathcliff's run off with her!' cried the girl.

The girl had been to the village, and had met the boy who brought the milk. He had told of how a gentleman and a lady had stopped to have a horseshoe fixed two miles out of Gimmerton not long after midnight. There was no mistaking Heathcliff, and the covering over the lady's head had fallen back when she took a drink, and shown her face clearly.

'Shall we try and fetch her back?' I asked. 'What should we do?'

'She went of her own free will,' answered the master. 'Trouble me no more about her. In future she is my sister in name only.'

He made no further mention of her to me, except to direct me to send what property she had in the house to her new home, wherever it was, when I knew it.

Chapter 16   Two Bad Months

For two months the runaway pair remained absent, and during those two months Mrs Linton suffered and gradually recovered from the worst shock of what was found to be a brain fever. Day and night Edgar watched over her, patiently bearing all the difficulties of temper caused by illness of both body and mind. The doctor warned him that his own health and strength were being destroyed for nothing, because his wife would never be the same again, but his joy knew no limits when Catherine's life was declared out of danger. There was double cause for joy, as another life depended on hers; and we hoped that in a little time Mr Linton's heart would be gladdened, and his lands made safe from the hands of a stranger, by the birth of a son.

The first time she left her room was at the beginning of March. Mr Linton had put a handful of flowers beside her bed in the morning. Her eye caught the bright colour on waking, and shone with pleasure.

'These are the earliest flowers at the Heights,' she exclaimed. 'They remind me of soft winds and warm sunshine and nearly melted snow.'

'The snow has quite gone, my dearest,' said her husband. 'Catherine, last spring I was looking forward eagerly to having you under this roof. Now I wish you were a mile or two up those hills. The air blows so sweetly, I feel it would cure you.'

The master told me to light a fire in the sitting room and place a chair in the sunshine. He brought her down, and she sat a for while, enjoying the heat. By evening, although very tired, she refused to return upstairs, so another room was prepared for her on the same floor. She was soon strong enough to move from one to the other, leaning on Edgar's arm.

About six weeks after Isabella had left, she sent her brother a note, announcing her marriage to Heathcliff. It appeared dry and cold, but at the bottom was a line in pencil, expressing her sorrow for what she had done and a desire for forgiveness. Linton did not reply, and two weeks later I got a letter from the unhappy girl, which I have kept until now.

'Dear Ellen,' it began, 'I came last night to Wuthering Heights and heard for the first time that Catherine has been, and is still, very ill. I must not write to her, I suppose, and my brother is either too angry or too unhappy to answer what I send him.

'Inform Edgar that my heart returned to the Grange twenty-four hours after I left. I can't follow it, though.

'I do not know how you managed, when you lived here, to remain human. Is Heathcliff mad or is he a devil? I beg you to explain, if you can, what I have married.

'We got here after sunset. Joseph brought out a light, gave me an ugly look, and took away the horses. Heathcliff stayed to speak to him, and I entered the kitchen, a dirty, untidy hole. I dare say you wouldn't recognize it: it is so changed since it was in your care. By the fire stood a rough-looking, dirty child, rather like Catherine in the eyes and around the mouth, whom I realized must be Hareton. I tried to make friends, but he first cursed and then set a dog on me.

'I wandered round the yard, and knocked at a door. It was opened by a tall man, very untidily dressed, with long uncut hair. He, too, was like our Catherine. It was her brother. He let me in and shut the door. I saw I was in the large room that used to look so bright and cheerful when I visited it years ago. Now it is dusty and uncared for. I asked if I could call a servant and be shown to a bedroom. Mr Earnshaw did not answer. He appeared to have forgotten my presence, and seemed so strange and unwelcoming that I did not want to interrupt him again.

'I remembered that four miles away lay my lovely home, containing the only people I love on earth; but there might as well be the ocean between us!

'Finally I repeated my question.

'"We have no female servants," said Earnshaw. "You must look after yourself."

'"Where must I sleep, then?" I wept. I was tired and miserable.

'"Joseph will show you Heathcliff's room" he replied. "I would be grateful if you would turn your key and lock the door."

'"But why, Mr Earnshaw?" I asked.

'"Look here!" he said, pulling a small gun from his pocket. "I can't help going up with this every night and trying his door. If once I find it open, he'll be a dead man!"

'"What has Heathcliff done to you?" I asked. "Wouldn't it be wiser to order him to leave the house?"

'"No!" shouted Earnshaw. "Am I to lose all my money, without a chance of winning it back? Is Hareton to have nothing? I will have it back, and I'll have his gold, too, and his blood!"

'You know your old master's habits, Ellen. He is clearly close to madness. I'm afraid to be near him.

'Heathcliff's room was locked. I went to sleep in a chair in the sitting room until he came in with the news of Catherine's illness and accused my brother of causing it. He promised to punish me instead of him, until he could get hold of him.

'I am miserable – I have been foolish! Say nothing of this to anyone at the Grange. Call and see me, Ellen, very soon. I shall expect you every day – don't disappoint me!

ISABELLA.'

Chapter 17 A Visit to Wuthering Heights

As soon as I had finished Isabella's letter, I went to the master and gave him the news of his sister and her wish for some sign of his forgiveness.

'I have nothing to say to her, Ellen,' was his reply. 'You may call this afternoon and say I'm sorry I've lost her. We are now divided for ever.'

Mr Edgar's coldness saddened me very greatly, and all the way to Wuthering Heights I worried my brains as to how to soften his answer.

There was never such a miserable scene as the house, formerly so cheerful, presented on my arrival. The young lady already shared the appearance of disorder that surrounded her. Her pretty face was pale and expressionless, her hair uncurled, some hanging down and some carelessly twisted round her head. Probably she had not tidied her dress since the evening before.

Hindley was not there, but Mr Heathcliff sat at a table. He rose and offered me a chair. He was the only thing that seemed respectable, and I thought he had never looked better. A stranger would have thought him a born gentleman and his wife a person of low origin.

She came forward, half expecting a letter, and I had to tell her her brother's words. Her lip trembled and she returned to her seat.

Her husband began questioning me about Catherine.

'Mrs Linton is now just recovering,' I told him. 'She'll never be like she was, but her life is saved. Her appearance is greatly changed, her character more so, and the person who is forced to be her companion will only keep up his love for her by remembering what she was formerly, and by pity and a sense of duty.'

Heathcliff forced himself to appear calm.

'Do you imagine I shall leave Catherine to your master's duty and pity! Nelly, I must have a promise from you that you'll arrange for me to see her. Agree or refuse, I *will* see her! What do you say?'

'I say, Mr Heathcliff,' I replied, 'that another meeting and quarrel between you and Mr Linton would kill her altogether.'

'With your help that may be avoided,' he said. 'The fear that she would suffer from his loss keeps me from doing my worst. And there you see the difference between our feelings. If he had been in my place, and I in his, I would never have raised a hand against him as long as she desired his company. The moment her feeling had ended, I would have torn his heart out, but until then – I would have died before I touched a single hair of his head!'

'Even so,' I interrupted, 'you don't care about ruining her chances of returning to health, by seeing her when she has nearly forgotten you.'

'Oh, Nelly! You know she has not! You know as well as I do that for every thought she spends on Linton, she spends a thousand on me! I feared last summer that she might have forgotten me, but now only her own words would make me believe such a horrible idea. And then – Linton would be nothing, or Hindley, or all the other dreams of revenge that I ever dreamed. One word would represent my future – *death*. But Catherine has a heart as deep as I have. Linton is hardly a degree nearer to her than her dog, or her horse. It is not in him to be loved like me: how then can she love in him what he has not?'

'Catherine and Edgar are as fond of each other as any two people can be!' cried Isabella, with a sudden return to life. 'I won't hear my brother spoken of so lightly!'

'Your brother is very fond of you, isn't he?' said Heathcliff scornfully.

'My young lady is looking sadly the worse for her change of condition,' I said. 'I hope you will consider that she is used to

206

being looked after. You must let her have a servant. Whatever you think of Mr Edgar, you cannot doubt her powers of love, or she would never have given up the comforts of her home to live in this wild place with you.'

'She gave them up under a false idea of me as the sort of man she has read about in stories,' he answered. 'I can hardly look on her as being sensible, so fixed is the idea she has formed of my character. But at last I think she is beginning to know me. I don't care who knows that the feeling was all on one side, and I never lied to her about it. The first thing she saw me do, on coming out of the Grange, was to hang up her little dog, but even that didn't make her hate me. Tell your master, Nelly, that I never in all my life met such a poor-spirited thing as she is. She brings shame even on the name of Linton!'

'He says he married me on purpose to gain power over Edgar,' cried Isabella. 'But he shan't do so! I just hope he'll kill me! The only pleasure I can imagine is to die, or to see him dead!'

'If you're called on in a court of law, you'll remember her language, Nelly!' said Heathcliff coldly. 'And take a good look at her face: she's near the point that would suit me. You're not responsible for your actions now, Isabella, and I, as your lawful husband, must keep you safe. Go upstairs. I have something to say to Ellen in private.'

He pushed her from the room.

'I have no pity,' he murmured. 'I have no pity! The more the worms suffer, the more I desire to crush them.'

I rose to go.

'Stop!' he said. 'Come here, Nelly. I must either persuade or force you to help me to see Catherine. I don't wish to cause any quarrels. I'd warn you when I came, and then you might let me in unnoticed, as soon as she was alone.'

I argued and complained, and firmly refused him fifty times, but in the end Heathcliff forced me to an agreement. I was to carry a letter from him to my mistress, and, if she agreed, to send him news of Linton's next absence from home, when he could come and see her.

Chapter 18   The Meeting

That evening I knew, as well as if I saw him, that Mr Heathcliff was around the Grange, and I avoided going outside because I was still carrying his letter in my pocket. Until my master went somewhere, I did not want to give it, because I could not guess how it would affect my mistress. It did not reach her, therefore, until three days had passed.

The fourth was Sunday, and I brought it into her room after the household had gone to church.

Catherine sat in a loose white dress, at the open window as usual. Her long hair, cut shorter during her illness, was simply combed over her forehead and neck. Her appearance was changed, but when she was calm there seemed a strange beauty in the change. The flash in her eyes had given place to a dreamy softness. The paleness of her face, and the strange expression resulting from her state of mind, added to the interest she awakened, but to me they were unmistakable signs that her future was an early death.

Gimmerton church bells were still ringing, and the full flow of the little stream in the valley came sweetly to the ear. Catherine seemed to be listening, but she had the dreamy, distant look that I have mentioned.

'There's a letter for you, Mrs Linton,' I said, gently placing it in her hand. 'You must read it now, because it needs an answer. Shall I open it?'

'Yes,' she answered, without changing the direction of her eyes.

I did so, and gave it to her. She pulled away her hand and let it fall.

I replaced it on her knee, and stood waiting.

At last I said, 'Must I read it? It is from Mr Heathcliff.'

There was a sudden movement, and a troubled flash of memory, and a struggle to arrange her ideas. She lifted the letter and seemed to read it, and when she came to the name at the end she drew in her breath: but still I found she had not understood its meaning. She pointed to the name, and fixed her eyes on me with sad and questioning eagerness.

'He wishes to see you,' I said. 'He's probably in the garden by this time and impatient to know your answer.'

As I spoke, I noticed a large dog, lying on the sunny grass below, raise its ears and then, smoothing them back, show by a movement of the tail that someone was coming whom it did not consider a stranger. Mrs Linton bent forward and listened breathlessly.

A step was heard in the hall. With indescribable eagerness Catherine directed her eyes towards the entrance to her room. In a moment Heathcliff was at her side and had her in his arms.

He neither spoke nor loosed his hold for several minutes. I saw he could hardly bear, for pure misery, to look into her face! He felt, from the moment he saw her, that there was no hope that she would recover. Her future was decided; she was sure to die.

'Oh, Cathy! Oh, my life! How can I bear it?' was the first sentence he spoke. And now he looked at her so deeply that I thought it would bring tears to his eyes; but they burned with pain, they did not melt.

'What now?' said Catherine, leaning back, and returning his look with one of sudden anger. 'You and Edgar have broken my heart, Heathcliff! And now you both come to cry pity on me, as if you were the people in need of sympathy! I shall not pity you, not I. You have killed me – and are all the stronger for it, I think.

How many years do you mean to live after I am gone?'

Heathcliff had knelt on one knee. He attempted to rise, but she seized his hair and kept him down.

'I wish I could hold you,' she continued bitterly, 'until we were both dead! I wouldn't care what you suffered. Why shouldn't you suffer? I do! Will you forget me? Will you be happy when I am in the earth?'

'Don't make me as mad as yourself!' he cried, forcing his head free. 'Are you possessed by a devil, to talk like that when you are dying? Do you realize that all those words will be burned into my memory? You know it is not true that I have killed you: and Catherine, you know that I could as easily forget you as my own existence! Is it not enough for your cursed selfishness that while you are at peace I shall be in misery?'

'I shall not be at peace,' murmured Catherine, brought back to a sense of weakness by the violent uneven beating of her heart. She said no more until the attack was over, then she continued, more kindly: 'I'm not wishing you greater pain than I have, Heathcliff. I only wish us never to be parted: and if the memory of any word of mine should give you pain in the future, think that I feel the same pain beneath the earth, and forgive me! Come here and kneel down again! You have never harmed me in your life.'

Heathcliff went to the back of her chair and leaned over, but not so far as to let her see his face, which was deathly white. She bent round to look at him; he would not allow it. Turning quickly he walked to the fireplace, where he stood silent with his back towards us. Catherine looked at him, then after a pause she spoke to me in an offended voice.

'You see, Nelly, he will not give way for a moment. That is how I'm loved. Well, never mind. That is not my Heathcliff. I shall love mine still. I am surprised he won't be near me,' she went on to herself. 'I thought he wished it. Heathcliff, dear, do come to me.'

In her eagerness she rose and supported herself on the arm of the chair. At that request he turned to her, looking completely miserable. For a moment they stayed apart, then how they met I hardly saw. Catherine seemed to jump, and he caught her and held her as if he would never let her go again. I thought my mistress had fainted, but when I approached to see he turned on me and pulled her closer to him, half mad with jealousy, so I stood to one side, not knowing what to do.

Soon a movement of Catherine's made me feel a little happier. She put her hand to his neck to bring his cheek to hers, while he said wildly: 'You teach me how cruel you've been – cruel and false! Why did you scorn me? Why were you false to your own heart, Cathy? I have not one word of comfort. You deserve this! You have killed yourself. Yes, you may kiss me, and cry, and force me to do the same – it is your punishment. You loved me – then what *right* had you to leave me? Because misery, and degradation, and death could not have parted us, *you* did it! I have not broken your heart – you have broken it, and in breaking it, you have broken mine. It is only the worse for me that I am strong. Do I want to live? Would *you* want to live with your soul in the grave?'

'Leave me alone,' wept Catherine. 'If I've done wrong, I'm dying for it. You left me too, but I forgive you. Forgive me!'

'It is hard, but I forgive you what you have done to me. I love my murderer – but yours! How can I?'

They were silent, their faces hidden against each other and washed by each other's tears. I became very uncomfortable, as the afternoon was passing and I could see in the sunshine up the valley a crowd of people outside the church.

'The service is over,' I said. 'Master will be here in half an hour.'

Heathcliff cursed and pulled Catherine closer. She never moved.

Soon I saw a group of the servants coming up the road. Then

Edgar Linton opened the gate and walked through.

'Now he's here,' I exclaimed.

'I must go, Cathy,' said Heathcliff, 'but, as sure as I'm alive, I'll see you again before you are asleep. I shall be near your window.'

'You must not go!' she answered, holding him as firmly as her strength allowed.

'For one hour!' he begged.

'Not for one minute,' she replied.

'I must. Linton will be up immediately.'

He would have risen, but she hung fast. There was madness in her face. 'No! Oh, don't, don't go. It is the last time.'

Heathcliff murmured a curse on Edgar, and sank back into his seat.

'Quiet, my dearest! I'll stay. If he shot me now, I'd die happy.'

I heard my master coming up the stairs.

'She doesn't know what she says!' I cried. 'Will you ruin her, because she has not sense enough to help herself? Get up! We are all finished!'

Mr Linton heard the noise and came faster. I saw that Catherine's arms had fallen, and her head hung down.

'Either she's fainted or she's dead,' I thought.

Edgar jumped on his uninvited guest, white with shock and fury. What he meant to do, I cannot tell, but the other stopped him by placing the lifeless-looking form in his arms.

'Unless you are a devil,' he said, 'help her first – then speak to me.'

He walked into the sitting room. Edgar Linton called me, and with great difficulty we managed to bring Catherine back to life, though she recognized no one. Edgar, in his anxiety, forgot her hated friend. At the earliest opportunity I went to urge him to leave, saying that she was better and I would give him further news in the morning.

'I shall stay in the garden,' he answered. 'And, Nelly, if you do not keep your word, I shall pay another visit, whether Linton is in or not.'

Chapter 19   Heathcliff's Curse

At twelve o'clock that night a second Catherine, a weak, seven-month child, was born; and two hours after that the mother died, having never recovered enough consciousness to miss Heathcliff or to recognize Edgar. Her husband's grief was painful to see, and was greatly increased, in my opinion, by his being left without a son. In my mind I blamed old Mr Linton for fondly leaving his property, after Edgar's death, to his own daughter, and not to his son's daughter.

Soon after sunrise I went out wishing, though fearing, to find Heathcliff. He was leaning against a tree, his hair wet with the morning mist.

'She's dead,' he said. 'I've not waited for you to learn that. Put away your handkerchief. She wants none of your tears. How did–', he struggled with his grief, 'how did she die?'

'Poor unhappy soul,' I thought, 'you have a heart and feelings the same as other men!' I then replied aloud, 'Quietly as a lamb.'

'And – did she ever mention me?'

'Her senses never returned. She recognized no one from the time you left her. She lies with a sweet smile on her face, and her last spoken thoughts wandered back to pleasant days of her childhood.'

'May she wake in misery!' he cried, with terrible violence. 'She's a liar to the end! I pray one prayer – Catherine Earnshaw, may you not rest as long as I am living! You said that I killed you – be with me always, then! – take any form – drive me mad! Only do not leave me here, where I cannot find you! Oh God, I cannot live without my life!'

He struck his head against the tree trunk, not like a man but like a wild animal. The moment he recovered enough to notice me, he thundered a command for me to go, and I obeyed.

Catherine's funeral was planned for the Friday following her death. Until then, her coffin lay uncovered in the largest room downstairs. Edgar spent his days and nights there, a sleepless protector, while Heathcliff, as only I knew, watched, equally sleepless, outside.

On the Tuesday, a little after dark, when my master, extremely tired from watching, had gone to rest for an hour or two, I went and opened one of the windows to give Heathcliff a chance to say a last goodbye.

That he had silently done so I knew, when later I noticed on the floor a curl of fair hair, torn from the little heart-shaped gold case that hung on a chain round Catherine's neck. It was her husband's, and Heathcliff had thrown it out and replaced it by black hair of his own. I twisted the two, and enclosed them together.

Mr Earnshaw was invited to see the body of his sister to the grave, but he never came. Isabella was not asked.

Catherine was laid in the earth, to the surprise of the villagers, neither in the church with the Linton family, nor outside with her own relations. Her grave was dug on a green slope in a corner of the churchyard where the wall is so low that wild plants have climbed over it from the moor.

That Friday was the last of our fine days for a month. In the evening the weather changed. The wind brought first rain and then snow. It seemed that winter had returned.

The next day my master remained in his room. I was in the lonely sitting room, with the crying baby, when suddenly the door opened and someone entered, breathless and laughing. It was Isabella Heathcliff.

She came forward to the fire, holding her hand to her side.

'I've run the whole way from Wuthering Heights,' she said. 'Don't worry! I'll explain in a moment, only just be so kind as to step out and order transport to take me on to Gimmerton, and tell a servant to find a few of my clothes.'

Her hair streamed on her shoulders, wet with snow and water. She was dressed in the girlish silk dress she usually wore, more suited to her age than her position. It was very wet. She had a deep cut under one ear, and her face had the marks of a blow.

When I had treated her wound and helped her to change her clothes, and she was seated by the fire with a cup of tea, she began to talk, but first she begged me to take poor Catherine's baby into another room.

'I don't like to see it!' she said. 'You mustn't think I care little for Catherine, because I behaved so foolishly on entering. I've cried too, bitterly. But I wasn't going to sympathize with Heathcliff. This is the last thing of his that I have with me.'

She slipped the gold ring from her third finger and threw it into the fire with childish hate.

'Necessity forced me to come here for shelter, but I daren't stay,' she went on. 'Heathcliff is quite likely to follow in search of me, to annoy Edgar. And besides, Edgar has not been kind, has he? I won't come begging for help, and I won't bring him more trouble. Heathcliff hates the sight of me, and I feel fairly certain that he wouldn't chase me across England, if I managed a clear escape, so I must get far away from here.'

I inquired what had urged her to come away from Wuthering Heights in such a condition.

'I was forced to do so,' she replied. 'I had succeeded in exciting his fury beyond his ability to control himself. Since last Sunday he has not eaten a meal with us. He has been out every night, has come home in the early morning and locked himself in his room. Though I was full of grief for Catherine, it was impossible to avoid thinking of the week as a holiday. I was able to move freely about the house and to sit in peace by the fire.

'Last night I stayed up late reading. Hindley, who was less drunk than usual, sat opposite, his head in his hands. He is quieter now than formerly, if nobody annoys him. The silence was broken at last by the sound of Heathcliff at the kitchen door. I suppose he had returned earlier on account of the weather.

'The door was locked. My companion turned and looked at me.

'"I'll keep him out for five minutes," he exclaimed. "You and I each have a great debt to settle with the man outside. Are you as soft as your brother? Are you prepared to suffer to the end, without revenge?"

'"I'm tired of suffering," I answered, "and I'd be glad of a revenge that would not bring harm to myself; but violence wounds those who use it."

'"I'll ask you to do nothing," he replied, "but sit still and be silent. Promise to hold your tongue, and before that clock strikes – it is three minutes to one – you're a free woman!"

'He pulled from inside his coat the little gun which he had shown me on the night of our arrival. He then began to blow out the candles. I pulled his arm.

'"I'll not hold my tongue," I said. "You mustn't touch him. Be quiet!"

'"I've made up my mind," he cried. "It's time to make an end."

'It was useless for me to struggle with him. I could only run and open the window.

'"You'd better find shelter somewhere else," I called out, rather joyfully. "Mr Earnshaw is planning to shoot you."

'Heathcliff, with a curse, ordered me to let him in. I shut the window and returned to my place by the fire. Hindley swore at me, saying that I still loved the devil.

'A blow from Heathcliff broke the window and his dark face looked furiously through. The bars were too close together for his body to follow, and I smiled, imagining myself safe.

'"Isabella, let me in," he commanded.

'"I can't be responsible for murder," I answered. "Hindley stands waiting with a loaded gun. And that's a poor love of yours that cannot bear a little snow. Heathcliff, if I were you, I'd go and stretch myself over her grave and die like a loyal dog!"

'I could not move with terror at the results of my insulting words, when Heathcliff leaned in and seized Hindley's weapon from him. The gun exploded. Heathcliff took a stone and broke down the wooden frame between two windows, and jumped in.'

Chapter 20 Isabella Escapes

'Hindley had fallen unconscious with pain. Blood flowed from a large wound in his arm. Heathcliff kicked him, holding me with one hand to prevent me from fetching Joseph. At last, he dragged the seemingly lifeless body on to a chair, and put a cloth round the wound with cruel roughness. Freed for the moment, I went in search of the old servant.

'"Your master's mad," shouted Heathcliff, "and if he lives for another month, I'll have him put in a madhouse. Wash that away." He gave Joseph a push on to his knees in the middle of the blood, and turned to me.

'"You shall help, too," he said. "You join with him against me, do you?"

'He shook me violently.

'Later, Hindley showed signs of life, and Heathcliff, knowing that he could not remember the treatment received while he was unconscious, blamed him for being drunk, and advised him to get to bed.

'This morning, when I came down, Hindley was sitting by the fire, deathly sick. His enemy, looking almost as ill, leaned against the chimney. Heathcliff did not look at me. His eyes were dull with sleeplessness and weeping, and his lips closed in an expression of indescribable sadness. If it had been anyone else, I would have covered my face in the presence of such grief. In his case, I felt pleasure. I couldn't miss this chance of causing him pain.

'Hindley wanted some water. I handed him a glass, and asked him how he was feeling.

'"Not as ill as I wish," he replied. "But besides my arm, every bit of my body is sore."

'"Your enemy kicked you last night, and threw you on the floor," I told him. "It's enough that he has murdered one of you," I went on aloud. "At the Grange, everyone knows that your sister would have been living now, if it had not been for Mr Heathcliff."

'Heathcliff's attention was awakened. He wept, and I laughed.

'"Get out of my sight!" he said.

'"If poor Catherine had trusted you, and accepted the degrading title of Mrs Heathcliff," I continued, "she would soon have sunk into a state similar to her brother's. She wouldn't have borne your shameful behaviour quietly!"

'Heathcliff made a sudden movement. He picked up a dinner knife from the table and threw it at my head. It struck me beneath my ear and stopped the words I was about to say. I ran to the door. The last sight I had of him was a furious rush by him, prevented by Hindley. They both fell together. I ran through the kitchen, knocking over Hareton, and escaped down the steep road, then straight across the moor, rolling over banks, struggling through pools of water, aiming for the shelter of the Grange. And I would rather it were my fate to live for ever in misery than, even for one night, remain beneath the roof of Wuthering Heights again.'

Isabella ended her story and took a drink of tea. Then she rose and, taking no notice of my wish that she should remain for another hour, stepped on to a chair, kissed the pictures of Edgar

218

and Catherine hanging on the wall, did the same to me, and went downstairs.

She was driven away, never to revisit the area, but when things were more settled there was a regular exchange of letters between her and my master. I believe she lived in the south, near London. There she had a son born a few months later. It was named Linton, and from the first it was a weak, complaining little thing.

Heathcliff, meeting me one day in the village, inquired where she lived. I refused to tell him, but he discovered, through some of the other servants, both where she was and of the existence of the child. Still he left her alone, though he often asked how the baby was.

'I'll have it when I want it,' he said.

Fortunately, the mother died before that time came.

◆

Grief, and a dislike of going anywhere that he was likely to meet Heathcliff, caused my master to lead a lonely life. He avoided the village, remaining within the limits of his own grounds, except for walks by himself on the moors and visits to the grave of his dead wife. Time gradually closed the wound, with the help of his daughter, who soon became queen of his heart. She was named Catherine, but he always called her Cathy, to make her name different from her mother's.

The end of Hindley was what might have been expected. It followed six months after his sister's. I found it hard to realize that he was only twenty-seven at the time.

When I requested permission to go to Wuthering Heights and help in the last duties to the dead, Mr Linton did not want to agree, but I spoke of Hindley's friendless condition, and said that my old master had a claim on my services as strong as his own. Besides, I reminded him, the child Hareton was his wife's nephew, and he ought to take care of him. He must inquire how the property was left, and find out the state of his brother-in-law's affairs. He told me to speak to Mr Green, his lawyer, and finally allowed me to go.

His lawyer had been Hindley's too. I called at the village, and asked him to go with me. He shook his head and advised that Heathcliff should be left alone, saying that, if the truth were known, Hareton would receive nothing from Hindley.

'His father died in debt,' he said. 'The whole property is held by someone else, and the only chance for the son is to allow him an opportunity of persuading that person to deal generously with him.'

When I reached the Heights, Joseph appeared glad to see me. Heathcliff said he did not consider my presence necessary, but as I had come I could stay and arrange for the funeral if I wished.

'The fool locked the doors of the house against me yesterday, and spent the night drinking himself to death,' he said. 'Joseph and I broke in this morning. He was both dead and cold, so it was useless to go to further trouble about him.'

I insisted on the funeral being respectable. Heathcliff let me have my own way, but warned me to remember that the money for the whole affair came out of his pocket. His behaviour all through this was hard and cold, showing neither joy nor sorrow. It expressed, if anything, a stony satisfaction at a difficult piece of work well done. I noticed once, in fact, something like pride in his face.

It was when he was about to follow the coffin from the house. He lifted the unfortunate Hareton on to the table and murmured with strange pleasure, 'Now, my pretty boy, you are mine! We'll see if one tree won't grow as twisted as another, if it is blown by the same wind!'

The poor little thing was pleased, and touched his cheek fondly, but I guessed the meaning of his words and remarked, 'The boy must go back with me to Thrushcross Grange, sir.'

'Does Linton say so?' he demanded.

'Of course – he has ordered me to take him.'

'Well, you may tell your master that I have a wish to try my skill at bringing up a young one, so if he attempts to remove this one, my own must take its place.'

This threat to Isabella's child was enough to tie our hands. Edgar Linton, little interested at the beginning, spoke no more of taking Hareton.

The guest was now master of Wuthering Heights. He held firm possession, and proved to the lawyer that Hindley had given into his keeping every yard of land he possessed, for money to supply his mad fondness for card playing.

In that manner Hareton, who should now be the most important gentleman in the area, was reduced to a state of complete dependence on his father's enemy, and lives in his own house as a servant without wages, unable to do anything to help himself because of his friendlessness and his ignorance that he has been wronged.

PART 3   THE SECOND CATHERINE (1784–1801)

Continued by Mrs Ellen Dean

Chapter 21   Cathy Rides Out

The twelve years that followed were the happiest of my life. My greatest troubles came from our little lady's small illnesses, which she had to experience like any other child. For the rest, after the first six months, she grew tall and straight, and could walk, and talk too in her own way, before the flowers came out for the second summer on her mother's grave. She was the loveliest thing that ever brought sunshine into an unhappy house: a real beauty, with

221

the Earnshaws' dark eyes but the Lintons' fair skin and delicate face and yellow curling hair. Her spirits were high, but not rough, and her heart was kind and loving. It must be admitted that she had her faults, and she was as spoilt as any child that always got her way. I don't believe her father ever spoke a severe word to her. He took complete charge of her education. Curiosity and a quick intelligence made her a good pupil. She learned rapidly and did honour to his teaching.

Until she reached the age of thirteen, she had not once been beyond the park by herself. Her father would take her with him outside, on rare occasions, but he trusted her to no one else. She had never been to the village, and the church was the only building she had entered. Wuthering Heights and Mr Heathcliff did not exist for her.

Although she seemed happy enough with her sheltered life, she would sometimes stare out of her window upstairs and ask: 'How long will it be before I can walk to the top of those hills, Ellen? What are those rocks like when you stand under them?'

One of the servants told her about the wonderful underground hollow in the rocks. Our little lady begged her father to let her go, and he promised that she could go when she was older. But Miss Cathy measured her age by months, not years, and was continually repeating her request. The road to these rocks ran close to Wuthering Heights. Edgar could not bear to pass the place, so he continued to refuse.

The Linton family were by nature delicate. Isabella lived only twelve years after leaving her husband. When her last illness came on her, she wrote to her brother and begged him to come to her, if possible, as she wished to say goodbye to him and deliver her son safely into his hands. Her hope was that the boy could be left with him, and that the father would show no interest.

Although my master did not like to leave home for ordinary calls, he did not think twice now. He set out immediately, leaving

Cathy in my particular care, with repeated orders that she must not wander out of the park, even if I went with her.

He was away three weeks. For the first day or two, my little lady sat in a corner in the library, too sad to read or play, and too quiet to give trouble. This was followed by a time of restlessness and, as I was too busy to run up and down amusing her, I got into the habit of sending her on her travels round the grounds, sometimes on foot and sometimes on a horse. When she returned I would listen with patience to the story of her adventures, real and imaginary.

I did not fear her leaving the grounds, because the gates were usually locked, and I thought that even if they were not, she would not dare to go out alone. In this belief I was wrong.

Cathy came to me one morning, at eight o'clock, and said that she was that day an Arab traveller, going to cross the desert, and I must give her plenty of food for herself and her horse and her three dogs. She rode off with the basket, laughing when I told her to be back early.

The naughty thing never made her appearance at teatime. One traveller, the oldest dog, returned, but there was no sign of Cathy or her horse. I sent people out to search in all directions, and at last went myself. A workman was busy at a fence on the edge of the grounds. I asked if he had seen our young mistress.

'I saw her in the morning,' he replied. 'She made her horse jump over the fence just here, where it is lowest, and rode out of sight.'

Chapter 22   First Visit to the Heights

I realized at once that Miss Cathy must have started for the rocks. I pushed through a space which the man was repairing, and walked mile after mile until I was in view of the Heights, but I could see no sign of her. The rocks lie about a mile and a half beyond the Heights, and I began to fear that night would fall before I could reach them.

'I wonder whether she has slipped while climbing,' I thought, 'and been killed, or broken her bones?'

My anxiety was painful, and at first I was truly glad to recognize, in hurrying past the farmhouse, the fiercest of our dogs lying under a window with a bleeding ear. I opened the gate and knocked violently at the door. A woman I knew, who had been a servant at the Heights since the death of Mr Hindley, answered.

'Ah!' she said. 'You've come looking for your little mistress. Don't be frightened. She's here safe, but I'm glad you're not the master.'

'He's not home, then?' I asked.

'No, no,' she replied. 'He won't return for an hour or more. Step in and rest a bit.'

I entered, and found my wandering lamb seated by the fire, in a little chair that had been her mother's. Her hat was hung against the wall, and she seemed perfectly at home, laughing and talking in the happiest manner imaginable to Hareton – now a great strong youth of eighteen – who was looking at her with a good deal of curiosity and surprise.

'Well, miss,' I exclaimed, hiding my joy under an angry look. 'This is your last ride, until your father comes back. I'll not trust you outside the house again, you naughty, naughty girl! Put that hat on and come home now.'

'What have I done?' she wept, losing her high spirits at once. 'Papa won't be cross with me – he's never unpleasant like you, Ellen.'

'No,' said the servant, 'don't be hard on the pretty one, Mrs Dean. We made her stop. She wished to ride back, afraid that you would be anxious, but Hareton offered to go with her and I thought he should as it's a rough road.'

'How long do I have to wait?' I went on, taking no notice. 'It will be dark in ten minutes.'

I picked up her hat, and moved towards her to put it on her, but she, seeing quite well that the people in the house were on her side, began dancing round the room. When I gave chase, she ran like a mouse over and under and behind the furniture. Hareton and the woman laughed, and Cathy joined them, making fun of me until I cried in great annoyance: 'Well, Miss Cathy, if you knew whose house this is, you'd be glad to get out.'

'It's your father's, isn't it?' she said, turning to Hareton.

'No,' he replied, looking down as his face turned red.

'Whose then – your master's?' she asked.

His face became redder still, and he turned away.

'I thought he was the owner's son,' the naughty girl continued to me. 'He talked of "our" house, and he never said "miss" to me. He should have done, shouldn't he, if he's a servant?'

Hareton looked as black as a thundercloud.

'Now get my horse,' she said, 'and you may come with me. Hurry! What's the matter?'

With a curse, the youth told her he was not her servant.

Cathy could not believe what she had heard. She, who was always "queen" and "dearest" at home, to be insulted!

'But Ellen,' she cried, 'how dare he speak to me like that? You wicked thing, I shall tell my father what you said!'

Hareton did not seem to feel this threat, so tears came to her eyes.

'You bring my horse,' she exclaimed, turning to the woman.

'Take care, miss,' she answered. 'You'll lose nothing by being polite. Mr Hareton is your cousin, and I was never hired to serve you.'

'*He* my cousin!' cried Cathy, with a scornful laugh. 'My father has gone to fetch my cousin from London.'

I was much annoyed with her and the servant for what they

had made known to one another. I had no doubt that the expected arrival of Isabella's son would be reported to Mr Heathcliff, and I felt sure that on her father's return Cathy's first thought would be to ask an explanation of Hareton's claim to be a relation.

Hareton, recovering from his disgust at being mistaken for a servant, fetched her horse to the door and took, to please her, a fine little dog from the yard. Placing it in her arms, he told her that he did not mean any harm. She looked at him in disgust, and began to weep.

I could hardly help smiling that she should turn away from the poor fellow, who was an active youth, good-looking, strong and healthy, though dressed in clothes suited to his daily business of working on the farm. Still, I thought I could see in his face better qualities than his father ever possessed. Mr Heathcliff, I believed, had not done him any bodily harm, as a result of his fearless nature. He had directed all his energies to keeping the boy uneducated; he was never taught to read or write, never cured of any bad habit.

Miss Cathy refused the peace offering of the little dog, and we started for home. I could not find out from my little lady how she had spent her day except that, as I had thought, she had set out for the rocks, and that as she passed the farmhouse gate, Hareton had come out and his dogs had attacked hers. There was a fierce battle before their owners could separate them, and that formed an introduction. Cathy asked Hareton the way to the rocks, and he finally went with her.

I saw that Hareton had been a favourite until she had hurt his feelings. It took me a long time before I could persuade her not to mention the matter to her father. I explained how he objected to everybody at Wuthering Heights, and how sorry he would be to hear that she had been there, and how, if she told him I had disobeyed his orders, perhaps he would be so angry that I would have to leave. Cathy could not bear this last possibility, so she promised to be silent and she kept her word. After all, she was a sweet little girl.

Chapter 23   Heathcliff Claims His Own

A letter edged in black announced the day of my master's return. Isabella was dead, and he wrote to tell me to arrange a room for his young nephew. Cathy was wild with joy at the idea of welcoming her father back, and meeting her 'real' cousin.

The day came, and my little mistress was so impatient that she made me walk all through the park to meet them.

They came into view at last. Miss Cathy shouted and held out her arms. Her father got down, nearly as eager as herself. While they exchanged loving greetings, I took a look at Linton. He was asleep, wrapped up in furs as if it were winter. He was a pale, delicate, girlish-looking boy, who might have been mistaken for my master's younger brother, they were so alike; but he had a sickly unpleasant look that Edgar Linton never had.

The sleeper, being woken at the house, was lifted to the ground by his uncle.

'This is your cousin Cathy, Linton,' he said, putting their little hands together. 'She's fond of you already. Try to be cheerful, now. The travelling is at an end.'

The boy stepped back from Cathy's welcome and put his fingers to his eyes. All three entered the house and went upstairs to the library, where tea was laid ready. I took off Linton's outdoor clothes and placed him at the table, but he began to cry.

'I can't sit on a hard chair,' he complained.

'Go to a more comfortable one, then, and Ellen will bring you your tea there,' said his uncle patiently.

Cathy carried a little seat and her cup to his side. At first she was silent, but that could not go on for long. She was determined to make a pet of her cousin, and she began touching his curls fondly, and kissing his cheek, and offering him tea from her cup, like a baby. This pleased him. He dried his eyes and smiled faintly.

'He'll do very well, if we can keep him, Ellen,' said the master to me, after watching them for a minute. 'The company of a child of his own age will put new life into him.'

'Yes, if only we can keep him,' I thought to myself, but I felt there was slight hope of that. I had no idea how the weak child would live at Wuthering Heights, between his father and Hareton.

Our doubts were soon decided.

I had just taken the children upstairs, and seen Linton asleep, when a servant stepped out of the kitchen and informed me that Mr Heathcliff's man Joseph was at the door and wished to speak to the master.

Very slowly I went up to the library and announced the unwanted visitor. Joseph followed close on my heels and without invitation pushed past me, saying: 'Heathcliff sent me for his boy, and I mustn't go back without him.'

Edgar Linton was silent for a minute. An expression of great sorrow spread over his face. He felt bitter grief at the idea of giving up the boy, but could not see any way of keeping him.

'Tell Mr Heathcliff,' he answered calmly, 'that his son shall come tomorrow to Wuthering Heights. He is in bed, and too tired to go the distance now.'

With some difficulty Joseph was persuaded to go away empty-handed, but with the parting threat that Heathcliff himself would come over the next day to get his son.

To avoid the danger of this threat being carried out, Mr Linton ordered me to take the boy home early, on Cathy's horse. He added: 'You must say nothing to my daughter of where he has gone.

She cannot see him in future. Simply tell her that his father sent for him suddenly, and he has had to leave us.'

Young Linton was very unhappy about being woken from his sleep at five o'clock in the morning, and surprised to find he must prepare for further travelling. I softened the matter by saying that he was going to spend some time with his father, who wanted to see him without delay.

'My father!' cried the boy. 'I never knew that I had a father. Why didn't my mother and he live together, as other people do?'

'He had business to keep him in the north,' I answered, 'and your mother's health made it necessary for her to live in the south.'

The boy was not satisfied.

'She didn't speak to me about him,' he repeated. 'She often talked of Uncle, and I learned to love him. How can I love my father?'

'All children love their parents,' I said. 'Let's hurry. An early ride on a beautiful morning is better than another hour's sleep.'

'Is she going with us – the little girl I saw yesterday?'

'Not now.'

'Is Uncle?'

'No. I shall be your companion.'

Linton sank back on his pillow. 'I won't go without Uncle,' he said.

I had to call for my master's help in getting him out of bed. The poor thing was got off in the end with promises that his visit would be short, that his uncle and Cathy would visit him, and other promises, equally without truth, that I invented from time to time. At last, in the pure air and the sunshine, he began to brighten on the way and to put questions about his new home. Was Wuthering Heights as pleasant a place as Thrushcross Grange? Was his father as good-looking as his uncle?

'The house is not quite so large,' I told him, 'but it is the

229

second in the neighbourhood. Your father is as young as your uncle, but he has black hair and eyes and looks more severe. He'll not seem so kind and gentle at first, perhaps, because it's not his nature, but of course he'll be fonder of you than any uncle, since you are his own.'

The boy was fully occupied with his own thoughts for the rest of the ride. It was half past six when we arrived. The household had just finished breakfast. The servant was taking away the things.

'Hullo, Nelly!' cried Mr Heathcliff when he saw me. 'You've brought my property, have you? Let me see it.'

He got up and came to the door. Hareton and Joseph followed, full of curiosity. Poor Linton took a quick, frightened look at all three.

'Surely,' said Joseph, after a careful examination, 'he's changed with you, master, and sent you his girl!'

Heathcliff gave a scornful laugh, and a curse.

'What a beauty! What a pretty little thing!' he exclaimed. 'It's worse than I expected!'

I told the trembling child to get down and enter. He did not quite understand his father's speech, and he was still not quite certain that this hard, scornful stranger was his father, but he held on to me with growing fear, and when Mr Heathcliff took a seat and ordered him to come to him, he hid his face in my shoulder and wept.

'Come!' said Heathcliff, stretching out a hand and dragging him roughly between his knees. 'None of that nonsense. We're not going to hurt you, Linton — isn't that your name? You're completely like your mother. Where is my share in you?'

He took off the boy's cap and pushed back his thick fair curls and felt his thin arms and small fingers. Linton stopped crying and lifted his great blue eyes to examine the examiner.

'Do you know me?' asked Heathcliff.

'No,' said Linton, with a look of fear.

'No? What a shame your mother never helped you to love me! You are my son. Be a good boy, and I'll look after you. Nelly, if you are tired, sit down. If not, get home. This thing won't be settled while you're still about.'

'Well,' I replied, 'I hope you'll be kind to the boy, Mr Heathcliff, or he won't live long.'

'I'll be *very* kind to him, you needn't fear,' he said, laughing. 'And to begin my kindness – Joseph! Bring the boy some breakfast. Hareton! Get to your work.'

'Yes,' he added when they had gone, 'my son is the future owner of your place, and I would not wish him to die until I am certain of receiving it from him. Besides, he's *mine*, and I want the pleasure of seeing my son fairly lord of *their* property, *my* child hiring their children to look after their fathers' lands for wages. It's only such a thought that makes me able to bear the miserable thing. He's worthless in himself, and I hate him for the memories he brings back! But he's safe with me. I have a room upstairs, finely decorated for him. I've hired a teacher to come three times a week. I've ordered Hareton to obey him. In fact, I've arranged everything to keep him a gentleman. It is a pity, though, that he so little deserves the trouble. If I wished for anything in the world, it was to find him a worthy object of pride, and I'm bitterly disappointed in the milk-faced baby!'

While he was speaking, Joseph returned with some food and placed it in front of Linton. Linton looked at the food with disgust and declared he could not eat it. Joseph was angry, but Heathcliff ordered the housekeeper to give him whatever he wanted to eat. Having no excuse for staying any longer, I slipped out while Linton was looking at a friendly sheepdog. But as I closed the door, I heard a cry and a repetition of the words: 'Don't leave me! I won't stay here! I won't stay here!'

Chapter 24 'Will You Walk into My House?'

We had sad work with little Cathy that day. She rose in a state of excitement, eager to join her cousin, and floods of tears followed the news that he had gone.

Whenever I chanced, from time to time, to meet the housekeeper from Wuthering Heights in the village, I used to ask how the young master was, as he lived almost as sheltered a life as Cathy herself and was never to be seen. I learned that he was in weak health and was a difficult person to look after. Mr Heathcliff seemed to dislike him more and more, though he took some trouble to hide it. He could not bear to be in the same room as him for long. Linton learned his lessons and spent his evenings in a small room of his own, or else lay in bed all day, as he was continually getting coughs and colds, and aches and pains of all sorts.

This housekeeper left two years after he came and another, whom I did not know, took her place.

Time passed at the Grange in its former pleasant way until Miss Cathy reached the age of sixteen. On her birthday we never had any kind of party, because it was also the day of her mother's death. Her father always spent it alone, and walked to the grave, so Cathy was left to amuse herself.

This was a beautiful spring day, and my young lady came down early, dressed for going out, saying that her father had given her permission to go on the edge of the moors with me, if we only went a short distance.

'So hurry, Ellen!' she said. 'There are some young birds up there. I want to see if they have made their nests yet.'

'That must be some distance away,' I answered. 'They don't nest on the edge of the moor.'

'No, it's not,' she said. 'I've gone very near with Papa.'

Thinking no more of the matter, I got myself ready and we set out. She ran backwards and forwards along the path, and at first I

found plenty of entertainment in listening to the birds singing far
and near, and enjoying the warm sunshine, and watching my little
dear, with her golden curls flying loose behind, and her bright
cheek, as soft and pure as a rose, and her eyes shining with pleasure.
She was a happy being in those days.

'Well,' I said, 'where are your birds, Miss Cathy? We have come
a long way.'

'Only a little farther – a little farther,' was her answer
continually.

At last I began to grow tired, and called to her that we must
go back. She did not listen, and I was forced to follow. She
disappeared ahead of me into a hollow and when I next came in
sight of her, she was two miles nearer Wuthering Heights than her
own home. I saw two people stop her, one of whom was Mr
Heathcliff.

Cathy had been caught stealing, or at least hunting for the
birds on the Heights. This was Mr Heathcliff's land, and he was
warning her. She showed him her empty hands.

'I've neither taken nor found any,' she said. 'My father told me
there were plenty up here, and I wished to see the eggs.'

With an evil smile, Heathcliff asked who her father was.

'Mr Linton of Thrushcross Grange,' she replied. 'I thought you
did not know me, or you wouldn't have spoken in that way.'

'You suppose that your father is highly respected?' he said
scornfully.

'And who are you?' inquired Cathy. 'Is that man your son?'

She pointed at Hareton, who looked bigger and stronger than
ever, but just as rough and awkward.

'Miss Cathy,' I interrupted, 'we must be getting back home
now.'

'No, that man is not my son,' answered Heathcliff, paying no
attention to me. 'But I have one, whom you have seen before. I
think both you and your nurse will feel better after a little rest.

Will you walk into my house? You shall receive a kind welcome.'

I whispered to Miss Cathy that she must on no account accept this invitation, but she ran on, and Heathcliff had seized my arm.

'Mr Heathcliff, it's very wrong,' I said. 'You know you mean no good. And as soon as we return, I shall get the blame for this.'

'I want her to see Linton,' he replied. 'He's looking better these last few days. I want the two cousins to fall in love and get married. It's generous of me, as the girl will have nothing when her father dies.'

'Linton's life is quite uncertain,' I said, 'and if he died, Cathy would become the owner of the place.'

'No, she would not,' he returned. 'There is no arrangement in the will of that kind. The property would go to me, but to prevent arguments I desire them to marry.'

And he led me to the gate, where Miss Cathy was waiting for us.

Chapter 25   A Second Visit to the Heights

Cathy gave Mr Heathcliff some strange looks, as if she could not exactly decide what to think of him, but now he smiled and softened his voice when addressing her, and I was foolish enough to imagine that the memory of her mother might persuade him not to do her harm.

Linton stood by the fireplace. He had been walking in the fields, and was calling for Joseph to bring him dry shoes. He had grown tall, his face was still pretty, and his eyes and skin were healthier than I remembered.

'Now, who is that?' asked Mr Heathcliff, turning to Cathy.

Cathy looked doubtfully from one to the other.

'Your son?' she said.

'Yes,' he answered. 'You have a short memory. Linton, don't

you remember your cousin, whom you were always wishing to see?'

'What, Linton!' cried Cathy, in joyful surprise. 'Is that really little Linton? He's taller than I am!'

She ran forward and kissed him. They stared in wonder at the changes that time had made in their appearance. Cathy had reached her full height, and she shone with health. Linton's looks and movements lacked energy, but there was a certain attractiveness in his manner.

Cathy turned to Heathcliff. 'And you are my uncle, then!' she cried, reaching up to kiss him also. 'I thought I liked you, though you were unpleasant at first. Why don't you visit the Grange with Linton? Naughty Ellen!' she continued, turning to me. 'Wicked Ellen, to try to stop me from entering!'

'Don't waste your kisses on me,' said her uncle. 'I think I'd better tell you. Mr Linton has a low opinion of me. We quarrelled at one time in our lives. If you mention your visit here, he will forbid you to come again.'

'Why did you quarrel?' asked Cathy, surprised and disappointed.

'He thought me too poor to marry his sister,' answered Heathcliff, 'and was upset when I got her.'

'That's wrong!' said the young lady. 'Some time I'll tell him so. But Linton and I have no share in your quarrel. I'll not come here, but he shall come to the Grange.'

'It is too far,' said her cousin. 'To walk four miles would kill me.'

The father looked with bitter scorn at his son.

'Have you nothing to show your cousin?' he said. 'Take her into the garden before you change your shoes.'

'Wouldn't you rather sit here?' Linton asked Cathy.

'I don't know,' she replied, with a quick look at the door.

He kept his seat, and moved closer to the fire. Heathcliff rose and called out for Hareton. Hareton replied and soon appeared. He had been washing himself, as was noticeable by his shining cheeks and his wet hair.

'He's not my cousin, Uncle, is he?' cried Cathy.

'Yes,' he replied. 'Your mother's nephew. Don't you like him?'

Cathy looked uncertain. She reached up and whispered a sentence in Heathcliff's ear. He laughed, and Hareton's face became dark. But his master chased the displeasure away by exclaiming: 'You'll be the favourite among us, Hareton! She said something very nice about you. Go round the farm with her, and behave like a gentleman. Don't use any bad words, don't fix your eyes on her, speak slowly, and keep your hands out of your pockets.'

He watched the pair walking past the window. Hareton did not look at his companion. 'I've tied his tongue,' remarked Heathcliff with satisfaction. 'He'll be afraid to say a word. Nelly, you remember me at his age – no, a few years younger – did I ever look so stupid?'

'Worse,' I replied, 'because you were more evil-tempered.'

'I take pleasure in him,' he continued. 'If he were a born fool I would not enjoy it half as much. I can sympathize with all his feelings, having felt them myself. He'll never be able to escape from his roughness and ignorance, because I've taught him to take a pride in his condition. I control him more tightly than his father ever controlled me. And the best of it is, Hareton is extremely fond of me. If his father could rise from the grave and tell me I've wronged his child, that child would fight him to protect me as his one friend in the world!'

He gave a wicked laugh. Linton, perhaps unhappy about the loss of Cathy's company, began to be restless. He got up and went outside.

Cathy was asking Hareton what the words over the door were. Hareton looked up and stared at them.

'Some writing,' he answered. 'I can't read it.'

Linton gave a silly little laugh.

'He doesn't even know his letters,' he said to Cathy. 'Did you ever see anyone so ignorant? There's nothing the matter but laziness, is there, Hareton? Have you noticed his bad pronunciation? He scorns "book-learning", as he calls it.'

'Why? What's the use of it?' said Hareton.

Linton and Cathy burst into a noisy fit of laughter, and the poor, angry youth went away, his face burning with fury and shame. Mr Heathcliff smiled as he saw him go, but afterwards I saw him direct a look of hate at the heartless pair, who continued to enjoy their sense of superiority. I began to dislike, more than to pity Linton, and to excuse his father in some degree for thinking badly of him.

◆

We stayed until the afternoon. I could not get Miss Cathy away before. Luckily my master had remained in his room and knew nothing of our long absence.

Next day, though, the truth came out. I was not completely sorry. I thought the responsibility of directing and warning my young lady could be borne better by her father than by me, but he was too careful in giving reasons why she should avoid the people at the Heights, and Cathy liked good reasons for anything that prevented her having her own way. Finally Mr Linton told her of Heathcliff's treatment of Isabella. She appeared so surprised and upset at this new view of human nature that he thought it unnecessary to say any more about it.

She kissed her father and sat down quietly to her lessons for an hour or two; then she went with him for a walk in the grounds, and the whole day passed as usual. In the evening, though, when I went upstairs to help her undress, I found her crying on her knees by the bedside.

'Silly child!' I exclaimed. 'If you had any real griefs, you'd be ashamed to waste a tear on a little thing like this.'

'I'm not crying for myself, Ellen,' she answered. 'It's for Linton. He'll be so disappointed if he doesn't see me again.'

'Nonsense!' I said. 'He will guess what has happened and trouble himself no further about you.'

'But may I not write a few words to tell him why I can't come? And just send those books I promised to lend him?'

'No, you can't,' I replied decisively. 'Then he would write to you, and there would never be an end to it.'

'But how can one little letter–'

'Silence!' I interrupted. 'We'll not discuss your letters. Get into bed.'

She gave me a very naughty look, so naughty that at first I refused to kiss her goodnight. I covered her up and went away, shutting the door; but a little later, feeling sorry, I returned softly, and found Miss Cathy standing at the table with a piece of paper and a pencil in her hand, which she guiltily slipped out of sight when I came forward.

'You'll get nobody to take that, if you write it,' I said.

I put out her candle as I spoke, receiving as I did a little blow on my hand, and the name of 'cruel thing'.

Weeks passed, and Cathy recovered her temper, though she became very fond of creeping off into corners by herself and reading some book which she would bend over to hide if I came near, and which seemed to have sheets of paper pushed between the leaves. She also got into the habit of coming down early in the morning to the kitchen, as if she were expecting something, and she had a small drawer in a cupboard in the library which she would examine for hours, and whose key she took special care to remove when she left.

One day, as she examined this drawer, I noticed that the little playthings and other small possessions that had formerly been kept in it had mysteriously been changed into bits of folded paper. I wondered what she was keeping secret, and worried for her, so at night I found among my keys one that would fit the lock, and made an examination of her hiding place.

The drawer contained a pile of daily letters from Linton Heathcliff, answers to messages written by my young lady. I tied them up in a handkerchief and relocked the empty drawer.

Next morning I watched Miss Cathy go down to the kitchen and rush to the door on the arrival of a little boy who came to fetch milk. While the serving-girl filled his can, Miss Cathy put something in his pocket, and took something else out. I followed the boy out into the garden and succeeded in seizing the letter, though he fought bravely to defend his trust. I remained under the wall and read it. It was more simple and sincere than those of her cousin: very pretty and very silly.

The day was wet, so at the end of her morning studies Cathy went straight to her drawer to amuse herself. Her father sat reading at the table, and I, on purpose, was mending the border of a curtain by the window, keeping my eye fixed on all that happened.

Never did any bird flying back to a nest robbed of its young ones express more complete misery in all its cries than she by her single 'Oh!'

Mr Linton looked up.

'What is the matter, my dear?' he said. 'Have you hurt yourself?'

'No, Father,' she replied with difficulty. 'Ellen! Ellen! Come upstairs – I'm sick!'

I obeyed her call.

'Oh, Ellen, you have got them,' she began at once. 'Oh, give them to me, and don't tell my father! I've been extremely naughty, but I won't do it any more!'

'I'm going with them to the library,' I replied, 'and we'll see what your father says about this nonsense.'

She tried to take them from me, but I held them above my head. She begged that I would burn them – do anything rather than show them. At last, since I was as ready to laugh as to be cross, I said: 'Will you promise me not to send or receive a letter again, or a book, or curls of hair, or rings, or playthings?'

'We don't send playthings,' cried Cathy, her pride defeating her shame.

'Not anything at all, then, my lady!' I said.

'I promise, Ellen!' she cried, catching hold of my dress.

But when I began to put them on the fire, their destruction was too painful.

'Can't I keep one or two Ellen?'

I continued to drop them on the flames.

'I *will* have one, you cruel thing!' she exclaimed, putting her hand into the fire, and drawing out some half-burnt pieces, with some damage to her fingers.

'Very well – then I'll have some to show your father!'

At that, she emptied her blackened pieces into the flames and without speaking went away to her own room. I went down to tell my master that the young lady's attack of sickness was almost gone, but I judged it best for her to lie down for a time. At tea she appeared, pale and red about the eyes, and unusually quiet.

Next morning, I replied to Linton's letter with a short note: 'Master Heathcliff is requested to send no more letters to Miss Linton, as she will not receive them.'

And from that time, the little boy came and went with empty pockets.

Chapter 26 The Result of Climbing a Wall

Summer came to an end. The crops were brought in late that year. Mr Linton and his daughter frequently walked among the workers in the fields, and on the last day they stayed until night fell. As a result of this my master caught a bad cold, which settled on his lungs, keeping him indoors all through the winter.

Poor Cathy, frightened from her little love affair, had been sadder and duller since it had ended, and her father encouraged her to read less and take more exercise. She no longer had his companionship, and though I tried to make up for this, I had only two or three hours free from my many daily duties.

One afternoon at the beginning of November, when it looked likely to rain, I asked my young lady to give up her walk. She refused, so I put on my outdoor clothes to go with her to the bottom of the park. This was a walk she chose when she was feeling low-spirited, as now, when my master was worse than usual.

As we neared a door which opened on to the road, my lady became more cheerful, and climbed up and seated herself on top of the wall to pick some berries. She reached up to get them, and her hat fell off on the outer side. Since the door was locked, she suggested dropping down to get it. I told her to be careful of falling, and she disappeared.

But the return was not so easy. The stones of the wall outside were smooth and well joined. I didn't remember this until I heard her laughing and calling out: 'Ellen, you'll have to fetch the key, or else I must run round to the main gate.'

'Stay where you are,' I answered. 'I have my bunch of keys in my pocket. Perhaps I can manage to open it.'

I had tried all the keys without success when I heard the sound of a horse and Cathy whispered anxiously through the door: 'Ellen, I wish you could open it.'

'Hullo, Miss Linton!' cried a deep voice. 'I'm glad to meet you. I have an explanation to ask of you.'

'I shan't speak to you, Mr Heathcliff,' answered Cathy. 'Father says you are a wicked man, and you hate him and me; Ellen says the same.'

'That is not the point,' said Heathcliff. 'I don't hate my son, I suppose, and it is concerning him that I demand your attention. Yes! You have cause to go red! Two or three months ago, you were in the habit of writing to Linton. I've got your letters, and if you will not listen to me, I'll show them to your father. I suppose you grew tired of the amusement? Well, Linton was serious. He's dying for you – breaking his heart at your cruelty. He gets worse every day, and unless you do something to help him, he'll be under the ground before next summer.'

'How can you lie so shamelessly to the poor child!' I called out. 'Miss Cathy, I'll break this lock open with a stone in a minute. Don't believe his nonsense.'

'I didn't know that there was anyone listening,' murmured Heathcliff. 'Mrs Dean, how can you lie so shamelessly! Miss Linton, I shall be away from home all this week. Go and see if I have not spoken the truth.'

The lock broke, and I came out.

'Come in,' I said, taking Cathy by the arm, and half forcing her to enter, as she was looking with troubled eyes at the speaker.

I closed the door and, since the rain had begun, we hurried home in silence.

That evening, as we sat by the fire, she wept to herself. I argued with her without success. Heathcliff had done his work too skilfully.

'You may be right, Ellen,' she said, 'but I shall never feel at peace until I know.'

What use were anger and argument? Next day saw me on the road to Wuthering Heights, by the side of my young mistress's horse. I couldn't bear her sorrow, her pale face and heavy eye. I gave in, in the faint hope that Linton might prove, by his way of receiving her, how little truth there was in his father's words.

Chapter 27   Linton Is Difficult

The rainy night was followed by a misty morning, and the rushing streams from the hills crossed our path. My feet were thoroughly wet, and I felt uncomfortable and unwell. We entered the farmhouse by the kitchen door, to be sure that Heathcliff was really absent.

Joseph was sitting alone, in front of a huge fire, with his pipe in his mouth. He answered our questions with his usual bad temper.

'Joseph!' cried a complaining voice from the inner room. 'How often do I have to call you? The fire is going out.'

Joseph took no notice. The housekeeper and Hareton were not around, both probably at their work elsewhere. We recognized Linton's voice and entered.

His cousin flew to his side.

'Is that you, Miss Linton?' he said, raising his head from the arm of the great chair in which he was lying. 'Will you shut the door, please? You left it open, and those hateful people won't bring coal for the fire. It's so cold!'

I attended to the fire, and fetched some coal myself. The sick boy complained of being covered in ashes, but he had a bad cough and looked feverish and ill, so I did not blame him.

'Well, Linton,' said Cathy, 'are you glad to see me?'

'Why didn't you come before?' was his reply. 'You should have come, instead of writing. It tired me so much, writing those long letters. Now I can neither bear to talk, nor anything else. I wonder where Zillah is! Will you' – looking at me – 'step into the kitchen and see?'

243

I had received no thanks for my other service, so I remained where I was, replying, 'There is no one there except Joseph.'

'I want to drink,' he exclaimed, turning away. 'Zillah is always going off to Gimmerton since my father left. And I'm forced to come down here – they pretend not to hear me upstairs.'

Cathy began searching for some water. She filled a glass and brought it. He told her to add a spoonful of wine from a bottle on the table and, having swallowed a little, seemed better and said she was very kind.

'Are you glad to see me?' repeated Cathy, pleased that he was smiling faintly.

'Yes, I am,' he replied. 'But I have been annoyed that you haven't come before. And Father swore it was my fault. He called me a worthless thing, and said if he had been in my place, he would be more master of the Grange than your father by this time.'

'I dare not come while your father is here,' said Cathy. 'If I could get my father's permission, I'd spend half my time with you. I wish you were my brother!'

'And then you would like me as well as your father?' he remarked, more cheerfully. 'But Father says you would love me better than anyone else, if you were my wife.'

'People hate their wives sometimes,' said Cathy, 'but not their brothers and sisters.'

Linton declared that people never hated their wives, but Cathy repeated that they did, and gave as an example his own father's dislike of her aunt. I tried to stop her thoughtless tongue, but everything she knew came out.

Linton declared that her story was false.

'Father told me, and he does not tell untruths,' she answered angrily.

'My father scorns yours!' cried Linton.

'And yours is a wicked man!' replied Cathy.

'Well, I'll tell you something,' said Linton. 'Your mother hated your father: now then!'

'Oh!' exclaimed Cathy, too furious to continue.

'And she loved mine!' he added.

'It's not true!' she shouted. 'I hate you now.'

'She did! She did!' sang Linton, sinking back to enjoy the unhappiness of his companion, who stood behind him.

Cathy, losing control of herself, gave the chair a violent push and caused him to fall against one arm. At once he was seized with a cough that stopped his breath and soon ended his moment of victory. It lasted so long that it frightened even me. As to his cousin, she wept violently, though she said nothing. I held him until the attack ended. Then he pushed me away, and leaned his head down silently. Cathy took a seat opposite, and looked into the fire.

'How do you feel now, Master Heathcliff?' I asked after about ten minutes.

'I wish she felt as I do!' he replied, 'Cruel, unkind thing!'

He continued to complain for a quarter of an hour.

'I'm sorry I hurt you, Linton,' his cousin said at last. 'But I wouldn't have been hurt by that little push, and I didn't imagine that you would have been. It wasn't much, was it?'

'I can't speak to you,' he murmured. 'You've hurt me so much that I shall lie awake all night with this cough.' And he began to weep.

'Must I go then?' asked Cathy sadly.

'Leave me alone.'

She waited a long time. He neither looked up nor spoke. At last she made a movement to the door, and I followed. We were brought back by a shout. Linton had slid from his seat on to the floor, and lay twisting himself about, determined to be as annoying as possible. Cathy knelt down and cried.

'I shall lift him up onto the seat,' I said, 'and he may roll about as much as he pleases. We can't stop to watch him. I hope you are satisfied, Miss Cathy, that you are not the person to improve his health.'

She offered him water. He refused the drink, but he would not let her leave him. She sang him a number of songs, and so they went on until the clock struck twelve.

'And tomorrow, Cathy, will you be here tomorrow?' Linton asked, holding her dress as she rose to go.

She whispered in his ear, and at last we left.

'You won't go tomorrow, miss?' I began, as soon as we were out of the house.

She smiled.

'I'll take good care,' I continued. 'I'll have the lock on that door mended.'

'I can get over the wall,' she said, laughing. 'The Grange isn't a prison, and besides, I'm almost seventeen. I'm certain Linton would recover more quickly if he had me to look after him.'

'Listen, miss,' I replied. 'If you attempt going to Wuthering Heights again, I shall inform Mr Linton.'

We reached home before our dinnertime. My master asked no explanation of our absence. He thought we had been wandering in the park. As soon as I entered, I hurried to change my wet shoes, but sitting for such a long time at the Heights had done me harm, and the next morning I was ill. For three weeks I was in bed, unable to carry out my duties.

My little mistress was very kind to me during this lonely time. The moment she left her father's room, she appeared at my bedside. Her day was divided between us. She paid no attention to her meals, her study or her play.

It is true that my master went to sleep early, and I generally needed nothing after six o'clock. I never considered what Cathy did with herself after tea. And though frequently, when she looked in to say goodnight, I noticed a fresh colour in her cheeks, instead of thinking it the result of a cold ride on the moors I imagined it was from a hot fire in the library.

◆

At last I was able to leave my room and move about the house. The first time I sat up in the evening, I asked Cathy to read to me because my eyes were weak. She did so without any pleasure, and after half an hour began to question me: 'Ellen, aren't you tired? Hadn't you better lie down now?'

'No, no, dear, I'm not tired,' I answered, several times.

She then opened her own mouth sleepily and stretched herself, rubbing her eyes and looking at her watch. Finally, she went to her room.

The next night she seemed more impatient still, and on the third she complained of a headache and left me. I thought her behaviour strange, and having remained alone for some time, went up to see if she was feeling better. I could discover no Cathy, upstairs or down. The servants had not seen her, and all was silent in Mr Edgar's room. I returned to my young lady's room, put out my candle, and seated myself at the window.

The moon shone brightly, and I asked myself if she had decided to walk around the garden. I saw a figure creeping along the inner fence of the park, but this was one of the servants. He stood watching the road through the grounds for some time, then suddenly disappeared, to reappear later leading Miss Cathy's horse, and there she was, having just got down and walking by its side.

She entered the sitting room by the long window, and came noiselessly upstairs to her room. She closed the door gently, slipped off her snowy shoes, untied her hat, and was about to remove her outdoor clothes when I suddenly stood up and showed myself. She froze with surprise.

'My dear Miss Cathy,' I began, 'where have you been riding at this time of night? And why should you try to deceive me by telling lies?'

'To the bottom of the park,' she said, uncomfortably.

'And nowhere else?'

'No,' was the reply, in a low voice.

'Oh, Cathy,' I cried sorrowfully, 'you know you have been doing wrong. I'd rather be ill for three months than hear you tell a lie!'

She ran forward and, bursting into tears, threw her arms around my neck.

'Well, Ellen, I'm so afraid of your being angry,' she said. 'Promise that you won't be, and you shall know the truth. I hate to hide it. I've been to Wuthering Heights. I had to keep my promise to Linton. I got possession of the key when the door in the park was being locked again, and I've hardly missed a day since you fell ill. It wasn't to amuse myself that I went. I was often miserable all the time. Now and then I was happy: once in a week, perhaps.

'On my second visit Linton seemed in good spirits. We laughed and talked quite happily for an hour. Then I got tired of sitting, and suggested a game. He agreed to play ball with me. I won every time, and then he became unpleasant again, and coughed, and returned to his chair. He easily recovered his good temper when I sang some pretty songs. That night I came riding home as light as air.

'The next night, Hareton met me and took my horse in. I told him to leave my horse alone. He moved off and, looking up at the letters in stone over the front door, said with a stupid mixture of awkwardness and pride, "Miss Cathy, I can read that now."

'"Wonderful," I exclaimed, "let me hear you – you are getting clever!"

'He slowly spelt out the name, "Hareton Earnshaw".

'"And the figures?" I cried, encouragingly.

'"I cannot tell them yet," he answered.

'I laughed loudly, and told him to walk away, as I had come to see Linton, not him. He became red in the face, and went off annoyed. I suppose he thought himself as educated as Linton!'

'Miss Cathy, dear,' I interrupted, 'you should remember that Hareton is as much your cousin as Master Linton, and you should respect his desire to learn. You made him ashamed of his ignorance before, and he tried to cure it to please you. If you had been brought up as he has, would you have been any better? He was as quick and intelligent a child as you ever were.'

'But wait, Ellen, and hear the rest.

'I entered. Linton was lying on the high-backed seat in the kitchen, and said that he was ill. He asked me to read to him for a bit, and I was going to begin when Hareton pushed the door open, seized Linton by the arm, and swung him off the seat.

'"Get to your own room," he said, in a voice of fury. "Take her there, if she comes to see you. You shan't keep me out of this place!"

'He swore, and nearly threw Linton out. I followed, dropping my book. He kicked it after me, and shut us out.

'Linton stood there white and trembling. He was not pretty then, Ellen. His eyes were full of an expression of mad, powerless fury. He shook the handle of the door. It was locked. He shouted out the most furious threats.

'I took hold of his hands, and tried to pull him away. In the end his cries were stopped by a terrible fit of coughing. Blood rushed from his mouth, and he fell to the ground. I ran into the yard, calling for Zillah. Meanwhile Hareton carried Linton upstairs. Joseph locked the door, and all three of them said I must go home.

'Hareton appeared again, a little way along the roadside. "Miss Cathy," he began "I'm sorry–"

'I struck him with my whip, and rode off.

'I didn't go the Heights the next evening. I had a fear that

Linton was dead. On the third day, I took courage and went. I found him, to my great joy, lying on a bed in a small, tidy room upstairs, reading one of my books. He would neither speak to me nor look at me for an hour, Ellen. And when he did open his mouth, it was to blame me, not Hareton, for what had happened! I got up and left the room, determined to visit him no more.

'It was so miserable going to bed, and getting up, and never hearing anything about him, that I could not stay away and, two days later, I rode over there. I told him that as he thought I came to hurt him, I had now come to say goodbye, and he must tell his father so.

'"You are so much happier than I, Cathy," he said, "that you ought to be better. Sometimes I *am* worthless and bad-tempered. But believe me, if I could be as sweet, kind, and good as you are, I would be. Your kindness has made me love you more deeply than if I deserved your love, and though I can't help showing my nature to you, I shall be sorry until I die!"

'I felt he spoke the truth, and I forgave him.

'About three times since then, we have been happy and hopeful. The rest of my visits have been dull and unhappy, partly from his selfishness and bad nature, partly from his sufferings. I've learned to bear them all. Mr Heathcliff purposely avoids me. I have hardly seen him.

'Now, Ellen, you've heard everything. You'll not tell Papa, will you?'

I thought the matter over, and then went straight to my master's room and told him the whole story. Mr Linton was anxious and upset. Cathy learned that her visits were to end. She wept, but without success. All she got to comfort her was a promise that her father would write and give her cousin permission to come to the Grange when he pleased. Perhaps, if he had realized his nephew's true nature and state of health, details of which I had kept from him, he would not have allowed even that.

Chapter 28   A Meeting on the Moors

Cathy was obedient to her father's commands. Her love for him was still the first feeling in her heart. He had spoken to her without anger, and with the deep emotion of one who is about to leave his dearest daughter among dangers and enemies. A few days later, he said to me: 'I wish my nephew would write, Ellen, or call. Tell me, sincerely, what you think of him. Is he changed for the better, or is there hope of improvement as he grows up?'

'He's very delicate, sir,' I replied, 'and hardly likely to reach manhood, but this I can say: he is not like his father, and if Miss Cathy had the misfortune to marry him, he would not be beyond her control.'

Edgar walked to the window and looked out towards Gimmerton church.

'I've often prayed,' he said, 'for the time to come when I would be laid beside my wife over there. But now I'm beginning to fear it. What can I do for Cathy? How can I leave her? I'd not care for one moment that Linton is Heathcliff's son, if he could comfort her for my loss. But if he should be unworthy – only a weak slave to his father – I cannot leave her to him!'

Spring arrived, but my master gained no real strength. He began once more his walks in the grounds with his daughter and, to her inexperienced eye, the colour in his cheeks and the brightness in his eyes were signs of a return to health.

He wrote once more to his nephew, expressing his desire to see him, and if the sick boy had been really fit to go out so far, I've no doubt his father would have allowed him to come. As it was, Linton replied saying that Mr Heathcliff objected to his visiting the Grange, but that he himself hoped to meet his uncle on his walks, and his cousin too.

Edgar, though he sympathized with the boy, could not at that time of year agree to his request, because he himself could not be

Cathy's companion. When summer came, and June still found him losing strength, he was at last persuaded to let the cousins ride or walk together, about once a week, under my protection. Though he had saved a yearly part of his income so that Cathy would have enough money when he died, he had a natural desire that she might keep, or at least return in a short time to, her old family home, and he considered her only chance of doing that was by a marriage with the young man who was going to own it.

He had no idea that his nephew was failing in health almost as fast as himself; nor had anyone, I believe. No doctor visited the Heights, and no one saw Master Heathcliff to report his condition to us. I myself began to imagine that my fears were false, and that he must actually be growing stronger, when he suggested riding and walking on the moors. I did not realize how wickedly his father treated him when he saw that his heartless plans were threatened with defeat by death.

It was already past midsummer when Cathy and I set out on her first ride to join her cousin. It was a heavy day, without sunshine. Our meeting place had been fixed where two roads met, but when we arrived there a little farm boy, sent as messenger, told us that Master Heathcliff was just this side of the Heights and would be very grateful if we would go on a little farther.

We found him only a quarter of a mile from his own door. He lay on the ground, waiting for us to come to him, and did not rise until we were within a few yards. He walked with difficulty, and looked very pale.

Cathy looked at him in grief and surprise, and asked whether he was worse than usual.

'No, better – better,' he replied, breathlessly, trembling and holding on to her hand, as if he needed support.

'But you look worse,' repeated his cousin. 'You are thinner and–'

'I'm tired,' he interrupted, hurriedly. 'It's too hot for walking. Let's rest here. I often feel sick. Father says I'm growing too fast.'

Cathy sat down, and he lay beside her. She talked, and he listened. He clearly had great difficulty in keeping up any kind of conversation. His lack of interest in what was said to him, and his lack of power to amuse her in any way, were so clear that she could not hide her disappointment.

A change had come over his whole person and manner. The unpleasant look had given place to a dull weakness: there was less childish temper and more of the self-pitying low spirits of a continually sick person. Cathy noticed as well as I did that he felt it a punishment, rather than a pleasure, to suffer our company, and she was quick to suggest, a little later, that she should leave.

This suggestion, unexpectedly, excited Linton and threw him into a strange state of fear. He looked anxiously towards the Heights, begging that she would remain another half-hour at least.

'Stay to rest yourself,' he said. 'And, Cathy, don't think or say that I am very unwell. It's the heavy weather and heat that makes me dull. I walked around, before you came, a great deal. Tell Uncle I'm in rather good health, will you?'

'I'll tell him that *you* say so,' replied my young lady, uncertainly.

'And be here again next Thursday,' he continued, avoiding her strange look. 'And – and, if you *do* meet my father, don't let him suppose that I've been silent and stupid. Don't look sad, or he'll be angry.'

'Is he severe to you now, Master Heathcliff?' I inquired.

Linton looked at me, but he did not answer. After another ten minutes, during which his head fell sleepily on his breast, and he did nothing but complain of tiredness or pain, Cathy began to pick berries to amuse herself.

'Why did he wish to see me?' she asked, in a low voice. 'It's just as if it were a duty he was forced to do, for fear that his father would be angry with him. But I'm not here to give Mr Heathcliff pleasure.'

Linton suddenly awoke.

'I thought I heard my father!' he exclaimed. 'Be quiet! He's coming.' And he held on to Cathy's arm.

Cathy freed herself and called to her horse.

'I'll be here next Thursday,' she cried, jumping up. 'Goodbye. Quick, Ellen.'

When we reached home, my master requested an account of the meeting. Both Cathy and I said little: Cathy, because she thought that her cousin was pretending as usual that his sufferings were greater than they were, and I, because I hardly knew what to hide, and what to tell.

Chapter 29   The Trap

Seven days passed, every one marking its passing by the rapid worsening of Edgar Linton's condition. We would have kept the truth from Cathy, but her own quick intelligence guessed what was coming. When Thursday came round, she could not bear to mention her ride. I did so, and obtained permission to order her out of doors, since her father's sick room had become her whole world and she spent every moment by his side. Her face had become pale with watching and sorrow, and my master gladly sent her off to what he imagined to be a happy change of scene.

He had a fixed idea that as his nephew was like him in appearance, he must be like him in mind, because Linton's letters, written, no doubt, under his father's eyes, gave few signs of his real character. Through understandable weakness, I did not correct this belief, asking myself what good there would be in disturbing my master's last days with information he was powerless to use.

Cathy's poor little heart was sad as we set out in the afternoon.

Linton was waiting in the same place as before. There was more life in his manner of receiving us this time, but not the life of high spirits nor of joy. It looked to me more like fear.

'It's late,' he said, speaking sharply and with difficulty. 'Is your father very ill? I thought you wouldn't come.'

Cathy's greeting froze on her lips.

'My father *is* very ill,' she said. 'Why didn't you send to free me from my promise, if you wished I wouldn't keep it? Come! I want an explanation. Playing and nonsense are completely driven out of my mind now; I've no time for pretence.'

Linton shivered, and looked at her, half ashamed.

'Pretence!' he said, in a low voice. 'Please, Cathy, don't look so angry. Scorn me as much as you please; I'm worthless, but I'm too weak for your anger – hate my father, and not me!'

'Nonsense!' cried Cathy, angrily. 'He's trembling, as if I were going to touch him! Get off! Let go of my dress!'

With tears pouring down his face, Linton had thrown himself on the ground. He seemed helpless with terror.

'Oh!' he wept, 'I can't bear it! Cathy, I am behaving falsely to you, too, and I dare not tell you now! But leave me, and I shall be killed! Dear Cathy, my life is in your hands! You have said you loved me, so perhaps you *will* agree – and he'll let me die with you!'

My young lady was thoroughly upset and afraid. She bent to raise him up.

'Agree to what?' she asked. 'To stay? Explain the meaning of this talk. Tell me at once what is weighing on your heart. You wouldn't do me any harm, would you? You wouldn't let anyone hurt your best friend, if you could prevent it?'

'But my father threatened me,' cried the boy with difficulty. 'I *dare* not tell.'

'Keep your secret, then,' said Cathy, with scornful pity. 'Save yourself; I'm not afraid.'

I heard a movement, and saw Heathcliff. He didn't look at my companions but, calling to me in an almost friendly way, said: 'It is something to see you so near my house, Nelly. How are they at the Grange?' he added, in a lower voice. 'It is said that Edgar Linton is on his deathbed: perhaps that's not true?'

'No, my master is dying,' I replied. 'It is true enough.'

'How long will he last, do you think?' he asked.

'I don't know.'

'Because,' he continued, looking at the two young people, 'that boy seems determined to defeat me. I'd thank his uncle to be quick and go before him.'

'I would say,' I remarked, 'that instead of wandering on the hills, he ought to be in bed, in the care of a doctor.'

'Get up, Linton!' he shouted. 'Don't twist about on the ground – up, this moment!'

Linton had sunk down again, in helpless fear, when his father looked at him. He tried several times to obey, but his strength failed him.

'I will, Father,' he said breathlessly. 'But leave me alone – I've done as you wished, I'm sure. Ah! Stay with me, Cathy. Give me your hand.'

'Take mine,' said his father, 'and stand on your feet. There, now. You would imagine I was cruel to him, Miss Cathy, to excite such terror. Be kind enough to walk home with him: he trembles if I touch him.'

'I can't go to Wuthering Heights,' said Cathy. 'My father has forbidden it. Linton, dear, your father won't harm you. Why are you so afraid?'

'Very well,' answered Heathcliff, 'we'll respect Cathy's decision. Come then, my brave boy! Are you willing to return in my company?'

He made a movement to seize the boy, but Linton, stepping back, held on to his cousin, and begged her in such a miserable manner to go with him that she could not refuse him. What frightened him, we could not imagine. We reached the door. Cathy walked in, and I stood waiting until she led the sick boy to a chair, expecting her to come straight out again.

Mr Heathcliff pushed me forward, made me sit down, and then turned and locked the door.

'I am by myself, and would like a little company,' he said. 'You shall have some tea. Hareton has gone with some cattle to the fields, and Zillah and Joseph are also out. Miss Linton, I give you what I have, though the present is hardly worth accepting. It is Linton I mean. Take your seat next to him.'

Cathy stepped close to Heathcliff, her dark eyes flashing.

'I'm not afraid of you,' she said. 'Give me that key! I wouldn't eat or drink here if I were dying of hunger!'

Heathcliff looked up with a sort of surprise at her anger; or possibly reminded by her voice and expression of the person from whom she got it. She had half succeeded in getting the key from his loosened fingers, when he recovered it.

'Now, Catherine Linton,' he said, 'stand back, or I shall knock you down.'

Taking no notice of his warning, she seized his closed hand, and finding that her nails had no effect, dug her teeth in rather sharply. Heathcliff gave me a look that prevented me from speaking for a moment. He opened his fingers suddenly, seized her, and gave her a number of blows on both sides of the head.

I rushed at him furiously.

'You devil!' I began.

A push on my chest silenced me. I am overweight and soon get out of breath. With the blow, and with fury, I fell back unsteadily, my lungs feeling ready to burst.

The scene was over in two minutes. Cathy, freed, put her two hands to her head. She trembled, poor thing, and leaned against the table in complete confusion.

'I know how to punish children, you see,' said the heartless man. 'Go to Linton now, as I told you, and cry as you like. I shall be your father tomorrow – all the father you'll have in a few days – and you will be punished again and again if you need it.'

Cathy ran to me instead of Linton, and knelt down and put her burning cheek on my knee, weeping aloud. Her cousin had moved back into a corner of his seat, as quiet as a mouse – pleased, I dare say, that punishment had been given not to him, but another. Heathcliff rose and made tea. He poured it out and handed me a cup.

'Wash away your anger,' he said, 'and help your own naughty pet and mine. I'm going to find your horses.'

Our first thought, when he left, was to force a way out. The kitchen door was locked outside and the windows were too narrow even for Cathy's little figure.

'Master Linton,' I cried, seeing that we could not escape, 'you know what your wicked father intends to do, and you shall tell us.'

'Yes, Linton,' said Cathy. 'It was for you I came, and it will be ungrateful if you refuse.'

'Give me some tea, I'm thirsty; then I'll tell you,' he answered. 'Mrs Dean, go away. I don't like you standing over me. Now, Cathy, you are letting your tears fall into my cup! I won't drink that. Give me another.'

Cathy pushed another to him, and dried her eyes. I was displeased by the miserable boy's calmness, since he was no longer in terror himself. His wild anxiety had disappeared as soon as we entered the Heights, so I guessed that he had been threatened with a terrible punishment if he failed to trick us into coming.

'Father wants us to be married,' he explained, after drinking some of the liquid. 'And he's afraid that I shall die if we wait, so we are to be married in the morning, and you are to stay here tonight.'

'*You* marry?' I exclaimed. 'Why – do you imagine that beautiful young lady, that healthy active girl, will tie herself to a little monkey like you?'

'Stay all night!' said Cathy, looking slowly round. 'Ellen, I'll burn the door down and get out.'

Linton was frightened again for his dear self.

'Won't you have me, and save me? Oh sweetest Cathy, you mustn't go and leave me! You *must* obey my father, you *must*!'

'I must obey my own,' she replied, 'and save him from this cruel anxiety. The whole night! What would he think! Be quiet! You're in no danger!'

Heathcliff now re-entered.

'Your animals have wandered off,' he said. 'Now, Linton, go to your room. Zillah won't be here tonight, so you must undress yourself.'

He held the door open, and his son rushed out like a frightened little dog. The door was locked again.

Heathcliff came closer to the fire, where my mistress and I stood silently. Cathy looked up and raised her hand to her cheek. Anyone else would have found it impossible to see this childish act with severity, but he looked fiercely at her and said: 'Oh, you aren't afraid of me? Your courage is well hidden!'

'I *am* afraid now,' she replied, 'because if I stay, my father will be miserable. Mr Heathcliff, let me go home! I promise to marry Linton. Papa would like me to, and I love him. Why should you force me to do what I'll do of my own free will?'

'Let him dare to force you!' I cried. 'There's law in the land, thank God, though we live in an out-of-the-way place.'

'Silence!' said the wicked man. 'I don't want *you* to speak! Miss Linton, I shall enjoy myself greatly in thinking that your father will be miserable. As to your promise to marry Linton, you will not leave this place until it is carried out.'

'Send Ellen, then, to let Papa know I'm safe!' exclaimed Cathy, weeping. 'Ellen, he'll think we are lost. What shall we do?'

'Not he! He'll think you were tired of looking after him, and ran off for a little amusement,' answered Heathcliff. 'You must admit that you entered my house of your own free will, in disobedience of his wishes. Weep as much as you like! It's nothing to me!'

'Mr Heathcliff, if Father thought I had left him on purpose, and if he died before I returned, how could I bear to live? I'm going to kneel here before you. You can't help pitying me!'

Heathcliff pushed her away with a curse. I was going to tell him what I thought of his behaviour, but I was silenced in the middle of a sentence by a threat that I would be shown into a room by myself, the next word I spoke.

It was getting dark. We heard a sound of voices at the gate. Our host hurried out immediately: *he* was quick to understand and act; *we* were not. There was talk for two or three minutes, and he returned alone.

'I thought it was your cousin Hareton,' I said to Cathy. 'Who knows – perhaps he might help you.'

'It was three servants sent to search for you from the Grange,' said Heathcliff. 'You should have opened the window and called out.'

At learning of this chance that we had missed, we both wept uncontrollably. He allowed us to weep on until nine o'clock, when he ordered us to go upstairs to Zillah's room.

Neither of us lay down. Cathy took up her position by the narrow window and watched for morning. I seated myself on a chair and blamed myself for failing in my duty.

At seven o'clock Heathcliff called Cathy out. I rose to follow, but he turned the key again.

'Be patient,' he said. 'I'll send up your breakfast.' And he left me still a prisoner in the room.

After two or three hours I heard a footstep. Hareton entered, bearing enough food for me all day.

'Stay one minute!' I began.

'No,' he cried, and went away.

And there I remained the whole day, and the whole of the next night; and another, and another. Five nights and four days I remained there, seeing nobody but Hareton, once every morning, and he was silent and paid no attention to any attempt to move him to pity.

Chapter 30   Mr Green Is Too Late

On the fifth morning, or rather afternoon, I heard a different step – lighter and shorter – and Zillah entered the room.

'Oh, my dear Mrs Dean,' she exclaimed. 'Well! There is talk about you in Gimmerton. I thought you were drowned in a pool, and Miss Cathy with you, until master told me you'd been found and he'd given you shelter here. And how long were you in the water? How are you feeling? Did master save you, Mrs Dean?'

'Your master is a true devil!' I replied.

'What do you mean?' asked Zillah. 'It's not his story: it's what they say in the village. When the master heard it, he just smiled and said the water had got into your head and made you a little mad, so he kept you safe until you recovered. He told me to unlock the door and tell you to go to the Grange, and to carry a message from him that your young lady will follow in time to attend your master's funeral.'

'Mr Edgar isn't dead?' I exclaimed. 'Oh! Zillah!'

'No, no. Sit down a moment, you're still sick from the accident, poor thing! He's not dead. The doctor thinks he may last one more day. I met him on the road and asked.'

I seized my outdoor things and hurried downstairs. There was no one around to tell me where Cathy might be. The place was full of sunshine and the door stood wide open. I stood there for a moment, when a slight cough drew my attention. Linton lay on a seat, sucking a stick of sugar.

'Where is Miss Cathy?' I demanded.

He sucked on like a baby.

'Has she gone?' I asked.

'No,' he replied. 'She's upstairs. She's not to go. We won't let her.'

'You won't let her!' I exclaimed. 'Direct me to her room immediately!'

'Father says I'm not to be soft with Cathy,' he answered. 'She's my wife, and it's shameful she should wish to leave me. He says she wants me to die so that she may have all my money, but she can't have it and she can't go home. She may cry and be sick as much as she pleases.'

He started on his sugar again, and closed his eyes.

'Master Heathcliff,' I went on, 'have you forgotten all Cathy's kindness to you last winter, when you said you loved her, and she brought you books, and sang you songs, and came to see you, in spite of bad weather? And now you believe what your father says, and join him against her!'

The corner of Linton's mouth fell, and he took the sweet from his lips.

'I can't stay with her,' he said. 'She cries so much that I can't bear it. She complains all night, and I can't sleep.'

'Is Mr Heathcliff out?' I inquired.

'He's in the yard,' he replied, 'talking to the doctor, who says that Uncle is dying at last. I'm glad, because I shall be master of the Grange after him – and Cathy always spoke of it as her house! It's mine: Papa says everything she has is mine. She offered me all her nice books, and her pretty birds, and her horse, if I would get the key of our room and let her out, but I told her she had nothing to give – they were mine, all mine. And then she cried, and took a little picture from her neck, two pictures in a gold case – on one side her mother, and on the other, Uncle, when they were young. I said they were mine, too, and tried to get them from her. The nasty thing pushed me off and hurt me. But when she heard Father coming she was afraid, and divided the case, and gave me her mother's picture and tried to hide the other, but Father took the one from me, and crushed the other under his foot, and struck Cathy down.'

'And were you pleased?' I asked.

'I didn't look,' he said. 'I shut my eyes every time my father strikes anything, he does it so hard. But she deserved punishing for pushing me. But when he had gone, she showed me her cheek cut on the inside, and collected up the bits of the picture, and has not spoken to me since. Perhaps she can't speak, because of the pain. I don't like to think so.'

'Can you get the key?' I asked.

'Yes, when I'm upstairs, but I can't walk upstairs now.'

'Which room is she in?'

'Oh, I shan't tell you that! It is our secret.'

He turned his face on to his arm, and shut his eyes again.

I considered it best to leave without seeing Mr Heathcliff, and to bring help for my young lady from the Grange. When I arrived home, my fellow servants were very surprised to see me, and happy to hear that their little mistress was safe.

I hurried to Edgar Linton's door.

How changed I found him, even in those few days! He thought of Cathy, and murmured her name.

'Cathy is coming, dear master,' I whispered. 'She is alive and well, and will be here, I hope, tonight.'

He half rose up, looked eagerly round the room, and then fell back unconscious. When he had recovered, I told him what had happened, and the reason for it. I said as little as possible against Linton, and I did not describe all his father's cruel behaviour.

263

He guessed that one of his enemy's purposes was to get hold of his money, as well as the land and house, for his son, or rather for himself. But my master could not understand why he did not wait for his death, having no idea how ill his nephew really was. He felt, though, that his will had better be changed. Instead of leaving Cathy's money in her own hands, he decided to put it in the care of some responsible people for her use during her life, and for her children if she had any, after her death. By that means, it could not pass to Heathcliff if Linton died.

I sent a man to fetch the lawyer, and four more, with suitable weapons, to the Heights, to demand the return of Cathy. Both parties were a long time returning. The first man returned to say that Mr Green had been out, and when he came would have a little business to do in the village, but he would be at the Grange before morning. The four men also came back without my mistress. They brought word that Cathy was ill and could not leave her room. I cursed the stupid men for believing such a story, and decided to go myself, at dawn, with a whole lot of men, and get her.

Happily I was saved the journey. At three o'clock in the morning I heard a knock at the door. Thinking it was the lawyer, I went down myself to admit him. My own sweet little mistress fell on my neck, weeping and crying: 'Ellen! Ellen! Is Papa still alive?'

I couldn't bear to be present at their meeting. After a quarter of an hour, I went in. Cathy's misery was as silent as her father's joy. He died, kissing her cheek.

Cathy remained by the deathbed until I managed to persuade her to come away and take some rest. At dinnertime the lawyer appeared, too late. He had called at Wuthering Heights and sold himself to Heathcliff, which was the cause of his delay.

He made himself busy ordering everything and everybody around the place. All the servants except myself were dismissed, and the funeral was hurried over. Cathy, Mrs Linton Heathcliff now, was allowed to stay at the Grange until her father's body had been laid side by side with her mother's, on the edge of the moor.

◆

The evening after the funeral, my young lady and I were seated in the library. Cathy had told me of how she had at last persuaded Linton to help her to escape. We had just agreed that the best thing that could happen to her would be to have permission to go on living at the Grange, at least during Linton's lifetime – he being allowed to join her there, and I to remain as housekeeper – when one of the dismissed servants who had not yet left, rushed in to say that Heathcliff was coming through the yard.

He made no ceremony of knocking or sending in his name. He was master, and walked straight in, without saying a word.

It was the same room into which he had been shown, as a guest, eighteen years before. Time had changed his appearance very little. He was the same man, his dark face rather more under control, his body a little heavier, perhaps. Cathy had risen, with the idea of rushing out, when she saw him.

'Stop!' he said, holding her by the arm. 'No more running away! I've come to fetch you home, and I hope you'll be an obedient daughter, and not encourage my son to further disobedience. He's suffered for that, I can tell you.'

'Why not let Cathy continue here,' I begged, 'and send Master Linton to her?'

'I'm looking for a tenant for the Grange,' he answered, 'and I want my children with me. Besides, that girl owes me her services for her food and room. I'm not going to keep her in laziness and rich living. Hurry and get ready.'

'I shall,' said Catherine. 'Linton is all I have to love in the world, and though you have done what you could to make us hate each other, you cannot succeed!'

'It is not I who will make him hateful to you – it is his own spirit. He's bitter about your going off, and I heard him draw a pleasant picture of what he would do to you if he were stronger.'

'I know he has a bad nature,' said Cathy. 'He's your son. But I'm glad that mine is better, to forgive it. And I know that he loves me, and for that reason I love him. Mr Heathcliff, *you* have *nobody* to love you. You *are* miserable, aren't you?'

'You will be sorry for yourself soon,' said Heathcliff, 'if you stand there another minute. Go and get your things.'

She went, and in her absence I began to beg for Zillah's place at the Heights but he would not agree. He told me to be silent and then, for the first time, looked round the room and at the pictures.

Having studied the painting of Mrs Linton, he said: 'I shall have that at home. Not because I need it, but . . .'

He turned quickly to the fire and, with a strange smile, continued, 'I'll tell you what I did yesterday! I got the man who was digging Edgar Linton's grave to remove the earth from *her* coffin lid and I opened it. It is still her face, but the gravedigger said it would change if the air blew on it, so I covered it again. Then I broke off one side of the coffin – not on her husband's side, curse him! – and I paid the man to break off one side of mine, the side nearest to her, when I'm laid there beside her.'

'You were very wicked, Mr Heathcliff,' I exclaimed. 'Weren't you ashamed to play such games with the dead?'

'Play games with her? No! *She* has been playing games with *me*, night and day, for eighteen years – without pause, without pity – until last night; and last night I was at peace. I dreamed I was sleeping the last sleep beside that sleeper, with my heart stopped and my cheek frozen against hers.

'It began strangely, that feeling,' he went on. 'You know I was wild after she died, and always, day after day, praying her spirit to return to me. I have a strong belief in ghosts. I am certain that they can and do exist among us! The day she was buried, there came a fall of snow. In the evening, I went to the churchyard. It was bitterly cold and, being alone, I said to myself, "I'll have her in my arms again!" I got a spade and began to dig. I had reached the coffin, and was on the point of opening it, when it seemed that I heard a murmur from someone above, close to the edge of the grave and, bending down, I thought, "If only I can get this off, I wish they would cover us both over with the earth." There was another murmur close to my ear. I appeared to feel warm breath. I knew that no living thing of flesh and blood was near, but I felt with complete certainty that Cathy was there, not under me, but on the earth. A sudden sense of happiness flowed through my heart, through every part of my body. I was indescribably comforted. Her presence was with me while I refilled the grave, and it led me home. You may laugh if you will, but I was sure I would see her there! The door was locked – that fool Hindley and my wife tried to stop me entering. I remember stopping to kick him, and then hurrying upstairs. I looked round impatiently – I felt her by me – I could almost see her, but I could not! And, since then, sometimes more and sometimes less, I've suffered from that unbearable misery! When I sat in the house, it seemed that if I went out I would meet her; when on the moors, that I would meet her coming in. She *must* be somewhere at the Heights, I was certain! And when I slept in her room, the moment I closed my eyes, she was either outside the window, or entering the room, or even resting her dear body on the same bed as she did as a child. I opened my eyes a hundred times a night – always to be disappointed! For eighteen years she was killing me slowly, with the ghost of a hope. Now, since I've seen her, I'm at peace – a little.'

Mr Heathcliff paused, and dried his forehead. His eyes were fixed on the fire; the expression on his face was strangely troubled, but less severe than usual. He only half addressed me, and I kept silent. After a short period, he looked once again at the picture, took it down, and leaned it against a chair.

As he was doing so, Cathy entered, announcing that she was ready when her horse was.

'Send the picture over tomorrow,' said Heathcliff to me. Then, turning to her, he added, 'You can do without your horse. Your own feet will serve you. Come along.'

'Goodbye, Ellen,' whispered my dear mistress. 'Come and see me.'

'Take care you do no such thing,' said her new father.

And, fixing Cathy's arm under his own, he hurried her away.

Chapter 31   Proud as a Princess

It was only last summer that Miss Cathy was married. I have paid a visit to the Heights, but I have not seen her since she went. Joseph would not let me enter, saying that she was not well and the master was not in. Zillah has told me something of the way in which they live. She thinks Cathy proud, and doesn't like her.

'The first thing she did,' Zillah said, 'on her arrival, was to run upstairs without even wishing Joseph and myself good evening. She shut herself up in Linton's room, and remained until morning. Then, while the master and Hareton were at breakfast, she entered and asked if the doctor could be sent for, as her cousin was very ill.

'"We know that," answered Heathcliff, "but his life is worth nothing, and I won't spend anything on him."

'"But I can't tell what to do," she said, "and if no one will help me, he'll die!"

'"Leave us!" cried the master. "No one here cares what happens to him. If you do, act the nurse; if you don't, lock him up and leave him."

'Then she began to ask me for help, and I said I'd had enough trouble with the boy. We each had our work to do, and hers was to look after Linton.

'How they managed, I don't know. He seemed to be complaining day and night, and she had very little rest, judging by her white face and heavy eyes. She sometimes came into the kitchen as if she would beg for help, but I never dare disobey the master, Mrs Dean, and it was no business of mine. I did pity her, I'm sure, but I didn't want to lose my post, you know.

'At last, one night, she came into my room, saying, "Tell Mr Heathcliff that his son is dying. Get up now and tell him!"

'She disappeared. I lay for a quarter of an hour, but heard nothing.

'"She's mistaken," I said to myself.

'My sleep was disturbed a second time by a sharp ringing of Linton's bell. The master called me to see what was the matter. I gave him Cathy's message.

'In a few minutes he came out with a lighted candle and went to their room. Mrs Heathcliff was seated by the bedside. Mr Heathcliff went up, held the light to Linton's dead face, and touched him. Afterwards, he turned to Cathy.

'"Now," he said, "how do you feel?"

'"He's safe, and I'm free; but you have left me to struggle so long against death, alone, that I feel and see only death."

'I gave her a little wine. Hareton and Joseph, woken by the noise, entered. Joseph was glad of the boy's removal, I think. Hareton seemed a bit upset, though he was more occupied with staring at Cathy.

'In the morning she said she was ill. She stayed upstairs for two weeks.'

Zillah visited her twice a day, and would have been rather more friendly, but her attempts at increasing kindness were proudly refused.

Heathcliff went up once, to show her Linton's will. He had left the whole of his, and what had been her money, to his father. The miserable boy was persuaded, or threatened, into that act during her week's absence, when his uncle died. He could not change the lands, being under age, but Mr Heathcliff has claimed and kept them in his wife's right, and his own also. I suppose that since Cathy has no friends or money to support her case, she can do nothing about this.

'Nobody,' Zillah went on, 'ever went near her door, except on that one occasion, other than myself. The first time she came down was a Sunday afternoon. She said she could not bear the cold upstairs any longer. Heathcliff had gone off to Thrushcross Grange, and Joseph was at church. I told Hareton his cousin would probably sit with us. He became red in the face, and passed his eyes over his hands and clothes. I saw he wanted to look respectable, so, laughing, I offered to help him. He was uncertain at first, but I talked him into accepting my help.

'The mistress walked in, as cold as ice and as proud as a princess. I got up and offered her my seat in the armchair. No, she turned up her nose at my politeness. Hareton rose too, asking her to come and sit close to the fire. She got a chair for herself, and placed it at a distance from both of us.

'Having sat until she was warm, she began to look around and discovered a number of books on a shelf. They were too high up for her to reach, and her cousin, after watching for a while, at last found the courage to help her.

'She didn't thank him, but she had accepted his help, and he was brave enough to stand behind as she examined the books, and even to point out what pleased him best in certain old pictures. Nor was he discouraged by the sharp manner in which she drew the page away from his finger. He was happy to look at her instead of the book. His attention, by degrees, became fixed on the study of her thick, silky hair. He couldn't see her face, and she couldn't see him. And, like a child, he went on from staring to touching. He put out his hand and passed it over one curl as gently as if it were a bird. If he had stuck a knife into her neck, she could not have turned on him in such a fury.

'"Get away this moment! How dare you touch me! I can't bear you!"

'Hareton moved away, looking foolish. He sat down very quietly, and she continued turning over the pages of books. Finally he came over to me and whispered, 'Will you ask her to read to us, Zillah? I should like to hear her.'

'"Mr Hareton wishes you to read to us," I said at once. "He'd be very grateful."

'She looked angry and answered, "The whole set of you will be good enough to understand that I will accept no pretence of kindness from you! When I would have given my life for one kind word, you avoided me. I'm driven down here by the cold, not to amuse you or enjoy your company."

'"But I offered more than once, and asked," said Hareton. "I asked Mr Heathcliff to let me nurse for you when Linton was sick—"

'"Be silent! I'll go out of doors, rather than have your unpleasant voice in my ears!" said my lady.

'The icy weather continued, and she was forced to keep us company more and more. But since then I've been as unfriendly as herself, and she has no one among us who likes her, and she doesn't deserve one.'

On hearing this account from Zillah, I decided to leave my employment, and take a small house, and get Cathy to come and live with me. But Mr Heathcliff would never allow it, and I can see no way out unless she could marry again.

And that, Mr Lockwood, is the present state of affairs at Wuthering Heights.

Told by Mr Lockwood

Chapter 32 - I Revisit the Heights

Soon after recovering from my illness last year, I left Thrushcross Grange and returned to London. The loneliness and wildness of the place had not suited me at all, and soon I had almost forgotten my stay there.

But this September I was invited to the north for the shooting season and, on my journey to my friend's property, I unexpectedly came within fifteen miles of Gimmerton. A sudden desire to visit Thrushcross Grange again seized me.

It seemed to me I might as well pass the night under my own roof as at a hotel. Besides, I could easily take a day to arrange matters with my landlord, as I had warned him that when my agreed year as his tenant was at an end in October, I did not intend to keep the house.

I rode into the courtyard at the Grange and saw an old woman sitting on the steps.

'Is Mrs Dean inside?' I asked.

'Mrs Dean? No!' she answered. 'She doesn't live here. She's up at the Heights now.'

I made arrangements for the night, and then climbed the stony road to Mr Heathcliff's home just as the sun was setting.

This time I did not have to unchain the gate, or to knock. A sweet scent of garden flowers hung on the air. The doors and windows were open, and two members of the household, seated just inside, could be both seen and heard. I paused.

A voice, as sweet as a silver bell, was ordering someone else to read some sentences correctly.

A deep male voice began to read. The speaker was a young man, respectably dressed and seated at a table with a book in front of him. His good-looking face shone with pleasure, and his eyes kept wandering impatiently from the page to a small white hand over his shoulder. Its owner stood behind, her light, shining curls touching, now and then, his brown hair, as she bent to examine his studies. It was lucky he could not see her pretty face, or he would never have been so steady.

The lesson was completed, not free from mistakes, but the pupil claimed a reward and received kisses that he generously returned. Then Cathy and Hareton, for it was them that I was watching, came to the door, and from their conversation I judged they were about to go for a walk on the moor. Clearly, an interruption by me would not be welcome.

I went round to find the kitchen. Here, too, the door was open, and at it sat my old friend Nelly Dean, sewing and singing a song, which was often interrupted from inside by the complaining voice of old Joseph.

Mrs Dean jumped to her feet, crying: 'Why, it's Mr Lockwood! How could you think of returning in this way? All's shut up at the Grange.'

'I am leaving again tomorrow,' I answered. 'And how have you come here?'

'Zillah left, and Mr Heathcliff wished me to come, soon after you went to London, sir. Have you walked from Gimmerton?'

'From the Grange. And while they prepare my rooms there, I want to finish my business with your master.'

'What business, sir? He's gone out at present.'

'About the rent.'

'Oh! Then it is with Mrs Heathcliff you must settle, or rather with me. She hasn't learned to manage her affairs yet, and I act for her: there's nobody else.'

I looked surprised.

'Ah! You haven't heard of Heathcliff's death, I see,' she continued.

'Heathcliff dead? How long ago?'

'Three months. Sit down, and I'll tell you all about it. But wait! You've had nothing to eat, have you?'

'I want nothing. I have ordered supper at home. You sit down, too. I never thought of his dying. You don't expect them back for some time – the young people?'

'No, I have to be cross with them every evening about their late wanderings, but they don't listen to me.'

And then she told me about the strange end of Heathcliff.

PART 5   THE FRUIT OF REVENGE IS TASTELESS
(FEBRUARY–APRIL 1802)

Told by Mrs Ellen Dean

Chapter 33   Cathy Is Bored

When, within two weeks of your leaving the Grange, Mr Lockwood, I was sent for to go to Wuthering Heights, I obeyed joyfully, for Cathy. My first meeting with her upset me and filled me with grief: she had changed so much since our separation. Mr Heathcliff did not explain why he had changed his mind about my coming. He only said he was tired of seeing Cathy, so I must make the little room upstairs, which had belonged to Linton, into my sitting room and keep her with me. She seemed pleased with this arrangement and, a little at a time, I secretly brought over from the Grange a number of books and other things.

Cathy was happy enough at first, but after a short time she became restless and difficult to please. For one thing, she was forbidden to move out of the garden. For another, in looking after the house, I was forced to leave her frequently, and she complained of loneliness. She preferred quarrelling with Joseph in the kitchen to sitting in peace by herself. I did not mind this, but Hareton often had to be in the kitchen too. Though at the beginning she either left when he arrived, or quietly joined me in my work, taking no notice of him at all, after a time she changed her behaviour and was unable to leave him alone – she talked about him, remarking on his laziness and stupidity, asking herself how he could bear the life he led.

'He's just like a dog, isn't he, Ellen?' she once remarked, 'or a horse? He does his work, eats his food, and sleeps. Do you ever dream, Hareton? Can't you speak to me?'

She looked at him, but he refused to look at her.

'I know why Hareton never speaks when I am in the kitchen,' she exclaimed on another occasion. 'He's afraid I'll laugh at him. Ellen, what do you think? He began to teach himself to read once, and because I laughed he burned his books and gave it up. Wasn't he a fool?'

'Weren't you naughty?' I said. 'Answer me that.'

'Perhaps I was,' she went on, 'but I didn't expect him to be so silly. Hareton, if I gave you a book, would you take it now?'

She placed one in his hand. He threw it away and threatened her.

'Well, I shall put it in the table drawer,' she said, 'and I'm going to bed.'

She whispered to me to watch whether he touched it when she went out. He would not come near it, to her great disappointment. I saw she was sorry about his continued unfriendliness and knew that it was her fault for frightening him off improving himself.

She tried hard to put right the harm she had done. While I was at work in the kitchen she would bring in some pleasant book and read aloud to me. When Hareton was there, she would pause at some interesting point and leave the book open at the page. She did this repeatedly, but he was determined to ignore it, and in the wet weather he got into the habit of smoking with Joseph, while on fine evenings he went off shooting.

All the time, Cathy complained and worried me to talk to her, and said that her life was useless.

◆

Mr Heathcliff, who found any sort of society less and less desirable, had almost forbidden Hareton to enter his room. The young man, owing to an accident at the beginning of March, had to remain at home in the kitchen for several days. His gun had exploded while he was out on the hills by himself. His arm was hurt, and he had lost a good deal of blood. It suited Cathy to have him by the fireside, or at least made her hate her room upstairs more.

On Easter Monday, Joseph went to Gimmerton market with some cattle, and in the afternoon I was busy ironing clothes in the kitchen. Hareton sat in silence as usual in the chimney corner, and my little mistress was drawing pictures on the windows, and amusing herself by little bursts of song and whispered exclamations and quick looks of impatience in the direction of her cousin, who went on smoking and looking into the fire.

I paid little attention to her actions, but soon I heard her begin: 'I've found out, Hareton, that I want – that I'm glad – that I would like you to be my cousin, now, if you hadn't become so unpleasant to me, and rough.'

Hareton gave no answer.

'Hareton! Hareton! Hareton! Do you hear?'

'Get off with you!' he said fiercely.

'Let me take that pipe,' she said, slowly stretching her hand out, and removing it from his mouth.

Before he could attempt to get it back, it was broken and

thrown in the fire. He swore at her, and seized another.

'Stop!' she cried. 'You must listen to me first, and I can't speak with those clouds floating in my face.'

'Will you go away,' he exclaimed, 'and leave me alone!'

'No,' she replied. 'Come, you must take notice of me. You are my cousin, and must recognize me. When I call you stupid, I don't mean I'm scornful of you.'

'I shall have nothing to do with you, and your cursed making fun of me,' he answered, 'and I'll never look at you again. Move out of the way, now, this minute!'

Cathy went to the window seat, biting her lip and trying not to weep.

'You should be friends with your cousin, Mr Hareton,' I said, 'as she is sorry for her past behaviour. It would do you a great deal of good, to have her for a companion.'

'A companion?' he cried. 'When she hates me, and doesn't think me fit to clean her shoes?'

'It's not I who hate you, it's you who hate me!' Cathy said, now openly weeping. 'You hate me more than Mr Heathcliff does.'

'That's not true,' began Hareton. 'Why then have I made him angry, by defending you a hundred times – and even when you laughed at me, and scorned me!'

'I didn't know you defended me,' she answered, drying her eyes, 'and I was angry and bitter at everybody. But now I thank you, and beg you to forgive me.'

She came to the fire, and offered her hand. His face grew as dark as a thundercloud, and he would not see it or take it.

Cathy must have guessed that it was pride, and not dislike, that caused the refusal because, after remaining a moment undecided, she bent down and gave his cheek a gentle kiss. The naughty thing thought I had not seen her and, moving away, took her former seat by the window. I shook my head disapprovingly, and she went red.

Hareton was very careful, for some minutes, that his face should not be seen, and when he did raise it, he did not know where to turn his eyes.

Cathy passed the time in wrapping a fine book neatly in white paper and, having tied it with string, and addressed it to 'Mr Hareton Earnshaw', she asked me to be her messenger and bear the present to him.

'And tell him, if he'll take it, I'll come and teach him to read it,' she said, 'and if he refuses, I'll go upstairs and never trouble him again.'

I carried it, and repeated the message. Hareton would not open his fingers, so I laid it on his knee. I returned to my work.

Cathy leaned her head and arms on the table until she heard the slight noise of the covering being removed, then she crept away and seated herself quietly by her cousin. He trembled, and his face shone. All his rudeness had left him. He could not at first find the courage to say a word in reply to her questioning look.

'Say you forgive me, Hareton, do!'

He murmured something that could not be heard.

'And you'll be my friend?'

'But you'll be ashamed of me every day of your life,' he answered, 'and I can't bear it.'

'So you won't be my friend?' she said, smiling sweet as sugar.

I could hear no further talk but, on looking round again, I saw two happy shining faces bent over the pages of the accepted book.

The friendship grew rapidly, though there were sometimes interruptions. Hareton could not be educated with a wish, and my young lady was not a model of patience. But as both their minds had the same idea – one loving and desiring good opinion, the other loving and desiring to give praise – they managed in the end to make a success of their relationship.

Chapter 34   Two or Three Bushes

On the day following that Monday, Cathy arrived downstairs before me and went out into the garden, where she had seen her cousin doing some light work. When I called her in to breakfast, I saw that she had persuaded him to clear a large area of ground of some fruit bushes, and they were busy planning to bring some plants over from the Grange.

I was worried at the change that had been made in a short half-hour. The fruit bushes were Joseph's work and she had fixed her choice of a flowerbed in the middle of them.

'There! That will be shown to the master!' I exclaimed. 'We shall have a fine explosion, see if we don't!'

'I'd forgotten they were Joseph's,' answered Hareton, 'but I'll tell him I did it.'

We always ate our meals with Mr Heathcliff. I took the mistress's place in making tea and serving the meat. Cathy usually sat by me, but today she crept nearer to Hareton.

'Now mind you don't talk to and notice your cousin too much,' was my whispered advice as we entered the room. 'It will certainly annoy Mr Heathcliff, and he'll be angry with you both.'

'I'm not going to,' she answered.

A minute later, she had moved closer to him and was pushing flowers into the food on his plate.

He dared not speak, he dared hardly look, but she went on until he could not keep back a smile. I looked disapproving, and she looked in the direction of the master, whose mind was occupied with other matters, as his expression showed. She became serious, but soon afterwards she started her nonsense again. At last, Hareton laughed softly.

Mr Heathcliff turned and looked at our faces. Cathy met his eye with her usual look of fear mixed with scorn.

'It is just as well that you are out of my reach,' he exclaimed. 'What makes you stare at me with those eyes? Down with them! I thought I had cured you of laughing.'

'It was I,' murmured Hareton.

Mr Heathcliff looked at him for a bit, and then silently went on with his breakfast. We had nearly finished when Joseph appeared at the door, showing plainly by his trembling lip and furious eyes that the attack on his precious bushes had been discovered. His jaws worked like those of a cow, and his speech was difficult to understand. Heathcliff listened impatiently to his long string of complaints.

'Is the fool drunk?' he asked at last. 'Hareton, is it you he's finding fault with?'

'I've pulled up two or three bushes,' replied the young man.

'And why have you pulled them up?'

Cathy put in her word.

'We wanted to plant some flowers there,' she said. 'I'm the only person to blame.'

'And who gave you permission to touch a thing about the place?' demanded Heathcliff, greatly surprised. 'And who ordered you to obey her?' he added, turning to Hareton.

The young man was speechless. His cousin replied: 'You shouldn't mind me having a few yards of earth to make pretty, when you have taken all my land!'

'Your land! You never had any!'

'And my money,' she continued, returning his angry look and biting into the last piece of her breakfast.

'Silence!' he exclaimed. 'Finish, and go!'

'And Hareton's land, and his money,' she went on. 'Hareton and I are friends now, and I shall tell him all about you!'

The master seemed unable to reply for a moment. He became pale and stood up, eyeing her with an expression of murderous hate.

'If you strike me, Hareton will strike you,' she said, 'so you may as well sit down!'

Hareton tried in a whisper to persuade her to go.

'He'll not obey you any more, you wicked man,' said Cathy, 'and he'll soon hate you as much as I do!'

'Be quiet!' murmured the young man. 'I won't hear you speak like that to him.'

'But you'll not let him strike me?'

'Come away,' he whispered.

It was too late. Heathcliff had caught hold of her. He had his hand in her hair. Hareton attempted to free the curls, begging him not to hurt her this time. Heathcliff's black eyes flashed. He seemed ready to tear Cathy to pieces. I was just coming to help her, when all of a sudden his fingers loosened. He moved them to her arm and stared fixedly at her face. Then he pushed his hand over his eyes, stood a moment to control himself and, turning to Cathy, said with forced calmness: 'You must learn to avoid putting me into a fury, or I shall really murder you some time! Go to Mrs Dean, and stay with her. As to Hareton, if I see him listen to you, I'll send him to earn his living where he can get it. Your love will lose him the little he has! Leave me, all of you!'

I led my young lady out. She was too glad to escape to protest.

At dinnertime I advised her to have her meal upstairs, but as soon as he saw her empty seat Heathcliff sent me to call her.

He spoke to none of us, ate very little and went out directly afterwards, saying that he would not return before the evening.

Chapter 35 'A Poor Ending to My Struggles'

During Heathcliff's absence that day, the two new friends settled themselves in the house, and I heard Hareton speak firmly to his cousin, when she offered to tell the story of Heathcliff's behaviour towards his father. He said he would not allow a word to be spoken to him against Heathcliff. It did not matter what Heathcliff was like; he would stand by him, and he would rather she spoke badly of himself, as she used to do, than begin on Heathcliff. Cathy got annoyed at this, but he asked how she would like him to speak badly of *her* father, and then she understood that Hareton was joined to the master of Wuthering Heights by ties stronger than reason could break – chains, formed by habit, that it would be cruel to attempt to loosen. She showed a good heart, from that time, in avoiding both complaints and expressions of hate concerning Heathcliff, and admitted to me her sorrow that she had tried to raise bad feeling between him and Hareton. In fact, I don't believe she has ever breathed a word, in her cousin's hearing, against her enemy since.

When this slight disagreement was over, they were friends again and returned to being pupil and teacher. I came to sit with them, and I felt so comforted to watch them, that I did not notice how time was passing. You know, they both appeared to me, in some degree, as my children. I had been proud of one for a long time, and now, I was sure, the other would be an equal cause of satisfaction. His honest, warm and intelligent nature rapidly shook off the clouds of ignorance and degradation in which he had been brought up, and Cathy's sincere praise encouraged his steady progress. His brightening mind brightened his face too. I could hardly believe it was the same person I had seen on the day when I discovered my little lady at Wuthering Heights after her ride to the rocks.

While I admired, and they worked on, evening came and the master returned. He came on us unexpectedly, entering by the front way, and he had a full view of the three of us before we could raise our heads. I thought there was never a pleasanter or more harmless sight. The red firelight shone gently on the two young heads and showed their faces lit up with the eager interest of children, because though he was twenty-three and she eighteen, each had so much that was new to learn and to feel that neither appeared grown-up.

They lifted their heads together. Perhaps you haven't noticed that their eyes are exactly alike, and they are those of Catherine Earnshaw. The present Cathy has no other likeness to her, except a certain width of forehead. With Hareton, the likeness goes further, and at that moment it was particularly clear because his mind was unusually active. I suppose that this likeness affected Mr Heathcliff. He walked to the fireplace, noticeably upset. He looked at the young man and took the book from his hand, looking quickly at the page and returning it without any remark. He made a sign to Cathy to leave. Her companion soon followed, and I too was about to go but he ordered me to sit still.

'It's a poor ending, isn't it,' he remarked, after a minute of silence, 'an unsatisfactory ending to my struggles? I turn all my energies to planning the destruction of the two families, and when everything is ready I find that the will to act has disappeared! My old enemies have not beaten me, and now would be the exact moment to revenge myself on their children. I could do it and no one could prevent me! But what is the use? It's not that I am showing generosity – I have lost the power to enjoy their destruction, and I am too lazy to destroy for nothing.

'Nelly, a strange change is taking place. I'm in its shadow at present. I take so little interest in my daily life that I hardly remember to eat and drink. Those two who have left the room are the only objects that have a clear appearance to me and that appearance causes me pain. About *her* I won't speak, and I don't desire to think. Her presence maddens me. *He* affects me differently.

'Five minutes ago, Hareton seemed a living picture of my youth. I felt for him in a variety of ways. In the first place, his extreme likeness to Catherine connected him with her in my mind. Not that this is his most powerful effect on my imagination, because what is *not* connected with her, to me? I cannot look down at this floor without seeing her face shaped on the stones! In every cloud, in every tree, I see her! The most ordinary faces of men and women deceive me with a likeness. The whole world is a horrible collection of reminders that she did exist, and that I have lost her!

'Well, Hareton's appearance was the ghost of my undying love, of my degradation, my pride, my happiness and my suffering . . . but it is madness to repeat these thoughts to you!'

'What do you mean by a change, Mr Heathcliff?' I said, worried by his manner, though he was neither in danger of losing his senses nor of dying. According to my judgement, he was quite strong and healthy and, as to his imagination, he had always from childhood taken pleasure in strange ideas. He might have strange fixed ideas on the subject of his lost love, but on every other point his brain was as sharp as mine.

'I shall not know until it comes,' he said.

'You have no feeling of illness, have you?'

'No, Nelly, I have not.'

'Then you are not afraid of death?'

'Afraid? No!' he replied. 'I have neither fear nor hope of death. Why should I? With my strength and healthy way of life, I ought to remain on the earth until there is hardly a black hair on my head! But I can't continue in this condition! I have to remind myself to breathe – almost to remind my heart to beat! I have a single desire, and my whole being is eager to realize it! I'm certain that it will be realized – and soon – because it has eaten up my existence. Oh, God! It is a long fight. I wish it were over.'

He began to walk restlessly up and down, murmuring terrible things to himself, until I began to believe that a sense of guilt had filled his heart with pain. I asked myself how it would end.

Chapter 36   The Change Comes

For some days after that evening, Mr Heathcliff avoided meeting us at meals, but he would not agree to allow Hareton and Cathy to eat elsewhere. He disliked giving way so completely to his feelings, preferring instead to be absent himself, and taking food about once in twenty-four hours.

One night, after the family were in bed, I heard him go downstairs and out of the front door. In the morning he was still away. It was April then, the weather was sweet and warm, the grass green, and the two apple trees on the southern wall in full flower. Cathy suggested that I bring a chair and do my work outside, and she persuaded Hareton to dig and arrange her little garden, now moved to this corner to satisfy Joseph. I was enjoying the blue sky and the warm sun when my young lady, who had run down near the gate to get some flower roots for a border, returned and informed us that Mr Heathcliff was coming in.

'And he spoke to me,' she said, with surprise. 'He told me to get away as fast as I could. But he looked so different that I stopped for a moment to stare at him.'

'How?' asked Hareton.

'Why, almost bright and cheerful – no, more than that – very much excited, and wild, and glad!'

I made an excuse to go in. Heathcliff stood at the open door. He was pale, and he trembled, but he had a strange joyful light in his eyes.

'Will you have some breakfast?' I said. 'You must be hungry.'

'No, I'm not hungry,' he answered, rather scornfully.

'I don't think it right to wander out of doors at night. It isn't wise, at least, in this wet season. You'll catch a bad cold.'

'Nothing that I can't bear.'

I noticed that he was breathing very fast and hard.

At midday he sat down to dinner with us and received a plate of food from my hands. He took his knife and fork, and was going to begin, when he suddenly laid them on the table, looked eagerly towards the window, then rose and went out. We saw him walking in the garden, and soon Hareton said he would go and ask him why he would not eat. He thought we had upset him in some way.

'Well, is he coming?' cried Cathy, when her cousin returned.

'No, but he's not angry. He told me to return to you, and asked how I could want the company of anybody else.'

I set his plate to keep warm by the fire. After an hour or two he re-entered, the same unnatural appearance of joy under his dark forehead, the same bloodless colour, and his teeth showing now and then in a kind of smile, his body shivering, not as one shivers from cold and weakness, but as a tight-stretched string trembles at a touch.

'Have you heard any good news lately, Mr Heathcliff?' I exclaimed. 'You look strangely excited.'

'Where would good news come from to me? And Nelly, once and for all, let me beg you to warn Hareton and the other one to keep away from me. I wish to have this place to myself.'

'Tell me why you are so strange, Mr Heathcliff!'

'I'll tell you. Last night, I was in misery. Today I am within sight of my heaven. I have my eyes on it. Only three feet separate me from it! And now you'd better go.'

I took away his uneaten dinner, more uncertain than ever.

He did not leave the house again, and at eight o'clock I thought I had better carry a candle and supper to him.

He was leaning against the edge of an open window. The fire had burned to ashes, and the room was filled with the cold, wet air, so still that the murmur of the stream down at Gimmerton could be heard. I began shutting the windows, one after another, until I came to him.

'Must I close this?' I asked, in order to call his attention.

The light flashed on his face as I spoke. What a terrible shock I got! Those deep black eyes, that smile, that deathly paleness! It appeared to me to be not Mr Heathcliff but an evil spirit, and in my terror I let the candle go out, and it left me in darkness.

'Yes, close it,' he said, in his familiar voice. 'There, that was foolish of you. Be quick, and bring another candle.'

I hurried out in a state of fear, and told Joseph to take a light. He went, and came back at once with the supper in his hand, explaining that the master was going to bed, and would not eat until morning.

We heard him go upstairs immediately. He did not enter his usual room, but turned into the one with the big closed-in wooden bed, where Catherine Earnshaw used to sleep.

It was a troubled night for me. In my mind I went over and over the strange life and nature of Heathcliff, remembering how I had looked after him as a child and watched him grow up.

'But where did he come from, the little dark thing, sheltered by a good man to the ruin of his family?' I asked myself. And I began, half dreaming, to imagine some suitable parents for him.

◆

Next morning, I prepared breakfast as usual for the household, and as Cathy and Hareton preferred taking theirs out of doors, I laid a little table for their use.

On re-entering, I found Mr Heathcliff downstairs. He and Joseph were talking about some farming business. He gave clear, exact directions concerning the matter discussed, but he spoke rapidly and had the same excited expression as on the day before. When Joseph left the room, he took his usual seat and I put coffee in front of him. He pulled it nearer, and then rested his arms on the table and looked at the opposite wall, fixing his feverish eyes on one particular place with such eager interest that he stopped breathing for half a minute.

'Come, now,' I exclaimed, pushing some bread against his hand. 'Eat, and drink that, while it is still hot.'

He didn't notice me, but still he smiled.

'Mr Heathcliff! Master!' I cried. 'Don't, I beg you, stare as if you saw a ghost!'

'Don't, I beg you, shout so loud,' he replied. 'Turn round, and tell me, are we by ourselves?'

'Of course.'

With a quick movement of his hand he made a space in front among the breakfast things, and leaned forward to stare more comfortably.

Now, I saw, he was not looking at the wall. It seemed that he kept his eyes fixed on something about two yards away. And whatever it was, it communicated, seemingly, both pleasure and pain, in extremes; at least the expression on his face suggested that idea. The imagined object was not fixed either.

His eyes followed it with unfailing watchfulness and, even when he was speaking to me, were never turned away. I reminded him of his food, but without success.

I sat, a model of patience, trying to attract his attention, until he became annoyed and got up. He left the house, passed slowly down the garden path, and disappeared through the gate.

The hours crept by. Another evening came. I did not go to rest until late, and when I did I couldn't sleep.

Heathcliff returned after midnight and shut himself up in the sitting room. I listened and, after a time, dressed and came downstairs.

I could hear Heathcliff walking restlessly up and down in the room. The silence was frequently broken by strange cries and the sound of murmured speech. The only word I could catch was the name of Catherine, joined with some wild word of love or suffering, and spoken as one would speak to a person who was present – low and serious and torn from the depths of his soul.

I hadn't the courage to walk in, so I made a noise while attending to the kitchen fire. He opened the door then and said: 'Nelly, come here. Is it morning?'

'It is striking four,' I answered.

'Come and light me a fire.'

He wandered up and down, breathing rapidly.

'When day breaks, I'll send for Green,' he said. 'I wish to make inquiries of him concerning some matters of law, while I can still act calmly. I have not made my will yet, and I cannot decide how to leave my property. I wish I could destroy it from the face of the earth!'

'I wouldn't talk so, Mr Heathcliff,' I said. 'Leave your will for a time. You'll still live to be sorry for your many unjust acts! You're in a nervous state, and the way you've passed these three days would take anyone's strength away. Do take some food, and some rest.'

'You might as well urge a man struggling in the water to rest within arm's length of the shore! I must reach it first, and then I'll rest. Well, never mind Mr Green. As to my unjust acts, I've done none and I'm sorry for nothing. I'm too happy, but I'm not happy enough. My soul's happiness kills my body, but does not satisfy itself.'

'Happy, master?' I cried. 'If you would hear me without being angry, I might offer you some advice.'

'Give it.'

'You should know, Mr Heathcliff, that from the time you were about thirteen years old, you have led a wicked, irreligious life. Could it be harmful now to send for a priest to guide you, and help you to a change of heart?'

'I'm more grateful than angry, Nelly, as you have reminded me of the manner in which I desire to be buried. It is to be carried to the churchyard in the evening, and to be laid by her side. You and Hareton may follow my body, and make sure, particularly, that the gravedigger obeys my directions concerning the two coffins! No priest need come, nor need any prayer be said over my grave. I tell you, I have nearly reached my heaven.'

Hearing the other members of the household getting up, he rose and went to his own room.

Chapter 37   The End of Heathcliff

That same afternoon, while Joseph and Hareton were at their work, he came into the kitchen and, with a wild look, told me to come and sit with him, as he wanted somebody there. I refused, telling him plainly that his strange talk frightened me.

'I believe you think I'm an evil spirit,' he said, 'something too horrible to live under a respectable roof!' Then, turning to Cathy, who hid behind me, he added, half jokingly, 'Will *you* come, girl? I'll not hurt you. No! To you, I've made myself hateful. Well, there is *one* who will not move away from my company! Oh, God! She's without pity! It's too much for flesh and blood to bear, even mine.'

He asked no one else to stay with him. At sunset he went to his room, and all through the night we heard him murmuring to himself. Hareton was anxious to enter, but I told him to fetch the doctor.

When he came, Heathcliff would not open the door. He said he was better and wanted to be left alone, so Doctor Kenneth went away.

The following evening was very wet. It poured until daybreak and, as I took my morning walk round the house, I noticed the master's window was open and the rain blowing straight in. He must be up, I thought. He could not be in bed, as the rain would be all over it. I decided to go and look.

Having succeeded in gaining entrance with another key, I ran to open the doors of the old bed, as the room was empty. Quickly pushing them to one side, I looked in. Mr Heathcliff was there – lying on his back. His eyes met mine, so steady and fierce, that I made a movement of fear, and then he seemed to smile.

I could not think that he was dead, but his face and throat were washed with rain, the bedclothes were wet through, and he was perfectly still. I put my fingers on one of his hands. Then my doubts left me.

I cried out for Joseph, who came and fell on his knees and gave thanks that the lawful master and the ancient family were once more in possession of their rights.

I felt unhappy and upset by the terrible event, and my memory returned to former times with a sort of unbearable sadness. But poor Hareton, the most wronged, was the only one who really suffered much. He sat by the body all night and kissed the fierce, scornful face that everybody avoided looking at, and suffered the strong grief that comes naturally from a generous heart.

PART 6   GOODBYE TO WUTHERING HEIGHTS

Mr Lockwood's last words

Chapter 38   The Dead Are at Peace

Mrs Dean was silent for a minute at the end of her story.

'They are going to the Grange, then?' I asked.

'Yes, as soon as they are married, and that will be on New Year's Day.'

'And who will live here?'

'Well, Joseph will take care of the house, with perhaps a boy to keep him company. They will live in the kitchen, and the rest of the house will be shut up.'

'For the use of any ghosts that choose to return to it,' I remarked.

'No, Mr Lockwood,' said Nelly, shaking her head, 'I believe that the dead are at peace.'

At that moment the garden gate opened. The wanderers were returning.

'They are afraid of nothing,' I said.

As they stepped up to the door and paused to take a last look at the moon, or rather at each other, by her light, I felt a desire to avoid them and, quickly saying goodbye to Mrs Dean, I passed through the kitchen and left.

My walk home was lengthened by a turn in the direction of the churchyard. I looked for, and soon discovered, the three stones at the head of the graves on the slope next to the moor: the middle one grey, and half buried in wild plants; Edgar Linton's only covered at the foot with grass, and Heathcliff's still brown earth.

I remained near them. I watched the insects among the wild flowers. I listened to the soft wind breathing through the grass. And I asked myself how anyone could ever imagine unquiet rest for the sleepers below that quiet ground.

ACTIVITIES

Chapters 1–4

Before you read

1 Check the meanings of these words in your dictionary.

   candle   household   moor   tenant   fierce

   landlord   murmur   wicked   gypsy   mistress   shiver

   a Which words refer to people?

   b What is the relationship between a landlord and a tenant?

   Are these sentences true or false? Correct the false ones.

   c A *moor* is an area of land which is covered with forests.

   d A *mouse* is a very fierce animal.

   e You use a *candle* to give light.

   f You *shiver* when you are hungry.

   g If you *murmur* something, you say it very loudly.

   h A person who is *wicked* behaves in a way that is morally wrong.

After you read

2 Who are these people?

   a Mr Lockwood

   b Mr Heathcliff

   c Joseph and Zillah

   d Mrs Dean

   e Catherine Earnshaw

   f Hareton Earnshaw

3 Discuss what you know about Heathcliff's appearance and character and his past and present lifestyles.

4 Take the parts of Mrs Dean and Mr Lockwood.

   Student A: You are Mrs Dean. Ask Mr Lockwood questions about the night he spent at Wuthering Heights.

   Student B: You are Mr Lockwood. Answer Mrs Dean's questions and discuss your experiences with her.

Chapters 5–10

Before you read

5 The title of the next part of the book is 'The First Catherine'.
What do you think Mrs Dean's story will be about?

6 Find these words in your dictionary. They are all in the story.

creep   degrade   exclaim   fury   misery   naughty
scorn   superior   weep

Match the words with the correct meanings.

a great unhappiness
b disobedient
c treat someone without respect
d move quietly and carefully
e cry
f say something suddenly and loudly
g better than another person or thing
h extreme anger
i feeling that someone is stupid or not as good as someone
else

After you read

7 Who is speaking to whom, and what are they talking about?

a 'You must take this as a gift of God, though it's as dark as if
it came from the devil.'
b 'I'd not exchange my condition here for Edgar Linton's at
Thrushcross Grange, not for a thousand lives!'
c 'Away, you gypsy! What! Are you trying to make yourself
look like your superiors!'
d 'I don't care how long I wait, if only I can do it in the end.'
e 'It's no company at all, when people know nothing, and say
nothing.'
f 'Can I stay after you have struck me?'
g 'In my soul and in my heart, I'm certain I'm wrong.'

8 Discuss the relationship between Catherine and Heathcliff.
How realistic do you find it? How can it be explained?

9 Take the parts of Catherine and Heathcliff and act out the conversation that you think they will have at their next meeting.

10 Compare life at Wuthering Heights with life at Thrushcross Grange.

Chapters 11–20

Before you read

11 Look in the Contents list at the titles of Chapters 11–20. What do you think the main events of this part of the book will be?

12 Find these words in your dictionary:
coffin   ignorant
a What shape is a *coffin*?
b If you are *ignorant* about something, you have no .... about it.

After you read

13 Answer the questions.
a How long does Heathcliff stay away for?
b Where does he live on his return?
c What are the effects of his influence on young Hareton?
d What causes Catherine to quarrel with Heathcliff?
e Where does Isabella go when she leaves Thrushcross Grange?
f Why does Hindley Earnshaw allow Heathcliff to stay with him?
g How does Catherine die?
h Who are her last conscious words addressed to?
i What is her last, unconscious speech about?
j Whose hair does she take to the grave?
k Why does Isabella leave Wuthering Heights?
l How does Heathcliff treat Hindley?

14 How does Heathcliff manage to claim:
a Hindley's property, including Wuthering Heights?
b Hareton Earnshaw?

15 Explain Heathcliff's remark to Catherine:
'I love my murderer – but yours! How can I?'

Chapters 21–28

Before you read

16 Who are Cathy Linton's parents? Who are the parents of her two cousins? What do we know about these last two children?

After you read

17 Complete these sentences with the right names.

a When .... dies, Edgar Linton goes to fetch ....

b .... lives at Thrushcross Grange in the care of her father and ....

c Wuthering Heights is the home of .... and ....; .... is also forced to live there.

d .... and .... write secret notes to each other.

e It is ....'s plan that .... and .... should marry.

f During ....'s illness, ... makes frequent visits alone to Wuthering Heights.

g .... finally agrees that the cousins should meet under the protection of ....

h .... and .... are both very ill.

i When .... dies, Thrushcross Grange will belong to .... When he dies, it will belong to ....

18 Compare the characters and appearances of Hareton and Linton.

Chapters 29–38

Before you read

19 At this stage in the story, which of the characters do you feel sorry for and why? Which, if any, of the characters do you like?

After you read

20 Explain why:

a Heathcliff wants Edgar to die before Linton.

b Heathcliff hits Cathy and pushes Nelly over.

c Edgar Linton is unable to make a new will.

    d Heathcliff damages Catherine's coffin.

    e Cathy does not leave Wuthering Heights after Linton's death.

    f Cathy finally decides to be friends with Hareton.

    g Hareton cannot hate Heathcliff.

    h Heathcliff goes mad.

21 Imagine you are Nelly. After Heathcliff's death, explain to Hareton how and why Heathcliff cheated him.

Writing

22 Is it true that Heathcliff is an evil man for whom the reader can have no sympathy?

23 Compare the two Catherines. How are their characters similar? How are they different?

24 How does Heathcliff use violence and fear to achieve his aims?

25 How effective is Heathcliff's influence on Hareton?

26 Write a letter from Edgar Linton, as he is dying, to his daughter Cathy, expressing his hopes and fears for her future.

27 How important to the story is the setting of the lonely houses and the wild moors?

The Warden

ANTHONY TROLLOPE

Level 5

Retold by J. Y. K. Kerr
Series Editors: Andy Hopkins and Jocelyn Potter

Contents

Introduction

'If it can be proved that I have an honest right to my income, I am just as ready as any other person to enjoy it. But if it cannot be proved, I will give up my position here. I cannot suffer all this pain.'

For nearly ten years, Septimus Harding has been the warden of the hospital for old men at Barchester. It is a well-paid job, although there isn't very much to do. The men have a comfortable home, good meals and some money – and they are happy. But suddenly the Church and its ways are under attack. Young John Bold begins to look closely at the warden's job and believes that Harding should be paid less and the old men more. A powerful national newspaper joins the attack on the Church. Harding would love to resign but his masters won't let him. Can this bitter argument somehow be settled?

Anthony Trollope was born in 1815 in London. His family was poor because of his father's failure in business. Trollope worked for the post office and rose to a high position. He was sent to Ireland in 1841 and wrote his first novel there. But his first real success was *The Warden* (1855), based on a real case concerning the Hospital of St Cross, near Winchester. This was the first of six 'Barsetshire' novels, set in a cathedral town in the south-west of England. These novels are still very popular, especially *Barchester Towers* (1857). Trollope was a very energetic writer and produced over sixty books. Forty-seven of these are novels. He died in 1882.

Chapter 1   Hiram's Hospital

A few years ago there was a clergyman★ called Septimus Harding, who lived in the quiet cathedral town of Barchester, in the west of England. Barchester is more famous for its beautiful cathedral and various fine old buildings than as a commercial centre; and its most important citizens are considered to be the bishop★ and the other clergymen of the cathedral, together with their wives and daughters.

Mr Harding had come to Barchester early in life. He had a fine singing-voice and a deep love of church music. For many years he remained an unimportant member of the cathedral staff, where his work was light but not well paid. At the age of forty he was put in charge of a small church close to the town, which increased both his work and his income, and at the age of fifty he was appointed precentor★ of the cathedral.

Mr Harding had married young and was the father of two daughters. The elder, Susan, was born soon after his marriage; the younger, Eleanor, not till ten years later. At the time when this story begins, Mr Harding was already the precentor at Barchester and was living with his younger daughter, having been a widower for many years. His elder daughter had married the bishop's son just before her father's appointment, and unkind tongues in Barchester whispered that his daughter's good looks had got him his job as precentor; but in this they were probably wrong. The fact remains that Susan Harding had married Dr Theophilus Grantly, the son of the bishop, archdeacon★ of

★ A clergyman is any church official. In the Church of England the head of a cathedral is a bishop, who lives in the bishop's palace. His senior manager is the archdeacon. The precentor is responsible for music at the cathedral services.

Barchester and the clergyman responsible for the church at Plumstead Episcopi, a village outside the town.

There are unusual circumstances connected with the position of the precentor which must be explained. In the year 1434 a rich man called John Hiram died, having made his money as a buyer and seller of wool. In his will he left his house and some of his lands near the town as a charity for the support of twelve old men. His will said that these men must be people who had lived all their lives in Barchester and who had worked in the wool business before old age and ill health forced them to retire. John Hiram also ordered the building of a hospital, or old people's home, for the twelve to live in, and, beside it, a house suitable for a warden for the hospital, who would also receive annually a certain amount of money from the rents of Hiram's land. Finally the will said that the position of warden should be filled by the cathedral precentor, if the bishop agreed to the appointment.

Ever since that time this arrangement had continued. The wool industry no longer existed in the town, so the bishop, the archdeacon and the warden took turns in choosing suitable old men – old workmen who were grateful to receive a comfortable home and one shilling★ and fourpence a day, the amount fixed by John Hiram's will. About fifty years earlier they had received only sixpence a day as well as their meals, but, by general agreement, the change to a daily figure of one shilling and fourpence a day was made.

This then was the situation at the time when Mr Harding became warden, and the old men thought themselves lucky to be so well fed and looked after. But the situation of the warden himself was even more fortunate. The lands once owned by Hiram had greatly increased in value over the centuries and were

★ A shilling is twelve old pence or a twentieth part of a pound.

now covered with houses. A gentleman called Mr Chadwick was employed as the manager of Hiram's land and buildings, and the money received in rents from these was paid to the warden. After making the daily payments to the twelve old men and giving them their meals, the warden was left with an income of eight hundred pounds a year, not including the value of his house; by contrast, his position as precentor brought him only eighty pounds annually. Some people did sometimes whisper that John Hiram's money was not fairly divided, and such whispers had come to Mr Harding's ears; but being a fair-minded, generous man, and feeling that there might be some truth in these observations, he had decided to give each man another twopence a day, paying this amount from his own pocket. He explained to the men that this extra money was a gift from himself and that future wardens would not perhaps continue it; but the men expressed themselves quite satisfied with the new arrangement. Mr Harding's generous decision, however, did not please everyone: Mr Chadwick, for example, considered it to be unwise, and the warden's strong-minded son-in-law, the archdeacon (the one person whom Mr Harding was really rather afraid of), was violently against it. But the warden had already informed the men at the hospital about the increase, so it was too late for the archdeacon to interfere.

Hiram's Hospital, as the place is generally known, is a pleasant old building which stands on the bank of a little river that runs near the cathedral. Beside it sits the handsome old house of the warden, with a pretty garden round it, and here Mr Harding lived at the age of nearly sixty, his hair beginning to turn grey, dressed always in black, with his glasses on his nose or in his hand. He was not exactly a hard-working person, although he had written a book about old church music, which was his greatest love. He had greatly improved the singing in Barchester cathedral, which was now as good as any in England; and his strong voice led the church services. More than anything he loved to play the cello – with or without an audience. Mr Harding did have one weakness, however: he had no head for money matters. He was generous to all and especially to the twelve old men in his care; yet he lived in continual fear of Archdeacon Theophilus Grantly, his son-in-law, who watched over his finances with the greatest attention.

Mr Harding had been precentor at Barchester for ten years when rumours about Hiram's Hospital and its finances began again, as part of a movement by various people in different parts of the country to criticize the Church of England. Mr Harding himself had no guilty feelings either about his work as warden or about the eight hundred pounds he received for it, but two of the old men in the hospital were beginning to say that, if old John Hiram's will was carried out properly, they would each be enjoying a hundred pounds a year. One of this discontented pair was called Abel Handy, a man to whom the warden himself had given the first vacant place that appeared at the hospital.

Also living in Barchester at that time was a young man called John Bold, who did much to encourage the dissatisfaction expressed by some of the old men. He and Mr Harding knew each other well and could even be called old friends, in spite of the difference in their ages. Dr Grantly, on the other hand, considered John Bold a trouble-maker and thought of him as his enemy.

John Bold's father had been a successful doctor in London. When he died he left most of his money to his son, who had just finished his medical studies. John, who was then only twenty-four years old, decided to set up house in Barchester with his unmarried sister Mary and to begin work as a doctor in the town. Barchester, however, already had nine other doctors, and after three years Bold found that he still had very few patients. He was a clever, rather daring young man. Having enough money to live on, he interested himself in putting right all sorts of social injustices. He defended the poor against the rich, the weak against the strong. He was quick to act and sure of the rightness of his actions, as any well-educated, self-confident young man can be.

Dr Grantly observed Bold's actions with alarm and thought him a dangerous rebel, but Mr Harding remembered how young Johnny had come to his garden as a child and listened to him playing his cello, and he could not bring himself to dislike him. In fact he was not the only person in his family who took an interest in the young doctor. His daughter Eleanor disliked hearing John criticized by others, though she dared not defend him to her brother-in-law. She encouraged her father to continue receiving Bold, in spite of his political views. She was unwilling to go to houses where she would not meet him and, in a word, she was in love. Nor was there any good reason why Eleanor Harding should not love John Bold, since he had all those qualities likely to touch a girl's heart. He was brave, enthusiastic and amusing, well-made and good-looking, young and active. His character was excellent. He had a large enough income to support a wife; he was her father's friend; and, most important of all, he was in love with her.

Dr Grantly was quick to notice the way the wind was blowing and was not at all happy about it. He had not yet spoken to his father-in-law on the subject because he knew that the warden's love for his daughter was so great that he could not refuse her anything; but he brought the matter up in private with his dear wife, as they lay in bed together in their bedroom at Plumstead Episcopi. Dr Grantly was a gentleman of impressive appearance and the highest principles.

In public he was a greatly respected figure: his forceful manner and strongly held opinions created fear, even terror, in the hearts of the people of Barchester. It was only when he took off his shining black clergyman's clothes and put on his nightshirt that he began to talk, look and think like an ordinary man.

'My dear,' he said, gathering his nightshirt around him, 'that John Bold was at your father's house again today. I must say that your father is most unwise to receive him.'

'He has never been very wise,' replied Mrs Grantly from her comfortable position under the blankets. 'There's nothing new in that.'

'No, my dear, I admit that. But at the present time his foolishness is – is – I'll tell you this, my dear: if he's not very careful, young John Bold will be off with Eleanor.'

'I think he will too, whether papa is careful or whether he isn't; and why not?'

'Why not!' almost screamed the archdeacon, 'why not! That bad-mannered, interfering adventurer – the least respectful young person I've ever met! Do you know that he's putting his nose in your father the warden's business in a completely unacceptable, most – ' Unable to find words strong enough to express his feelings, he finished his sentence with 'Good heavens!', spoken in a manner which always caused a great impression at church meetings.

'I cannot agree with you, archdeacon, that he is badly behaved. I certainly don't like Mr Bold; I think he is much too pleased with himself. But if Eleanor likes him, and they decide to get married, that would be the best possible thing for papa. Bold will never cause trouble over Hiram's Hospital if he's papa's son-in-law.' And the lady then turned over in bed in a way which showed that she had no wish to discuss the subject any further that night.

Dr Grantly was not a bad man. He was quite intelligent enough for the work he had to do. He carried out his duties at Plumstead Episcopi faithfully, but it was as archdeacon that he really shone. In most cases where there is both a bishop and an archdeacon, one does all the work and the other does very little. In the case of Barchester, the worker was the archdeacon. He was confident, a good speaker, quick to make decisions and firmly fixed in his opinions. Above all, he was always determined to defend the interests of the Church from outside attack with everything in his power.

As for Mr Harding, he saw no reason why his daughter should not love John Bold. He had noticed her tenderness for him, and his main regret over the action which Bold was about to take concerning the hospital was that this might separate him from his daughter, or else separate her from the man she loved. He was certainly not going to turn his back on the man his daughter loved just because he held opinions which were different from his own.

Until now Bold had not taken any action concerning the hospital, but he had heard of the complaints made by some of the old men there. He had also heard that the income from Hiram's land and buildings was very large. He decided therefore to call upon the manager, Mr Chadwick, and ask for information about how the whole organization was financed. He soon discovered that, if he interfered with Mr Chadwick as the manager, he must also interfere with Mr Harding as the warden. This situation was regrettable, but he was not a man who could allow personal considerations to decide his actions.

Having now become interested in the matter, he began to examine it with his usual energy. He got a copy of John Hiram's will and studied the wording with great care. He found information about the houses built on Hiram's lands and their value, and worked out how the income from them was divided up. With this information he called one day on Mr Chadwick and asked for details of the income and of the amounts of money spent on the hospital over the last twenty-five years. Mr Chadwick naturally refused the request and said that he did not have permission to make these facts public.

'And who is able to give this permission?' asked Bold.

Mr Chadwick informed him that he must turn to the hospital's lawyers, Messrs Cox and Cummins of Lincoln's Inn. Mr Bold wrote down the address, said the weather was cold for the time of year and wished him good morning. Chadwick agreed about the weather and showed him to the door.

Bold went immediately to his own lawyer, Mr Finney. Finney advised him to write to Cox and Cummins at once, demanding a complete history of the hospital's finances.

'Should I not see Mr Harding first?' suggested Bold.

'Yes, yes, of course,' agreed Finney. 'Mr Harding is not a man with experience of business matters, but I don't think that seeing him can do any harm.' Mr Finney could see from the expression on John Bold's face that he intended to do things his own way.

Chapter 2   A Shadow of Doubt

Bold at once set off to the hospital. He knew that Eleanor usually went for a drive at this time, so he would probably find Mr Harding alone. It was a pleasant June evening. The little gate to the warden's garden stood open and, as Bold went in, he could hear the sweet sound of Mr Harding's cello. The warden was sitting on a garden chair, playing some of the much-loved church music he had collected in his book. Around him sat, lay or stood ten of the twelve old men who lived under the hospital roof. The two rebels were not there. Recently they had kept away from the warden, whose music was no longer to their taste.

One of the listeners was Mr Bunce, a big handsome figure of a man, although he was over eighty. Bunce was the unofficial leader of the twelve and made no secret of his loyal and affectionate feelings for Mr Harding. The warden was equally fond of Bunce and would often ask him in to drink a glass or two of wine with him on cold winter evenings. Bunce now sat listening and looking at the warden admiringly, as he played his heavenly music.

When he saw Bold walking towards him the warden immediately stopped playing and began to make him welcome.

'Please, Mr Harding, don't let me interrupt you,' said Bold. 'You know how fond I am of church music.'

Mr Harding had been expecting a pleasant social chat and he looked rather puzzled and displeased when Bold told him that he had come to discuss business matters. 'I wish to speak to you about the hospital,' said Bold, 'and most particularly about the hospital finances.'

'My dear friend, I can tell you nothing. I am like a child in such matters. I only know that I am paid eight hundred pounds a year. Go and talk to Chadwick; he knows all about the financial situation. But tell me now, how is Mary Jones with her bad leg?'

'She's improving. But Mr Harding, I hope you won't be displeased by listening to what I have to say about the hospital.'

Mr Harding gave a deep sigh. He was very much displeased at the idea of discussing this subject with John Bold, but, not knowing how to avoid it, he sighed again and said nothing.

'I have the greatest respect for you, Mr Harding, and I do not want you to think that what I'm going to do comes from any personal dislike on my part . . .'

'Personal dislike! That's unthinkable!'

'I believe that the Church is not properly carrying out John Hiram's will and I wish to examine the matter.'

'Very well, I have no reason to refuse you, if that is what you want; and now we need not say another word about it.'

'Just one word more, warden. Chadwick has given me the names of your lawyers and I consider it my duty to ask them for details of the hospital finances. If this seems to you to be interference, I hope you will forgive me.'

'Mr Bold,' said the other, 'if you act fairly, speak nothing but the truth and do not try to deceive us in carrying out your purpose, I shall have nothing to forgive. I suppose you think that I do not deserve the income which I receive from the hospital and that this money should be given to others. Believe me, I shall never think badly of you just because you hold an opinion different from my own. Do what you believe to be your duty. But here comes Eleanor with her horses, so let us go in and have tea.'

Bold, however, felt uncomfortable at the idea of sitting down with Mr Harding and his daughter after such a conversation and so he excused himself with embarrassed apologies. He simply lifted his hat to Eleanor in greeting as he passed her, leaving her surprised and disappointed by his departure.

Mr Harding's calm manner impressed Bold, making him think that the warden was sure of his position and that he was about to interfere in the private matters of a fair-minded and respectable man. But Mr Harding himself was far from satisfied with his own view of the case. Could it possibly be that John

'I believe that the Church is not properly carrying out John Hiram's will and I wish to examine the matter.'

Bold was right and that for the past ten years the warden had been receiving an income that legally belonged to others? For the first time in his quiet, happy, respectable life a shadow of doubt fell across his mind and for many, many days to come our good warden was neither happy nor free of self-accusing thoughts.

Eleanor noticed that her father seemed unusually worried as he sat drinking his tea, but she was more concerned about John's sudden, unfriendly departure. She supposed that there had been some kind of quarrel between the two men and felt half angry with both of them, without being able to say why.

Mr Harding thought long and deeply, both before going to bed and afterwards, as he lay awake questioning the rights and wrongs of the income he enjoyed. Was John Hiram's will being fairly carried out? That was the real question. He knew how strongly Dr Grantly would support his position, but he did not want Dr Grantly's support. He decided instead to admit his doubts and share his thoughts with his old friend the bishop; and to the bishop he went, the morning after John Bold's unwelcome visit.

The bishop, now over seventy, was the very opposite of his son the archdeacon: not active and forceful but gentle and kind. The bishop and Mr Harding loved each other dearly. They had grown old together and over the years they had passed many hours considering the business of the Church in all its details. Now that their children had married and Mr Harding had become precentor and warden, they were all in all to each other.

Up to this time the bishop had heard nothing of the trouble at the hospital, so it was a long explanation which Mr Harding had to give before he could make the bishop understand his own view of the matter. At first the bishop's solution was to refer the whole problem to his son. 'No one understands the matter so well as the archdeacon.'

'But, bishop,' said the warden, 'did you ever read John Hiram's will?'

The bishop thought he might have done, about thirty-five years ago, but was not completely sure of the fact.

'But, bishop, the question is, who has the power to decide these things? If, as the young man says, the will demands that the income from Hiram's lands should be divided into more equal shares, who has the power to change it?'

The bishop thought that such changes could take place with the passing of time. He said something about tradition, and spoke of the proper difference between the needs of a clergyman in Mr Harding's position and those of a number of poor old men supported by the Church. He laid his hand on Mr Harding's knee and Mr Harding understood that he felt sympathetic towards his old friend in trouble. And this, thought Mr Harding, was the reward he had come for.

There was a silence for a little and then the bishop asked almost angrily whether this 'trouble-maker' (John Bold) had any friends in Barchester. Mr Harding had already decided to tell the bishop everything – to speak of his daughter's love as well as his own troubles – and now was the time to do so.

'Mr Bold is much liked in my family, bishop. Indeed, I like him very much myself. It is not impossible that he will one day be my son-in-law.'

The bishop's amazement was plain to see. He almost whistled aloud but, being a bishop, did not.

'I don't mean they are about to be married, just that they are very fond of each other,' said Mr Harding hurriedly.

'But, Harding, how can you stand against him if he is to be your son-in-law?'

'But I am not against him; it is he who is taking sides against me. If my position has to be defended, I suppose Chadwick will do it.'

'Oh, the archdeacon will see to that. The archdeacon will never allow family relationships to stand in the way of doing what he feels to be right.'

Mr Harding made the bishop promise to say nothing of Eleanor's love for John Bold, especially not to the archdeacon; and then he said goodbye, leaving his poor old friend feeling both amazed and puzzled.

◆

The case of Hiram's Hospital and its income, which was about to cause such a storm in Barchester, was slow to reach the twelve old men themselves; but Finney the lawyer had been mixing with them, helping to increase their dissatisfaction and feeding their hopes of getting rich. In fact the old men's important needs were already met: good food, clothes, a well-heated home and plenty of rest after the hard lives they had led; and a kind, true friend to look after them if they were ill or unhappy. John Bold himself sometimes had doubts about whether the old people's lives would really improve if they got one hundred pounds a year instead of one shilling and sixpence a day; but he quickly buried such thoughts.

'Each one of you ought by law to receive one hundred pounds a year' was the message which Mr Finney whispered in Abel Handy's ear. Handy was not slow to tell the other eleven and to win support. Mr Bunce, of course, could not be persuaded to change sides and with him two others remained loyal to the warden. Of the other men, five supported Handy and three were undecided. Mr Finney had prepared a petition which listed their wrongs and requested justice for their case, promising to send copies to all the important newspapers in London; but so far only six of the men had signed and this would not make a good impression. The undecided ones were Job Skulpit, Billy Gazy and Jonathan Crumple.

'Well, Job,' said Handy, 'you're ready to sign, I think. Here's the place, do you see?' and he pointed to the dirty piece of paper in front of them.

'Just think, Billy Gazy,' said another of Handy's supporters, 'a hundred a year and all to spend! Just think of that, old Billy!'

But Billy's only words were, 'I don't know. I just don't know.'

'Come on, Skulpit,' said Handy. 'You're not going to be like Bunce and let that old churchman rob us all. Take up the pen and ask for what is yours.'

'But then,' said Skulpit, apologizing for the delay in his signing, 'our Mr Harding's not so bad. He did give us twopence a day, didn't he now?'

'Twopence a day!' cried the others.

'Twopence a day!' shouted Handy. 'You want me to go hat in hand and thank the man for twopence a day when he owes me a hundred pounds a year? No, thank you!'

And so the old men argued this way and that until Gazy, Crumple and finally Job Skulpit were persuaded to put their marks on the page, since none of them could write.

'Well, now all nine of us are in the same boat,' said Handy, 'and old Bunce and his friends can – '

'Well, Handy, and what can old Bunce do?' The upright figure of Bunce himself appeared in the doorway.

'You've been doing no good here, Abel Handy, that's easy to see.'

'I keep to my own business, Mr Bunce,' said the other, 'and you should do the same. Your spying on us won't do any good either.'

'I suppose then, Job,' Bunce continued, 'you've put your name on their paper at last.' Skulpit looked ready to die of shame. 'I've known you, Job, since the day you were born,' said Bunce, 'and I tell you now you've done a foolish, wrong thing. You've turned your back on a man who's your best friend. You're playing the game of these others, who care nothing for him, whether he's rich or poor, well or ill, alive or dead. A hundred a year? Are the lot of you so soft in the head that you think you're all going to get it? Aren't you getting everything you hoped for, and more than you hoped for, already, when before you were too poor and weak to earn your daily bread?'

'We want what Hiram left us. We want what's ours by law.'

'Law!' said Bunce bitterly. 'Did you ever know a poor man made better by law or a lawyer? Will Mr Finney ever be as good to you, Job, as Mr Harding has been? Will he visit you when you're sick and offer you sympathy when you're depressed?'

'No, nor give you a glass of wine on cold winter nights. He won't do that, will he?' cried Abel Handy and, laughing at his own cleverness, he and his colleagues left the room victorious, carrying with them the now powerful piece of paper.

Chapter 3   Dr Grantly and the Petitioners

Though doubt and uncertainty gave our poor warden a sleepless night, his brave son-in-law suffered from no such weakness. Dr Grantly was fully confident of the rightness of his case. His greatest aim in life was to defend the interests of the Church against any kind of attack from its enemies. Such work demanded courage and energy, and the archdeacon certainly had plenty of both.

A day or two had passed since the signing of the petition. 'Well, Mr Chadwick,' he said, walking into the hospital manager's office, 'anything from Cox and Cummins this morning?'

Mr Chadwick handed him a letter, which the archdeacon read with great attention. Messrs Cox and Cummins simply reported that no word had yet been received from the opposite party and suggested that it would be wise to approach Sir Abraham Haphazard, the attorney-general.★

'I quite agree with them,' said Dr Grantly, giving back the letter. 'Haphazard is without a doubt the best man for the case. Of course we must have him.'

Having settled this point to his satisfaction, he walked over to the hospital to learn how matters were going there. The archdeacon, for all his good qualities, was not a man especially alert to other people's feelings and, after greeting the warden in his sitting-room, he did not hesitate to deliver an attack on the 'unspeakable' John Bold in front of Miss Harding, though he rightly guessed that the lady had a certain fondness for his enemy. Eleanor still knew nothing about Bold and the crisis over the hospital, but she sensed that things were somehow going wrong.

'We must do something – and soon,' said the archdeacon firmly. 'Of course you have heard of the petition?'

Mr Harding admitted rather unwillingly that he had heard of it.

'Well?' The archdeacon waited for Mr Harding to express an opinion, but none came. 'We can't allow these people to get an advantage over us while we simply sit and watch them.'

The warden continued to look at him in silence, while his

★ The attorney-general is the senior legal adviser to the government.

fingers made the movements of someone playing the cello – a sure sign that he was upset.

'Cox and Cummins say that we must employ Sir Abraham Haphazard for this case, and I quite agree with them,' went on the archdeacon.

The warden's fingers played a slow, sad tune. He thought uncomfortably of his income being examined, his modest life, his daily habits, his undemanding work.

'I suppose they've sent this petition to my father,' said Dr Grantly.

'I really don't know,' answered Mr Harding.

'What I can't understand is why you let them do it, when you are in charge of the place and have Bunce to help you.'

'Do what?' asked the warden.

'Why, let young Bold and his awful lawyer Finney prepare this petition. Why didn't you tell Bunce to destroy it?'

'That would hardly have been wise,' said the warden.

'It would have been very wise, if they had done it among themselves. I must go to the bishop's palace and answer it now, I suppose; and a very short answer it will be.'

'But why shouldn't they send a petition, archdeacon?'

'Why shouldn't they?' said the archdeacon impatiently, at the top of his voice. 'I'll let them know why they shouldn't! I want to say a few words to them all together.'

To the warden this idea was most unwelcome, because privately he had decided not to interfere in any action the men might take in the matter. He strongly wished neither to accuse them nor to defend himself. He realized that the archdeacon was now about to do exactly these things, which worried him greatly, but he did not know how to refuse permission to his son-in-law.

'I'd much rather remain quiet on the matter,' he said weakly, as if apologizing.

'Quiet?' said the archdeacon, his voice echoing round the room. 'Do you wish to be quietly reduced to poverty? Nonsense, warden, we must act. Have someone ring the bell and tell the men I shall speak to them outside, in the garden.'

Mr Harding was forced to obey and the unpleasant order was given. The archdeacon stood up, fully confident of his powers of persuasion.

'I wish to be excused,' said Mr Harding, preparing not to follow him.

'For heaven's sake, don't let us show them we're divided,' replied the archdeacon. 'We must all pull together. Come, warden, don't be afraid of your duty.'

Mr Harding was afraid, afraid that he was being led to do something which was far from his duty; but he weakly got up and followed his son-in-law outside.

The old men had gathered in groups. When the two church-men appeared, they all took off their hats, even the unwilling Abel Handy. Mr Bunce stepped forward and greeted the two gentlemen. The archdeacon then stepped forward to make his speech.

'Now, my men,' he began, 'I want to say a few words to you. Your good friend the warden here, and the bishop for whom I speak, would be very sorry if you had any reason to complain about your circumstances. Any good reason for a complaint would be removed by one of us without the need for you to send any petition to anyone.' Here he stopped for a moment, expecting some signs of grateful agreement from his audience; but no such signs came. Even Bunce sat silent, with tight lips. 'Without the need for a petition of any kind at all,' he repeated. 'But I'm told that you have already sent a petition to the bishop.'

'Yes, we have,' said Handy.

'And in it, I'm told that you say you do not receive what you think you should receive according to Hiram's will.'

'Yes, that's so,' said several voices.

'Now what is it you ask for? What is it that you haven't got already? What is it – '

'A hundred a year,' answered Greg Moody, Handy's friend.

'A hundred a year!' cried the archdeacon in amazement, stretching his arms to heaven. 'A hundred a year! Why, men, you must be mad! And you talk about John Hiram's will! When John Hiram built this hospital for poor, old, weak working men, do you think he meant to turn them into gentlemen? Do you think John Hiram intended to give a hundred a year to old men with no families, who earned in the best of their time no more than a shilling or two a day? No, men, I'll tell you what John Hiram meant. He meant that twelve old men should come here in their poverty to enjoy the care and protection offered by the Church; and here they should prepare themselves for death and make their peace with God. That was what he meant. You have not read John Hiram's will. I doubt whether those dishonest advisers of yours have read it. But I have. I know what his will was, and I tell you that that was his will and that was his intention.'

Not a sound came from the old men as they sat listening to the archdeacon. They simply stared at Dr Grantly's well-filled figure, giving no sign of the anger and disgust they must have felt.

'Now let me ask you this,' he continued. 'Do you think you live worse than John Hiram intended? Haven't you each got a room of your own, and time to enjoy yourselves? Your lives are twice as good, you have ten times more money in your pocket than you had when you were working. And yet you send us a petition asking for a hundred pounds a year! You have been badly advised, made fools of by people who are simply using you for their own purposes. You will never get a hundred pence more than what you have now. In fact it is very possible that you may get less. It is very possible that the good bishop and your warden may make changes – '

'No, no, no,' interrupted Mr Harding, who had been listening with increasing alarm and unhappiness to his son-in-law's speech. 'No, my friends, I want no changes – at least no changes that would make your lives worse.'

'May God be with you, Mr Harding,' said Bunce. 'We know you were always our friend.'

The archdeacon had not finished his speech, but he felt that he could not continue it now, so he led the way back to the house, followed by his father-in-law.

'Well,' he said, as soon as they were alone, 'I think I spoke to them plainly.'

'Yes, you were plain enough,' said the warden, without enthusiasm.

'And that's the important thing,' said Dr Grantly, clearly well pleased with himself. 'With people of this lower sort one must speak plainly or they will not understand. But they did understand, I'm sure. They knew what I meant.'

Privately, the warden thought they had understood too well.

'Now I'll just look in at Chadwick's office,' said the archdeacon, 'and then I'll go up to the palace and answer this petition of theirs.'

The warden's mind was very troubled. He had been greatly embarrassed by the archdeacon's speech but he was painfully afraid of a disagreement with any person on any subject. He thought he would give almost anything to avoid the storm which he felt sure was coming. He did not yet question the fact that he deserved his comfortable, quiet life, but he felt horror at the thought of being made the subject of common gossip and public criticism. He walked up and down his garden for hours, turning these thoughts over in his mind, feeling that he must soon make some kind of decision.

During this time the archdeacon went about his business well contented. Finding the petition in his father's library as he expected, he wrote a short answer to the men. He told them that they had no reason to complain but instead many reasons to be grateful. He made sure that the bishop signed this reply, called for his carriage and returned home to Mrs Grantly at Plumstead Episcopi.

♦

After much painful thinking Mr Harding was able to make only one firm decision: he would not show himself to be hurt over the hospital question or allow it to cause any quarrel either with Bold or with the old men themselves. Some time ago he had promised Eleanor that they would hold a little party – a musical evening – at their home and, although he did not really feel in the mood for this event, he did not wish to disappoint his daughter. When Eleanor asked him about it, she was glad to hear him say: 'I was thinking of asking Mr Bold, so I have already written him a note of invitation; but you must write one to his sister.'

Mary Bold was older than her brother, aged just over thirty. She was not beautiful or particularly clever but she had a clear sense of right and wrong and was extremely kind-hearted. People who knew her only on the surface were not greatly impressed but those who got to know her well became very fond of her, and Eleanor Harding was among the fondest of all her admirers. Eleanor had never talked openly to Mary about her brother but each understood the other's feelings about him. Brother and sister were at home together when the two invitations arrived.

'How odd that they should send two notes,' said Mary. 'I wonder why.'

Her brother understood immediately that Mr Harding's note

to him was a peace-offering, but it is always easier for the victim to be generous. John Bold felt that, as things stood, he could not go to the warden's party.

'Well, ' said Mary, 'I suppose we must both write separate letters of acceptance.'

'You'll go, of course, Mary,' said John, 'but I cannot, though I wish I could with all my heart.'

'And why not, John?' asked Mary. 'Don't tell me that you've quarrelled with Eleanor!'

'No indeed,' said her brother. 'I've no quarrel with her.'

'What is it, John?' said Mary, looking at him with a troubled, loving face.

'Well, you see, Mary,' he said at last, 'I've taken up the case of those twelve old men at Hiram's Hospital and of course that brings me into a difficult relationship with Mr Harding.' He then began to explain the whole problem to his sister.

'But why are you doing this, you who have known Mr Harding so long? Surely, John, as his friend, as a young friend – '

'Age has nothing to do with it, Mary. If an action is the right one, personal feelings must not be allowed to interfere. Of course I greatly like Mr Harding, but that is no reason for failing in my duty to those old men.'

'And Eleanor, John?' said Mary, looking at him shyly.

'Eleanor, that is, Miss Harding, if she wishes – but there is no need to talk about Eleanor Harding now. I do know that she would never blame me for doing what I know is my duty.'

Mary sat silent for some time. She wrote the first words of her reply, but then she stopped and looked at her brother.

'Oh, John, I beg you to think again about all this.'

'About what?' he said

'About the hospital and Mr Harding and the old men. Oh, John, think of Eleanor. You'll break her heart and your own too. You are going to make yourself and Eleanor and her father terribly unhappy – and for what? For a dream of turning wrong into right.'

'You don't understand, my dear girl,' said John.

'I do understand, John. I know how much you love Eleanor. At least let me say that you will go to this party. Do not break with the Hardings, if your mind is in any doubt.'

'My mind is not in doubt,' said John, after a pause. 'I could never respect myself again if I were to give in now, just because Eleanor Harding is beautiful. I do love her and I would give anything to feel sure that she loves me but I cannot for her sake step back from the work I have begun.'

So poor Mary Bold sat down and sadly finished her note, accepting for herself and making excuses for her brother.

◆

The party eventually took place as arranged. Fat old ladies chatted with fine old gentlemen, and pretty young ladies were admired by rather stiff young gentlemen, while everyone drank quantities of excellent tea and ate pieces of delicious cake. Later, lamps were brought, music desks put up and Mr Harding played his cello, joined by a young fellow-musician on the piano, to the great satisfaction of his invited audience. Then the young men began to entertain the young ladies while the older guests settled down to play cards, until it was time for everyone to express their thanks and make their way home.

Finally Mr Harding was left alone with his daughter. 'Well, Eleanor,' he said, 'are you ready for bed?'

'Yes,' she said, 'but, papa, Mr Bold was not here tonight. Do you know why?'

'Well, Eleanor, I can only guess.'

'Oh, papa, do tell me,' she cried, throwing her arms around him. 'What is going on? What is it all about? Is there any – ' she was unsure of the word to use – 'any danger?'

'Danger, my dear? What sort of danger?'

'Danger to you, danger of losing – oh, papa, why haven't you told me all this before?'

Mr Harding knew all about his daughter's love for John Bold. As a loving father he naturally thought that it was her own problems and not his that were troubling her. He looked at her in silence and then gave her a tender kiss. 'Tell me, Nelly, do you like Mr Bold very much?'

This question took Eleanor by surprise, because her feelings about John were complicated. She admitted to herself that she loved him and she knew that he admired her but she was angry that, in spite of this, he was ready to turn against her father and threaten his peaceful way of life. So when she spoke of danger, she meant danger to him, not to herself.

'So, Nelly, do you like him? That's a poor word: do you love him?'

Eleanor lay in her father's arms without answering.

'Come, my love,' her father said, 'tell me how you feel about John and I shall tell you all about my problems with the hospital.'

So Mr Harding told his daughter the whole story, taking great care to praise John Bold and not to blame him; and then, reminding her that it was late, he sent her up to her room with tearful eyes and a suffering heart.

♦

At breakfast next morning there was no further discussion of the matter. The following day John Bold met Miss Harding walking along a quiet leafy path near the cathedral, where he had hoped to find her.

'My sister tells me,' he said rather hurriedly, 'that you had a delightful party the other evening. I was so sorry I could not be there.'

'We were all sorry,' said Eleanor coolly.

'I believe, Miss Harding, you understand why at this moment – ' Bold hesitated, started again, paused but could not continue his carefully prepared speech.

Eleanor made no attempt to help him. 'Please don't apologize, Mr Bold. My father, I know, will always be glad to see you, if you visit him; his feelings towards you are quite unchanged. Where your own opinions are concerned, you are of course the best judge of those.'

'Your father is always kind and generous. But you, Miss Harding, I hope you will not think badly of me because – '

'Mr Bold,' she said, 'you may be sure of one thing: I shall always consider my father to be right and those who are against him to be wrong. If some of these people do not really know him, there can be some excuse; but those people who ought to know him well, and to love and respect him – of them I am forced to form a very different opinion. I wish you good day, Mr Bold.'

And with a cold look she stepped quickly past him, leaving her admirer in a far from comfortable mood.

Chapter 4   Uncertainty, Suffering and Doubt

Though Eleanor Harding seemed to leave John Bold with self-confidence, her heart was in a very different condition from the self-control her appearance suggested. Her father had told her repeatedly that Bold was doing nothing unfair or ungenerous, so why should she feel so cold towards him? As she walked away, she would have given the world to take him by the hand, using her feminine arts to persuade him to give up his plan, and so save her father at the cost of herself; but she had been too proud to do this and had left him without one look of love or one kind word.

'But you, Miss Harding, I hope you will not think badly of me
because – '

Poor Bold walked away in low spirits, his self-confidence badly shaken. He felt that he would never win back Eleanor's respect unless he could agree to give up the matter which he had promised to support. However, it would not be easy to give up, and in any case how could a girl with Eleanor's high principles learn to love a man who turned away from the path of duty?

As far as his attempts to bring changes to the hospital were concerned, Bold had good reasons to feel pleased. All Barchester was talking about the problem and every day the case was growing in size and weight. But, most important of all, the daily *Jupiter*, that all-powerful national newspaper, had mentioned it:

We have been informed of a great injustice concerning the warden of an old hospital for poor people belonging to Barchester Cathedral. The hospital gets its income from rented lands and buildings. The old people for whom the hospital exists have received no advantage from the increase in the value of the houses and land over the last four centuries, since all this increase has gone into the warden's pocket. It is simply no answer to say that twelve old men receive enough for their daily needs. By what arguments of law or tradition can the warden explain why he receives such a large income for doing nothing? Does he ever ask himself just what are the services he is being paid for? Or does the idea never enter his head? With shock and shame we must express our opinion that only in the Church of England, and only among its officials, can an example of such selfishness be found.

It is easy to imagine how troubled Mr Harding's mind was after reading this newspaper article. How was he to answer this? How could he explain to those thousands of newspaper readers that he was no robber, but a simple, modest man who had innocently accepted what was innocently offered to him?

'Write to the *Jupiter*,' said the bishop. The archdeacon did not

330

agree. 'In such matters the *Jupiter* is all-powerful. By writing to protest, you will simply put yourself more in the wrong and become open to further attack.'

The article in the *Jupiter*, although it deeply upset the warden, was seen as an enormous success by the opposite side. Bold was sorry that the attack on Mr Harding had been so personal, but he was delighted that such a powerful independent voice had taken up his cause. Finney, his lawyer, felt enormous pleasure at being on the same side as the *Jupiter*.

The old men at the hospital had also heard about the newspaper article and were impressed that this great instrument of truth had taken up their case. Abel Handy went from room to room, repeating everything he understood was printed there (though he was unable to read it himself), with some extra ideas of his own which he felt should be added. Jonathan Crumple dreamed of soon being rich and Job Skulpit realized how right he had been to sign the petition, and said so twenty times. Even Billy Gazy became restless, and Mr Bunce kept alone, with sadness in his heart, because he guessed that evil days were coming.

Sir Abraham's opinion on the Hiram's Hospital crisis was still unknown, and the uncertainty, suffering and doubt of the people of Barchester remained extreme.

◆

Our story now moves once more to the archdeacon's bedroom at Plumstead. The lady of the house was making up her face, while the archdeacon was next door in his dressing-room.

'It's your fault,' called Mrs Grantly through the half-open door. 'I told you from the beginning how it would end, and papa has no one to thank but you.'

'Good heavens, dear,' said the clergyman from the doorway, wiping his face with a towel, 'how can you say that? I am doing my best.'

'I wish you had never done so much,' said his wife bitterly. 'If you had just let John Bold come and go at the hospital, as he and papa wanted, he and Eleanor would be married by now and we would not have heard one word more about the whole hospital business.'

'But, my dear – '

'Oh, it's all very well, archdeacon, and of course you're right: you never admit that you could be wrong. But the fact is that, by protesting so loudly, you've just made the young man more stubbornly determined.'

'But, my love – '

'And all because you didn't want John Bold as a brother-in-law. How is poor Eleanor going to find someone better? Papa hasn't got a shilling of his own and, though you can say she's pleasant-looking, she's not the sort to turn men's heads. I don't know how she can marry someone better than John Bold, or even someone half as suitable.'

Dr Grantly felt this attack was most unfair, but what could he say? A few months ago the idea of having Bold as a brother-in-law would have made him very angry. Since then, matters had changed. Bold's show of power had quite impressed the arch-deacon and he was beginning to think that such a marriage would not have been a bad thing. However, he still believed firmly in 'no surrender'. He tried to encourage Mrs Grantly once more and for the twentieth time he began to tell her of the talents of Sir Abraham Haphazard.

'Oh, Sir Abraham!' she said, picking up her house keys before making her way downstairs. 'Sir Abraham won't get Eleanor a husband! Sir Abraham won't get papa another income when they've driven him out of the hospital! Listen to me, archdeacon. While you and Sir Abraham are fighting this case, papa will lose his position and what will you do then, I'd like to know, with him and Eleanor on your hands?

And anyway, who's going to pay Sir Abraham? I suppose he will not take on this case for nothing.' And with these words the good lady went downstairs to join her children and servants at family prayers, the model of a good, obedient wife.

After an excellent breakfast the archdeacon went off to that most private place, his workroom, telling the family that he was going to be very busy but that he would see Mr Chadwick if he called. When he reached his workroom he took out paper, pen and ink and laid them on his desk. Then he yawned, stretched and walked across the room to lock the door. Having made these preparations, he threw himself into a comfortable chair, opened a secret drawer beneath his table, took out a tasty French novel and began to read.

After an hour or two there was a knock at the door and Mr Chadwick's name was given. Immediately the French novel went back into the secret drawer and the comfortable chair was pushed into the shadows and, when the archdeacon unlocked the door, he was found by the manager working as usual on important Church matters. Mr Chadwick had just come from London and was known to be bringing important news.

'We've got Sir Abraham's opinion at last,' said Chadwick, passing him a copy of what the attorney-general had written. 'He has recognized a weak point in the opposite party's argument. They are directing their case against Mr Harding and myself, but Sir Abraham believes that we are only paid servants. The defendants in the case should have been either Barchester city or the Church or your father the bishop.'

'So Mr Bold is taking aim in the wrong direction, is he?' said the archdeacon.

'Haphazard thinks that any direction would be the wrong one. A lawsuit brought against the bishop might be the most dangerous, but, as Sir Abraham says, by arguing and delaying you could involve the other side in costs of fifteen thousand pounds before the matter was properly settled.'

The archdeacon clapped his hands together delightedly, thinking of the serious problems that his enemies would soon be facing.

'Don't let anyone see this document, though, archdeacon, because people will talk. We don't want the other side to find out how to fight their own battle, do we? No one in Barchester except you and me ought to see it.'

'No, no, certainly no one else,' said the archdeacon. He opened his secret drawer and carefully put Sir Abraham's opinion away, on top of the French novel.

'We must of course tell your father and Mr Harding as much of all this as will satisfy them that the matter is doing well,' said Chadwick.

'I shall meet them both tomorrow,' said Dr Grantly. 'I shall tell them all that they need to know. You can't stay to lunch, Mr Chadwick? Well, I realize your time is valuable.' And with these words the Doctor shook hands with the manager and saw him to the door.

The archdeacon was delighted. He knew that Mr Harding could never afford to pay the legal costs, which would be enormous, and that he and his father would have to pay most of them. But this did not discourage him. More important still was the victory of the Church, and this was the end to which all his energies were employed.

Chapter 5   A Council of War

The following day a meeting was arranged between Dr Grantly, his father the bishop and Mr Harding. The archdeacon arrived

The following day a meeting was arranged between Dr Grantly,
his father the bishop and Mr Harding.

first and had little difficulty in persuading his father that all was going well. On his arrival the warden took up his usual place at the bishop's elbow, affectionately asking after his old friend's health.

'Sir Abraham's opinion has come at last,' began the archdeacon.

'It is quite encouraging,' said the bishop, pressing his friend's arm. 'I'm so glad.'

'Yes,' said the archdeacon, 'Sir Abraham has paid very close attention to this case and his opinion is that the other side hasn't got a leg to stand on.'

'But how is that, archdeacon?'

'Well, under Hiram's will two paid officials have been chosen for the hospital: one to look after the men and the other to look after the money. You and Chadwick are these two servants and no one can criticize either of you for receiving a fixed wage for your work.'

'That does seem clear,' said the bishop.

'Yes, quite clear,' agreed the archdeacon. 'The amount of pay such servants receive depends on the market value of the services at any time; and those who manage the hospital should be the only judges of this.'

'And who does manage the hospital?' asked the warden.

'Oh, let them find that out; that's a quite different question. They are bringing this lawsuit against you and Chadwick, and now you have a full and perfect defence.'

'But according to that,' said Mr Harding, 'I might just as easily have sixteen hundred a year as eight, if the managers decide to give me that amount. And if I myself am one of the managers, in fact the chief manager, that can hardly be a fair arrangement.'

'Oh, that really has nothing to do with it. The main thing is to stop this young man and his cheating lawyers from interfering in an arrangement which everybody knows is fair and serviceable to the Church.'

Mr Harding sat silent for some time. At last he said, 'Did you see Sir Abraham's opinion, archdeacon?'

The archdeacon said that he had not – that is to say, he had, but he had not seen the opinion itself, he had seen what might be called a copy, whether of the whole or part of it.

'I would like to see the opinion,' said the warden, 'or at least a copy of it.'

'I suppose you can, if you insist; but I don't see the use myself. It is extremely important that no one should know its content, and so we do not wish to make extra copies.'

'Why should no one know its content?' asked the warden in puzzlement.

'What a question to ask!' cried the archdeacon, throwing up his hands in horror. 'But it is just like you – you are as innocent as a child in matters of business. Can't you see that we must do nothing to inform or help the enemy?'

'You mean that we are not to make public the fact that we have asked advice from this famous lawyer and that he has told us that Hiram's will is fully and fairly carried out?'

'Good heavens,' said the archdeacon, 'why should we say anything about Hiram's will?'

The warden now got up and began to walk nervously up and down the room. 'What about the *Jupiter*?' he asked suddenly, showing that his mind had certainly not been put at rest.

'Oh, the *Jupiter*,' answered the archdeacon. 'That can't do any real damage; you must just suffer that. In any case the matter is too unimportant to be mentioned again unless we ourselves bring it up.'

The warden continued his walking up and down. The hard, stinging words of the newspaper were fresh in his memory. 'If it

337

can be proved,' he burst out at last, 'that I have an honest right to my income, as I have always believed I had, I am just as ready as any other person to enjoy it. I am eager to clear my name and prove to the world that I have been on the side of right. But if it cannot be proved, I will give up my position here. I cannot suffer all this pain. Could you expect me to suffer it?' he asked the bishop, almost in tears.

'No, no, dear friend,' replied the bishop tenderly, 'you must only do what your heart tells you to be right.' Unwisely he asked his son to support his point of view.

The archdeacon could not feel sympathetic, but he could advise. 'If you were to give up the wardenship just to show that you can live without it, you would be giving encouragement to rebels of every kind to make similar attacks on the Church. It would be weak. It would be wrong. It would be simply cowardly.'

'Cowardly?' cried the bishop in protest.

'Well, is it not cowardly if one cannot face the evil things one is falsely accused of? No one who really knows you will think the worse of you because of what the *Jupiter* says.'

The poor warden gave a heavy sigh and his friend the bishop echoed the sigh more gently but the archdeacon paid no attention. 'You simply cannot give up this position. You owe it to my father, who offered it to you, to those who held the wardenship in the past and to those who may hold it in the future; and you owe it to us, your brothers in the Church.' The archdeacon having finished his speech, stood observing its effects on his two listeners.

The poor warden felt unable to breathe. The archdeacon's speech had silenced him, shaken him, almost destroyed him; but it had not satisfied him. He could not see the future clearly, but he saw a battle being prepared – a battle which would take away the few comfortable things left in his life.

He sat and looked at the archdeacon, as a bird might look at a snake.

'I hope you agree with me,' said the archdeacon at last, breaking the silence. 'And, Bishop, I hope *you* agree with me too.'

'Yes, I suppose so,' said his old father slowly.

'And you, warden?'

'Do not press me for an answer just at present. I shall do nothing without careful thought, and I will give you and the bishop notice before I do it.'

Without another word he left the room. He did not breathe freely until he found himself alone outside the palace. He walked slowly, for a long time, thinking about his troubled situation, trying without success to find some weakness in the archdeacon's arguments. Then he made his way home, having decided to suffer it all, the shame and the pain, as he had been pressed to do by those whom he believed best able to advise him.

♦

Mr Harding had never been a sadder man than when he returned to his own house that day. He wandered into the sitting-room, where his daughter was, but he felt unable to speak to her and went instead to the library. He was not quick enough to escape Eleanor's sharp eyes, however. She saw that he was upset and after a few moments she followed him. She found him sitting in his chair with no book or pen or music in front of him. He was doing nothing, looking at nothing, thinking of nothing: he was simply suffering.

'Leave me, my dear, because I am busy,' he said.

Eleanor, seeing how upset he was, went back to the sitting-room. Once again she found herself shut out of her father's troubles. She no longer expected to make him happy but simply wanted to be allowed to share his problems. It was not his conversation that she wanted but his trust.

She decided to pay a visit to Mary Bold, as she now did almost every day. John Bold was up in London, busy seeing lawyers and others involved in the case. Eleanor talked to Mary Bold about her poor father while Mary listened kindly, and then Mary told Eleanor about her brother's doings, which perhaps was kinder still.

Back at the hospital the warden sat alone, with his back against the arm of his chair. He was still sitting in the same chair, in the same position, when Eleanor came back from her visit.

Their tea was as gloomy as dinner had been. When the meal was over, Eleanor put her arms round the warden's neck and said, 'Papa, won't you tell me what it is?'

'What what is, my dear?'

'This new unhappiness of yours.'

'Oh, it's not new, my dear. We all have troubles sometimes,' he said, trying to smile.

'Papa, I will not leave you till you talk to me.'

The father kissed his daughter but still said nothing; he was shy even with his own child.

'Oh, papa, do tell me what it is. If you have sad news, let us be sad together. We are all in all to each other now.'

'My child,' he answered, 'why should you also be unhappy before it is necessary? It may be that we must leave this place; but why should you be worried till that time comes?'

'Give up your position, papa,' cried Eleanor, looking boldly into his face. 'Give it up, papa.'

It was tragic to see that look of hope and carefree happiness disappear from the warden's face as the memory of the arch-deacon came back to him. If only he could give it up, what an easy way out of all his troubles that would be!

Eleanor put her arms round the warden's neck and said, 'Papa, won't you tell me what it is?'

'Papa, don't think that you must stay here because of me. I can be happy with just a couple of rooms, if I see you come in and go out with a light heart.'

At these words the warden's tears fell like rain from his old eyes. When he was able to speak again, he told Eleanor all the arguments of the archdeacon, explaining how he was unable to oppose them. Eleanor for her part encouraged him to express every feeling and to open every secret in his heart to her. And finally they began to talk about John Bold, and Eleanor told how she had loved him once but could not do so now, since he had become her father's enemy. But the warden protested that Bold was no enemy of his, and spoke of happier days when their troubles would all be over. He would never allow her love for John to be changed by this quarrel. So each supported and encouraged the other, and both went to bed in a much calmer mood than they had known for some time.

Chapter 6   Eleanor's Own Petition

As Eleanor lay awake in bed that night, she was determined to free her father from his unhappy situation; she therefore formed a plan. She would go personally to John Bold and beg him to drop the legal action which he had begun, for her father's sake. Of course she could not offer herself as a reward – that would be quite improper. Though she might continue secretly to love John Bold, any question of marriage was naturally at an end.

Finally she slept and she rose with renewed hopes the following morning. She knew that John Bold was in London but was expected home soon, so she went to visit Mary, to arrange with her a plan for a meeting with her brother. However, on entering the Bolds' sitting-room she was surprised to see John's stick and coat and various bags, which showed that he had returned.

'John came back very suddenly,' said Mary. 'He has been travelling all night.'

'Then I'll come again some other time,' said Eleanor, in some confusion.

'He will be out for the next two hours,' said Mary. 'He's with that horrible Mr Finney. He came only to see him and he goes back again to London on the night train.'

Eleanor, who had not meant to have her interview with Bold that day, realized that such a meeting must be held now or never.

'Mary,' she began, 'I must see John before he goes back.'

'Of course,' said Mary, secretly rather surprised. 'I know he'll be delighted to see you.'

'I must see him now, today, and beg him to do me a special service,' went on Eleanor with great seriousness. 'But when I have done so, there can never be anything further between us.' And she began to explain her plan for saving her father.

It was clear that Mary Bold did not follow her line of thought. It seemed quite natural that Eleanor should try to speak to Bold's better feelings with reference to her father, and it seemed to Mary quite natural that John should give way, moved by such sincere tears and pretty looks. But why his good nature should not be rewarded, when the reward would help everyone and hurt no one, was a point which her practical nature could not understand, and she said so.

'But I am sure you love him, don't you?' argued Mary. 'And I am sure he loves you better than anything in the world.'

Eleanor tried to answer, but her eyes filled with tears, so she walked to the window, pretending to blow her nose, and when she recovered herself she said as firmly as she could, 'Mary, this is nonsense.'

'But you do love him,' Mary insisted. 'You love him with all your heart. You cannot deny it.'

'I – ' began Eleanor, and finally burst into tears, admitting to Mary that she did love John but that it would make no difference to her decision.

While they were still talking, Bold returned and Eleanor was forced to take action. She decided to carry out her original plan and ran into her friend's bedroom to wash the marks of tears from her eyes.

'Tell him that I am here,' she said to Mary, 'and that I shall join you both soon. And remember, whatever you do, don't leave us alone together.' Eleanor then washed her face with extreme care, thinking always of her poor father; and yet she also managed to improve the arrangement of a curl or two and give some added colour to her lips, to be sure that she would make a good impression.

John Bold had not seen her since the day they had met walking near the cathedral, yet during this time he had often thought of her and considered a hundred ways of showing her how pure his love was. Sometimes when he woke in the morning he even felt like blowing his brains out but this was usually after a late-night party with Tom Towers, his friend who was a reporter for the *Jupiter*.

How beautiful Eleanor seemed to him as she walked slowly into the room. The care she had taken with her appearance was now having its effect. She had never looked more lovely to her admirer than she did now. Her face was serious but full of movement, and her full, dark eyes shone with nervous energy.

He began to talk – about London, about Barchester, about the weather, and then asked about Mr Harding's health.

'My father is not very well,' said Eleanor. 'I specially want to speak to you about my father, Mr Bold. Papa is very unhappy, very unhappy indeed, about this business of the hospital. You would pity him, Mr Bold, if you could see the suffering it has caused him.'

'Oh, Miss Harding!'

'He is a changed man. And if this goes on, he will die; he will break his heart and die. I am sure it was not you, Mr Bold, who wrote those cruel things in the newspaper.'

'Indeed it was not,' cried John Bold, who was beginning to feel extremely guilty about his friendship with Tom Towers.

'No I'm sure it was not; you would not be so cruel. But they have called my father greedy and dishonest, and they say that he is robbing the old men and taking the money of the hospital for nothing.'

'I have never said so, Miss Harding. I – '

'No,' continued Eleanor, interrupting him, the tide of her feelings carrying her on. 'No, I am sure you have not, but others have said so. And if such things are said or written again, they will kill papa! You know, I'm sure, that he is not interested in money.'

Brother and sister were both quick to agree on this point.

'It is kind of you to say so, Mary, and of you too, Mr Bold. He would leave the hospital tomorrow, and give up his house and the income and everything, if the archdeacon – ' Here she almost said 'would allow it' but instead gave a deep sigh and added, 'How I wish he would!'

'No one who knows Mr Harding personally can possibly accuse him of doing wrong,' said Bold.

'But he is the one whom you are punishing. He is the one who is suffering,' said Eleanor. 'He has never had an unkind thought in his life, never spoken an unkind word.' At this moment she burst into tears so violent that she could not speak.

For the fifth or sixth time Bold tried to say that neither he nor his friends blamed Mr Harding personally.

'Then why are you punishing him?' cried Eleanor through her tears. 'Why are you wrecking his life? Oh, Mr Bold, why did you begin all this? You whom we all so – so – valued!'

John Bold tried his best to excuse himself, with references to his public duty, and repeated how highly he valued Mr Harding's character.

By now Eleanor was again in control of herself. 'Mr Bold,' she said, 'I have come here to beg you to give up this action.'

He stood up from his seat and looked inexpressibly unhappy and uncomfortable.

'I beg you to give it up, I beg you to spare my father, to spare his life and his health, before one or the other is destroyed. I know how much I am asking and how little right I have to ask anything, but it is not for myself – it is for my father. Oh, Mr Bold, I beg you, do this for us; do not drive to desperation a man who has loved you so well.'

She did not actually kneel in front of him, but she let her soft hands rest pitifully on his arm. What pleasure this would have given him in different circumstances! But what could he say to her now? How to explain that the matter was probably beyond his control, that he could not now silence the storm which he had created?

'Surely, John, you cannot refuse her,' said his sister.

'I would give my life itself,' he said, 'if it would be of use to her.'

'Oh, Mr Bold, do not say that. I ask nothing for myself, and what I ask for my father is something which is in your power to give.'

'I would give her anything,' said Mr Bold wildly, still talking to his sister. 'Everything I have is hers if she will accept it: my house, my heart. Every hope I have is fixed on her. Her smiles are

346

sweeter to me than the sun, and when I see her sad as she is now, every nerve in my body aches. No man can love her better than I love her.'

'No, no, no,' cried Eleanor, 'there can be no talk of love between us. Will you protect my father from the evil which you have brought upon him?'

'Oh, Eleanor, I will do anything. Let me tell you how I love you.'

'No, no, no,' she almost screamed. 'This is improper of you, Mr Bold. Will you leave my father to die in peace, quietly in his quiet home? I will not leave you till you promise me.' She held on to his arm as she followed him across the room. 'Promise me, promise me,' she cried. 'Say that my father is safe. One word will do. I know how true you are; say one word and I will let you go.' Still she held him, looking eagerly into his face. Her hair was loose, her eyes were red and yet he thought he had never seen her look so lovely. 'Promise me,' she said. 'I will not leave you till you promise me.'

'I will,' he said at last. 'All I can do, I will do.'

'Then may God protect you!' said Eleanor, and began to cry like a child. Exhausted, she wanted to go now, but Bold wished to explain the situation concerning her father, and she felt the need to stay and listen to him.

Bold explained that the action against the hospital was something which he alone had started; but that now many other people had become interested in the matter, some of whom were much more powerful than himself. However, the lawyers turned to him for their instructions and, more importantly, for the payment of their bills, and he promised that he would tell them at once that he wished to give up the case. He then suggested that he would ride over to see Dr Grantly that same afternoon, to tell him of the change in his intentions, and for this reason he would delay his immediate return to London.

All of this was indeed pleasant to hear, and Eleanor began to enjoy the satisfaction of feeling that she had succeeded in her purpose. She now got up to fetch her hat.

'Are you going so soon?' said Bold. 'May I not say one word for myself?'

'*I'll* fetch your hat, Eleanor,' said Mary, leaving the room.

'Mary, Mary, don't go!' cried Eleanor, but it was too late.

Now they were alone, John Bold poured out the feelings of his heart and this time Eleanor's 'no, no, no,' had no effect. She was pressed to say whether her father would be against their marriage; whether she found him acceptable; whether she preferred someone else; whether she could possibly love him; and so on. To each of these questions she was forced to give replies, so when she finally left the Bolds' home she felt that she had succeeded very well in part of her intention (to save her father) but had completely failed in the other part (to refuse any further contact with John).

Eleanor returned home not unhappy but yet not completely satisfied with herself. She felt annoyed with Mary, who had proved less dependable than expected. All she could do now, she thought, was to inform her father that John Bold was her accepted lover.

◆

John Bold got on his horse and rode off to Plumstead Episcopi, feeling rather nervous about the coming interview. From time to time he remembered the meeting with Eleanor which had just ended. On the one hand he felt the thrill of a lover who knows that he is loved; on the other hand he felt ashamed that his determination had given in so quickly to the tears of a pretty woman. How was he to face his lawyer? What was he to say to his friend Tom Towers?

On arrival he was shown into the archdeacon's workroom, with its desks and comfortable chairs. The archdeacon was standing with his back to the fireplace, ready to receive him, and his expression was one of satisfaction.

'Well, Mr Bold,' he said, 'what can I do for you? I am happy to help such an old friend of my father-in-law.'

'Please excuse my calling on you like this, Dr Grantly.'

'Certainly, certainly.'

Dr Grantly did not invite Bold to sit down, so he had to tell his story standing, with his hat in his hand. He did, however, manage to tell it, without any interruption from the archdeacon.

'And so, Mr Bold, I understand that you wish to bring this attack on Mr Harding to an end.'

'Oh, there has been no question of an attack, believe me . . .'

'Well, we won't quarrel about words. Most people would call this attempt to take away a man's income an attack, but we can call it instead a little game, if you prefer.'

'I intend to put an end to the legal action which I have begun,' said Bold stiffly.

'I understand,' said the archdeacon; 'you've already had enough of it. Well, I'm not really surprised: supporting a lost cause when there is nothing to win and everything to pay cannot be very pleasant.'

At this Bold turned very red in the face. 'You misunderstand the principles on which my actions depend, but that does not matter very much. I did not come here to discuss principles with you but to inform you of a matter of fact. Good day, Dr Grantly.'

'One moment, I have something to say in reply. You are going to end this lawsuit?'

'Yes, Dr Grantly, I am.'

'So first you allowed a gentleman who was one of your father's oldest friends to suffer all the insults which the press could throw at him; you have said publicly that it was your duty to protect those old fools in the hospital whom you have so shamefully deceived; and now you find that your game costs more than it is worth and you have decided to put an end to it. A wise decision, Mr Bold; it is just a pity that you have taken so long to reach it. Have you considered, though, that *we* may not wish to give up the case? that *we* may find it necessary to punish you for the injury you have done to us?'

Bold was now bright red with anger but he said nothing.

'We have found it necessary to employ the best advice that money can buy. You understand that these heavy costs must now come out of your own pocket. We shall not allow you to withdraw this matter from the courts.'

'You can do as you wish, Dr Grantly. Good day.'

'Let me finish, sir,' said the archdeacon. 'I have here the latest opinion from Sir Abraham Haphazard. I expect you have heard of this already, and that is the reason for your visit here today.'

'I know nothing at all of Sir Abraham Haphazard or his opinion.'

'In any case I shall tell you what it is: he considers that you do not have a leg to stand on in this matter, and that your attempts to destroy Mr Harding are completely useless. Here,' and he slapped the paper on the table in front of him. 'I have this opinion from the first lawyer in the land. Your case is in pieces, sir. And now I wish you good day, because I am busy.'

Bold had been almost speechless with anger, but now he felt so wounded and insulted that he could not leave the room without some kind of reply. 'I came here, Dr Grantly, with the warmest, kindest feelings – '

'Oh, of course you did; nobody doubts that.'

' – and you have injured me by your behaviour – '

'Of course. The damage you have done to my father-in-law must have caused you much pain.'

'The time will come, Dr Grantly, when you will understand why I called on you today.'

'No doubt, no doubt. Good day to you, Mr Bold.' And the doctor went off, closing the door behind him and making it quite impossible for John Bold to speak another word.

This was certainly the bitterest moment in John Bold's life. Not even the memory of his success in love could calm him. In fact he felt that his love for Eleanor was at the heart of the problem: it had caused him to give up the lawsuit and to be insulted; it had caused his actions to be misunderstood. This visit to the archdeacon had been a terrible mistake.

When he reached home, he rushed upstairs to the room where his sister Mary was sitting.

'If a devil really exists on earth,' he said, 'then it has the form of Dr Grantly.' He said nothing more but simply grabbed his hat, hurried out of the house and set off for London without another word.

Chapter 7   Mr Harding's Decision

The meeting between Eleanor and her father was not as stormy as the one just described but it was hardly more successful. On her return from Bold's house she found her father in a strange mood. He was walking quickly up and down the garden and she could see that he was greatly excited.

'I am going to London, my dear,' he said at once. 'I must settle this business somehow. There are some things I cannot bear.'

'Oh, papa, what is it?' she said, leading him by the arm into the house. 'I had such good news for you and now I'm afraid I'm too late.' Then she told him that the legal action was over and that Bold had asked her to tell her father that it would not be continued. She did not mention the new relationship she had formed with John Bold.

The warden did not seem particularly grateful for this news and, though Eleanor was not expecting to be warmly thanked, she felt hurt at the way in which her information was received.

'Mr Bold can do what he thinks proper, my love,' said Mr Harding. 'If he has done wrong, of course he will stop what he is doing, but that cannot change my purpose.'

'Oh, papa!' she cried, almost in tears, 'I thought you would be so happy – and that everything would now be all right.'

'Read that, my dear,' said the warden, giving her the latest number of the *Jupiter*, folded in such a way as to show a particular article. The topic was once again the wrongs committed by the Church. The writer heavily criticized families and individuals grown rich on income which they had not earned. It named the sons of some bishops and the grandsons of others and, having discussed these well-known personalities and their crimes, it turned finally to the subject of Mr Harding:

A few weeks ago we mentioned a case of similar injustice, though at a more modest level, in which the warden of a poor people's hospital in Barchester was receiving the greater part of the hospital's income. We refer to the question of the Barchester hospital again because we understand that a certain gentleman has taken out a lawsuit against Warden Harding on the part of the twelve old men, acting purely in the public interest. The argument for the defence is one which all fair-minded people will find completely unacceptable, namely that Mr Harding takes nothing except what he receives as a servant of the hospital, and that he is not personally responsible for deciding how much he should be paid for his work. If this defence is to be offered, we hope that Mr Harding will be called as a witness to describe: the nature of his employment; the amount of work that he does; the income which he receives; and how he was given this position. We do not think he will receive much public support.

As Eleanor read this column, her face grew red with anger and, when she finished it, she was almost afraid to look at her father.

'Well, my dear,' he said, 'is it worth being a warden at that price?'

'Oh, papa, dear papa.'

'Mr Bold can't unwrite that, my dear. Mr Bold can't stop people from reading it. And what's more, my dear,' he continued, 'Mr Bold can't disprove the truth of every word you have just read – and neither can I.' Eleanor stared at him, hardly understanding what he was saying. 'I have thought deeply about all this since we were together last night,' said her father, and he came and put his arm around her waist as he had done then. 'I have thought a lot about what the archdeacon has said and what this newspaper says, and I do believe I have no right to be here.'

'No right to be warden of the hospital, papa?'

'No right to be warden with eight hundred a year, no right to such a house as this, or to spend on luxuries money that was intended for charity. Mr Bold may do as he likes about his lawsuit but I hope he will not give it up for my sake.'

Poor Eleanor! Believing till now that she had done so much, she suddenly felt that her attempts had resulted in nothing; it was not a pleasant feeling.

'They must not put forward this argument in my defence,' continued the warden. 'The man who wrote the article is right

353

when he says that such a defence is disgusting to an honest mind. I will go up to London, my dear, and see these lawyers myself; and if no better excuse can be made for me than that, I must leave the hospital.'

'But the archdeacon, papa?'

'It can't be avoided, my dear. There are some things which a man cannot bear; I cannot bear that.' And he put his hand on the newspaper.

'But will the archdeacon go with you?'

'No, I think not,' he said. 'I think I shall start before the archdeacon is ready. I shall go early tomorrow morning.'

'That will be best, papa,' said Eleanor, understanding very well her father's way of thinking.

'The fact is, my dear, I wish to do all this before the archdeacon can – can interfere. He will accuse me of being weak and cowardly, but I know that I ought not to remain here. So, Nelly, we shall have to leave this pretty place.'

Eleanor's face grew bright as she told her father how completely she agreed with him. She could see that he was once more his usual happy self.

'We shall live at Crabtree Parva. That also has a very pretty garden.' Crabtree Parva was a church where Mr Harding had been a clergyman in the past and which was now looked after by a younger colleague, a married man with half a dozen children. The house at Crabtree was very modest, as the income was – only eighty pounds a year.

Eleanor told her father that she herself would have no regrets about leaving the house or giving up the horses; she was simply happy that he would escape from all the troubles which surrounded him at present.

'But we will take the music, my dear.'

And so they went on planning their future happiness. Finally the warden did thank Eleanor for what she had done and

Eleanor did find an opportunity to tell him her secret. Her father showed that he was delighted and said that the man she loved was honest, true and kind-hearted – 'a man to whom I can trust my dear child with safety'.

Eleanor ran upstairs to prepare her father's clothes for the journey, and the warden returned to his garden to say goodbye to every tree and plant that he knew so well.

♦

Still suffering from the archdeacon's insults and deeply annoyed with himself, Bold returned to London. His interview with the archdeacon had gone badly wrong, but he still felt it necessary to keep his promise to Eleanor and he set off to do this with a heavy heart.

The lawyers whom he had employed in London received his instructions with surprise and considerable doubt but they were forced to obey, expressing their regret that the heavy costs would fall on their own employer when it would not have been difficult to throw them on the opposite side.

He next thought of the newspapers. The leader of the attack was of course the *Jupiter*. He knew Tom Towers very well and had often discussed with him the matter of the hospital. Bold could not say whether the pieces which had appeared in the newspaper were written by his friend; Towers was always very cautious in such matters and unwilling to talk about the newspaper's plans. However, Bold believed he had written the words which had caused such pain in Barchester and he felt it was his duty to prevent him from repeating them. This idea led him from the lawyers' office to the place which formed the centre of Tom Towers's operations.

Tom Towers lived comfortably in an apartment in the Temple.*

* The Temple is a part of London where lawyers have their offices.

The room in which he usually worked was filled with books and works of art. He was enjoying a final cup of tea, surrounded by a sea of newspapers, when his servant brought in John Bold's visiting-card. Tom Towers told the boy to show his friend in. The two men were about the same age and had known each other since Tom was a poor law student, struggling to earn a living as a newspaper reporter. Tom Towers was now more powerful than most politicians, though few people knew his name. Some people believed that Tom Towers was the most powerful man in Europe, with the appearance of an ordinary person but the powers of a god.

Chapter 8   Persuading the Press

'Ah, Bold! How are you?' cried his friend.

'And how are you? I suppose you're busy?' inquired Bold.

'Yes, but if I have a free hour in the day, this is it.'

'I want to ask you if you can help me in a certain matter.'

Towers understood from his friend's voice that he was referring to the newspaper. He smiled but made no promise.

'You know the lawsuit I've been busy with?' said Bold. 'Well, I've given it up.'

Tom Towers simply lifted one eyebrow and waited for his friend to continue.

'Yes, I've given it up. The fact is that the behaviour of Mr Harding – Mr Harding is the – '

'Oh yes, you mean the warden – the man who takes all the money and does nothing,' said Tom Towers, interrupting him.

'Well, I'm not sure about that. But he has behaved so extremely well in this matter, so unselfishly, so openly, that I cannot continue with the case and so cause him harm.' Bold's heart remembered Eleanor as he said this, but he felt that what he said was not untrue.

'It's the old story of the traditional rights of the person holding the position,' said Towers. 'But what happens if that person holds a traditional wrong, and the traditional rights lie with the poor people, if only they knew how to get at them? Isn't this case something like that?'

Bold could not deny it but thought that it was one of those cases which needed careful management before any real good could be done.

'It will cost you a fair amount, I'm afraid,' said Towers.

'A few hundred pounds – perhaps three hundred,' said Bold. 'I can't help that and I'm prepared for it.'

'That's philosophical! It's quite unusual to hear a man talking of his hundreds in such an unemotional manner. But I am sorry that you are giving up the case; it damages your good name if you start something like this and don't bring it to a finish.'

'I couldn't continue it,' said John Bold, 'because I found I was in the wrong.'

Tom Towers seemed rather unconcerned. 'In that case,' he said, 'of course you must give it up.'

'And I have called this morning to ask you also to give it up,' said Bold, trying to hide his embarrassment.

'To ask me?' said Tom Towers, with the most gentle smile and a look of innocent surprise.

'Yes,' said Bold, showing great hesitation. 'The *Jupiter*, you know, has taken the case up very strongly. Mr Harding has felt its criticisms deeply. I thought if I could explain to you that he personally has not been to blame, these newspaper articles might be discontinued.'

Tom Towers's face was a model of calmness as this suggestion was made. He showed no sign either of agreement or

357

disagreement. 'My dear friend,' he said, when Bold had finished speaking, 'I really am not responsible for what the *Jupiter* does.'

'Come on, Towers,' said Bold, taking courage as he remembered his promise to Eleanor, 'I have no doubt in my own mind that you wrote the articles yourself, and they were very well written. All I am asking is that in future, for my sake, you will make no personal reference to Mr Harding.'

'My dear Bold,' said Tom Towers, 'I have known you for many years and value your friendship. I hope you will let me explain to you that none of us connected with the press can properly allow any kind of interference.'

'Interference!' cried Bold. 'I don't want to interfere.'

'Indeed you do, my friend. What else do you call it? You think that I am able to keep certain remarks out of a newspaper. Your information is probably incorrect but you think I have such power and you are asking me to use it; that is called interference. Now, if I had this power, as you believe, and was ready to use it as you want me to, would that not be very improper? It is the independence of great newspapers like the *Jupiter* which has earned them so much respect in the eyes of the public. Think about this carefully and you'll see that I am right.'

Bold realized that it was useless to argue further. He said goodbye and left the room as quickly as he could, in his own mind accusing his friend of obvious dishonesty. 'I know he wrote those articles,' said Bold to himself, 'and I know he got his information from me. He was quite willing to believe my word absolutely when it suited his own opinions but when I offer him information which offends his views, he tells me that private considerations are damaging to the high principles of the press! What is any public question but a collection of private interests? What is any newspaper article but the expression of the views held by one side?' It was the completely unshakeable position

'My dear friend, I really am not responsible for what
the Jupiter does.'

which his friend held on what was right and wrong that made Bold so angry, and this same quality which made such a position secretly so attractive.

◆

The good warden had to use his modest ability to deceive to get out of Barchester without being stopped on the way. The evening before he had written a note to the archdeacon, explaining his intentions of making this journey and, if possible, of seeing the attorney-general. He excused himself for not informing Dr Grantly earlier, saying that his decision had been a very sudden one. He then gave the note to Eleanor, on the understanding that it would be sent over, but not too quickly, to Plumstead Episcopi.

The warden had also prepared a note for Sir Abraham Haphazard, explaining who he was and begging the great gentleman to spare him a ten-minute interview at any time on the following day. Mr Harding knew that the archdeacon would follow him to London as soon as he received his note but he judged that for this one day he was safe. If he could manage to see Sir Abraham that day, he would have carried out his purpose before the archdeacon could interfere.

On arriving in London the warden drove to the hotel near St Paul's* where he had stayed in the past. He ordered dinner and then set off to visit the attorney-general in his office. There he was told that Sir Abraham was in court. Mr Harding left his note. He asked to have an answer that same evening and said he would return to receive it. When he returned he was given his own note back again, with this message written in pencil on it: 'Tomorrow, 10.00 p.m., my office. A.H.' 10.00 p.m.! What an hour to choose for a legal interview!

* The famous cathedral church in London.

The next day he had breakfast at nine and told the waiter, 'If anyone calls for me, I am going to eat out and I shall return about eleven o'clock this evening.'

We shall not describe the nervous wanderings in which the poor warden spent the next twelve hours until the time of his appointment, though they seemed endless. A clock was striking ten as he knocked on Sir Abraham's door, where a clerk informed him that the great man would be with him immediately.

Chapter 9   The Law Gives its Opinion

Mr Harding was shown into a comfortable library and was not kept waiting long. After ten or fifteen minutes the attorney-general entered.

'Very sorry to keep you waiting, Mr Warden,' said Sir Abraham, shaking hands with him, 'and sorry too about the lateness of the hour, but it was the best I could do.'

Sir Abraham was a tall, thin man whose hair was grey but who did not look old in other ways. His hard face gave him the appearance of a machine with a mind, full of intelligence but empty of natural feelings. He was as bright and sharp and cold as a diamond. He knew everyone whom it was useful to know and yet he had no friends. The one thing which he respected was success and he knew of no one as successful as himself.

'And so, Mr Warden,' said Sir Abraham, 'all our troubles with this lawsuit are at an end. You need trouble yourself no further about it. Of course they must pay the costs, so the cost to you and Dr Grantly will be very small.'

'I'm afraid I don't quite understand you, Sir Abraham.'

'Don't you know that their lawyers have advised us that they have withdrawn the lawsuit?'

Mr Harding explained that he knew nothing of this, though

he had heard of some such intention. Finally he also succeeded in making Sir Abraham understand that even this did not satisfy him; and he began to explain his point of view.

'I know I have no right to trouble you personally with this matter, but as it is of the greatest importance to me, as all my happiness is concerned with it, I thought I might dare ask your advice. The truth is, Sir Abraham, that I am not fully satisfied with this matter as it stands at present. I can clearly see that the finances of the hospital are not arranged according to the will of John Hiram.'

'No such organizations are, Mr Harding, nor can they be. The changed circumstances in which we live make it impossible.'

'That is quite true, but I can't see how those changed circum-stances give me the right to eight hundred a year. I don't know whether I have ever read John Hiram's will but if I read it now, I would not understand it. What I want you to tell me, Sir Abraham, is this: do I as warden have a legal right to what remains of the income after the twelve old men have been fully taken care of?'

Sir Abraham said that he couldn't exactly say it in so many words that Mr Harding had a legal right, etc, etc, etc, and ended by expressing his strong opinion that it would be madness to ask any further questions on the matter as the lawsuit was going to be – in fact already was – withdrawn.

Mr Harding, sitting in his chair, began to play an imaginary cello. 'I can resign,' said Mr Harding, slowly playing away with one hand.

'What! Give up your position completely?' said the attorney-general, looking at him in total amazement.

'Did you see those articles in the *Jupiter*?' said Mr Harding, almost sure that Sir Abraham would be sympathetic to the embarrassment he had felt.

Sir Abraham said that he had seen them. The idea that this poor little clergyman could be forced to resign because of a newspaper article was so insane that he hardly knew how to talk to him as a sensible human being.

'Wouldn't it be better to wait,' he said, 'until Dr Grantly comes to town? Wouldn't it be better to delay your decision until you are able to get his advice?'

Mr Harding said firmly that he could not wait and Sir Abraham began seriously to doubt that he was sane. 'Of course,' he said, 'if you have a private income large enough to cover your needs and if this – '

'I haven't a sixpence of my own, Sir Abraham,' said the warden.

'Good heavens! Then Mr Harding, how do you intend to live?'

Mr Harding explained that he would continue to receive eighty pounds a year for his work as precentor and that he had a right to the clergyman's place at Crabtree, which would bring him another eighty pounds. He mentioned that these two positions involved duties which might be difficult to carry out at the same time but that there was the possibility of changing places with a colleague.

Sir Abraham listened in pitying amazement. 'I really think, Mr Harding, that you should wait for the archdeacon. This is a very serious step – one which, in my opinion, you have absolutely no need to take. A man is never the best judge of his own situation.'

'A man is the best judge of what he himself feels. I would rather be poor for the rest of my life than read another article like the two which have appeared, feeling, as I do, that the writer has truth on his side.'

'Don't you have a daughter, Mr Harding – an unmarried daughter?'

'I have, Sir Abraham, and she and I are in complete agreement on this subject.'

'Excuse me for saying so, Mr Harding, but shouldn't you be more conscious of your daughter's happiness? For her sake, give up this idea.'

'But if this income is not lawfully mine, then she and I will both have to beg,' said the warden, in a voice much sharper than before.

'My dear sir, nobody questions its lawfulness.'

'Yes, Sir Abraham, one person does question it – I question it myself. It may seem strange to you, Sir Abraham, that I lived for ten years without giving any thought to these matters until they were made violently known to me by a public newspaper. But now my sense of right and wrong is fully awake, I must obey it. When I came here today I did not know that Mr Bold had withdrawn his lawsuit, and my purpose was to ask you to give up my defence. As there is now no action, there can be no defence. I would like you to know that, from tomorrow, I shall no longer be warden of the hospital.' And as he finished speaking he played a complicated tune with wild movements of his arms.

Sir Abraham looked at him with great surprise: a few minutes ago so shy and hesitant and now so full of strong, even violent feelings. 'You'll sleep on this, Mr Harding, and tomorrow – '

'I have done more than sleep on it.' said the warden. 'I have lain awake on it, night after night. I could not sleep on it then but I hope to do so now.'

The attorney-general had no answer to make to this, so Mr Harding finally withdrew, thanking the great man for his kind attention.

Mr Harding felt a certain amount of satisfaction as he left Sir Abraham's office. He knew that the attorney-general thought he was a fool, but he did not care. He now had to face the

'Yes, Sir Abraham, one person does question it – I question
it myself.'

archdeacon, so he walked slowly back to his hotel. He rang the bell softly, his heart beating. He almost thought of escaping round the corner and delaying the storm a little longer, but he heard the slow steps of the old waiter approaching to unlock the door.

'Dr Grantly is here,' he was told, 'and Mrs Grantly. They are in the sitting-room upstairs, waiting for you.'

The warden tried to appear unconcerned as he replied, 'Oh, indeed! I'll go upstairs at once,' but he failed completely.

As the warden entered the sitting-room, the archdeacon was standing in the middle of the room with a deeply sad expression, while his patient wife sat on a sofa behind him.

'Papa, I thought you were never coming back,' said the lady. 'It's twelve o'clock.'

'Yes, my dear,' said the warden. 'The attorney-general could not see me until ten. It is late, but what could I do?' He gave his daughter a kiss, shook hands with his son-in-law and again tried to look unconcerned.

'And you have been with the attorney-general?' asked the archdeacon.

Mr Harding said that he had.

'But, papa, what did you say to Sir Abraham?' asked his daughter.

'I asked him, my dear, to explain John Hiram's will to me. He couldn't explain it in the only way that would have satisfied me, and so I resigned the wardenship.'

'Resigned it! Good heavens!' and the good archdeacon sank back in horror into an armchair. 'I'm sure Sir Abraham must have advised you to ask for guidance from your friends.'

Mr Harding said that this was correct.

'Then your threatening to resign amounts to nothing and we are just where we were before.'

Mr Harding was now moving uncomfortably from one foot to the other. In fact he did not have the least doubt in his mind about resignation, though he did have doubts about his ability to defend his decision against his son-in-law.

The archdeacon was marching up and down the room, signalling by certain shakings of his head the complete stupidity of his father-in-law. 'Why,' he said at last, 'why did you leave Barchester so suddenly? Why didn't you tell us what you were planning to do?'

The warden hung his head and made no reply. 'I think I'll go to bed,' he said at last.

'At least you'll promise me to take no further step without discussing the matter first,' said the archdeacon.

Mr Harding gave no answer but slowly lit his lamp.

'Come, warden,' said the archdeacon, 'promise Susan to give up this idea of resigning the wardenship.'

The warden looked at his daughter and said, 'I'm sure Susan will not ask me to break my word or do what I know to be wrong.'

'Papa,' she said, 'it would be madness to give up your position. What are you going to live on?'

'God who feeds the wild birds will take care of me also,' said Mr Harding with a smile. 'And I shall have my place at Crabtree,' he added.

'Eighty pounds a year!' cried the archdeacon.

'And the position of precentor,' said his father-in-law.

'My dear warden,' said Dr Grantly, 'this is all nonsense. Whether you have eighty pounds or one hundred and sixty, you still can't live on it. You can't destroy Eleanor's future like that. You simply can't resign: the bishop will not accept it. The whole thing is settled. What we must prevent now is any more newspaper articles.'

'But I shall resign,' said the warden, very, very softly.

'Then, Mr Harding, there is nothing but disaster in front of you,' said the archdeacon, unable to contain himself any longer. 'How do you mean to pay for the enormous expenses of this action?'

'I will sell my furniture,' said the warden.

'Furniture!' cried the archdeacon, marching up and down the room. 'Your father is like a child,' he said to his wife. 'Eight hundred pounds a year, with nothing to do! And he throws it away because some journalist writes an article in a newspaper! Well, I have done my duty. If he chooses to destroy his child, it is not my fault.'

There was a pause for about a minute and then the warden picked up his lamp and quietly said, 'Good night.'

'Good night, papa,' said Mrs Grantly.

As Mr Harding closed the door he heard the familiar remark – slower, heavier and gloomier than ever – 'Good heavens!'

Chapter 10   The Warden Resigns

The three met again the next morning at breakfast, a gloomy event. The archdeacon ate his toast in silence, turning over bitter thoughts in his mind. The warden tried to talk to his daughter and she tried to answer him but they both failed.

'I think I shall go back home at three o'clock today,' the warden said.

'I must go to Cox and Cummins,' said the archdeacon. 'I must once more beg you to take no further steps till you see my father. At least you owe him that much.' And without waiting for a reply Dr Grantly set off. Shortly afterwards Susan also left the room.

The warden now wrote his letter of resignation, which went like this:

My Lord Bishop,

It is with the greatest pain that I feel it necessary to resign into your hands the wardenship of the hospital at Barchester, to which you so kindly appointed me nearly twelve years ago.

I need not explain the circumstances which have made this step necessary to me. You know that a question has been asked about the right of the warden to the income which goes with the wardenship. It seems to me that this right is not built on very solid ground, and I hesitate to run the risk of accepting an income which is legally doubtful.

The position of precentor of the cathedral is, as you know, traditionally joined to that of the warden. However, unless you disagree with such an arrangement, I would like to continue the work of the precentor.

You will realize that my resignation of the wardenship does not prevent the position from being offered to someone else. I do not wish to suggest that there is harm in another person filling it or that such a person will not command my greatest respect.

I cannot finish this official letter without again thanking you for all your great kindness, and I beg to sign myself

Your most obedient servant,
Septimus Harding,
Warden and Precentor

He then wrote the following private note:

My dear Bishop

I cannot send you this official letter, which may perhaps be made public, without sending you also a warmer expression of thanks for all your kindness to me. You will, I know, understand the feelings and perhaps pity the weakness that make me resign my position at the hospital. I am not a person whose character is strong enough *to stand firm against public attack. If I were sure that I was absolutely in the right, I should consider it my duty to defend my position under any circumstances; but I do not have this complete certainty and I cannot believe that you will think me wrong in what I am doing.*

My dear friend, let me have a line from you to say that you do not blame me for what I am doing and that the clergyman of Crabtree Parva will be the same friend to you as the warden of the hospital.

I thank you from my heart for the appointment which I am now giving up and for all your kindness; and am, dear bishop, now as always,

Yours most sincerely,
Septimus Harding

Having written these letters, Mr Harding, no longer the warden, realized that it was nearly two o'clock and that he must prepare for his journey. He packed his bag and paid his bill. He was then driven to the station with a warm glow of success in his heart. Indeed, had he not for the first time in his life held his ground against his much-feared son-in-law and against the archdeacon's wife also? Was not this a great victory?

Eleanor was waiting at Barchester station when the train came in to the platform.

'Dear papa,' she said, as soon as he told her the news, 'I'm so glad.'

◆

The morning after Mr Harding's return home, he received a note from the bishop. 'Please come and see me at once,' wrote the bishop, 'so that we may see what can be done.'

Mr Harding did go to see the bishop and there were long discussions between the two old friends. The bishop's first suggestion was that they should live together at the palace. He told Mr Harding that he needed another helper, a companion with whom to discuss Church matters. It was difficult for Mr Harding to make his friend understand that this arrangement would not suit him: he could not resign from his present appointment and then become a regular guest at the bishop's table. Mr Harding, though deeply grateful, refused this offer. His wish was to support himself, not to be supported by the charity of others.

The bishop considered that Mr Harding could continue to hold the position of precentor, an opinion with which everyone agreed.

Mr Harding allowed himself no rest until everything was prepared for his departure from the hospital. The lawyers' bill, which the archdeacon had used to frighten his father-in-law, was not as great as he had feared and was paid by the bishop, on the instructions of the archdeacon. For the present Mr Harding rented rooms in Barchester, and his music, books and instruments were taken there, together with his own armchair and Eleanor's favourite sofa. Eleanor had prepared a little bedroom for herself in one of the rooms above the chemist's shop where she and her father were going to stay.

The day for the move was fixed and all Barchester was greatly excited. Opinion was divided about the correctness of Mr Harding's action. The businessmen, the officers of the town and most of the ladies were loud in his praise; he was gentlemanly, generous, upright. But the professional people, especially the lawyers and clergymen, had a different way of thinking. They said that Mr Harding had shown weakness, an absence of fellow-feeling. His resignation would do much harm and very little good.

On the evening before he left he asked all the old men to his sitting-room to say goodbye. The wine and glasses were on the table and the chairs arranged round the room. The sound of old feet could be heard approaching.

'Come in, my friends, come in,' said the warden. 'Come and sit down.' And he took Abel Handy by the hand and led the old rebel to a chair.

The others followed slowly – some hardly able to walk, some almost blind. Now their old faces were covered with shame, and every kind word from their master simply increased their guilty feelings. When the news had first reached them that Mr Harding was going to leave the hospital, it was seen as a kind of victory. He had admitted that he had no right to the money about which they had petitioned, and, as it did not belong to him, it must of course belong to them. The one hundred a year owed to each of them was actually becoming a reality. Abel Handy was a hero and Bunce a false companion who had taken the enemy's side. But other rumours soon made their way into the old men's rooms. First they were told that the income given up by Mr Harding would not come to them, and the lawyer Finney told them that this was true. They were then told that Mr Harding's place would be immediately filled by someone else. They knew that a new warden could not be kinder than Mr Harding and imagined that he would be much less friendly. And then came the bitter news that from the moment of Mr Harding's departure his own special gift of twopence a day would no longer be given out. So this was to be the end of their great struggle, of their fight for their rights, of their petition, their arguments and their hopes! They were to change the best of masters for a possible bad one and to lose twopence a day each man!

'Sit down, sit down, my friends,' said the warden. 'I want to say a word to you and to drink your healths before I say goodbye. My dear old friends,' he said, 'you all know that I am going to leave you. There has been some misunderstanding between us recently. You have thought, I believe, that you did not get all that you deserved and that the income from the hospital has not been properly shared out. I myself am unable to say how this money should be divided or managed, and so I have thought it best to go.'

'We never wanted you to leave us, sir,' said Handy.

'No indeed, sir,' said Skulpit, 'we never thought it would end like this.'

'No,' went on Mr Harding, 'I am sure you did not wish to turn me out, but I thought it best to resign. And now that I am about to leave you, I dare to offer you my advice.'

The men all said that such advice would be most welcome.

'Another gentleman will probably take my place here very soon, and I strongly advise you to receive him in a friendly manner and not to discuss among yourselves the amount of his income. You are well looked after here and I do not think that your position can be improved.'

'It's true, sir, what you say. We see it all now,' cried one of the old men.

'Yes, Mr Harding,' said Bunce, speaking for the first time. 'I believe they do understand it now, now that they have driven from under their roof the best warden that they will ever know – and just when they stand in most need of a friend.'

'Come, come, Bunce,' said Mr Harding, blowing his nose and wiping his eyes.

'Oh, none of us ever wanted to do Mr Harding any harm,' said Handy. 'If he's leaving now, it's not because of us. And I don't see why Mr Bunce speaks against us like that.'

'You've spoiled your lives and you've spoiled mine too, and that's why,' said Bunce.

'Nonsense, Bunce,' said Mr Harding, 'nobody's life is spoiled. I hope that we shall all leave as friends, that you'll all drink a glass of wine in a friendly spirit with me and with one another. You'll have a good friend too in your new warden, I'm sure. And remember that I'm not going so far away that I shall not be able to come and see you sometimes.'

Mr Harding filled all the glasses, and himself gave one to each man. Then, lifting his own, he said, 'I hope you may all live contented, trusting in God and thankful for the good things he has given you.'

These poor old men felt guilty and ashamed to have driven the good warden from his happy home to spend his old age in some strange place. They did their best, however; they drank the wine and left. Mr Harding shook hands and spoke a kind word to each one as he departed. Finally only Bunce remained.

Mr Harding went sadly back to his sitting-room and Bunce went with him. The good warden did what he could to make his old friend happier but poor old Bunce felt that his days of happiness were gone. 'My life is over,' he said. 'I have now to forgive those who have injured me – and then die.'

And so the old man departed and Mr Harding himself finally burst into tears.

Chapter 11 Happiness

The following morning Mr Harding walked out of the hospital arm in arm with his daughter and quietly entered his new apartment in town. There was a tear in Eleanor's eye as she left, but Mr Harding walked with a firm step and a look of satisfaction on his face.

It was not long before the archdeacon brought up the subject of a new warden with his father. Naturally he expected to be asked to recommend someone, and he had three or four suitable clergymen on his list. He was greatly amazed when his father decided that no one would be appointed in Mr Harding's place. 'If we can put matters right, Mr Harding will return,' he said, 'and if we cannot, it would be wrong to put any other gentleman into so cruel a position.' It was useless for the archdeacon to argue, to insist and even to threaten; nothing could persuade his father to fill the vacant place.

The hospital itself has suffered over the years since Mr Harding left it. No one now lives in the warden's house. Six of the old men have died and their places remain unfilled. Quarrels divide the six who are left. The hospital building has been kept in good condition by Mr Chadwick, who still acts as manager, but the whole place has become untidy and ugly. The warden's garden is uncared-for and wild, the flower beds empty and the grass uncut. A few years ago it was the prettiest place in Barchester and now it is a matter of shame to the city.

◆

Mr Harding did not go to Crabtree Parva in the end. Instead, he was put in charge of a tiny church within the walls of the city. It is no bigger than an ordinary room, but it is still a perfect church. Here he holds the afternoon service every Sunday, and always in the front row is to be seen the faithful Mr Bunce. Mr Harding is still the precentor in the cathedral. He leads a contented life. He still lives in the rooms he rented when he left the hospital, but now he has them to himself. Three months after the move Eleanor became Mrs Bold and of course went off to live with her husband.

The marriage itself created some difficulties. The archdeacon, whose feelings were still strong, could not agree to be present at the event himself, although he allowed his wife and children to go. The marriage took place at the palace and the bishop himself took the service. About six months after the wedding, the archdeacon agreed to meet John Bold at a dinner party and since that time they have become almost friends. The archdeacon firmly believes that marriage has opened John Bold's eyes to the great truths of religion, and Bold has come to think that time has softened the rougher parts of the archdeacon's character.

Mr Harding, then, is a happy man. His time is spent mainly at his daughter's or at the palace. He is never left alone for long, and within a year of Eleanor's marriage his determination to live alone had changed enough for him to allow his cello to be kept ready for him at his daughter's house.

Every other day a message is brought to him from the bishop. 'The bishop is not very well today and he hopes Mr Harding will dine with him.' In fact, although the bishop is over eighty, he is never ill. Mr Harding does dine with him very often, which means going to the palace at three and remaining there till ten; and if he does not go, the bishop is in a complaining mood and goes off to bed an hour before his usual time.

It took a long time for the people of Barchester to stop calling Mr Harding 'Mr Warden'. Today if someone calls him by that name, he always says with a smile, 'Not warden now, only precentor.'

ACTIVITIES

Chapters 1–5

Before you read

1 Look at the pictures in this book. How long ago does the story take place? How can you tell?

2 These words all come in this part of the story. Use a dictionary to check their meaning.

article   carriage   cello   charity
lawsuit   petition   warden   will

Now match each word with one of the meanings below:

a a musical instrument with strings
b written instructions about what to do with your property after you die
c a formal request
d a vehicle pulled by horses
e a piece of writing in a newspaper or magazine
f an organization created for the good of others
g a legal action in the courts
h the head of a school or college

After you read

3 Can you identify these people?

a energetic, confident, a good speaker, decisive
b brave, enthusiastic, amusing, young, active
c fair-minded, generous, not hard-working, musical
d not beautiful, kind-hearted, with a clear sense of right and wrong
e pleasant-looking, seemingly self-confident, very fond of her father, in love

4 Answer these questions:

a Who are the petitioners and what do they want?
b What actions does Dr Grantly take over the petition?
c In Chapter 4, what upsets Mr Harding's peace of mind?
d Why does he feel better at the end of Chapter 5?

Chapters 6–11

Before you read

5 Is Mr Harding being fair or weak over the question of his job and salary? What would *you* do in his situation? Discuss this with other students.

6 Dr Grantly says: 'We shall not allow you to withdraw the matter.' *Withdraw* means:

   a to remove
   b to delay
   c to discuss

7 Mr Harding says: 'I can resign.' *Resign* means:

   a to sign another document
   b to give up my position
   c to deny the previous statement

After you read

8 Who says these things? Who to?

   a 'But he is the one you are punishing.'
   b 'It's quite unusual to hear a man talking of his hundreds in such an unemotional manner.'
   c 'God who feeds the wild birds will take care of me also.'

Writing

9 Explain the terms of John Hiram's will concerning the hospital.

10 Imagine that you live in Barchester. You read the article in the Jupiter given on page 330. Write a letter to the newspaper, defending Mr Harding and the church's position.

11 Trollope makes some indirect criticisms of the church, the law and the press in his novel. Describe some of them.

Jude the Obscure

THOMAS HARDY

Level 5

Retold by Katherine Mattock
Series Editors: Andy Hopkins and Jocelyn Potter

Contents

Introduction

'We loved each other too much, too selfishly, you and I, Jude; and now we're punished . . .'

Young Jude Fawley lives in the sleepy village of Marygreen but he often looks across the fields to the roofs and spires of the city of Christminster. He promises himself that one day he will leave his obscure life in Marygreen and go there. He will study at the university, enter the church and become a great man.

But it is not easy for a poor boy to follow the path Jude has chosen, and life has many surprises for him. First, there is Arabella Donn, the beautiful country girl who is looking for a husband. And then there is Sue Bridehead, whom Jude loves.

Thomas Hardy was born in 1840, in Upper Bockhampton, a village near Dorchester in the south-west of England. His father was a stone-mason and builder. Thomas was educated at local schools and then got a job in a local architect's office, where he remained for ten years. In 1861, he moved to London and studied at evening classes. He began to write stories. One of his early books was *Under the Greenwood Tree* (1872). The book was quite successful, and Hardy decided to give up architecture and become a professional writer. In 1874, he completed *Far from the Madding Crowd*. This novel already has some of the sadness and seriousness that are to be found in Hardy's later work. Other novels followed, all set in 'Wessex', the south-west of England where he grew up: *The Mayor of Casterbridge* (1886), *The Woodlanders* (1887), *Tess of the D'Urbervilles* (1891) and *Jude the Obscure* (1896).

Hardy died in 1928 at the age of eighty-eight.

PART 1   AT MARYGREEN

Chapter 1   Goodbye, Mr Phillotson

The schoolmaster was leaving the village and everybody seemed sorry. As his belongings were brought out of the schoolhouse, tears came into the eyes of a small boy of eleven, one of his night-school pupils.

'Why are you going to Christminster, Mr Phillotson?' asked the boy.

'You wouldn't understand, Jude,' the schoolmaster said kindly.

'You will, perhaps, when you are older.'

'I think I would understand now, Mr Phillotson.'

'Well then,' said the teacher. 'I'm going to Christminster to be near the university. My dream is to go to university and then to enter the Church.'

Jude helped to lift Phillotson's things onto a cart, all except a piano. 'Aunt can look after that,' the boy suggested, 'until you send for it.'

At nine o'clock, the schoolmaster got up into the cart beside his box of books. 'Goodbye, my friends,' he said. 'Be a good boy, Jude. Be kind to animals and read all you can. And if you ever come to Christminster, hunt me out.'

The horse and cart moved off across the village green, past the well and the old cottages and the new church. Jude looked sadly down into the well at the water far below. 'He was too clever to stay here any longer,' he said to himself. 'A small, sleepy village like Marygreen!'

'Bring me that water, you lazy young good-for-nothing!' A thin old woman had come to the door of her cottage.

Jude waved, picked up his buckets and walked across the green.

A little blue sign over the door of the cottage said, 'Drusilla Fawley, baker'. This was Jude's great-aunt, his grandfather's sister. As he emptied the buckets, he could hear her talking inside to some of the other village women.

'And who's *he*?' asked a newcomer when Jude entered.

'My great-nephew,' replied Miss Fawley. 'He came up to me from South Wessex a year ago, when his father died. Poor useless boy! But he has to earn a penny wherever he can. Just now, he keeps the birds away for Farmer Troutham.'

'And he can help you with the baking, I suppose.'

'Hmph!' said Miss Fawley. 'It's a pity the schoolmaster didn't take him with him to Christminster. The boy's crazy for books. His cousin Sue's the same, I've heard, though I've hardly seen her since her mother – well, I won't go into that. Jude,' she said, turning to him, 'don't *you* ever marry. The Fawleys shouldn't marry.'

Jude went out to the bakehouse and ate the cake put out for his breakfast. Then he climbed over a hedge onto a path that led down to a large, lonely field planted with crops.

Clackety-clack. Clackety-clack. Every few seconds, the boy banged together two pieces of wood to frighten the birds away. Then, feeling tired and sorry for them, he threw down the clacker. 'Farmer Troutham can afford to let you have *some* dinner,' he said aloud. 'Eat, my dear little birdies!' The birds, black shapes on the brown earth, stayed and ate.

WHAM-CLACK! Jude and the birds rose together into the air as a red-faced farmer hit the boy on the seat of his trousers with his own clacker. 'So!' shouted Troutham, hitting him again and again on his behind. 'It's "Eat, my dear birdies", is it, young man? That's how you earn your sixpence a day keeping the birds off my crops!' He stopped at last. 'Here's your payment for today. Now, go home and don't let me ever see you on my fields again!'

Jude found his aunt at home selling a loaf to a little girl.

'Why are you back so early?' the old woman demanded.

'Mr Troutham has sent me away because I let the birds eat a little bit. There are the last wages I shall ever earn!' Jude threw the sixpence tragically onto the table.

'Ah! Why didn't you go to Christminster with that schoolmaster of yours?'

Jude helped his aunt for the rest of the morning. Then he went into the village and asked a man where Christminster was.

'Over there, about twenty miles away.' The man pointed to the north-east, past Farmer Troutham's field.

Jude's curiosity increased. The railway had brought him from the south up to Marygreen, but he had never been north beyond it. Quietly, he went back down to Troutham's field and up the far side, to where the path joined the main road. To his surprise, he found he was looking down on miles of flat lowland.

Not far from the road stood a farm building known as the Brown House. Jude stopped when he noticed a ladder and two men repairing the roof.

'I want to know where Christminster is, please,' he said.

'It's out across there, past those trees.' One of the men pointed. 'You can see it on a clear day.'

'The best time to see it,' said the other man, looking in the same direction, 'is when the sun's going down, all flaming red. But you can't see it now. It's too cloudy.'

In the evening, when Jude passed the Brown House again on his way home, the ladder was still there though the men had gone. He climbed up it, prayed, and waited.

About quarter of an hour before sunset, the clouds thinned in the west. Jude looked to the north-east as the men had told him. There, now, he could see points of light. The air became clearer still. Now the points of light showed themselves as the windows and shiny wet roofs and spires of a city. It was Christminster!

The boy looked on and on, until suddenly the shine went and the city was hidden again. The sun had set.

Jude went to the Brown House whenever he could and looked eagerly into the distance.

Jude climbed quickly down the ladder and began to run towards Marygreen, trying not to think about ghosts.

Chapter 2　Preparing for Christminster

From this time on, Jude went to the Brown House whenever he could and looked eagerly into the distance. One evening when he was there, a team of horses came slowly up the hill, pulling coal.

'Have you come from Christminster?' he asked the carter.

'No, not that far,' replied the carter pleasantly. He noticed the book of stories under the boy's arm. 'You couldn't understand the books they read in Christminster, young man,' he went on. 'It's all learning there, nothing but learning and religion! I'm

386

talking of the college life, of course. As for music, there's beautiful music everywhere in Christminster. And the buildings, well! There's nothing like them anywhere in the world . . .'

Jude walked home, deep in thought. 'Christminster is a city of light,' he said to himself. 'It's a place of learning and religion. It would just suit me.'

But how could he prepare himself for Christminster? He would start learning. Yes, he would learn Latin and Greek! But how could he get the right books?

At about this date, Phillotson sent for his piano and that gave Jude an idea. He wrote his hero a letter, asking him to get him some old grammar-books in Christminster; and he hid the letter inside the piano.

Every morning before his aunt was up, Jude then called at the village post office. At last, a packet arrived. He cut the string, opened the books – and discovered, to his horror, that every word of both Latin and Greek had to be individually learnt!

'I can't do it!' he cried. 'Why was I ever born?'

♦

Jude was now twelve years old. He quickly recovered from his disappointment over the grammar-books and began to make himself useful to his aunt. Her bakery grew, and they bought an old horse and cart. Jude used this horse and cart for delivering bread to cottages outside the village, and for studying his Latin and Greek at the same time.

At sixteen, he decided to concentrate on Christian studies. He read the New Testament in Greek; and on Sundays he visited all the local churches, translating anything he found in Latin.

He was as determined as ever to go to Christminster. But how could he support himself there while he studied? He had no income and no trade. Perhaps he could enter the building trade. The uncle he had never met, his cousin Susanna's father, did ecclesiastical metal work. Perhaps he, Jude, could do church work of some sort, too.

As soon as he had settled matters with his aunt, he went to the little market-town of Alfredston, on the main road north of the Brown House, and found work with a stone-mason there.

Jude now stayed in the town during the week, and walked the five miles back to Marygreen every Saturday. In this way, he reached and passed his nineteenth year.

Chapter 3   Arabella

One Saturday afternoon at this time, Jude was returning early to Marygreen with his basket of tools on his back. It was fine summer weather and he was feeling pleased with his progress.

'Now,' he said to himself as he wandered back past the village of Cresscombe, 'I must settle in Christminster where I can buy books more easily. I'll save money and get into a college. I might even become a leader of the Church . . .'

'Ha-ha-ha!' The sound of girls' laughter came over the hedge, but Jude did not notice.

'At Christminster, I must master ecclesiastical history . . .'

'Ha-ha-ha!'

'I can work hard. Christminster will be proud of me.'

Jude was still deep in his dream when something soft and cold hit him on the ear and fell at his feet. He looked down. It was part of a pig, the unmentionable part of a pig!

He looked over the hedge. There was a stream and a cottage with some pigs. Three young women were kneeling by the stream, washing lumps of meat in the running water.

'Thank you!' he said, as he wiped his face.

'I didn't throw it!' said one girl to her neighbour.

'Oh, Anny!' said the second.

'You didn't do it, oh no!' Jude said to the third. He was almost sure she was responsible.

'Shan't tell you.' The girl was dark-eyed, well-built, almost handsome.

Jude climbed over the hedge and the two met on a small bridge over the stream.

'Don't tell people it was I who threw it!' said the girl.

'How can I? I don't know your name.'

'Arabella Donn. I live here. My father sells pigs.'

They talked a little more, and a little more. Jude had never before looked at a woman as a woman. Now he looked from Arabella's eyes to her mouth, to her breast, to her round bare arms.

'You should see me on Sundays!' she said.

'I don't suppose I could? Tomorrow? Shall I call?'

'Yes.' The girl looked at him almost tenderly, and returned to the congratulations of her companions.

Jude, as he went on his way, breathed new air. Suddenly, his plans for reading, working and learning were pushed to one side. 'But it's only a bit of fun,' he said to himself.

♦

It was Sunday afternoon and Jude was in his room at his aunt's. He would not, he decided, go to meet the girl. He would read his Greek New Testament. He sat down at the table and, almost as soon, jumped up again. He could surely give up just one afternoon . . . In three minutes, he was out of the house in his best clothes and on his way down to Arabella Donn's, west of the Brown House.

A smell of pigs came from the back and a man called out in a business-like voice, 'Arabella! Your young man!'

Jude entered just as Arabella came downstairs in her Sunday best. She looked so handsome that he was glad he had come.

They walked up to the Brown House, but in his excitement Jude did not once look towards Christminster. This country girl in her Sunday dress had agreed to take a walk with him! Our student, our future leader of the Church, was quite overcome. The pair went on to Alfredston and, at Arabella's suggestion, had some beer at an inn.

It was getting dark when they started home, and they walked closer together. 'Take my arm,' said Jude, and Arabella took it, up to the shoulder.

As they climbed to the Brown House, she put her head on his shoulder. Jude took the hint and kissed her. When they were halfway up the hill, he kissed her again. They reached the top and he kissed her once more.

It was nine o'clock when they arrived at her home and later still when 'Arabella's young man' got back to Marygreen. In his room, the New Testament still lay open on the table in silent accusation.

◆

Jude left early next morning for his usual week in Alfredston. At the place where he had first kissed Arabella, he stopped and sighed. Six days before he could see her again!

A little later, Arabella came the same way with her two companions. She passed the place of the kiss without even noticing it.

'And what did he say next?'

'Then he said . . .' Arabella repeated some of Jude's tenderest words to her.

'You've made him care for you,' said the one called Anny.

'Yes,' answered Arabella in a low, hungry voice. 'But I want more than that. I want him to have me, to marry me!'

'Well he's an honest countryman. You can get him if you go about it in the right way.'

'What's the right way?'

The other two girls looked at each other. 'She doesn't know! Though she's lived in a town!'

'How do you mean? Tell me a sure way to catch a man, as a husband.'

Arabella's companions looked at each other again, and laughed. Then one spoke quietly in her ear.

'Ah!' Arabella said slowly. 'I didn't think of that.'

'Lots of girls do it,' said Anny.

Chapter 4   Tricked into Marriage

Every weekend that summer, Jude walked out with Arabella. He made no progress with his books – but neither did he make the sort of progress that Arabella wanted.

Suddenly, one Sunday morning, the girl said to her mother, 'There's a service at Fensworth church this evening. I want you and Father to walk to that.'

'What's going on tonight, then?'

'Nothing,' said Arabella. 'But he's shy, and he won't come in when you're here.'

In the afternoon, as usual, she met Jude. They walked on the high ground and the sound of church bells floated up from below. When the bells stopped, Arabella suggested that they went home.

'I won't come in, dear,' Jude said, as usual.

'They've gone to church,' she said. 'Now, you'll come in?'

'Certainly!'

They went indoors. Arabella took off her jacket and hat, and they sat down, close together.

'You may kiss my cheek,' she said softly.

'Your *cheek*!' protested Jude and reached towards her. There was a little struggle. He held her close.

'One proper kiss,' he said, 'and then I'll go.'

But Arabella had jumped up. 'You must find me first!' she cried and ran out of the room. It was now dark and her lover could not see. Then a laugh showed that she had rushed upstairs. Jude rushed up after her.

◆

In the next two months, the pair met constantly. Arabella seemed dissatisfied, always waiting, wondering.

Then, one evening, Jude told her that he was going away. 'It'll be better for both of us,' he said.

Arabella began to cry. 'But it's too late!'

'What?' asked Jude, turning pale. 'You're not . . .'

'Yes, and what shall I do if you leave me?'

'Oh, Arabella! You *know* I wouldn't leave you. I have almost no wages yet, and this ends my dream of Christminster – but certainly we'll marry, my dear. We must!'

That night, Jude went out alone and walked in the dark. He had to marry Arabella. So he must, he told himself, for his own peace of mind, think well of her.

◆

The marriage notice was sent out immediately. Jude's aunt made him a wedding-cake, saying it was the last thing she could do for the fool, and Arabella sent slices to her two friends, labelled 'In remembrance of good advice'.

On the wedding night, Jude took his wife to a lonely roadside cottage he had rented between the Brown House and Mary-green. In their own bedroom for the first time, Arabella unpinned a long tail of hair from her head and hung it on the mirror.

'What! It wasn't your own hair?' asked Jude in sudden disgust. 'You've enough of your own, surely?'

'Enough for the country,' she said. 'But in towns the men

'What! It wasn't your own hair?' asked Jude in sudden disgust.
'You've enough of your own, surely?' 'Enough for the country,'
Arabella said.

expect more. When I was a barmaid at Aldbrickham in North Wessex . . . '

'False hair? A barmaid?' Jude turned away.

♦

The couple were poor. Jude was still just a nineteen-year-old apprentice stone-mason. He had rented the lonely cottage only so that Arabella could help by keeping a pig.

But Mrs Jude Fawley was pleased with her new position in life. She had a husband: that was the important thing. And he would be able to buy her new dresses when he threw away those stupid books and concentrated on his trade.

One day, in Alfredston, she met her friend Anny for the first time since the wedding.

'So it was a good plan, you see,' said the girl to the wife 'And when do you expect . . . ?'

'Shhh! Not at all. I was mistaken.'

'Oh-ho, Arabella! "Mistaken"! That's clever! But he won't like it. He'll say it was a trick, a double trick.'

'Pooh! Anyway, what can he do about it? We're married now.' But Arabella did not look forward to telling Jude.

Then, one evening when he was tired after a hard day's work, he said as they went to bed, 'You'll soon have plenty of work yourself, dear, won't you?'

'How do you mean?'

'Well, I meant . . . little clothes to make . . . When will it be? Can't you tell me exactly yet?'

'There's nothing to tell. I made a mistake. Women get these things wrong sometimes.'

'Good God!' Jude lay down without another word.

When he woke up next morning, he seemed to see the world differently. But the marriage remained.

Chapter 5   Some Family History

Winter came and, one Saturday at dawn, Jude and his wife killed the pig she had fattened. The killing troubled Jude – the animal's cries and Arabella's cruel ways.

'You tender-hearted fool!' she said.

Jude set off for his work. The road to Alfredston now reminded him too much of his first walks with Arabella, so he read as he walked, to keep his eyes down.

As he walked home that evening, he heard girls' voices behind a wall, just as he had once heard them behind a hedge.

'If I hadn't suggested it to her, she wouldn't be his wife today.'

'I think she knew there was nothing the matter when she told him she was . . .'

The voices belonged to Arabella's old companions. They were talking about himself and her!

When Jude arrived home, Arabella was boiling up some fat from the pig. She wanted some money, she said. He ought to earn more. 'I don't know why you married, on your wages.'

'Arabella. That's unfair! You know why. Those friends of yours gave you bad advice.'

'What advice?'

Jude told her about the conversation he had heard.

'That was nothing.' Arabella laughed coldly. 'Every woman has the right to do that.'

'No, Bella. Not when it traps an honest man for life . . . Why are you boiling up that fat tonight? Please don't.'

'Then I must do it tomorrow morning,' she said angrily.

Next morning, Arabella went back to her pig fat, still in a bad temper. 'So that's the story about me, is it? That I trapped you?' She saw some of Jude's books on the table and began throwing them to the floor.

'Leave my books alone! Your hands are covered in fat!' Jude caught her by the arms.

'That's right!' she cried. 'Make me work on a Sunday, then complain about it! Ill-use me as your father ill-used your mother, and as his sister ill-used her husband!'

Jude looked at her in amazement. He left her and went, after a while, to call on his aunt at Marygreen. 'Aunt,' he demanded, 'did my father ill-use my mother? Tell me.'

'I suppose that wife of yours has said something,' Drusilla Fawley replied. 'Well, there isn't much to tell. Your parents weren't happy together. Coming home from Alfredston market one day, they had their last quarrel and they separated on the hill by the Brown House. Your mother drowned herself soon after and your father took you away to South Wessex. His sister quarrelled with her husband too and went off to London with little Sue . . . the Fawleys weren't made for marriage.'

Instead of returning to his own cottage, Jude walked to Alfredston where, at the same inn he had visited with Arabella, he drank for an hour or more. When he finally went home, laughing loudly and unsteady on his legs, he found a note from his wife: 'Have gone to my friends. Shall not return.'

Then a letter came. She was tired of him and their dull life, she said. She was leaving this stupid country. She was going to Australia with her parents.

Jude sent Arabella the money from the sale of their pig and everything else he had, and he went back into lodgings in Alfredston.

Eventually he heard of the family's departure for Australia and, the following evening, he walked by himself in the starlight, along the main road to the upland.

He felt like a boy again! But he was a man, he reminded himself, and a man who had separated from his wife. He came to the Brown House, where his own parents had separated and where he had first seen, or imagined, Christminster.

He looked to the north-east and saw, in the far distance, a ring of light. It was enough. He would go to Christminster, he decided, as soon as he finished his apprenticeship.

PART 2   AT CHRISTMINSTER

Chapter 6   The First Sight of Sue

Three years after Arabella's departure, Jude finally arrived at Christminster. He was now a serious and strong-faced young stone-mason, black-haired with a black beard. He hoped to find work in the city of his dreams and was pleased that he had not only a friend there, the schoolmaster Phillotson, but also a relation. He had seen a photograph of a pretty girl at his aunt's and she had said that it was his cousin Sue Bridehead, who now lived somewhere in Christminster.

Jude arrived at sunset and got himself lodgings in a suburb known as Beersheba. Excited, he went straight out to explore the place he had dreamed of for so long.

It was a windy, whispering, moonless night. Alone in the darkness, he wandered along streets and down obscure, forgotten alleys. He saw the old colleges. He heard their bells. He felt their aged stonework with his mason's fingers. As the leaves brushed against their walls in the wind, he met the ghosts of the university's great men . . .

Next morning, when Jude woke, the ghosts of the past had gone. He found a good job as a stone-mason and began earning and learning with enthusiasm, renewing the city's old stonework by day and studying his books by night. His whole aim was to enter the university. But, like most dreamers, he had no definite plan of action. He did, however, have the photograph of Sue. His aunt had sent it, but with a request that he would stay away from his Bridehead relations and not bring trouble into the family. Sue's father had gone to London, she added, but the girl was working as some sort of artist in a shop selling ecclesiastical objects.

Jude put up the photo in his room and felt, somehow, more at home. He walked past the ecclesiastical shops and saw, sitting behind a desk in one of them, a girl just like the one in the picture. She was doing some lettering on metal, so she must surely be his cousin, following her father's trade. Jude did not speak to her. His aunt had asked him not to. Besides, he was in his rough working-jacket – and she was so pretty! So he walked away and began day-dreaming about the girl instead.

A few weeks later, Jude saw her in the street, as he worked on the stonework of one of the colleges. She came so close that he turned shyly away, but of course she did not know him. She was light and slight, lovely, nervous, tender . . .

From this moment, the emotion which had been building up in Jude since his lonely arrival in the city of his dreams, began to centre on this girl. He knew that, despite his aunt's request, he would soon introduce himself. But he *must* think of her in just a family way, he told himself. He was, after all, a married man. And she was his cousin. And if Fawley marriages usually ended in sadness, a Fawley marriage between blood relations might end in something worse . . .

Jude saw her next at the 'high' Church of St Silas in Beersheba, where he was doing some work. She was led by the elderly lady who employed her and he did not dare to make himself known to her. Man cannot live by work alone, and Jude wanted someone to love. 'But it can't be!' he told himself. 'I already have a wife!'

As the days went by, however, he found himself thinking of Sue more instead of less. Indeed, he was always thinking of her.

Jude saw Sue next at the 'high' Church of St Silas in Beersheba.
She was led by the elderly lady who employed her.

Chapter 7 A Teaching Position

One afternoon at this time, a dark-haired girl walked into the place where Jude worked, lifting her skirts to avoid the stone- dust and asking for Mr Jude Fawley.

'Look,' said a man known as Uncle Joe, 'that's the daughter of that clever Bridehead man who did the ironwork at St Silas ten years ago and then went away to London.'

Jude was out, so the girl left a note for him. 'My dear cousin Jude,' she wrote, 'I have only just learnt that you are in Christminster. Why did you not let me know? I very much wanted to get to know you, but now I am probably going away . . .'

A cold sweat spread over Jude. He wrote back immediately, arranging to meet her in the city that same evening.

'I'm sorry,' he began shyly as Sue walked up to him, 'that I didn't call on you.'

'Oh, I don't mind that.' The voice was silvery. Sue looked Jude up and down, curiously. 'You seem to know me more than I know you,' she added.

'Yes, I've seen you now and then.'

'But you didn't speak? And now I'm going away!'

'Yes. That's sad. I know hardly anyone else. Well, I do have one very old friend here somewhere. I wonder if you know of him, Mr Phillotson?'

'I've sent books to a Mr Richard Phillotson at Lumsdon. He's the village schoolmaster there.'

'Only a schoolmaster still!' Jude's face fell. If his hero had failed in his dream of university, how could he, Jude, ever succeed? 'Let's go and call on him,' he said.

So they walked to Lumsdon, where a knock brought Phillotson to the schoolhouse door. He was now forty-five years old. His face was thin and worn, like his clothes, and Jude's schoolboy admiration turned to sympathy.

'I don't remember you at all,' said the schoolmaster doubtfully when Jude told him his name. 'You were one of my pupils, you say?'

'It was at Marygreen,' Jude replied.

'Yes, I was there a short time. And is this a pupil, too?'

'No, this is my cousin ... I wrote to you for some grammar-books, if you remember. And it was you who started me on that. On the morning you left Marygreen, you told me to try to go to university – it was the thing to do, you said.'

'I told you that?' Phillotson was suprised. 'I gave up the idea years ago.'

'I've never forgotten it,' said Jude; 'That's why I came to Christminster, and to see you tonight.'

'Come in,' said Phillotson, 'and your cousin, too.'

His visitors chatted pleasantly for a while, but they did not stay to supper. Sue lodged with her elderly employer and she had to be indoors before it was late.

'Why do you have to leave Christminster?' Jude asked her regretfully as they walked back. They had talked only on general subjects, and she had spoken to him only as to a friend, but this cousin of his was an amazement to him. She was so alive! Sometimes an exciting thought made her walk so fast that he could hardly keep up with her!

'I've quarrelled with Miss Fontover,' she said. 'I want some work in which I can be more independent.'

'Why don't you try teaching again? You taught in London once, you told Mr Phillotson. Let me ask him to have you at his school. If you like it and go on to a training college, you'll have twice as much income and freedom as any church artist employed by Miss Fontover!'

'Well, ask him. Goodbye, dear Jude. I'm so glad we've met at last. We needn't quarrel because our parents did, need we?'

How he agreed! Next day, he went to Lumsdon again and persuaded Phillotson to take on Sue Bridehead as a pupil-teacher.

◆

The schoolmaster sat in his little schoolhouse and looked at the cottage opposite. It was half-past eight in the morning and he was waiting to see Miss Bridehead come across the road for the morning's lessons.

She had been with him only for three or four weeks, but she was an excellent teacher, just as bright as Jude had described her. Already, he wished to keep her. Indeed, their work together had become a delight to him.

Phillotson had invited Jude to walk out and see them that Friday evening. It was raining and Jude set off with a feeling of gloom. He knew now that he loved Sue, but he also knew that this love was wrong.

As he entered the village, he saw Sue and Phillotson walking along the empty road in front of him under one umbrella. Then he saw Phillotson put his arm round the girl's waist. Gently, she moved it away. Phillotson replaced it and this time, looking round her quickly and doubtfully, she let it remain. In horror, Jude sank back against the hedge out of sight; and the couple entered the school.

'Oh, he's too old for her – too old!' Jude cried hopelessly. But he could not interfere. Was he not Arabella's husband?

Unable to go on, he returned to Christminster. 'And it was I,' he said bitterly, 'who introduced them!'

Chapter 8   The Hell of Failure

Jude's old aunt lay unwell at Marygreen, looked after by a neighbour, and that Sunday he went to see her.

'Was Sue born here?' he soon heard himself asking.

'In this room. So you've been seeing her!' said the old woman sharply.

'Yes.'

'Then don't! Her father brought her up to hate the Fawleys, and a town girl like that won't have any time for a working man like you.'

'But she's thoughtful and tender and — '

'Jude!' cried his aunt from her bed. 'It was bad enough for you to marry that woman Arabella. But it'll be even worse if you now go after Sue.'

The neighbour said she remembered Sue Bridehead at the village school, before she was taken to London. 'She was the smallest of them all,' said the Widow Edlin, 'but she could do things that only boys do usually. I've seen her slide with them on the ice in winter, with her little curls blowing. All boys except herself, and they used to cheer her! Then, suddenly, she used to run indoors and refuse to come out again . . .'

Jude left his aunt's that evening with a heavy heart.

'You're at a college by now?' called out a villager.

'No.' Jude slapped his pocket meaningly, and walked on.

But the question brought him down to earth at last. 'All this waiting outside the walls of the colleges won't do!' he told himself as he journeyed back to Christminster. 'I must get proper information.'

So he wrote to the Masters of several colleges, asking for advice. As he waited for their replies he heard news that Phillotson was leaving the Lumsdon school to go to a larger one further south. Was Sue involved? Was Phillotson wanting a bigger income for some reason to do with her? How could he now ask the schoolmaster's advice on his own situation?

Christminster, Jude realized, had had too powerful a grip on his imagination. It was not enough just to live there and study there. Without natural brilliance or proper teaching or a lot of money, he would never get into its university.

He always remembered the afternoon on which he awoke from his dream. He went high up into one of Christminster's many unusual buildings, a round theatre with windows that gave a view over the whole town. He looked down on all the colleges below – their spires, halls, churches, gardens – and saw, now, that they were not for him. His own future lay with the ordinary workers. Phillotson, he thought, must have had the same sort of disappointment. But Phillotson now had sweet Sue to cheer him.

That evening, one reply finally arrived from the Master of a college. 'Sir,' it said, 'I have read your letter with interest; and, judging from your description of yourself as a working man, I suggest that you will succeed better in life if you remain at your own trade . . .'

It was a hard blow after ten years of studying. Instead of reading as usual, Jude went down to the street, had a few glasses of beer at an inn and walked into town, looking for the real, ordinary Christminster.

♦

He did not go to his work next day. Again he looked for the real Christminster life. This time, he went to a low inn and sat there all day, drinking until his money had gone.

In the evening, the regular customers began to come in – Jude's fellow mason Uncle Joe, a man known as Tinker Taylor, an actor, two 'ladies', a couple of students . . . Jude, already drunk, said he was as good as any university Master and showed off his church Latin in return for another drink.

'*Credo in unum Deum, Patrem omnipotentem . . .*' Suddenly, he realized what he was doing. In self-disgust, he left the inn and went to the only person in the world who could help him.

'Sue! Sue!' Late in the evening, he knocked at the lighted window of her lodging opposite the Lumsdon school.

'Is it Jude? My dear, dear cousin, what's the matter?'

'I am so bad, Sue. My heart is neary broken. I've been drinking and speaking against God and . . .'

She took him indoors, sat him down and pulled off his boots. 'Sleep now,' she said. 'I'll come down early in the morning and get you some breakfast.'

Jude woke at dawn. Ashamed and unable to face her, he left the house. Whatever could he do? He must get away to some obscure place and hide, perhaps pray. The only place he could think of was his aunt's. She had sold the bakery business now, so her cottage was quiet enough.

He called at his lodgings and found a note of dismissal from his employer. Jobless and moneyless, he packed his things and walked the twenty miles to Marygreen, sleeping one night in a field outside Alfredston.

'Out of work?' asked his aunt, looking at his clothes.

'Yes,' said Jude heavily. He went up to his old room and lay down, still dressed. When he woke up, he felt that he was in hell – the hell of failure, both in ambition and in love. He could hear his aunt praying in the next room and, not for the first time, he thought of entering the Church.

PART 3   AT MELCHESTER

Chapter 9   Learning about Sue

Jude did some little local jobs, putting up headstones on graves, and continued to think about the ecclesiastical life. A man could do good, he told himself, without going to the colleges of Christminster. He could enter the Church in a more modest way and spend his life in an obscure village, helping others. *That* might be true religion. The idea encouraged him, but he did nothing about it until a letter arrived from Sue. She was going to enter a teacher's training college, she wrote, at Melchester in Mid-Wessex.

There was a theological college at Melchester also! Jude could work in the city, study, join the theological college and be ready to enter the Church at the age of thirty . . .

◆

Christmas came and went. Sue was already at Melchester and

Jude planned to go there in the spring. She had not once mentioned either his behaviour that night he arrived at her cottage or any involvement with Phillotson.

Suddenly, however, she sent for him. The college was even worse than the shop. Could Jude come immediately?

Her cousin packed up his things and left for Melchester with a lighter heart.

On his way from the station to see Sue, Jude paused under the walls of Melchester Cathedral. He looked up at its lovely spire and down at all the new stone lying on the ground. Here too, then, old stonework was being renewed and he might find exactly the employment he wanted.

As he came to the west front of the cathedral, a wave of warmth passed over him. Sue's college was opposite. That quick, bright-eyed girl with the pile of dark hair was here!

But the college was a college for young ladies, and the girl who came to greet him was different from before. She wore a plain, dark dress, her hair was twisted tightly up, her movements were quieter.

'I'm glad you've come!' Sue came prettily forwards, but there was no sign that she thought of Jude as a lover. He *must,* he said to himself, tell her about his marriage, but he did not want to.

The cousins walked into the town and Sue talked freely about everything except the subject that most interested Jude. When they sat for a while, he put his hand on hers. She smiled and looked coolly at his fingers. 'I like to see a man's hands rough from his work,' she said. ' . . . Well, I'm glad I came to Melchester, after all. See how independent I shall be after the two years' training! And then Mr Phillotson will help to get me a big school.'

She had mentioned him at last. 'I was afraid,' said Jude, 'that perhaps he wanted to marry you.'

'Now don't be so silly! An old man like that!'

'Oh, come, Sue! I saw him putting his arm round your waist.'

Sue bit her lip. 'You'll be angry if I tell you everything . . . But I *shall* tell you,' she said, with the sudden change of mood that was part of her. 'I — I've promised to marry him when I finish at the college. We'll then take a large school together and have a good income between us.'

'Oh, Sue!' Jude turned away.

'I knew you'd be angry! We'd better not meet again.'

That was the one thing Jude could not face. 'I'm your cousin,' he said quickly. 'I can see you when I want to!'

'Then don't let's talk of it any more. What does it matter, anyway? It's not going to happen for two years!'

Jude could not understand her. 'Shall we go and sit in the cathedral?' he asked.

'Cathedral? I'd rather sit in the railway station,' she answered in annoyance. 'That's the centre of town life now. I'm tired of old things!'

'How modern you are, Sue!'

'I must go back,' she said, 'or I'll be locked out.'

Jude took her to the college gate and said good night. His drunken visit to her at Lumsdon, he thought, had led to this promise to marry Phillotson.

Next day, he found the employment he wanted, on the cathedral repairs. Having also found respectable lodgings close by, he bought books and began to study Theology.

Chapter 10   A Night Away from College

One Friday, a few weeks after Jude's arrival, Sue had an afternoon's leave. Where should they go? After some discussion, the pair went by train into the countryside and started to walk across high, open land to the next station.

In their excitement, however, they missed the last train back and had to stay the night in a lonely cottage.

'Are you a married couple?' the son of the house asked Jude privately.

'Shhh, no!'

'Then she can go into Mother's room, and you and I can lie in the outer room after they've gone through. I'll call you early enough to catch the first train back in the morning.'

'I expect I'll get into trouble,' Sue said.

♦

The following evening, Jude was studying at his lodgings when a stone was thrown lightly at his window.

'Jude! It's Sue! Can I come up without anyone seeing me?' Judes heart leapt. Had she come to him in trouble as he had once come to her?

In a moment, his cousin entered his room. 'I'm so cold!' she said. 'Can I sit by your fire?'

'Whatever have you done, darling?' He had not meant to call her that.

'They locked me up because I stayed out with you. It seemed so unfair. So I got out of the window and escaped across a stream!' She was trying hard to sound independent.

'Dear Sue!' Jude took her hand. 'But you're very wet! I'll borrow some clothes from the lady of the house.'

'No! Don't let her know! They'll find me!'

'Then you must put on some of mine.' Jude gave her his Sunday suit and left the room.

When he returned, she was asleep in his suit in his only armchair, with her own clothes spread out to dry. He stood with his back to the small fire, looking at her, loving her.

Then, saying he had 'a young gentleman visitor', he asked for supper in his room.

'Eat this,' he commanded when Sue woke up, 'and stay where you are. Tomorrow is Sunday. I can sit here by the fire all night and read. Don't be frightened.'

'I have no fear of men, as such, nor of their books,' she said thoughtfully. 'I have mixed with them almost as one of their own sex. When I was eighteen and in Christminster, I became friendly with one student in particular: he taught me a lot and lent me many books.'

'Has your friendship finished?'

'Yes. He died, poor man. But we used to go about together – on walking tours, reading tours – like two men almost. I agreed to live with him after he graduated. But when I joined him in London, I found that he meant a different thing from what I meant, and so after a time we separated. He said I was breaking his heart. My father was in London, but he wouldn't have me back, so I returned to Christminster.'

Jude's voice shook. 'However you've lived, Sue, I believe you're innocent.'

'I've never given myself to any lover, if that's what you mean!' she said.

'Have you told Mr Phillotson about this friend of yours?'

'Yes, long ago. He just said I was everything to him, whatever I did.' There was a silence. 'Are you very annoyed with me, dear Jude?' she suddenly asked in a voice of extraordinary tenderness. 'I care as much for you as for anybody I ever met.'

'But you don't care *more*!' There was another silence. 'I'm studying Theology now, you know,' Jude said, to change the subject. 'Would you like to say evening prayers with me?'

'I'd rather not,' she said. 'My friend taught me to have no respect for all that tradition . . . But I won't upset your beliefs. Because we are going to be *very* nice with each other, aren't we?' She looked trustfully up at him.

Jude looked away. Was his heart going to be the next one that she broke? But she was so dear! If only he could forget her sex as she seemed able to forget his, what a companion she would make!

They talked on until Sue fell asleep again, deep inside his jacket. At six in the morning, when her clothes were dry, he touched her on the shoulder and went downstairs into the starlight.

When he returned, she was in her own clothes again. 'Things seem so different in the cold light of morning,' she said. 'I've run away from the college! Whatever will Mr Phillotson say? He's the only man in the world for whom I have any respect or fear . . . Well, that doesn't matter, I shall do as I choose!' She would go a few miles away, she said, to a village near the town of Shaston, to stay with the sister of a fellow-student until the college allowed her back.

They went quietly out of the house towards the station, watched equally quietly by a woman at an upstairs window.

'I want to tell you something; two things,' Jude said quickly as the train came in.

'I know one of them,' Sue said, 'and you mustn't! You mustn't love me. You must only like me! Goodbye!'

Chapter 11   To Love or Not?

Jude hated Melchester that Sunday, but next morning a letter arrived which changed everything.

'What a cruel and ungrateful woman I was at the station!' Sue wrote from the village near Shaston. *'If you want to love me, Jude, you may.'*

Jude wrote straight back, of course. Then, receiving no reply, he sent a message that he was coming out to see her the following Sunday.

410

He found her lying in bed. 'Sue, what's wrong?' he cried. 'You couldn't write?'

'They won't have me back at the college,' she answered. 'That's why I didn't write. Not the fact, but the reason! Somebody has sent them untrue reports – and they say you and I ought to marry as soon as possible, for the sake of my good name! But I don't think of you as a lover. At least, I hadn't quite begun to. And I never supposed *you* loved *me* till the other evening. Oh, you've been so unkind, not telling me!'

'I'm to blame, Sue,' Jude said simply, 'more than you think.' He had meant to tell her about Arabella, but still he could not. 'You belong to Mr Phillotson,' was all he said. 'I supppse he's been to see you?'

'Yes,' she said after a short pause. 'Though I didn't ask him to.'

Jude left in the afternoon, hopelessly unhappy.

But the next morning, another note arrived from the village near Shaston. 'Jude, I'm coming to Melchester on Saturday to collect my things from the college. I could walk with you for half an hour if you like.'

Jude asked her to call for him at the cathedral works.

◆

At Shaston itself, a dozen miles from Melchester, a middle-aged man was dreaming a dream of great beauty about the writer of the above note. Richard Phillotson had recently returned to his native town, to run a large school and make preparations for taking a wife.

Sue Bridehead had written to him, too. Whenever he was away from his pupils, he read and re-read her short notes from Melchester, kissing them like a boy of eighteen. But why, he puzzled, did she not want him to visit her?

One Saturday morning, unable to keep away any longer, he went to call on her. It was two weeks after her sudden departure

411

from the college, and Sue had told him nothing whatever about it. Shaken at the news the college now gave him, he entered the cathedral opposite – and saw Jude among the workmen inside.

Both men were embarrassed: Jude was expecting to see Sue that same day; Phillotson had just been told that Jude was Sue's lover.

'I hear,' said Phillotson, his eyes on the ground, 'that you have seen my little friend Sue recently. May I ask —?'

'About her escape from the training college?' Jude readily explained the whole series of adventures.

'You're telling me,' said Phillotson as he finished, 'that the college's accusation is untrue?'

'It is,' said Jude. 'Absolutely. I swear it before God!'

◆

The schoolmaster left the cathedral at about eleven, but Sue did not appear and Jude finally found her in the market square.

'You haven't seen Mr Phillotson today?' he asked.

'I haven't – but I refuse to answer questions about him! I've already written and said that you may love me . . .'

Jude knew that, as an honest man, he must now tell her about Arabella.

'Why didn't you tell me before!' Sue burst out when he had finished. 'Before I could write that note!'

'But I never thought you cared for me at all, till quite recently, so I felt it didn't matter! *Do* you care about me, Sue?'

She chose not to answer the question. 'I suppose she – your wife – is a very pretty woman, even if she's bad?'

'She's pretty enough – but I've not seen her for years.'

'How strange of you to stay away from her like this,' said Sue shakily. 'You, so religious, unlike me!'

Jude tried to put an arm round her waist.

'No, no!' she said, with tears in her eyes. 'You can't mean that as a cousin; and it mustn't be in any other way.'

They walked on, and she recovered. 'What does it matter?' she smiled. 'We have to stay separate, anyway. We're cousins, and I'm promised to somebody else.'

'There was another reason why I didn't tell you everything,' said Jude. 'My great-aunt has always told me that I ought not to marry, that Fawley marriages end badly.'

'That's strange. My father used to say the same!'

They stopped and looked at each other.

'Oh, it can't mean anything,' said Sue lightly. 'Our family's been unlucky in marriage, that's all.'

Chapter 12   With Fear in her Eyes

Sue returned to her friend's house near Shaston and, a day or two later, a letter came from her.

'My dear Jude,' she wrote, 'Mr Phillotson and I are to be married in three or four weeks. You must wish me happiness! Your affectionate cousin, *Susanna Bridehead*.'

Jude twisted in pain. Then he laughed a bitter laugh and went off to work. 'Oh, Susanna!' he said to himself. 'You don't know what marriage means!' Could the story of his own marriage have made her agree to this now?

A second letter followed. 'Jude, will you give me away at my wedding? You are my only married relation in the area, and it seems from the Prayer Book that somebody has to "give me" to my husband, like a she-animal. I suppose you too, O Churchman, have this high view of woman! Ever, *Susanna Bridehead*.'

What a fool that 'married relation' made him seem as her lover! Bravely, Jude wrote back: 'My dear Sue, of course I wish you happiness! And of course I will give you away. I suggest that you marry from my house since I am, as you say, your nearest relation. But I don't see why you sign your letter in such a distant way. Ever your affectionate, *Jude*.'

So it was all arranged. Jude moved into new and larger lodgings, away from the woman who had reported on his 'gentleman' visitor; and Sue came to stay in the same house.

They saw each other very little. Phillotson came frequently, usually when Jude was out. He would obviously be a kind and loving husband, but what did Sue feel? Jude was depressed that, having made a wrong marriage himself he was now helping the woman he loved to do the same.

On the morning of the wedding, the cousins went for a last walk together.

'That's the church where you'll be married,' Jude said, pointing.

'Indeed? Let's go in!'

They entered by the western door. Sue held Jude's arm, almost as if she loved him.

'I shall walk through the church like this with my husband in about two hours,' she said a little later, her hand still on his arm. 'Was it like this when you were married?'

'Good God, Sue, don't be so pitiless!'

'Forgive me, Jude!' Her eyes were wetter than his.

Why did she do these things? Later, Jude wondered this again during the wedding service. Why had she asked him to give her away – and why had he ever agreed? She was nervous, he could see. As he gave her away to Phillotson, she could hardly control herself. And, as the newly-married couple departed, Sue looked back at Jude with fear in her eyes.

Chapter 13   Arabella Reappears

She could not possibly go home with Phillotson! Surely she would return! Jude waited, but Sue did not come. He looked out of the window and imagined her journey to London, where they had gone for their holiday. He looked into the future and imagined her with children . . .

His depression deepened in the following days. Then he heard that his aunt was seriously ill at Marygreen, and that his old employer at Christminster had a job for him.

He went first to Marygreen, from where he wrote to Sue at Shaston. If she wanted to see her Aunt Drusilla alive, he said, she should come up immediately by train. He would meet her tomorrow evening, Monday, at Alfredston station, after he had seen his old employer in Christminster.

◆

The City of Learning looked beautiful, but Jude had lost all feeling for it. The only ghost it held now was the ghost of Sue. Her chair was still there in the shop, empty.

He went to see his old employer, but could not bring himself to return to this place of lost dreams. He met Tinker Taylor and, in his depression, went with him to the inn where he had got so drunk before.

With nothing to do until his train left for Alfredston, Jude sat on alone behind one of the inn's glass screens. A barmaid served someone on the other side. Jude looked up, and was amazed to see that the barmaid was Arabella. Arabella, in a black dress with a white collar, chatting happily.

'Well, have you heard from your husband, my dear?' her customer asked.

'I left him in Australia,' she replied, 'and I suppose he's still there.' She gave the man his change and he caught at her hand. There was a little struggle, a little laugh, and the man left.

Jude hesitated, then went around the screen.

'Well!' Arabella recognized him with surprise. 'I thought you must have died years ago! Have a drink, for old times' sake!'

'No, thanks, Arabella,' Jude said without a smile. 'How long have you been here?'

'About six weeks. I returned from Sydney three months ago, and I saw this job in an advertisement.'

'Why did you return?'

'Oh, I had my reasons. You're not at the university or in the Church?'

'No . . . ' Jude noticed a jewelled ring on her hand. 'So you tell people you have a living husband?'

'Yes. There might be problems if I called myself a widow. But we can't talk here. Can you come back at nine?'

'All right,' Jude said gloomily. 'I suppose we'd better arrange something.' He put down his unemptied glass and went out. He would not now be able to meet Sue at Alfredston, but he had no choice. In the eye of the law and the Church, this woman was his wife.

When he returned to the inn at nine, it was crowded. The barmaids were pink-cheeked and excited. Arabella insisted on pouring a drink for Jude as well as another for herself.

'Until we've come to some agreement, we shouldn't be seen together here,' she said. 'Let's take the train to Aldbrickham. Nobody will know us there for one night.'

'As you wish.'

They made the half-hour's journey to Aldbrickham, and entered an inn near the station in time for a late supper.

Chapter 14   Arabella's Second Choice

'You said when we were getting up this morning that you wished to tell me something.' Jude had just come back to Christminster on the train with Arabella.

'Two things,' she replied. 'One was about that gentleman I

mentioned last night, who managed the Sydney hotel. You promise to keep this a secret?' She spoke unusually quickly. 'Well, he kept asking me to marry him, and at last I did.'

Jude turned pale. 'What – marry him? Legally, in church?'

'Yes. And I lived with him till we had a quarrel and I came back here. He talks of coming to England for me, poor man!'

'So that was the "husband" you talked of in the bar. Why didn't you tell me last night! Arabella, you've committed a crime!'

'Crime? Pooh! He was very fond of me and we lived as respectably as any other married couple out there. There was one more thing I wanted to tell you, but that can wait. I'll think over what you said about your circumstances, and let you know.'

Jude watched her disappear into the inn where she worked and turned back towards the station, burning with shame at the memory of the last twelve hours.

Suddenly there in front of him was Sue. 'Oh, Jude, I'm so glad to find you!'

Emotionally, they took each other's hand and walked on together, each conscious that this was their first meeting since Sue's marriage.

She had come to Christminster early this morning to look for him, she said. 'I thought that perhaps you were upset that I was married and not here as I used to be, so you'd gone drinking again to drown your feelings!'

'And you came to save me, like a good angel! No, dear, at least I wasn't doing that. But I'm sorry I didn't meet you at Alfredston last night, as I arranged. I had a sudden appointment here at nine o'clock.' Looking at his loved one, so sweet and rare, Jude became even more ashamed of the hours he had spent with Arabella.

'Then where did you stay last night?' Sue asked the question in perfect innocence.

'At an inn.' How could he possibly explain?

They got on the next train to Alfredston, talking a little stiffly. Jude could not forget that Sue was now 'Mrs Phillotson', though she seemed unchanged. She had been married less than a month but, both on the train and as they walked from Alfredston to Marygreen, she avoided all conversation about herself. Jude became sure she was unhappy.

When they reached the cottage beyond the Brown House where he had lived with Arabella, he heard himself saying: 'That's the house I brought my wife home to.'

Sue looked at it. 'That cottage was to you as the schoolhouse at Shaston is to me.'

'But I wasn't happy there as you are. If you *are* happy, Mrs Phillotson.'

'He's good to me!' Sue burst out. 'If you think I'm not happy because he's too old for me, then you're wrong.'

Jude said no more. They walked down into the field where Farmer Troutham had beaten him as a boy, up the other side to the village – and found Mrs Edlin at their aunt's door.

'She's got out of bed!' she cried. 'I couldn't stop her!'

They entered and saw Drusilla Fawley sitting, wrapped in blankets, by the fire.

'You'll regret this marrying, too!' she screamed at Sue. 'And why that schoolmaster, of all men? You can't love him!'

Sue ran out, and Jude found her crying in the old bakehouse. 'It's true!' she said.

'God – you don't like him?'

'I don't mean that,' she said quickly. 'But perhaps I was wrong to marry.' Then she dried her eyes and said, as she left for Shaston, that Jude must not come to see her, not yet.

♦

Jude stayed on at his aunt's, studying his Theology and trying desperately to forget his love for Sue.

While he was there, a letter arrived from Arabella. Her Australian husband had come to London, she wrote, and wanted her to run an inn with him in Lambeth. He said he still loved her, and she felt she belonged to him more than to Jude, so she had just gone to join him. She wished Jude goodbye and hoped he would not inform against her.

Then, on the Thursday before Easter, when Jude had returned to Melchester, a note came from Sue. She was now teaching at her husband's school, she said, and of course Jude must visit them. He could come that afternoon if he wished.

PART 4   AT SHASTON

Chapter 15   'We Two Are in Tune'

Jude climbed up from the station to the hilltop town of Shaston and found the schoolroom empty. Mr Phillotson was away at a meeting, said a girl cleaning the floor, but Mrs Phillotson would be back in a few minutes.

There was a piano in the room, the same piano that Phillotson had had at Marygreen. Jude, as he waited, played a tune he had heard at a church in Melchester.

Lightly, someone touched his left hand. 'I like that tune,' said Sue. 'I learnt it at the training college.'

'Then you play it for me.'

Sue sat down and played. When she had finished, they again touched hands. 'I wonder why we did that?' she said.

'I suppose because we two are in tune!'

'We'll have some tea,' Sue said quickly. 'Are you still studying Theology?'

'Yes, harder than ever.'

'I could come and see you at one of your churches next week.'

'No. Don't come!'

'What have I done? I thought we two —'

'Sue, I sometimes think you're playing with my affections,' Jude said angrily.

She jumped up. 'Oh, Jude, that was a cruel thing to say! Some women need love so much, and they may not always be able to give their love to the person licensed by the Church to receive it! But you're too straight to understand . . . Now you must go. I'm sorry my husband's not at home.'

'Are you?' Jude went out.

'Jude! Jude!' Sue called pitifully from the window. 'I'm really all alone! Come and see me again. Come next week.'

'All right,' said Jude.

◆

Two days later, Sue changed her mind. 'Don't come next week,' she wrote to Jude. 'We were too free. You must try to forget me.'

'You're right,' Jude wrote back. 'It's a lesson I ought to learn at this Easter season.'

Their decisions seemed final, but on Easter Monday Drusilla Fawley died and it was necessary for Jude to inform Sue. 'Aunt Drusilla is dead,' he wrote from Marygreen. 'She will be buried on Friday afternoon.'

Sue came, alone and nervous, and the cousins went together to the burial service.

'She was always against marriage, wasn't she?' asked Sue afterwards, when they were back at the familiar cottage.

'Yes. Particularly for members of our family.'

Sue looked at Jude. 'Would a woman be very bad, do you

'What have I done? I thought we two —'
'Sue, I sometimes think you're playing with my affections,' Jude
said angrily.

think, if she didn't like living with her husband just because she had, well, a physical feeling against it?'

Jude looked away. 'Sue, you're not happy in your marriage, are you?'

'Of course I am! . . . But I have to go back by the six o'clock train.'

'That train won't take you to Shaston. You'll have to stay here until tomorrow. Mrs Edlin has a room if you don't wish to stay in this house.'

Sue's hand lay on the tea-table. Jude put his hand on it, but Sue took hers away. 'That's silly, Sue!' he cried. 'It was a totally innocent action!'

'Then I must tell Richard that you hold my hand,' she said. 'Unless you are sure that you mean it only as my cousin?'

'Absolutely sure. I have no feelings of love now.'

'Oh! How has that happened?'

'I saw Arabella when I was at Christminster.'

'So she's come back and you never told me! I suppose you'll live with her now?'

'Of course – just as you live with your husband.'

There were tears in Sue's eyes. 'How could your heart go back to Arabella so soon? . . . But I must be as honest with you as you've been with me. Though I like Mr Phillotson as a friend, I hate living with him as a husband! There, now I've told you.' She bent her face down onto her hands and cried until the little table shook.

'I *thought* there was something wrong, Sue.'

'There's nothing wrong, except the awful contract to give myself to this man whenever he wishes. *He* does nothing wrong, except that he has become a little cold since he found out my feelings. That's why he didn't come today. Oh, I'm so unhappy! Don't come near me, Jude. You mustn't!'

But Jude had jumped up and put his face against hers. 'It all happened because I was married before we met, didn't it? That's the only reason you became *his* wife, Sue, isn't it?'

Instead of replying, Sue left the house and went across to Mrs Edlin's cottage.

♦

Next morning, Jude walked with Sue as far as the main road to Alfredston. He must not kiss her goodbye, she said, unless he promised that he kissed her only as a cousin and friend. No, he would not promise that. So they separated. But then both looked round at the same time – and ran back into each other's arms, kissing close and long.

The kiss was a turning-point for Jude. To him it seemed the purest moment of his life, but to his Church it would seem nothing of the sort. He realized that he could not possibly continue in his unlicensed love for Sue *and* hope to become a teacher of religion.

That evening, he lit a fire in the garden and calmly put all his theological books on the flames.

Chapter 16   Separate Lives

Phillotson met his troubled wife at the station and tried to interest her. His schoolmaster friend Gillingham had called for the first time since their marriage, he said, and —

'Richard, I let Mr Fawley hold my hand. Was that wrong?'

'I hope it pleased him,' was all Phillotson said.

Sue did not mention the kiss. That evening, she went to bed early, saying she was tired. Her husband worked on school matters and did not go to their room until nearly midnight. Sue was not there.

'I'm not sleepy now. I'm reading by the fire.' Her voice came from the back of the house, near the kitchen.

Phillotson went to bed, but when he woke up some time later, she was still not there. He went downstairs. 'Sue?'

'Yes.' The voice, very small, now seemed to come from a clothes-cupboard under the stairs.

'Whatever are you doing in there? There's no bed, no air!' He pulled at the door. Sue was lying on some cushions in her white night-dress.

'Oh, please, go away!' She knelt, wide-eyed and pitiful.

'But I've been kind to you and given you every freedom. It's awful that you feel this way!'

'Yes, I know,' she said, crying. 'Life is so cruel!'

423

'Shhh! The servant will hear. I hate such odd behaviour, Sue. You give in too much to your feelings.' And so he left her, only advising her not to shut the door too tightly.

At breakfast the next morning, Sue asked her husband to let her live away from him. 'Will you let me go? Will you?'

'But we married, Susanna.'

'We made a contract. Surely we can unmake it? Then we could be friends, and meet without pain. Richard, have pity!'

'But you promised to love me.'

'It's foolish to promise always to love one person!'

'And does "living away" from me mean living by yourself?'

'Well, if you insisted yes. But I meant living with Jude.'

'As his wife?'

'As I choose.'

Phillotson gripped the table. 'I can't allow you to go and live with your lover. We would lose everyone's respect.'

'Then allow me to live in your house in a separate way.'

To that, finally, the schoolmaster agreed. He watched his pretty wife teaching in his school, and felt very lonely.

◆

Phillotson kept his promise and moved to a room on the other side of the house. But then, one night, he absentmindedly entered their old room and began to undress. There was a cry from the bed and a quick movement towards the window. Sue leapt out.

In horror, he ran down and gathered up in his arms the white shape lying on the ground.

Sue was, in fact, scarcely hurt. 'I was asleep, I think!' she began, turning her pale face away from him. 'And something frightened me – a terrible dream. I thought I saw you —'

Sick at heart, Phillotson watched her go slowly upstairs. He sat with his head in his hands for a long, long time. Then, next day after school, he walked down to the little town of Leddenton and knocked at the door of his old friend, Gillingham.

♦

'Now, George, when a woman jumps out of a window and doesn't care whether she breaks her neck or not, the meaning is clear. And so I'm going to do as she asks.'

'What, Dick, you'll let her go?' Gillingham was amazed. 'And with her lover?'

'I shall. I can't defend my decision religiously or any other way, but I think I'm doing wrong to refuse her . . . I had no idea that simply taking a woman to church and putting a ring on her finger could involve one in such a daily tragedy! I shall let her go.'

'But with a lover!'

'She hasn't definitely said she'll live with him as a wife. And it's not just animal feeling between the two: I think their affection will last. One day, in the first jealous weeks of my marriage, I heard them talking together at the school. There was an extraordinary sympathy between the pair . . .'

'But what about family life? What about neighbours, society? Good God, what will Shaston say?' Gillingham walked to the door with his friend, 'Stick to her!' were his final words.

Next morning, Phillotson told Sue that he agreed to her departure. Only he did not wish to hear, he said, anything about Jude Fawley or about where she was going.

Having made the decision, he felt a new sense of peace.

Chapter 17   Two Rooms at the Inn

Sue left Shaston one evening after dark, taking with her only one small trunk. Phillotson put her on the station bus, then returned to the schoolhouse and packed away all her remaining things.

Jude met her at Melchester station, carrying a black bag and looking handsome in his Sunday suit. His eyes shone with love. 'There wasn't time to tell you, dear one,' he said, getting onto the train. 'We can't stay here, where we're known. I've given up my cathedral work. We're going on to Aldbrickham. I've booked a room for us at a hotel.'

'One room? Oh, Jude, I didn't mean that!' Seeing his shock, Sue put her face against his cheek. 'Don't be angry, dear. Perhaps I *am* free to live with you from this moment, but Richard has been so generous and if I loved him ever so little as a wife, I'd go back to him even now . . . But I don't love him.'

'And you don't love me either, I half fear. Sue, I sometimes think you are incapable of real love.'

Sue moved away from him, looking out into the darkness. 'My liking for you is not as some women's, perhaps,' she said in a hurt voice. 'But I do love to be with you. I've let you kiss me and that tells enough.'

Jude sat back, remembering the poor Christminster graduate. Then he forgave her, as he always did, and they sat side by side with joined hands. 'You know you're all the world to me, Sue,' he said gently, 'whatever you do.'

It was about ten o'clock when they reached Aldbrickham. Sue would not go to the hotel, so a boy wheeled their luggage to the George Inn, where they took two rooms.

'Your relation came here once before, late just like this, with his wife,' said a maid chatting to Sue. 'About a month or two ago. A big, handsome woman.'

Sue was quiet throughout supper. 'You came here lately with Arabella,' she accused Jude as they went upstairs afterwards.

Jude looked round him. 'Why, yes, it is the same place! I really didn't know it, Sue.'

'When were you here? Tell me!'

'The day before you and I met in Christminster and we went back to Marygreen together. I told you I had met her again.'

'But you didn't tell me everything. You've been false to me!'

She was so upset that Jude had to take her into her room.

'But, Sue, you had a new husband and she was my legal wife —'

'Was it this room? Yes, I see by your face that it was!'

Sue buried her face in the bed. 'I thought you cared for nobody in the world except me!'

'It's true. I did not, and I don't now,' said Jude.

'I thought that a separation – like yours from her and mine from him – ended a marriage.'

'I don't want to speak against Arabella, but I must tell you one thing which settles the matter. She has married another man! I knew nothing about it until after she and I came here. And now she's asked me for a divorce, so that she can remarry this man legally. So I'm not likely to see her again.'

Sue got up. 'Then I forgive you. And you may kiss me just once, here, on my cheek. You do care for me very much, don't you, in spite of my not – you know?'

'Yes, sweet,' Jude said with a sigh. 'Good night.'

Chapter 18   Phillotson Dismissed

'Shaston' soon began to talk about Sue's absence. A month after she left, Phillotson was questioned about it by the school governors and he was too honest to lie. 'She asked my permission to go away with her lover, and I gave it,' he told them. 'Why shouldn't I? She wasn't my prisoner.'

But he had young people in his care! He must not appear to encourage such behaviour! Consider the effect on the town!

427

The governors asked Phillotson to leave the school. Against his friend Gillingham's advice, he refused. So they dismissed him, and that led to an illness. Day after day, the schoolmaster lay in his bed: a middle-aged man, facing failure and sadness.

Gillingham came to see him and, after a time, mentioned Sue's name. 'Where are she and her lover living?' he asked.

'At Melchester, I suppose. That's where he was.'

Gillingham then wrote Sue an unsigned note, addressing the envelope to Jude. From Melchester, the note was sent on to Marygreen, from where Mrs Edlin sent it to Aldbrickham.

Three days later, the sick man heard a little knock at his bedroom door.

Sue entered, as light as a ghost. 'I heard that you were ill,' she said, 'and as I know that you recognize other feelings between man and woman than physical love, I've come.'

The amazed servant-girl brought up tea; and Phillotson and his wife talked of this and that. Sue had heard no news from Shaston and so he simply told her that he was leaving the school. He was not seriously ill, he said.

Sue went to the window. 'It's such a beautiful sunset, Richard,' she said thoughtfully.

'Is it? It doesn't shine into this dark corner.'

'I'll help you to see it,' she said, and moved a mirror to a place by the window where it caught the sunshine. 'There – you can see the great red sun now!'

Phillotson smiled sadly at her child-like kindness. 'You *are* an odd little thing!' he said, as the sun glowed in his eyes. 'To come and see me after what has happened!'

'I must go home now,' she said quickly. Jude doesn't know where I am.' She went to the door, and he noticed tears on her face.

'Sue!' He had not meant to call her back. 'Do you wish to stay? I'll forgive you everything.'

'Oh, you can't!' she said. 'Jude is getting a divorce from his wife, Arabella.'

'His wife! It's news to me that he has a wife.'

'It was a bad marriage. But he's divorcing her as a kindness because she wants to remarry. I *must* go now.' Sue's fear had returned, and she did not tell her husband that she was still not living with Jude as a wife.

'She's his, from lips to toe!' said Phillotson as she left.

Next time Gillingham came, Phillotson seemed better. He told his friend about Sue's visit and said that he had decided, in kindness, to divorce her.

'Freedom will give her a chance of happiness,' he said. 'Because then they'll be able to marry.'

PART 5   AT ALDBRICKHAM
AND ELSEWHERE

Chapter 19   'The Little Bird Is Caught at Last'

The following year, Sue and Jude were still living separately, in a little house in Spring Street, Aldbrickham, that was rented by Jude. A sign on the door said, 'Jude Fawley: Mason'. He now made headstones, cheaply, for which Sue marked out the letters.

One Sunday morning in February, at breakfast, Sue held up an envelope. The courts, she said as Jude kissed her, had agreed to her divorce from Phillotson. Jude's divorce had come through a month before. 'But I feel that I got *my* freedom under false pretences,' Sue worried. 'If the courts had known the truth about you and me, they would not have given Richard the divorce.'

Jude had to smile. 'Well, you have only yourself to blame for the false pretences, darling!'

His happiness at their new freedom made Sue happier too. She suggested that they should go into the countryside for a walk, and she put on a bright dress to celebrate.

'So, my dear, we can marry at last,' Jude said as they made their way towards the wintry fields.

'I suppose we can,' said Sue without enthusiasm. 'But I have the same old fear of a marriage contract. Remember our parents! I might begin to be afraid of you, dear Jude, when you had a Government licence to love me!'

'My own sweet love, I don't want to force you into any thing! For the rest of our walk, we'll talk only about the weather.'

♦

One Friday evening at the end of that month, there was a knock at the front door. Jude opened his window and saw a woman under the street-light.

'Is that Mr Fawley?' The voice was Arabella's!

'Whatever do you want, Arabella?'

Sue came into Jude's room, immediately upset.

'I'm sorry to call so late, Jude,' Arabella said, 'but I'm in trouble.' Her man hadn't married her after all, she went on, and she had a sudden responsibility that had arrived from Australia. If Jude could walk with her towards the Prince Inn where she was staying for the night, she would explain.

'Don't, don't go tonight, dear!' Sue was shaking. 'She only does it to trap you again. She's such a low sort of woman – I can see it in her shape, and hear it in her voice!'

'I shall go,' said Jude. 'God knows I love her little enough now, but I don't want to be cruel.' He moved towards the stairs.

'But she's not your wife!' cried Sue wildly. 'And I —'

'And you're not either, dear, yet,' said Jude. 'I've waited with patience, but we're living here in one house, both of us free, and *still* you will not be mine!'

Sue was now crying as if her heart would break. 'Very well

then, I will be. Only I didn't mean to! And I didn't want to marry again! But I do love you.' She ran across and threw her arms round his neck. 'I give in!'

'And so I'll arrange for our marriage.'

'Yes, Jude.'

'Then I'll let her go,' he said softly. 'Don't cry any more. There, there and there.' He kissed Sue on one side, and on the other, and in the middle – and closed the window.

◆

The next morning was wet.

'Now, dear,' said Jude happily. 'I'll take along the marriage notice so that it can be made public tomorrow.'

'I was so selfish about Arabella!' said Sue. 'Perhaps she really did have a problem. Perhaps I should go and see her?'

'Arabella can look after herself,' said Jude calmly. 'Still, go to the inn if you want to. And then we'll take the marriage notice together.'

Sue went off under an umbrella, letting Jude kiss her and returning his kisses in a way she had never done before. 'The little bird is caught at last!' she said with a sad smile.

At the inn, saying she was a friend from Spring Street, Sue was asked to go upstairs. She found Arabella still in bed. 'I've just looked in to see if you're all right,' she said gently.

'Oh!' Arabella was disappointed. 'I thought my visitor was your friend, your husband – Mrs Fawley, as I suppose you call yourself?'

'Indeed I don't,' said Sue stiffly. She looked at Arabella's tail of hair hanging on the mirror and at the rain, and felt depressed.

Just then a maid brought in a telegram for 'Mrs Cartlett'. Arabella read it and brightened. 'From Lambeth!' she said. 'My man agrees to keep his promise to marry me again. I sent him a telegram saying I'd almost got together with Jude again, and that frightened him! Well, I don't need Jude now, so I advise you, my dear, to persuade him to marry you as soon as possible.'

'He's waiting to, particularly since last night —' Sue went pink.

'So my visit helped it on – ha-ha!' laughed Arabella. 'Go on, let him marry you! Then, if he throws you out, the law will protect you; and if he leaves you, you'll have the furniture.' She put her hand on Sue's arm. 'I really did want Jude's advice on a little business matter. I'll write to him from London.'

When Sue reached home, Jude was waiting at the door. But she persuaded him not to take the marriage notice, not yet. Arabella, she said, had made her feel more than ever that legal marriage was a trap to catch a man.

'Sue, you're beginning to frighten me off marriage too! All right, let's go in and think about it.'

Chapter 20   Little Father Time

Three weeks later, while they were still thinking about it, a newspaper and a letter arrived from Arabella.

The newspaper, which Sue opened, reported the marriage of 'Cartlett - Donn' in Lambeth. 'Well, at least we don't have to worry about her now,' said Sue easily.

But Jude's attention was on the letter. 'Listen to this! " . . . The fact is, Jude, that a son was born of our marriage eight months after I left you, when I was at Sydney with my parents. They have looked after him ever since, but now they say they are sending him over to me. So I must ask you to take him when he arrives, because Cartlett might not like him. I swear he is your lawful son. *Arabella Cartlett*".'

Sue's eyes filled with tears.

'It *may* be true,' Jude said. 'But does it really matter whether a child is one's own by blood?'

At this, Sue jumped up and kissed Jude. 'We'll have him here, dearest! And if he isn't yours, all the better!'

' . . . Just imagine his life in a Lambeth drinking-house, with a mother who doesn't want him. The boy – my boy, perhaps might start asking, "Why was I ever born?"'

'Oh, no, Jude! We must have him. I'll be a mother to him.'

So Jude wrote straight back, telling Arabella to send the boy on to them – and they agreed to marry before he came.

◆

The next evening, a small pale child knocked at the door of the house in Spring Street. Arabella had postponed writing to Jude until the ship from Australia was due; and the boy reached London Docks on the same day as she received Jude's answer. So she gave him a good meal, a little money, and put him on the next train to Aldbrickham, before Cartlett could see him.

Hearing the knock, Sue came down from her room.

'Is this where Father, Mr Fawley, lives?' asked the child.

Sue looked at him and ran to fetch Jude, who picked him up with a sad tenderness.

'Arabella's speaking the truth!' Sue burst out. 'I see you in him!'

The boy looked across at her. 'Are you my real mother at last? Can I call you Mother?' He began to cry.

'Yes, if you wish, my poor dear.' Sue put her cheek against his to hide her own tears. 'I do want to be a mother to this child,' she said to Jude after they had put him to bed, 'and marriage might make it easier. Oh, Jude, you'll still love me afterwards, won't you?'

◆

The boy was very quiet and serious. People called him Little Father Time, he said, because he looked so old.

His father was disappointed that he was not called Jude. 'We'll have him properly named in church,' he said to Sue, 'the day we're married.'

The morning after his arrival, they took their marriage notice to the district office. But they did not marry. They could not make themselves do it, either at the office or in church, even though the Widow Edlin arrived for the wedding.

'Don't tell the child,' Sue told her. 'We've only postponed it. And if Jude and I are happy as we are, what does it matter?'

Chapter 21   At the Great Wessex Show

One day in June of that year, two trains arrived at the little town of Stoke Barehills, bringing visitors to the Great Wessex Agricultural Show. One train came from Aldbrickham. The other came from London and, among the crowd that got off it, were a well-built, rather red-faced woman in city clothes and a short, rather top-heavy man with a round stomach.

'Heavens, Cartlett!' cried the woman, looking at a couple coming off the other platform. 'There's Jude Fawley!'

'They seem fond of one another and of their child.'

'It isn't *their* child!' said Arabella jealously. 'They haven't been married long enough!' But Cartlett thought her child was still in Australia, so she said no more.

Jude and Sue walked on into the show-ground, enjoying their holiday and trying hard to make Father Time enjoy himself, too. Sue, in a new summer dress, holding up her white cotton sun-umbrella, was as light as a bird. Jude looked proud of her. Their delight in each other was obvious. They seemed like two halves of a single whole.

Arabella stayed close behind them. 'They can't be married,' she said, 'or they wouldn't be so much in love! See how —'

Cartlett lost interest and went off to the beer tent:

'Arabella!' She was greeted with a laugh by her girlhood friend Anny, who had come down for the day from Alfredston.

Jude and Sue walked on into the show-ground, enjoying their holiday and trying hard to make Father Time enjoy himself, too.

'Have you seen Jude and his young woman, or wife, or whatever she is?' said Arabella. 'There they are, by the horses!'

'She's pretty,' said Anny. 'He's nice-looking, too. Why didn't you stick to him, Arabella?'

'Yes, why didn't I?' She noticed Jude's hand reaching out to Sue's as the lovers stood close together.

'Happy?' Jude asked Sue, and Sue nodded.

'Silly fools – like two children!' Arabella said gloomily. She left them admiring some roses and went to join Cartlett, who was sitting at the bar, drinking and talking to one of the barmaids. 'Surely you didn't come fifty miles from your own bar just to stick in another?' she remarked, ready for a quarrel. 'Take me round the show as other men take their wives!'

Chapter 22   Disapproval

Arabella was not the only person who took an interest in Jude and Sue. When Father Time suddenly arrived, their neighbours began to talk about them. And when the child was called 'Jude' and sent to school, the pupils made hurtful remarks.

So the pair went off for several days 'to London'; and when they came back, they let people understand that they were legally married at last. Sue, who had been called Mrs Bridehead, now openly took the name of Mrs Fawley.

But it was all too secret, too late. People began to avoid them and to give fewer orders for headstones. In the autumn, when Sue was expecting a child of her own, the couple were even dismissed from a lettering job in a local church.

Jude decided then to give up the house and look for work elsewhere. 'We'll have a better chance where we're not known,' he said to Sue. 'I'm sickened by ecclesiastical work now. Perhaps if I went back to baking, our way of life would matter less to people!'

And so they left Aldbrickham. Jude did no more church work.

He now had few religious beliefs left and he did not want to earn money from people who disliked his ways. But he accepted other employment as a stone-mason wherever he found it; and, for the next two-and-a-half years, he and his growing family lived all over Wessex.

Chapter 23   Arabella Meets Phillotson

On a Saturday afternoon in May, almost three years after she saw Jude and Sue at the agricultural show, Arabella came to the busy town of Kennetbridge, a dozen miles south of Marygreen. Anny drove the horse and cart in which she came, and the two friends agreed to meet again in half an hour.

Arabella, all in black, walked around Kennetbridge market on her own, and stopped in surprise at a little bakery counter run by a young woman and an old-faced boy. 'Mrs Fawley!'

Sue recognized her and changed colour. 'How are you, Mrs Cartlett?' she said stiffly. Then, seeing Arabella's black clothes, she became sympathetic. 'Oh! You've lost —'

'My poor husband, yes. He died suddenly six weeks ago. I'm living at Alfredston with my friend Anny . . . And you, my little old man, I suppose you don't know me?'

'You're the woman I thought at first was my mother.'

Sue quickly sent the boy off with a basket of cakes to sell. 'He doesn't know yet,' she said. 'Jude's going to tell him when he's a little older.'

'Then you're living with Jude still? Married?'

'Yes.'

'Any children?'

'Two.' Sue hesitated.

'And another coming soon, I see. But why are you selling cakes now?' Unasked, Arabella took one and ate it. 'Jude used to be too proud a man for this.'

Sue bit her lip. 'My husband hasn't been well since he caught cold last winter, putting up some stonework for a music-hall in the rain. So now he makes these cakes, which he can do indoors. We call them Christminster cakes.'

'He still keeps on about Christminster then! But why,' Arabella's questioning continued, 'don't you go back to school-teaching? Because of the divorce?'

'That and other things. We gave up all ambition and were never so happy in our lives until Jude became ill.'

'Here's the boy again,' said Arabella. 'My boy and Jude's!'

◆

'Anny, I've heard of Jude again and seen *her*!' Arabella and Anny were driving back to Alfredston. 'I want him back!'

'Fight against it,' said Anny. 'He belongs to someone else.'

They drove on in silence across the upland until they saw the cottage where Arabella had once lived with Jude.

'He's more mine than hers,' Arabella burst out. 'I'd take him from her if I could!'

'Arabella! Your husband's only been dead six weeks!'

At the top of the hill by the Brown House, they gave a lift to a thin, elderly looking man.

Arabella looked at him when he was in the cart, and looked again. 'Mr Phillotson?' she asked.

'Yes,' said the traveller politely. 'And you are —?'

'I was one of your pupils. Arabella Donn. I used to walk up from Cresscombe to your school at Marygreen . . . And I married Jude Fawley, one of your night-school pupils.'

'*You* were Fawley's wife?' Phillotson lost his stiffness. He had recently returned to Marygreen, he said. It was the only school which would take him after his wife left him as she did.

Arabella told him that she had just seen Sue at Kennetbridge. 'She's not doing well. Her husband is ill and she's worried . . . You were wrong to divorce her.'

'No,' said Phillotson. 'I'm sure that I was right.'

'She was innocent. The divorce was wrongly given. I talked to her just afterwards and I'm sure of it.'

He gripped the side of the cart. 'But she wanted to go.'

'Yes. But you shouldn't have let her.'

◆

When Sue had sold all the Christminster cakes, she and the boy left the market with their empty baskets and walked to some old cottages with gardens and fruit-trees. The Widow Edlin came to the door of one, carrying a baby and holding a little girl by the hand.

Jude was sitting inside, in an armchair. 'You've sold them all?' he asked, a smile crossing his thin, pale face.

'Yes.' Sue told him about the market. Then, when they were alone, she kissed him and told him about Arabella.

'Arabella at Alfredston!' Jude looked worried. 'Perhaps it's a good thing that we've almost decided to move on. I'll be well enough to leave very soon. Then Mrs Edlin can go home again – dear, faithful, old Mrs Edlin!'

He had so far avoided all the old places, he said, but now he would like to go back to Christminster if Sue agreed. 'What does it matter if we're known there? It's still the centre of the world to me because of my early dream. I'd like to go back to live there, perhaps to die there! I'd like to be there by a particular day in June . . .'

PART 6   AT CHRISTMINSTER AGAIN

Chapter 24   In the Streets of Christminster

They arrived at Christminster on Remembrance Day, the day chosen by Jude.

'Let's go and watch the celebrations,' said Jude suddenly. 'We'll leave our luggage at the station and get lodgings later.'

He carried their baby son, Sue led their little daughter and Arabella's boy walked silently beside them until they arrived at a round theatre – the theatre from which Jude had looked out on the day he awoke from his Christminster dream.

Today, there were holiday crowds lining the open space between the theatre and the nearest college. 'Here's the best place! Here's where they'll pass!' cried Jude in excitement. He pushed his way close to the barrier, holding the baby in his arms. Graduates in red and black arrived at the college. The sky turned dark and it began to rain and thunder.

'It seems like Judgement Day!' whispered Father Time.

Jude would not leave. He explained details of the stonework to the people around him. Tinker Taylor and the stone-mason Uncle Joe called out to him. He spoke loudly to the crowd of his failure to enter the university.

'He does look ill and worn-out,' said a woman.

'I may do some good before I'm dead,' Jude went on, 'as a terrible example of what *not* to do —'

'Don't say that!' whispered Sue in tears. 'You've struggled so hard!' It was raining heavily now. 'Let's go on, dear. We haven't any lodgings, and you're not well yet.'

But Jude watched and waited until all the university doctors had walked across to the theatre. 'Well, I'm an outsider to the end of my days!' he sighed at last. 'But how pale you are, Sue!'

'I saw Richard among the crowd, and I felt afraid . . .'

'You're tired. Oh, I forgot, darling! We'll go at once.'

Chapter 25   'Because We Are Too Many'

Lodgings were difficult to find so late in the day. Eventually, a woman said she could take Sue and the children for a week if Jude could stay elsewhere.

But when Jude had left to collect their luggage and find

lodgings for himself at an inn, Sue heard the woman's husband shouting downstairs. Then the woman came up and said they would have to leave tomorrow. Her husband, she said, wanted no children in the house.

The boy was deeply upset. 'Mother, what shall we do?'

'I don't know. I'm afraid this will trouble your father, but we won't tell him tonight.'

'It's all because of us children, isn't it?'

'Well, people do dislike children sometimes.'

'If children are so much trouble, why do people have them? I was a trouble in Australia and I'm a trouble here. Why was I ever born? When children are born that are not wanted, they should be killed straight away.'

She hesitated. Then she decided to be honest. 'There's going to be another baby in our family soon,' she said.

'What!' The boy jumped up wildly. 'Oh, Mother, you've never sent for another! Why couldn't you wait until we've more money and Father's well?' He burst into tears.

'Forgive me, little Jude,' she begged him, crying too. 'I'll explain when you're older.'

'I won't forgive you, ever, ever! I'll never believe you love me or Father or any of us any more!'

He ran into the next little room, where a bed had been spread on the floor for the three children. 'If we children weren't here, there'd be no trouble!' she heard him say.

'Go to sleep now, dear!' she commanded.

◆

Sue woke early next morning and she ran across to the inn, to tell Jude about the problem with the lodgings. They had a quick meal and then returned together to prepare the children's breakfast. All was still quiet in the children's little room and, at half-past eight, Sue went in to call them.

Jude heard a scream and saw her fall to the floor, unconscious.

He ran forward, then looked down at the children's bed. It was empty. He looked round the room – and saw two little bodies hanging from the back of the door, like clothes, and the boy's body hanging from the ceiling.

In horror, he cut them down, laid Sue on her bed and ran for a doctor. But it was too late. The children had been hanging for more than an hour and all three were dead. 'Done because we are too many,' said a note in little Jude's writing.

Sue was conscious again but, at the sight of the note, her nerves gave way completely. Screaming and struggling, she was carried downstairs. She lay there, shaking and staring at the ceiling.

As soon as she could speak, she told Jude about her conversation with the boy the evening before. That must have caused the tragedy, she said. She was to blame.

'No,' said Jude, 'it was in his nature to do it, to wish not to live.' Then he too broke down.

'Oh, oh, my babies!' Sue cried. 'They had done no harm. Why were they taken, not I? We loved each other too much, too selfishly, you and I, Jude; and now we're punished . . .'

◆

She had to stay on at the now-hated lodgings. People came and went – police, lawyers, newspaper men. The law took its course.

At last, the children could be buried. But then Sue tried to stop the grave-digger from covering the grave with earth. 'I want to see them once more,' she cried. 'Oh, Jude, please, Jude, I want to see them! Just one little minute . . .'

Later that night, the child Sue was expecting was born dead.

Chapter 26   Separation

Sue hoped for death for herself too, but slowly she recovered. Jude returned to his old trade of stone-mason, and they moved to Beersheba, not far from the church of St Silas.

They talked endlessly that summer of their life together and of Life itself. Gradually, Jude realized that they had mentally travelled in opposite directions since the tragedy. Sue was no longer the fearless, independent thinker she had been. 'It's no use fighting against God,' she said. 'I must give up my selfish ways.' While Jude rarely went to church now, she went frequenty to St Silas.

Finally, one Sunday evening when she returned from a service there, she told Jude that she did not ever want to marry him. 'And, dear Jude, I don't think I ought to live as your wife any more.'

'What! But you *are* my wife, Sue, in all except law.'

'I'm Richard's wife,' she said. 'I feel more and more sure that I belong to him, or to nobody.'

◆

A few evenings later, Arabella called at the lodgings, behaving correctly but looking poorer than before.

'Thank you for writing,' she said. 'I've just come from the child's grave. As it's your trade, Jude, you'll be able to put up a handsome headstone . . . If he had been with me, perhaps it wouldn't have happened. But of course I didn't wish to take him from your wife.'

'I'm not his wife,' said Sue, and left the room.

'Why did she say that?' asked Arabella in a changed voice. 'She *is* your wife, isn't she? She once told me so.'

'I cannot tell you,' said Jude firmly.

'Ah, I see! Well, I thought I should call before I go back to Alfredston. Father has just come back from Australia. I'm living with him now. Mother died out there.'

As soon as she left, Jude looked for Sue. She was not in the house. He went to St Silas and found her lying there, in her black clothes, crying.

'I wanted to be alone,' she said, almost sharply. 'Why did you come?'

'Why?' he repeated, wounded to the heart. 'I, who love you better than my own self! Why did *you* come here, alone?'

'I felt so unhappy when Arabella came. She seems to be your wife still and Richard to be my husband. God has taken my babies from me to show me this. Arabella's child killed mine. That was God's judgement – the right killing the wrong.'

'This is terrible!' Jude replied. 'If your religion does this to you, then I hate it . . . Come home with me, dearest.'

He lifted her up, but she preferred to walk without his support and she stopped at a little coffee-house. 'Jude,' she said, 'will you get yourself lodgings here?'

'I will – if you really wish. But *do* you?' He took her home and followed her up to the door of their room. She put her hand in his and said, 'Good night, Jude'.

'You have never loved me as I love you!' he burst out.

'At first, Jude, I admit, I just wanted you to love me. But then I couldn't let you go – possibly to Arabella again – and so I began to love you. And now I love you as much as ever. But I mustn't love you any more. I joined myself to Richard for life.'

'Oh, Sue!' Jude suddenly sensed his own danger. 'I'm a weak man! Don't leave me just to save yourself!'

'I'll pray for you, Jude, night and day.'

'I mustn't stay? Not just once more, as it has been so many times? Oh, Sue, my wife, why not? . . . Very well. Perhaps it's all been my fault. Perhaps I spoilt one of the purest loves that ever existed between man and woman!' He went to the bed and threw one of its pair of pillows to the floor. 'Good night,' he said and started to go.

'This breaks my heart,' she said, her face wet with tears. 'Oh, kiss me!'

He took her in his arms and covered her tears with kisses.

'We'll see each other sometimes, won't we, Jude?' she said, freeing herself. 'We'll be dear friends just the same?'

Jude turned and went down the stairs.

Chapter 27   Remarriage

The man whom Sue now thought of as her husband still lived at Marygreen. He had seen her on Remembrance Day at Christminster. Then he had read in the newspaper about the tragedy, and had puzzled at the age of the eldest boy.

A few weeks later, Phillotson was at Alfredston for the Saturday market and he met Arabella. She told him that the eldest boy had been her son, and that Sue was not, after all, married to Jude. 'And now, I hear, she doesn't live with him any more. She says she's your wife in the eyes of God.'

'Indeed? Separated, have they?'

'Yes. As for me, I hope soon to be in a bar again at Christminster or some other big town.'

Phillotson asked for Sue's address. Arabella gave it and walked on, smiling to herself.

The schoolmaster still wanted Sue in his strange way. He could remarry her, he thought, on the respectable excuse that he had divorced her wrongly. Then society might accept him again.

So he wrote to Sue, suggesting that she should return to him. It was a careful letter. Physical love, he wrote, had little to do with the matter. He simply wished to make their lives less of a failure.

◆

One evening soon after, Sue walked to Jude's new lodgings and told him that she was going to remarry Phillotson.

Jude turned on her fiercely. 'But you're *my* wife!' he shouted. 'I loved you, and you loved me, and we made our own contract. We still love each other. I *know* it, Sue!'

445

Jude turned on her fiercely. 'But you're my wife!' he shouted.
'I loved you, and you loved me, and we made our own contract.'

'But I'm going to marry him again,' she answered, 'at the Marygreen church. And you should take back Arabella.'

'Good God, what next? What if you and I had married legally?'

'I'd have felt just the same.'

Jude shook his head hopelessly. Had the tragedy destroyed her reason? 'Wrong, all wrong! You don't love him.'

'I admit it. But I shall try to learn to, by obeying him.'

Jude argued and begged, but she was unshakeable. 'I didn't think you'd be so rough with me,' she said. 'I was going to ask you —'

'To give you away?'

'No. To come to the children's grave with me.'

So they went to the grave, and there they said goodbye.

The next day was a Friday. Sue left Christminster alone, having asked Phillotson not to come for her. She wanted to return to him freely, she said, just as she had freely left him.

She sent her luggage on in front of her and walked the last half mile into Marygreen in the early evening. 'I've come, Richard,' she said, looking pale and sinking into a chair in the new schoolhouse. 'Will you take me back?'

'Darling Susanna.' He bent and kissed her cheek – and Sue. moved nervously away. 'So you still dislike me!'

'Oh no, dear! I'm cold and wet from the journey, that's all. When is our wedding?'

'Tomorrow morning early, I thought. But it's not too late to refuse if you —'

'I want it done quickly.'

'Well, my friend Gillingham has already come up from Shaston to help us. Join us for supper and then I'll take you over to your room at Mrs Edlin's.'

◆

Morning came. A thick fog had moved up from the lowland and drifted by the trees on the village green covering them with big drops. At half-past eight, before many people were around, Sue and Phillotson were remarried.

Later in the day, Phillotson walked out a little way to say goodbye to Gillingham. Sue seemed nervous when he got back. 'Of course, my dear,' he said, 'I shall allow you to live just as privately as before.'

Sue brightened a little.

Chapter 28   Back with Arabella

The following evening, a woman in black stood on the doorstep of Jude's lodgings in the rain. 'Father's turned me out after borrowing all my money for his new business! Can you take me in, Jude, while I look for work?'

'No!' said Jude coldly. But Arabella cried, and finally he agreed to let her use a little room at the top of the house for a few days.

'You've heard the news, I suppose?' she said then. 'Anny writes that the wedding was arranged for yesterday.'

'I don't want to talk about it.'

At first, Arabella did not come near Jude. But, the next Sunday, she asked if she could join him for breakfast as she had broken her teapot.

They sat for a while in silence. Then she said that she could find out about the wedding if he wanted to know. She needed to go to Alfredston to see Anny – and Anny had relations at Marygreen.

Hating himself, Jude agreed. He paid for her journey and, impatiently, met her at the station in the evening.

'They're married,' she smiled. 'Mrs Edlin said Sue was so upset that she even burnt the prettiest things she'd worn with you. Still,' Arabella sighed, 'she feels that he's her only husband in the eyes of God.' She sighed again. 'I feel exactly the same!'

Jude left her without a word. In his depression, he walked to all the places in the city he had visited with Sue. Then he turned into an inn.

Hours later, Arabella went to the inn where she had once worked as a barmaid and, as she expected, found Jude sitting there, half drunk.

'I've come to look after you, dear boy. You're not well.' Arabella suddenly seemed to have some money again. She bought him more drinks, stronger drinks. And whenever Jude said, 'I don't care what happens to me,' she replied, 'But I do, very much!'

When closing time came, she guided him out onto the street. 'You can't go back to your lodgings in this condition. Come round to my father's. He's more friendly towards me now.'

'Anything, anywhere,' said Jude. 'What does it matter?'

And so she guided him to her father's new little pork-and-sausage shop, her arm around his waist and his arm, at last, through unsteadiness, around her.

'This way,' she said in the dark, after she had shut the door. 'I'll pull off your boots,' she whispered. 'Now, hold on to me. First stair, second stair, that's it . . .'

♦

Arabella looked at Jude's curly black hair and beard on the white pillow next morning, and felt well pleased.

'I've got a prize upstairs!' she told her father down in the shop. 'It's Jude. He's come back to me.'

She went off to Jude's lodgings and, unasked, brought away all his things and her own. Then, 'to advertise Father's new shop', she invited people like Uncle Joe and Tinker Taylor from the inn to a party. And, all the time, she kept Jude so drunk that he did not know where he was or what he did.

On the fourth day, in front of all the party guests, she said, 'Come along then, old darling, as you promised.'

'When did I promise anything?' asked Jude.

Arabella looked at her father. 'Now, Mr Fawley,' said Donn, 'you and my daughter have been living here together on the understanding that you were going to marry her.'

'If that's so,' said Jude hotly, standing up, 'then by God I *will* marry her!'

'Don't go,' Arabella said to the guests. 'We'll all have a good, strong cup of tea when we come back.'

'I like a woman that a breath of wind won't blow down,' said Tinker Taylor after the three had left for the church. 'Mrs Fawley, I suppose?' he said when they returned.

'Certainly,' said Arabella smoothly, pulling off her glove and holding out her left hand.

'She *said* I ought to marry you again,' said Jude thickly. 'True religion! Ha–ha–ha! Give me some more to drink!'

Chapter 29   To See Sue Again

After their remarriage, Jude and his wife moved to new lodgings nearer the centre of the city. At first, Jude was able to work, but by the autumn he was a sick man again.

'Why can't you stay healthy?' complained Arabella, as he coughed and coughed. 'Soon I'll have to sell sausages out on the street to support you!'

Jude laughed bitterly. 'I've been thinking of that pig you and I once had. I tried to finish it off as quickly as possible. If only someone would now do the same for me!'

He did not get any better, and one day he begged Arabella to write and tell Sue. 'You know I love her, and I'd like to see her once more. I've one foot in the grave, so what can it matter?'

'I won't have that loose woman in my house!'

Jude leapt up from his chair, forcing Arabella back onto a sofa. 'Say anything like that again and I'll kill you!'

'Kill me?' she laughed. 'You couldn't even kill that pig properly!'

Jude began to cough and had to let her go. But one morning soon afterwards, in heavy wind and rain, he left the house when she was out and went to the station.

Wrapped in a long coat and blanket, pale as a ghost, he travelled by train to Alfredston and from there he walked the five miles to Marygreen. At half-past three, he stood by the familiar well. He crossed the green, asked a boy to fetch Mrs Phillotson from the schoolhouse, and entered the church.

There was a light footstep. 'Oh, Jude, I didn't know it was you!' Sue tried to go back, but he begged her not to. 'Why did you come?' she asked, tears running down her face. 'I know – it was in the Alfredston newspaper – that you've done the right thing and married Arabella again.'

'God above, "the right thing"? It's the worst thing of my life, this contract with Arabella! *You're* my wife. How could you go back to Phillotson?'

'He's a kind husband to me. And I've struggled and prayed and I've nearly made myself accept him. You mustn't wake —'

'Oh, you darling little fool! Where has all that intelligence gone, that fighting spirit?'

'You insult me, Jude. Go away!' She turned.

'I will. Sue, you're not worth a man's love.'

She turned back. 'Don't! Kiss me, oh, kiss me, and say I'm not a coward!' She rushed to him. 'I must tell you, my darling love! My remarriage has been a marriage in name only. Richard himself suggested it.'

'Sue!' Pressing her to him, Jude hurt her mouth with kisses. 'I have a moment's happiness now. You do love me still?'

'You know it! But I *mustn't* kiss you back . . . And you look so ill —'

'So do you! There's one more kiss, in memory of our dead children, yours and mine.'

The words struck Sue like a blow. 'I *can't* go on with this . . . But there, darling, I give you back your kisses. I do, I do!'

'I ask you one last time. We were both out of our senses when we remarried. Let's run away together!'

'No; again, no! Why do you tempt me, Jude? Don't follow me, don't look at me. Leave me, for pity's sake!'

Sue ran to the east end of the church and knelt there. Jude picked up his blanket and went straight out, coughing. Sue hesitated, then put her hands over her ears. At the corner of the green, by the path to Farmer Troutham's old field, Jude looked back at Marygreen for the last time. Then he walked on.

When a cold wind is blowing, the coldest place in all Wessex is

Jude picked up his blanket and went straight out, coughing. Sue hesitated, then put her hands over her ears.

the top of the hill by the Brown House. Here Jude now walked, wet through, against a bitter, north-east wind. It was ten o'clock when he finally reached Christminster.

Arabella was waiting on the platform. 'You've been to see her?'

'I have. I've got my only two remaining wishes in the world: I've seen her and I've finished myself'.

All the way back to their lodgings, Jude saw the same ghosts of great men that he had seen on his first arrival at Christminster. 'They seem to be laughing at me now. But, Arabella, when I'm dead, you'll see my ghost among these!'

'Pooh! Come along and I'll buy you something warm to drink.'

◆

While Jude and Arabella were walking home, Sue was talking to Mrs Edlin in the schoolhouse. 'I've done wrong today, Mrs Edlin. Jude has been here and I find that I still love him . . . I'll never see him again, but I must now make things right with my husband. I shall go to his room tonight.'

'I wouldn't, my dear. He agrees to separate rooms, and it's gone on very well for three months as it is.'

'Yes, but I was wrong to accept the arrangement . . . Don't go, Mrs Edlin!' Sue begged nervously. 'Please stay in my room tonight.'

They went up the stairs together. Sue undressed in her own room. Then, with a frightened look at the widow, she crossed to her husband's room and half-opened the door.

'Is that you, Susanna?'

'Yes, Richard.' She almost sank to the floor. 'I've come to beg your pardon and ask you to let me in.'

'You know what it means?' Phillotson said firmly.

'Yes. I belong to you. Please let me in.'

Mrs Edlin closed the door of Sue's old room and got into bed. 'Poor little thing!' she said. 'How it blows and rains!'

◆

453

After Christmas, Jude again lay ill at home.

'You were clever,' said Arabella, 'to get yourself a nurse by marrying me! I suppose you want to see your Sue?'

'No. Don't tell her that I'm ill. Let her go!'

One day, however, Mrs Edlin came to see him. Arabella left the old woman alone with Jude, and he immediately asked about Sue. 'I suppose,' he said bluntly, 'they are still husband and wife in name only?'

Mrs Edlin hesitated. 'Well, no. It's been different since the day you came. She insisted. To punish herself.'

'Oh no, my Sue! . . . Mrs Edlin, she was once a woman who shone like a star. Then tragedy hit us, and she broke. Our ideas were fifty years too soon, and they brought disaster on us both!' Jude cursed the world angrily, and then began to cough.

Chapter 30   Remembrance Day

Summer came round again and, with it, the Remembrance celebrations. Jude lay on his bed, very sick.

One afternoon, while the bells rang out, Arabella sat waiting for her father to take her place as nurse. He did not come. She looked impatiently at Jude. He was asleep. So she went out anyway, to join the crowds.

It was a warm, cloudless day. The sound of concert music reached Jude's room as his cough started and woke him. 'A little water, please,' he said, his eyes still closed. 'Some water – Arabella – Sue – darling! Please!' No water came. 'Oh, God,' Jude whispered, 'why was I ever born?'

When Arabella returned, she was met outside by two or three of the stone-masons. 'We're going down to the river for the Remembrance games,' said Uncle Joe. 'But we've called on our way to ask how your husband is.'

'He's sleeping nicely, thank you,' said Arabella.

'Then why not come along with us for half an hour, Mrs Fawley? It would do you good.'

'I *wish* I could. Well, wait a minute. Father is with him, I believe, so I can probably come.'

She ran upstairs. Her father had not arrived, but Jude seemed to be sleeping, although he lay strangely still. Arabella went close to the bed. His face was quite white. His fingers were cold. She listened at his chest. His heart, after nearly thirty years, had stopped.

The happy rum-tum-tum of a band reached her ears from the river. 'Why did he die just now!' said Arabella, annoyed.

She thought for a moment. Then she softly closed the bedroom door again and went off with the men to the river.

'Oh, I'm glad I came!' she said, looking at all the boats and flags and people. 'And my absence can't hurt my husband.' A man she knew put his arm around her waist, and she pretended not to notice. 'Well, it's been good,' she cried later, when all the excitement was over. 'Now I must get back to my poor husband.'

By ten o'clock that night, Jude's body was laid out on the bed. Through the half-open window, the sound of dance music entered from one of the colleges.

♦

Two days later, two women stood looking down at Jude's face as the sounds of Remembrance Day itself came into the room from the round theatre.

'How beautiful he is!' said Mrs Edlin, red-eyed.

'Yes; handsome,' agreed Arabella. 'Do you think *she*'ll come?'

'I don't know. She swore not to see him again! Poor heart! She looks years and years older.'

'If Jude had seen her again, perhaps he wouldn't have cared for her any more . . . But he told me not to send for her.'

'Well, the poor little thing *says* she's found peace.'

'She may swear that on her knees,' said Arabella, 'but it's not true. She'll never find peace again until she's where he is now!'

ACTIVITIES

Chapters 1–8

Before you read

1　Look at the picture on the cover of this book. What does it suggest to you? What is the young man thinking about?

2　The words below all come from this part of the story. Use your dictionary to check their meaning.

　　apprentice　cottage　dismissal　lodgings
　　obscure　spire　stone-mason　trade

　　Now match each word with its meaning in the list below:

　　a　a small house in the country
　　b　dark, not well-known
　　c　a cutter of stone
　　d　a line of work, e.g. building
　　e　a pointed tower
　　f　being told to leave one's job
　　g　a room rented to live in
　　h　a young person in training for skilled work

3　Answer these questions:

　　a　What would a *barmaid* sell you?
　　b　What could you do at an *inn*?
　　c　What do you get from a *well*?
　　d　Where do people do *ecclesiastical* work?
　　e　Where do *hedges* grow?
　　f　What farm animal is used to pull a *cart*?

After you read

4　Answer these questions:

　　a　Why does Jude decide to marry Arabella?
　　b　Why does she leave him?
　　c　Where does she go?
　　d　Who is 'light and slight, lovely, nervous, tender'?
　　e　Who do Jude and his cousin visit at Lumsdon?
　　f　How does this person help the cousin to get a job?

456

g What does Jude see in Lumsdon one evening that fills him with horror?

Chapters 9–18

Before you read

5 At the end of Chapter 8, Jude suffers 'the hell of failure', both in ambition and love. What does this mean? What would you advise him to do to improve his life? Discuss your ideas with other students.

6 These words come in this part of the story. Use a dictionary to check their meaning.

divorce   headstone   theological

Now match each word to one of the meanings below:

a to do with religion

b the legal ending of a marriage between two people

c a piece of stone marking a grave

After you read

7 Answer these questions:

a Why is Sue told to leave the college at Melchester?

b Who does Jude spend the night with at an inn in Aldbrickham?

c 'The kiss was a turning point for Jude.' What does it cause him to do?

8 Who says these words? Who to?

a 'Something frightened me – a terrible dream.'

b 'I sometimes think you are incapable of real love.'

c 'Your relation came here once before . . . with his wife.'

Chapters 19–30

Before you read

9 Phillotson has decided to divorce Sue. Do you think that she will finally marry Jude? What other problems could possibly happen now?

After you read

10 Answer these questions:
  a Who are the parents of 'Little Father Time'?
  b What shocking thing does he do in the lodgings in Christminster?
  c When Arabella says, 'I've got a prize upstairs!', what does she mean?

11 Complete these sentences:
  a Although he is very ill, Jude returns to Marygreen because . . .
  b Sue decides to return to sharing her husband's room because . . .
  c Arabella says, 'My absence can't hurt my husband' because . . .

12 Just before he dies, Jude says: 'Our ideas were fifty years too soon and they brought disaster on us both.' What does he mean? Do you agree with him? Discuss these questions.

Writing

13 Read Chapter 6 again. Imagine you are Jude's Aunt Drusilla. Write the letter you send him with Sue's photo.

14 You are Jude. Look again at page 403. Write one of the letters to the master of a college, asking for information and advice about university studies.

15 Imagine that Jude is a young man born in the 1960s. How do you think his life story might be different? Tell the story in a few words.

16 Write a note to a friend about this book. Say what it is about, whether you liked it and whether or not your friend will like it. Give your reasons.

Sons and Lovers

D. H. LAWRENCE

Level 5

Retold by J. Y. K. Kerr
Series Editors: Andy Hopkins and Jocelyn Potter

Contents

Introduction

Gertrude Morel no longer loved her husband. She had not wanted this child and there it lay in her arms and pulled at her heart . . . It had come into the world unloved. She would love it all the more, now that it was here.

Gertrude Morel is poor and unhappily married. Her husband Walter is rough and insensitive, spending much of his free time in the pub. Mrs Morel turns instead to her children, especially her three sons. At first William, the eldest, is her favourite. But things happen, and Mrs Morel turns all her love and attention to Paul, the second son.

This moving story describes family life in a coalminer's family in the early twentieth century. It also describes the emotional development of Paul, torn between his passionate love for his mother and his romantic friendships with two young women, Miriam and Clara.

David Herbert Lawrence was born near Nottingham in 1885, the fourth of five children. He trained as a school teacher and taught at a school in the south of England for three years.

In 1911, his first novel, *The White Peacock*, came out. In the same year his mother died and he gave up teaching because of ill health. He went to Germany and Italy with Frieda Weekley, a married woman whom he married on his return to England in 1914.

Lawrence was now a full-time professional writer. Unhappy in England, where he was criticised for opposing the First World War and for the sexual openness of his books, Lawrence spent most of his time abroad with Frieda. He died in the south of France in 1930, aged forty-four.

Sons and Lovers (1913), one of Lawrence's most famous novels, is based on his own family life. Other important books include *The Rainbow* (1915), *Women in Love* (1920) and *Lady Chatterley's Lover* (1928).

Chapter 1   The Early Years

The Morel family lived in the village of Bestwood in a house built by the mining company for its employees. Gertrude Morel was thirty-one years old and had been married for eight years. Her husband, Walter, was a coalminer. There were two children: William, a boy of seven, and Annie, who was only five. Mrs Morel was expecting her third baby in two months' time. They could not afford to have this third: she did not want it. Its father spent most of his free time drinking in the pub. She had no respect for him but she was tied to him. She was sick of it, this struggle with poverty and ugliness and dirt.

Gertrude Morel was from a Nottingham family: educated, church-going people. Her father was an unsuccessful engineer. She had her mother's small, well-made figure and her father's clear blue eyes. When she was twenty-three years old, she met, at a Christmas party, a young man of twenty-seven. Walter had shining, black, wavy hair and a black beard. He laughed often and heartily, with a rich, ringing laugh. He was quick in his movements, an excellent dancer. He was so open and pleasant with everybody. Gertrude, who was not pleasure-loving like Walter, had never met anyone like him. His body burned with a soft golden flame, the flame of life, and seemed to her something wonderful.

Walter Morel was equally impressed by Gertrude: her blue eyes, her soft brown curls, her beautiful smile. She spoke in an educated way, she had the manners of a lady. The next Christmas they were married and for three months she was perfectly happy. She admired him for being a miner, risking his life daily. Sometimes when she herself was tired of lovetalk, she tried to open her heart seriously to him. He listened to her respectfully but without understanding. She realised that she could not share her deeper thoughts and ideas with him. Instead, he took pleasure in making and mending, doing little jobs around the house.

Her first big shock was when she found that the bills for their new furniture were not yet paid; and that he did not own their house, as he had told her, but was paying rent – and too high a rent – for it. Then he began to be rather late coming home.

'They're working very late these days, aren't they?' she said to a neighbour.

'No later than they always do,' she answered. 'But they stop to have a drink at the pub and then they get talking. Dinner stone cold and it's just what they deserve!'

'But Mr Morel doesn't drink.'

The woman looked hard at Mrs Morel, then went on with her work, saying nothing.

Mrs Morel was very ill when the first boy was born. Morel was good to her but she felt very lonely, miles away from her own people. When her husband was with her, it made the loneliness worse. The child was small and weak at first but he quickly grew strong. He was a beautiful baby, with dark golden curls and dark blue eyes, which gradually changed to a clear grey. He came just when her disappointment was at its greatest and her life seemed most empty. She gave all her attention to her child and the father was jealous. While the baby was still small, it often annoyed Morel, and sometimes he hit it. Then Mrs Morel hated her husband for days. Feeling unloved, Morel went out and drank. On his return she greeted him with fierce, stinging remarks about his drinking.

Morel always rose early, about five or six, even on a holiday. On Sunday morning he usually got up and prepared breakfast. The child rose with his father, while the mother lay resting for another hour or so. William was now one year old and his mother was proud of him, he was so pretty. One Sunday morning Mrs Morel lay listening to the two of them talking below. Then she fell asleep. When she came downstairs, there was a big fire burning and breakfast was laid. Morel sat in his armchair, looking rather shamefaced. The child stood between his legs, his head of hair cut short like a sheep; and on a newspaper spread out in front of the fire lay William's golden curls, shining in the firelight. Mrs Morel stood quite still and went very white.

'So what do you think of him?' laughed Morel, a little guiltily.

She came forward, ready to hit him. 'I could kill you, I could!' she said, so angry she could hardly speak. She picked up the child, buried her face in his shoulder and cried painfully. Morel sat looking at the fire in shock. Later she said she had been silly, the boy's hair had to be cut sooner or later. But she remembered this event for the rest of her life. Before, she had wanted to bring her husband closer to her. From now on he was an outsider. This made her life easier to accept. The pity was, she was too much his opposite. In trying to make him better than he was, she destroyed him.

◆

The Morels were poor. Morel was expected to give his wife thirty shillings★ a week to pay for everything: rent, food, clothes, insurance, doctors. Sometimes it was a little more, more often less. On Friday night, and Saturday and Sunday, Morel spent freely, mostly on beer. He rarely gave William an extra penny or a pound of apples.

One public holiday he decided to walk to Nottingham with Jerry Purdy, one of his drinking companions. They spent most of the day visiting pubs. Mrs Morel had stayed at home all day,

★ There were twenty shillings in a pound and twelve pence in a shilling.

'I could kill you, I could!' Mrs Morel said, so angry she could
hardly speak.

working in the house. In the evening Morel returned, kicking open the garden gate and breaking the lock. He entered the kitchen unsteadily and nearly upset a bowl of boiling liquid which was cooling on the table.

'God help us, coming home in his drunkenness!' cried Mrs Morel.

'Coming home in his what?' shouted her husband, his hat over one eye.

'Say you're *not* drunk!' she insisted.

'Only a nasty old cat like you could have such a thought,' answered Morel.

'You've been drinking all day, so if you're not drunk by eleven o'clock at night–' she replied. 'We know well enough what you do when you go out with your beautiful Jerry. There's money to drink with, if there's money for nothing else.'

'I've not spent two shillings all day,' he said.

'Well, if Jerry's been buying your drinks, tell him to spend his money on his children – they need it! And what about your own children? You can't afford to keep them, can you?'

'What's it got to do with you?' he shouted.

'Got to do with me? Why, a lot! You give me just twenty-five shillings to do everything with, you go off drinking all day, come rolling home at midnight–'

'It's a lie, it's a lie – shut your face, woman!'

The quarrel got fiercer and fiercer. Each forgot everything except their hatred of the other. She was just as angry as he.

'You're a liar!' he shouted, banging on the table with his hand. 'You're a liar! You're a liar!'

All the dislike she felt for him now came pouring out.

'You're nothing but dirt in this house!' she cried.

'Then get out of it – it's mine! It's me who brings the money home, not you. So get out! Get out!'

'And I would,' she cried in tears at her own powerlessness. 'I would have gone long ago, but for those children. Do you think I stay for *you*?'

He came up to her and held her arms tightly. She cried out, struggling to be free. He took her roughly to the outside door and pushed her out of the house, banging the door shut and locking it behind her. Then he sank exhausted into a chair and soon lost consciousness. She stood for a few moments staring helplessly in the August night, her body shaking, remembering the unborn child inside her. The darkness was full of the sweet smell of flowers. There was no noise anywhere. Then a train rushed across the valley miles away. She went to the back door and tried the handle. It was still locked. Through the window she could just see her husband's head on the table and his arms spread out. She knocked on the window more and more loudly but still he did not wake. Fearful for the unborn child, she walked up and down the garden path to keep warm, knocking every now and then on the window, telling herself that in the end he must wake. At last he heard the knocking and woke up.

'Open the door, Walter,' she said coldly.

Realising what he had done, he hurried to unlock the door. As Mrs Morel entered, she saw him disappearing shamefacedly up the stairs. When at last she herself went to bed, Morel was already asleep.

Chapter 2   The Birth of Paul

Before the baby was born, Mrs Morel cleaned the house from top to bottom. When Morel got home one evening, the child had already arrived. The delivery nurse met him in the kitchen.

'Your wife is in a bad way. It's a boy child.'

He hung up his coat and then dropped into his chair.

'Have you got a drink?' he asked. The nurse brought him one, then without a word served him his dinner and went back upstairs. He ate his meal, sat for twenty minutes, made up the fire and then unwillingly went up to the bedroom. His face was still black and sweaty as he stood at the end of the bed.

'Well, how are you then?' he asked.

'I shall be all right,' she answered.

'Hm. It's a boy.'

She turned down the blanket and showed him the baby. He pretended to be pleased but she knew he was not much interested. He wanted to kiss her but he did not dare, so he left the room.

Mrs Morel sat looking at her baby and the baby looked up at her. It had blue eyes like her own, which seemed to bring out her most secret thoughts. She no longer loved her husband. She had not wanted this child and there it lay in her arms and pulled at her heart. A wave of hot love went out of her towards the child. She held it close to her face and breast. It had come into the world unloved. She would love it all the more, now it was here.

◆

During these months Morel got angry at the slightest thing. He seemed exhausted by his work. He complained if the fire was low or his dinner was not to his liking. If the children made a noise, he shouted at them in a way that made their mother's blood boil. They hated him and his bad temper.

'Goodness me, man, there isn't a bit of peace while you're in the house,' said Mrs Morel at last.

'I know that. You're never happy till I'm out of your sight,' he answered, and hurried to escape. He was still not home by eleven o'clock. Finally she heard him coming. He had taken his revenge: he was drunk.

'Is there nothing to eat in the house?' he asked roughly.

'You know what there is,' she said coldly.

471

He leaned unsteadily on the table and pulled at the table drawer to get a knife to cut bread. The drawer stuck, so he pulled harder. It flew right out and spoons, forks, knives fell all over the floor. The baby woke at the noise.

'What are you doing, you drunken fool?' the mother cried.

In trying to fit the drawer back in, it fell, hurting his leg. In his anger he picked it up and threw it at his wife. One of the corners hit her above the eye. Blood ran into her eye and red drops fell on the baby's blanket.

'Did it hit you?' asked Morel, bending over her unsteadily.

'Go away!'

'Let me look at it, woman.'

She smelled the drink on his breath and weakly pushed him away.

He stood staring at her.

'What has it done to you, dear?' he asked.

'You can see what it's done,' she answered.

Mrs Morel would not let him touch her. She cleaned the wound herself and went upstairs, telling him to mend the fire and lock the door.

'It was her own fault,' he told himself afterwards. Having hurt her, he hated her.

By the following Wednesday he had no money left. He looked inside his wife's purse when she was in the garden with the baby, and took a sixpence. The next day Mrs Morel found the money missing and was sure he had taken it. When he had had his dinner, she said to him coldly: 'Did you take sixpence from my purse last night?'

Although he denied it, she knew he was lying.

'So you steal sixpence from my purse while I'm bringing the washing in,' she said accusingly.

'I'll make you pay for this,' answered Morel. He got washed and went upstairs with a determined expression on his face.

Soon afterwards he came down dressed, with his things tied up in an enormous blue handkerchief.

'You'll see me again when you do,' he said.

'It'll be before I want to,' his wife replied.

At that, he marched out of the house with his parcel.

William and Annie were surprised to find their father gone.

'Where's he going to?' asked William.

'I don't know,' said his mother. 'He's taken his things wrapped up in a handkerchief and he says he's not coming back.'

'What shall we do?' cried the boy in alarm.

'Don't worry, he won't go far.'

'But if he doesn't come back?' said Annie fearfully. She and William sat on the sofa and burst into tears. When Mrs Morel went to fetch coal from the coalhouse at the end of the garden, she felt something hidden behind the door. There in the dark was the big blue parcel. She laughed and went back to the house. William and Annie were crying again because she had left them.

'Silly babies,' she said. 'Go down to the coalhouse and look behind the door and *then* you'll see how far he's gone.'

Off they went to look. No longer worried, they went contentedly to bed.

Mrs Morel sat waiting. She was tired of him, tired to death. He had not even had the courage to take his things further than the bottom of the garden. At about nine o'clock he came in, looking guilty. She said nothing. He took off his coat and sat down to take off his boots.

'You'd better fetch your things from the coalhouse before you take your boots off,' she said quietly.

'You can thank your stars I've come back tonight,' he said trying to impress her. He looked such a fool she was not even angry with him; but her heart was bitter because he had once been the man she loved.

Chapter 3   William Takes the Lead

Some time later Morel became seriously ill. His wife nursed him and, being strong, he soon recovered. He depended on her almost like a child and she was more tolerant of him now because she loved him less. Instead, she turned for love and life to the children and he half accepted this, letting them take his place in her heart. When they sat together at night he was restless, feeling a sort of emptiness. Then he went off to bed and she settled down to enjoy herself alone, working, thinking, living.

The baby Paul hated to be touched by him. Usually a quiet baby, he went stiff in his father's arms and immediately started to scream. He was a pale, rather silent child, and his face often wore a worried or puzzled expression.

Now another baby was coming, the fruit of this time of peace between the parents. This new baby was again a boy, and they called him Arthur. He was very pretty, with a head of golden curls, and he loved his father from the first. Hearing his father's footsteps, he used to wave his arms and laugh.

At the same time William grew bigger and stronger and more active, while Paul, always rather slight, got thinner and followed his mother around like a shadow.

♦

When William was thirteen, his mother got him a job in the Cooperative Society office. His father wanted him to become a miner like himself.

'He's not going down the mine,' said Mrs Morel, 'and there's an end of it. If your mother put you in the mine at twelve, it's no reason why I should do the same with my boy.'

She was very proud of her son. He was a clever boy with an open nature and eyes of the brightest blue. He went to night-school and trained as a clerk. Then he became a teacher at the night-school. He could run like the wind: when he was twelve, he won first prize in a race. He could jump higher and throw farther than any boy in Bestwood.

William began to get ambitious. He gave all his money to his mother. He went about with the sons of shopkeepers and the schoolteacher. He enjoyed all the social and sporting life that Bestwood offered. He also liked dancing, in spite of his mother. He was a great favourite with the ladies and enjoyed telling Paul about his successes. About this time he began to study. With a friend of his he started to learn French and Latin and other things. He and Fred Simpson studied together till midnight, sometimes till one o'clock. Soon he grew pale and Mrs Morel, alarmed, begged him to take better care of his health.

When William was nineteen, he suddenly left the Co-operative office and got a job in Nottingham. Now he had thirty shillings a week instead of eighteen. His mother and father were proud of him. It seemed that he was going to succeed in life. William stayed at his job in Nottingham for a year. He was studying hard but he still went to all the dances and parties. Then he was offered a position in London at a hundred and twenty pounds a year.

'They want me in Lime Street on Monday week, mother,' he cried, his eyes shining as he read the letter. Mrs Morel felt everything go silent inside her.

'Didn't I tell you I could do it? Think of me in London! And I can give you twenty pounds a year, Mother. We shall all be rolling in money.'

'We shall, my son,' she answered sadly.

As the day of his departure came closer, she felt increasingly desperate. She loved him so much and now he was going away. She felt that he was going out of her heart, leaving her only pain and sadness.

Before he left – he was just twenty – William burned his file of love-letters from his lady-friends. Then he went off to London to start a new file.

Chapter 4 Paul's Childhood

Paul's figure was rather small and slight, like his mother's. His fair hair gradually became dark brown. His eyes were grey. He was a pale, quiet child, who seemed old for his years. He was sensitive to what other people felt, especially his mother. When she was upset, he understood and could have no peace.

About this time the family moved to another house near the top of a hill, commanding a fine view of the valley below. After dark Paul used to go out to play under the street lamp with the other children of their street. Then when the miners stopped coming home from the mine, he ran fearfully back to the kitchen. The lamp still burned, the fire shone red, Mrs Morel sat alone. Steam rose from the cooking pot, the dinner plate lay waiting on the table. The whole room seemed to be waiting, waiting for the man who was sitting in his coal dirt, dinnerless, a mile away from home across the darkness, drinking himself drunk.

When Morel did come home, everyone in the house kept quiet because he was dangerous. He ate his food roughly and, when he had finished, pushed all the pots away to lay his head and arms on the table. Then he went to sleep, heavy with beer and tiredness and bad temper.

Morel was shut out from family events. No one told him anything. He was an outsider. The only times he entered family life was when he found jobs to do around the house. Sometimes in the evening he mended boots, or the kettle or the metal bottle for cold tea which he took every day to the mine. Then he always wanted helpers and the children enjoyed helping him. He loved telling young Arthur stories about the little horses that the miners used down in the mine. But these happy evenings only took place if Morel had some job to do. Then he always went to bed early. The children felt safe when their father was in bed.

Mrs Morel had given most of her attention to William but when he went to work in Nottingham and was not so much at home, she made a companion of Paul. The two brothers were a little jealous of each other but at the same time they were good friends.

Friday night was baking night and market night, because the wages were paid on Fridays. It was the rule that Paul should stay at home and watch the bread in the oven. He loved to be by himself and draw or read. He was very fond of drawing. Mrs Morel enjoyed her marketing. The market place was always full of women shoppers. She usually quarrelled with the cloth-seller, chatted with the fruit man, laughed with the fish man, was coldly polite to the man selling pots. But this time a little dish decorated with blue flowers caught her eye. He told her it cost sevenpence. She put the dish down and walked away. Suddenly the pot man shouted: 'Do you want it for fivepence?'

She was surprised. She bent down and picked up the dish.

'I'll have it,' she said.

Paul was waiting for her. He loved her homecoming. She was always at her best, tired, happy, weighed down with parcels. She dropped her parcels and her string bag on the table.

'Is the bread done?' she asked, going to the oven.

'The last one is baking,' he replied. 'You needn't look. I haven't forgotten it.'

'How much do you think I bought this for?' she said, taking the dish out of its newspaper wrapping.

'One shilling and threepence,' said Paul.

'Five pence!'

The two stood together admiring the dish. She unfolded

another piece of newspaper and showed him some little flowering plants.

'Fourpence for these.'

'How cheap!' he cried.

'Yes, but I couldn't afford it this week of all weeks.' Yet she was full of satisfaction.

They were very poor that autumn. William had just gone to London and his mother missed his money. He sent ten shillings once or twice but he had many expenses. He wrote to his mother regularly once a week. He told her all his doings, how he made friends, how he was enjoying London. All day long as she cleaned the house, she thought of him. He was in London: he would do well.

William was coming home at Christmas for five days. There had never been such preparations. Paul and Arthur decorated the kitchen with green leaves. Annie made pretty strings of coloured paper. Mrs Morel baked a special fruit cake, a big rice cake, little cheese cakes. Everything was decorated. A great fire burned. The smell of fresh baking filled the kitchen. William was due at seven o'clock but he was late. The children had gone to the station to meet him. Morel sat in his armchair full of nervous excitement and Mrs Morel quietly went on with her baking. Neither one spoke. They waited and waited.

At last there was the sound of voices and footsteps.

'He's here!' cried Morel, jumping up.

The door burst open and William came in. He dropped his bag and took his mother in his arms. For two seconds, no longer, she held him and kissed him. Then she stood back and, trying to be normal, said: 'But how late you are!'

'Aren't I?' he cried, turning to his father. 'Well, Dad!'

'Well, my boy!' Morel's eyes were wet. 'We thought you were never coming.'

The two men shook hands.

'Everything's just as it was,' said William, looking round.

'Everything's just as it was,' said William, looking round.

Everybody was still for a second. Then he leaned forward, picked up a newly baked biscuit and put it whole into his mouth.

He had brought them endless presents. Every penny he had, he had spent on them. For his mother there was an umbrella with gold on the handle, which she kept till her dying day. There were pounds of wonderful sweets, quite unknown in Bestwood. Everybody in the family was mad with happiness.

People came in to see William, to see what a difference London had made to him. They all found him 'such a gentleman, such a fine young man, my word!'

When he went away again, the children were in tears, Morel took himself off to bed and Mrs Morel did all her housework mechanically, robbed of all feeling for days.

Chapter 5 Paul Faces Life

Morel was careless of danger. About a year after William went to London, and just after Paul had left school, before he got work, a great piece of rock fell on Morel's leg when he was working in the mine, and broke it in several places. He had a very bad time in hospital. For a week he was in a serious condition, then he began to mend. Knowing that he was going to recover, the family began to worry less and to be happy again. Mrs Morel talked to Paul almost as if she was thinking aloud, and he listened as best he could. In the end she shared almost everything with him. Together, they learned how perfectly peaceful the home could be.

Paul was now fourteen years old and looking for work. His face had lost its boyish roundness and was rather rough-looking but very expressive. He was quite a clever painter for a boy of his age and he knew some French, German and mathematics. He was not strong enough for hard physical work, his mother said.

He did not care for making things with his hands but preferred going for country walks, or reading, or painting.

'What do you want to be?' his mother asked. He had no idea. 'Anything.'

'That's no answer,' said Mrs Morel. But it was the only answer he could give.

'Then you must look in the paper for advertisements,' said his mother. He copied out some advertisements and took them to her.

'Yes,' she said, 'you may try.'

He used a letter which William had prepared for him to write to the different companies offering jobs. His handwriting was terrible.

♦

William wrote from London in a kind of fever. He seemed unsettled by the speed of his new life. His mother could feel him losing himself. He wrote of dances and going to the theatre, of boats on the river, of going out with friends. But she knew he sat up afterwards in his cold bedroom, studying Latin and learning all he could about the law, because he wanted to improve himself. He never sent his mother any money now. It was all taken, the little he had, for his own life. Mrs Morel still dreamed of William and what he could do; but in her heart she was worried.

He also wrote a lot now about a girl he had met at a dance, Lily Western. His pet name for her was 'Gypsy'. She was young, beautiful, very well-dressed and much admired by men. His mother congratulated him in her doubtful fashion. She imagined him tied to an expensive wife. 'I'm very likely an old silly,' she told herself, 'expecting the worst.' But the worry remained that William would do the wrong thing.

Soon Paul was asked to go for an interview at Thomas Jordan,

Maker of Medical Appliances, at 21, Spaniel Row, Nottingham. Mrs Morel was delighted.

'You see,' she cried, her eyes shining, 'You've only written four letters and the third is answered. I always said you were lucky.'

Paul looked at the picture of the wooden leg wearing an elastic stocking that appeared on Mr Jordan's notepaper. He had not known that elastic stockings existed.

Mother and son set off one very hot morning in August. Paul felt extremely nervous but he refused to tell his mother and she only partly guessed. They travelled the sixteen miles to Nottingham by train. Mother and son walked down Station Street, feeling the excitement of lovers sharing an adventure. They turned up a narrow street that led to the Castle and found the Thomas Jordan sign. They went through a big doorway into an open space full of boxes and packing stuff, and up two lots of stairs. In front of them was a dirty glass door with the company name on it. Mrs Morel pushed open the door and stood in pleased surprise. They were in a large work-shop with thick paper parcels piled everywhere, and clerks with their sleeves rolled up, calmly going about their business.

'Can I see Mr Jordan?' she asked one of the clerks.

'I'll fetch him,' answered the young man and went to a glass office at the far end of the room. A red-faced old man with white hair came towards them. He had short legs and was rather fat. They followed him to his office and were told to sit down.

'Did you write this letter?' he asked Paul, holding it up.

'Yes,' he answered.

'Where did you learn to write?'

Paul simply looked at him, too ashamed and nervous to speak.

'And you say you know French?' asked the little man sharply.

'A friend gave him lessons,' said Mrs Morel quickly.

Mr Jordan hesitated, then pulled a sheet of paper from his pocket and passed it to Paul.

'Read that,' he said.

It was a letter in French in strange, spidery, foreign hand-writing which was very difficult to read. Paul struggled with the words: 'Please send me . . . two pairs . . . of grey cotton stockings . . . without fingers . . .'

'Without toes!' the factory owner corrected him. 'Stockings don't have fingers.'

Paul hated the little man for making him look stupid.

'When can he start?' Mr Jordan asked his mother.

It was agreed that Paul would be employed as a junior clerk at eight shillings a week. As he followed his mother down the stairs on their way out, she looked at him with her blue eyes full of delighted love.

On the Monday morning Paul got up at six, to be ready for work. He had bought his season ticket for the train at a cost of one pound eleven shillings, and his mother had packed his dinner in a small basket. She stood in the road, watching him as he crossed the fields to the station. Now she had two sons in the world: a man in London and one in Nottingham. They came from her and their work would also be hers. All morning she thought of Paul.

At the factory Paul was told to work with Mr Pappleworth, an amusing man about thirty-six years old. Pappleworth showed him what to do. They had to read the letters ordering different appliances, note down each order in a big book, write out the exact details on a yellow order paper and take the order to one of the departments to be made. Most of the orders were for elastic stockings or bandages. Later, he was introduced to Polly and the girls downstairs, and then Fanny and the girls upstairs. At one o'clock Paul ate his dinner and then he went out into the brightness and freedom of the streets until two. In the afternoon there was not very much to do. At five o'clock all the men went downstairs and had tea. After tea the gas lights were lit. Paul had done his paperwork and now he had to pack up the finished goods in parcels, writing the address and putting the right stamps on each one. At last he was free to grab his dinner basket and run to the station in time for the 8.20 train. His day in the factory was exactly twelve hours long.

He did not get home that evening till twenty past nine. He was pale and tired but his mother saw that he was rather pleased. He told her everything, all he had seen, all he thought, every detail of the experience.

So the time passed happily enough. The factory was a friendly place. Nobody was rushed or driven too hard and every Friday night he put his eight shillings proudly on the kitchen table. Then he told his mother the happenings of the day. It was almost as if it was her own life.

Chapter 6   Death in the Family

Arthur Morel was growing up. He was quick and careless, rather like his father. He hated study and hard work. He was the flower of the family, a well-made boy with fair hair, fresh colouring and wonderful dark blue eyes. He had a quick temper and thought only of himself. He loved his mother but she got tired of him sometimes. He had loved his father, and Morel still thought the world of him but now Arthur had come to hate him. His father's manners in the home got worse and worse. When they got too much for him, Arthur used to jump up and leave the house. He got so bad-tempered that, when he won a place at the Grammar School in Nottingham, his mother sent him to live with one of her sisters, and so he only came home at weekends.

Annie was a junior teacher at Bestwood School, earning about four shillings a week. But soon she would get fifteen shillings, because she had passed her examination. That would make the financial situation in the home a bit easier.

William was now engaged to his girl and had bought her an engagement ring. He wanted to bring her home at Christmas. This time William arrived with the lady but with no presents. Mrs Morel had prepared supper. He kissed his mother hurriedly and then stood back to introduce a tall, handsome, young woman, very fashionably dressed.

'Here's Gyp!'

Miss Western held out her hand and showed her teeth in a small smile.

'Oh, how do you do, Mrs Morel,' she said.

'I'm afraid you will be hungry, said Mrs Morel.

'Oh no, we had dinner in the train.' She looked round the kitchen. It seemed small and curious to her, with the green leaves decorating the pictures and the rough little table. Annie showed her up to the front bedroom where the parents usually slept, then returned to fetch hot water. After half an hour Miss Western came down wearing another fine dress. Morel pressed her to take his armchair beside the fire. The three children sat round in silent admiration. At ten o'clock she shook hands all round and departed to bed, led by William. In five minutes he was downstairs again but he talked very little until he was alone with his mother. His heart was rather sore, he did not know why.

'Well, mother, do you like her?'

'Yes,' came the cautious reply.

'She's not like you, Mother. She's not serious, and she can't think. Her mother died when she was a child. She's had no love. I know she seems shallow. You have to forgive her a lot of things.'

'You mustn't judge too quickly,' said Mrs Morel.

But William remained uncomfortable within himself.

Lily continued to play the fine lady. She sat and let Annie or

Paul act as her servants. And yet she was not so fine. For a year now, she had been some sort of secretary or clerk in a London office.

At Easter William came home alone; and he discussed Lily endlessly with his mother.

'You know, mother, when I'm away from her, I don't care for her a bit. But then when I'm with her in the evenings, I'm awfully fond of her.'

'It's a strange sort of love to marry on,' said Mrs Morel, 'if she holds you no more than that.'

♦

Paul's wages had been increased at Christmas to ten shillings a week. He was quite happy at Jordan's but his health suffered from the long hours and the bad air. His mother wanted to help. His half-day holiday was on Monday afternoon. At breakfast one Monday in May, Mrs Morel told Paul that her friend Mrs Leivers had invited them to visit her at their new farm. It was agreed that mother and son would go that afternoon: a four mile walk. They set off in style, Mrs Morel with the umbrella William had given her, because of the sun.

After walking for a long time, they finally came to a group of low, red farm buildings. There were apple trees and a pool with ducks. Some cows stood under the trees. As they entered the garden, a girl appeared in the doorway of the house. She was about fourteen, with short, dark curls and dark eyes. She disappeared. In a minute another figure appeared, a small woman, also with great dark brown eyes.

'Oh!' she said smiling. 'You've come then. I *am* glad to see you.' She introduced the girl with the dark curls as her daughter Miriam. The four of them had tea together. Then they went out for a walk in the wood. Both mother and son were thrilled by the beauty of the place. When they got back to the house, they found Mr Leivers and Edgar, the eldest son, in the kitchen. Edgar was about eighteen. Then the two younger boys came in from school. The boys all went outside and played games. Miriam watched but did not join in. She was very shy.

Finally it was time for the Morels to go home. Mr and Mrs Leivers walked over the fields with them for part of the way. Paul was carrying a great bunch of flowers Mrs Leivers had given them. The hills were golden with evening: everywhere was perfectly still. Mrs Morel and Paul went on alone together.

'Wasn't it lovely, Mother?' he said quietly. He felt almost painfully happy.

◆

William came home again with his young lady for a week's holiday. There was a feeling of sadness and tenderness in the house while they were there. But William often got annoyed. For an eight days' stay, Lily had brought five dresses and six blouses.

'Oh, could you please wash these two blouses and these other things?' she said to Annie.

And Annie stayed washing while William and Lily went out. This made Mrs Morel extremely angry. William read a lot and had a quick, active mind; but Lily found reading difficult. She understood nothing but love-making and social chat. She could not give him real companionship.

'She wants to get married,' he told his mother, 'and I think we might get married next year.'

'A fine mess of a marriage it would be,' answered his mother. 'I should consider it again, my boy. Nothing is as bad as a failed marriage. Mine was bad enough, God knows.'

'I couldn't give her up now,' said William.

'Well, remember there are worse wrongs than breaking off an engagement.'

Before he left, William remarked to his mother: 'Gyp's

very fond of me now. But if I die, she'll forget me in three months.'

Mrs Morel was afraid. Her heart beat wildly, hearing the bitterness in her son's words.

He came home again in October, this time also alone. He was thinner than ever. He was doing extra work, trying to make some money to get married with. On the Sunday morning, as he was putting his collar on, he showed his mother an ugly red mark under his chin.

Three days after he left, a telegram came from London, saying that he was ill. Mrs Morel read the telegram, borrowed some money, put on her best clothes and set off. It was six o'clock when she arrived at William's address.

'How is he?' she asked the house-owner.

'No better,' she told her. William lay on the bed, his eyes red, his face discoloured. There was no fire in the room. No one had been with him. He looked at her but did not see her: he was quite unconscious.

'How long has he been like this?' asked Mrs Morel.

'He got home at six o'clock on Monday morning and slept all day. The next morning he asked for you, so I sent you a telegram and fetched the doctor.'

The doctor came again. It was a chest infection, he said, and 'erysipelas', a rare skin disease. He hoped it would not get to the brain.

Mrs Morel settled down to nurse. That night she prayed for William, prayed that at least he would recognise her but his condition got rapidly worse. At two o'clock in the morning he died. Mrs Morel sat perfectly still for an hour in William's bedroom. When day came, she sent a telegram.

'William died last night. Let father come. Bring money.'

Morel had only once before been in London. Nervously he set off to help his wife. They returned to Bestwood on Saturday night, having walked from the station. In the house Mrs Morel was white and silent. All she said was: 'The coffin will be here tonight, Walter. You'd better arrange for some help.' Then, turning to the children: 'We're bringing him home.'

In the front room Morel arranged six chairs opposite each other for the coffin to stand on. At ten o'clock there was the noise of wheels. Arthur held one candle, Annie another. Outside in the darkness Paul could see horses, a lamp and a few pale faces. Six miners in their shirtsleeves came up the narrow garden path, holding the coffin high.

'Steady, steady!' cried Morel, as if in pain. The six men struggled into the room with the great wooden box. Paul saw drops of sweat fall from his father's face onto the wooden top.

At last the family was alone in the room with the great coffin. The mother was stroking the shining wood.

'Oh my son, my son!' she cried softly. 'Oh my son, my son!'

They buried him on the hillside that looks over towards Bestwood. It was sunny. They laid a bunch of white flowers on the warm earth.

William had been right about Lily. She wrote to Mrs Morel at Christmas: 'I was at a party last night. Some charming people were there. I didn't miss a single dance . . .' After that Mrs Morel never heard from her again.

Then, on 23rd December, Paul came home and gave his Christmas money to his mother with shaking hands.

'I feel bad, Mother.'

She undressed him and put him to bed. He had a serious chest infection, the doctor said. Paul was very ill. His mother lay in bed with him at night. They could not afford a nurse. He grew worse and the crisis approached. Realising how much his mother was suffering, Paul used all his willpower to hold on to life and finally he began to recover. He was in bed for seven weeks and when he

Six miners in their shirtsleeves came up the narrow garden path,
holding the coffin high.

got up, he was weak and pale. Mrs Morel's life now fixed itself on Paul.

Chapter 7   Boy and Girl Love

Paul went to Willey Farm many times during the autumn. He made friends with the two younger Leiver boys. Edgar kept his distance at first and Miriam also did not let him approach her. She was deeply romantic by nature. Literature was important to her, and religion. She did not care much about being beautiful and in general she did not think highly of the male sex. But she saw in Paul a new type of male, quick and light, one who could be gentle and sad, who knew a lot and who had had a death in the family.

Gradually he began to spend more time with Miriam. They had a common feeling for things in nature: flowers, trees and birds. She and her mother admired his paintings and encouraged him. One dull afternoon when the others were out, the girl said to him, hesitating:

'Have you seen the swing?'

'No,' he answered. 'Where?'

'Come,' she said. 'I'll show you.'

In the cowhouse a great thick rope with a seat on the end hung from the roof. Paul sat down, eager to try it, then immediately rose.

'Come on then and have first go,' he said to her.

'No, I won't go first,' she answered. 'You go!'

'All right,' he said, sitting down again. 'Watch this!'

In a moment he was flying through the air, every bit of him swinging, diving like a bird in the pleasure of movement. He looked down at her. Her red woollen hat hung over her dark curls and her beautiful warm face was lifted towards him. He gradually swung more slowly and jumped off.

'This swing's a real winner!' he cried delightedly.

Miriam was amused that he took the swing so seriously.

'Don't you want to try it?' asked Paul.

'Well – not much. I'll have just a little one.'

He held the seat steady for her, then started her moving.

'Keep your feet up or you'll hit the wall.'

She felt him catch her and push her again and was afraid. Again came his push, at just the right moment.

'Ha,' she laughed in fear. 'No higher!'

'But you're not a *bit* high!' he complained.

'But no higher!'

He heard the fear in her voice and stopped pushing. She felt sure he was going to push her again but no: he left her alone. She swung more slowly and got down. Paul took her place and away he went. For a time he was nothing but a body swinging in space, there was no part of him that did not swing. She could never lose herself like that.

Later on they talked. She was very dissatisfied with her life.

'Just because I'm a girl, why must I stay at home? Why am I not allowed to do anything? What chance do I have?'

'Chance of what?'

'Of knowing anything – of learning – of doing anything. It's not fair, just because I'm a woman.'

'But it's as good to be a woman as a man,' said Paul.

'Ha! – is it? Men have everything.'

'But what do you want?' he asked.

'I want to learn. Why must I know nothing?'

'You mean mathematics and French?'

'Yes, why can't I learn mathematics?' she cried, her eyes widening.

492

Next time he went up to the farm, he found Miriam cleaning the kitchen.

'Ready to do some mathematics?' he asked, taking a little book from his pocket.

'But–' He could see she was doubtful.

'You said you wanted to,' he insisted.

'Yes, but tonight I wasn't expecting it.'

However, they made a start.

Paul taught Miriam regularly. She had always studied the work from the week before but things came slowly to her. He got angry with her, felt ashamed, continued the lesson, got angry again. She listened in silence. She rarely protested.

'You don't give me time to learn it.'

She was right. It was strange that no one else made him so angry. When he saw her suffering, again he felt pity.

His painting was improving. Mr Jordan had given him Wednesday afternoon off to go to the art school. He loved to sit at home, alone with his mother at night, working and working; but when a drawing was finished, he always wanted to take it to Miriam.

The Bestwood library was open on Thursday evenings. Paul and Miriam were in the habit of meeting there when they changed their library books. Afterwards Paul often went part of the way home with her. Always when he went with Miriam and it got rather late, he knew his mother was worrying and getting angry with him. She did not like Miriam. She felt that the girl was leading Paul away from her. 'She will never let him become a man, she never will,' she thought. So when he was away with Miriam, Mrs Morel got more and more annoyed.

'What are you so displeased about?' he asked. 'Is it because you don't like her?'

'I don't say I don't like her. But I don't agree with young boys and girls staying out late, and never did.'

He kissed her and went slowly to bed. He had forgotten Miriam. He saw only that his mother was somehow hurt.

Sometimes as they were walking together, Miriam put her arm shyly into his. But he always disliked it and she knew this. He himself did not know what was the matter. He was so young and their relationship was so unphysical, he did not know that he really wanted to press her to his breast to reduce the ache there. He was too ashamed to recognise the fact that he might want her as a man wants a woman. Neither of them could face such an idea. And the 'purity' of their feelings prevented even their first love kiss. It was as if she could scarcely accept the shock of physical love, while he was too shy and sensitive to give it.

Chapter 8   The Battle of Love

Out of kindness to his mother, Paul did not go much to Willey Farm for a while. He sent two pictures to the autumn exhibition of students' work at the Castle Museum and both of them won first prizes. He was most excited and his mother was enormously pleased. William had won sports prizes, which she still kept; she did not forgive his death. Arthur, now in the army, was handsome, warm and generous. He would probably do well in the end. But Paul was going to do something important in life. She believed in him more firmly because he himself did not seem to realise his own capabilities. Life for her was rich with promise. Her struggle had not been for nothing.

Several times during the exhibition Mrs Morel went to the Castle Museum, unknown to Paul. She wandered round the long room, looking at the other pictures. Some made her jealous, they were so good. Then suddenly she had a shock that made her heart beat. There hung Paul's picture!

Name – Paul Morel – First Prize.

She felt a proud woman. When she passed well-dressed ladies going home through the Park, she thought to herself: 'Yes, you look very fine but I wonder if *your* son has two first prizes in the exhibition.'

One day Paul met Miriam in the street in Nottingham. He had not expected to meet her in town. She was walking with a rather impressive young woman, fair-haired, with a discontented expression, who held herself boldly upright. It was strange how small Miriam looked beside this woman with the handsome shoulders. Miriam watched Paul closely: his eyes were on the stranger, not on her. She explained that she had driven in to market with her father.

'I've told you about Mrs Dawes,' she said nervously.

'Clara, do you know Paul?'

'I think I've seen him before,' replied Mrs Dawes, showing little interest as she shook hands. She had proud, grey eyes, a skin like white honey and a full mouth with a slightly lifted top lip. Her clothes were simple and rather dull. Clearly she was poor and, unlike Miriam, did not have much taste.

'Where have you seen me?' asked Paul.

'Walking with Louie Travers,' she replied. Louie was one of the girls in the factory.

'How do you know her?' he asked. She did not answer. The two women moved on towards the Castle.

Paul remembered that Clara was the daughter of an old friend of Mrs Leivers. She had once held one of the better jobs at Jordan's and her husband, Baxter Dawes, still worked there, making metal parts. But Mrs Dawes was separated from her husband and had taken up the cause of women. People said she was clever.

He knew Baxter Dawes from work, a big, well-built man of thirty-one or two. He had the same white skin as his wife and a golden moustache; but his eyes moved continually this way and that. He seemed to have little self-respect; usually he was rude and insulting. He and Paul met often enough in the factory and disliked each other. Clara Dawes had no children. She now lived with her mother.

The next time Miriam saw him, she asked: 'What did you think of Clara Dawes?'

'She has a good figure,' answered Paul, 'but she doesn't look very friendly. Is she unpleasant as a person?'

'I don't think so. I think she's discontented – still married to a man like Baxter. What other things did you like about her?'

'Oh, I don't know. Her passionate mouth, the shape of her throat, her skin. There's something fierce about her. I think I'd like to do a painting of her.'

Miriam seemed strangely lost in thought.

'You don't really like her, do you?' he asked her.

'Oh yes, I do,' she said.

'Perhaps you like her because she's so much against men.'

Paul was now twenty-one. Mr Jordan had put him in charge of the department where he worked, and had increased his wages to thirty shillings a week. At the Art School he was studying design. He was also helping Miriam to learn French. On Friday evenings, when his father went to the pub and his mother to the market, Paul was left at home to watch the baking of the bread. Annie, who was now engaged to be married to Leonard, her young man, was also out visiting. At a quarter past seven there was a low knock and Miriam came in. He showed her his latest artwork and corrected the French she had written for him. This week she had done well. He loved to talk about his work with Miriam. All his passion went into these conversations. Somehow she lit up his imagination.

'Aren't you forgetting the bread?' Miriam said suddenly.

Paul rushed to open the oven door. Out came bluish smoke. One loaf was hard as a brick, another was burned black along one side. Paul tried to scratch off the burnt part, then wrapped it in a wet towel and left it in the back kitchen. They went back to their French until it was time for Miriam to go home. Paul turned down the gas and they set off.

He did not get home again until a quarter to eleven. His mother was in her chair, reading the local newspaper. Annie was sitting in front of the fire, looking gloomy. The burnt loaf, unwrapped, stood on the table. Paul felt very uncomfortable. For some minutes he sat pretending to read. Then: 'I forgot that bread, mother.' There was no answer from either woman.

'You don't know how ill our mother is,' said Annie after a pause.

'Why is she so ill?' asked Paul sharply.

'She could hardly get home. I found her white as anything, sitting here,' said Annie in a tearful voice.

'I had so many parcels,' said Mrs Morel, 'the meat and the vegetables and a pair of curtains.'

'Let Annie fetch the meat,' said Paul.

'But how was I to know? You were off with Miriam instead of being here when Mother came.'

'And what's the matter with you?' Paul asked his mother.

'I suppose it's my heart,' she replied. She certainly looked bluish round the mouth.

'And have you felt it before?'

'Yes, often enough.'

'Then why haven't you told me, and why haven't you seen a doctor?'

'You'd never notice anything,' said Annie. 'You're too eager to be off with Miriam.'

'So that was why the bread was spoiled,' said Mrs Morel bitterly.

'No, it was not!' he replied angrily.

'I bought you a nice piece of cheese,' said his mother. He was too angry to go and look for it.

'I don't want anything,' he said.

'If I want you to go out on a Friday night, you say you're too tired,' she complained, 'but you're never too tired to go if *she* comes for you.'

'I can't let her go back alone.'

'Can't you? Then why does she come? Because you want her.'

'I do like to talk to her but I don't *love* her,' Paul explained. 'We talk about painting and books. You know you don't care whether a picture is decorative or not.'

'How do you know I don't care?'

'Oh, you're old, Mother, and we're young.'

He only meant that the interests of her age group were not the interests of his; but the moment he had spoken, he realised that he had said the wrong thing. It was too painful. He realised that he was life to her. And after all she was the chief thing to him, the only all-important thing.

'No, mother, I really don't love her. I talk to her but I want to come home to you.'

As he bent to kiss his mother, she threw her arms round his neck and cried in a desperate voice quite unlike her own: 'It's too much. I could let another woman but not her. And I've never – you know, Paul – I've never had a husband, not really–'

Immediately he hated Miriam bitterly. His mother kissed him, a kiss of passionate love. Without knowing, he gently stroked her face. At that moment Morel came in, walking unsteadily, his hat over one eye. He paused in the doorway.

'Making more trouble?' he said with an ugly look. Mrs Morel's feelings turned to sudden hatred of her drunken husband.

'At least I'm not drunk,' she said.

Morel disappeared and returned with a piece of cheese in his hand. It was what Mrs Morel had bought for Paul.

'And I didn't buy that for you. If you give me only twenty-five shillings, don't expect me to buy you cheese, when you're already full up with beer!'

'What!' shouted Morel, 'what – not for me?' He looked at the cheese in his hand and suddenly threw it into the fire. Paul jumped to his feet.

'Waste your own food!' he cried.

'What – what!' shouted Morel, taking up a threatening position. 'I'll show you, you cheeky young fool!'

'All right,' said Paul hotly. 'Show me!'

At that moment he wanted to hit his father violently.

'There!' cried Morel, delivering a great blow just past his son's face. Even so close, he did not dare to touch the younger man.

'Right!' said Paul and was preparing to hit his father on the mouth. He ached to land the blow; but he heard a frightened sound behind him. His mother was pale as death, and dark around the lips. Morel was dancing up to deliver another blow.

'Father,' said Paul urgently.

Morel shook and stood still.

'Mother!' cried the boy. 'Mother!'

She began to struggle with herself. She could not move. Gradually she got more control. Paul laid her down on the sofa and ran to fetch her something to drink. The tears were streaming down his face.

'What's the matter with her?' said Morel sitting on the opposite side of the room.

'She's fainted!' replied Paul.

Morel took his boots off and went unsteadily to his bed.

Paul knelt there, stroking his mother's hand.

'It's nothing, my boy,' she whispered.

Paul made up the fire, straightened the room, laid the things for breakfast and brought his mother's candle. He followed her up the stairs and kissed her once more.

'Goodnight, Mother.'

'Goodnight!' she said.

In the days that followed, everyone tried to forget what had taken place.

Chapter 9   The Defeat of Miriam

The Easter holiday began happily. Paul rode his bicycle up to Willey Farm. But he was in a hard, critical mood when he went out walking round the farm with Miriam. Paul kept on finding fault with her. They stopped to rest on a bed of dry grass.

'Why are you sad?' she asked gently.

'I'm not sad, why should I be?' he answered. 'I'm only normal.'

She wondered why he always called himself normal when he was unpleasant.

'But what's the matter?' she insisted.

'Nothing.'

He picked up a stick and dug the earth with it in a fever of bad temper. Gently but firmly, she put her hand on his.

'Don't!' she said. 'Put it away.'

He threw the stick into the grass and leaned back.

'What is it?' she asked again softly.

He lay quite still with only his eyes alive, and those full of unhappiness.

'You know,' he said finally, his voice rather tired, 'you know, we'd better break off.'

'Why?' she asked. 'What has happened?'

'Nothing has happened. I can only give friendship, I'm not

capable of anything more. It's not equal, our relationship. Let's end it.'

He meant that she loved him more than he loved her. She pitied him in his suffering. He felt so ashamed.

'But I don't understand,' she said.

'I know,' he cried, 'you never will. You'll never believe I can't – can't physically, any more than I can fly—'

'Can't what?' she whispered.

'Love you.'

'What have they been saying at home?' she asked.

'It's not that,' he answered.

But she knew it was. They did not talk much more that evening. Instead Paul and Edgar went off on their bicycles.

He had come back to his mother. Hers was the strongest tie in his life. Even Miriam seemed unreal when he thought about her. And in the same way his mother depended on him. Paul was going to change the face of the earth in some way that really mattered. And yet for Paul it was not enough. His new young life, so strong and commanding, was driving him on toward something else. It made him mad with restlessness.

◆

Miriam had not stopped hoping to win Paul back. He still visited the Leivers but spent most of his time with Edgar.

In May, she asked Paul to come to the farm and meet Mrs Dawes. He was rather excited at the idea of seeing Clara again.

Mrs Dawes came for the day. Her heavy, fair hair was twisted on top of her head. She wore a white blouse and a dark blue skirt. Paul did not come till the afternoon. As he got off his bicycle, Miriam saw him look round eagerly at the house.

'Hasn't Clara come yet?' he asked.

'Yes,' replied Miriam in her musical voice. 'She came this morning. She's reading.'

'And is she any pleasanter?' he asked again.

'You know I always think she's quite pleasant.'

Clara sat inside, reading. Paul saw the back of her white neck with the fine hair lifted up from it. She rose, looking at him without interest. When she shook hands, she seemed to keep him at a distance and yet offer him something. He noticed the roundness of her breasts inside her blouse and the fine curve of her shoulders.

'You've chosen a fine day,' he said.

'It seems so,' she answered.

The conversation continued for a little. Clara did not seem to find Paul's comments at all clever.

'Well, I think I'll go and see Edgar,' he said, and left them.

After tea Mrs Leivers said to Clara: 'And you find life happier now?'

'Much happier.'

'And are you satisfied?'

'If I can remain free and independent, yes.'

'And you don't miss anything in your life?' asked Mrs Leivers gently.

'I've put all that behind me.'

Paul had been listening to this conversation.

'You'll find you're always falling over the things you've put behind you,' he said, and left to find Edgar again. He felt he had been clever and was proud of himself. He whistled as he went.

A little later Miriam came to ask if he would go with her and Clara for a walk. Clara walked in front by herself for part of the way, her head bent. Paul was curious about her. He forgot Miriam, who was walking beside him, talking to him. She looked at him, finding he did not answer her. His eyes were fixed in front on Clara.

'Do you still think she is unpleasant?' she asked.

'Something's the matter with her,' he said.

'Yes,' said Miriam.

They came to a field hidden by trees round the edges. In the smooth grass, beautiful, bright yellow spring flowers were growing. Paul and Miriam started picking them. Clara wandered about looking depressed. Then she knelt down, bending forward to smell the flowers. Her neck looked such a beautiful thing, her breasts swung slightly in her blouse. The curve of her back was beautiful and strong. Suddenly, without realising, Paul was dropping a handful of flowers over her hair and neck. She looked up at him with fear in her grey eyes, wondering what he was doing. Suddenly, standing there above her, he felt uncomfortable. Clara laughed strangely and rose, picking the flowers from her hair. One flower remained caught in her hair. Paul saw but did not tell her. He collected the flowers he had dropped. Unexpectedly, she gave him a grateful smile.

Going down the path, they were all silent. As the evening deepened, they could see the mining village across the valley, little lights on a dark hill touching the sky.

'It's been nice, hasn't it?' said Paul.

Miriam agreed. Clara was silent. He could tell by the way she moved, pretending not to care, that she suffered.

At home he told his mother about Clara: that she was poor, that she lived with her mother, that she was thirty years old.

'And what's so charming about her, my boy?' asked his mother.

'I don't know that she's charming, Mother, but she's nice. She seems straight, you know, not a bit deep.'

Mrs Morel was not against the idea of Clara.

♦

Annie and Leonard were getting married. She had saved eleven pounds and Leonard twenty-three, so the wedding took place almost immediately. Arthur came home and looked sensational

Suddenly, without realising, Paul was dropping a handful of flowers over Clara's hair and neck.

in his army uniform. Annie looked nice in a grey dress she could also use for Sundays. Morel was cool to Leonard. Annie cried her eyes out in the kitchen on leaving her mother. Mrs Morel cried a little, then stroked her and said:

'Don't cry, child, he'll be good to you.'

Afterwards Paul and Mrs Morel were left alone.

'You're not sorry she's married, Mother, are you?'

'No, but it seems strange, now she's gone from me. When I think of my own wedding day, I can only hope that her life will be different.'

'I'll never marry while I've got you – I won't.'

He kissed her and went to bed.

Mrs Morel sat thinking, about her daughter, about Paul, about Arthur. She was upset at losing Annie. But Paul needed her and Arthur needed her too.

◆

Paul felt life changing around him. Annie was married, Arthur was living his own life of pleasure. For both of them life lay outside their mother's house. They only came home for holidays and rest. Paul dreamed of following them. Yet home for him was beside his mother. He grew more and more restless. Miriam did not satisfy him. His old wish to be with her grew weaker. Sometimes he met Clara in Nottingham, sometimes he saw her at Willey Farm; but between Paul and Clara and Miriam there was always a kind of struggle.

For Miriam's twenty-first birthday Paul wrote her a long, rather philosophical letter, which more or less brought their relationship to an end. He was now twenty-three years old and his sexual need was growing strong. Often when he talked to Clara Dawes, he was conscious of his blood flowing quicker, of something alive in him, of a new self, a new consciousness. He knew that sooner or later his need would have to be satisfied.

Chapter 10   Clara

When he was twenty-three, Paul sent in a painting to the winter exhibition at the Castle Museum. One morning the postman came when Mrs Morel was doing the washing. Suddenly Paul heard a wild noise from his mother. Rushing into the kitchen, he found her screaming and waving a letter, as if she had gone mad. The postman too came running back, afraid something bad had happened.

'His picture's got first prize, Fred,' she cried, 'and it's been sold for twenty pounds!'

'That looks like meaning something!' said the young postman.

'Didn't I say we would do it?' she said, pretending she was not crying.

Morel was greatly impressed. 'Twenty pounds for a bit of a painting that took him just an hour or two,' he said amazed. 'Yes, and that other boy would have done as much if they hadn't killed him,' he added quietly. The thought of William went through Mrs Morel like a sharp knife.

♦

Arthur left the army and immediately got married to Beatrice, whom he had known for years. The baby was born six months after the wedding. With the help of Beatrice's mother, Mrs Morel found furniture for a little two-room house. He was caught now. For a while he refused to settle down and got annoyed with his young wife, who loved him. He nearly went mad when the baby cried or gave trouble. He complained for hours to his mother, who only said: 'Well, my son, you did it yourself, now you must make the best of it.' And then the stronger side of his character appeared. He accepted his responsibilities, recognised that he belonged to his wife and child and made a good job of it.

♦

The months passed slowly. One day a friend of Clara's in Bestwood asked Paul to take a message to Mrs Dawes. In the evening after work he went to the house where she lived with her mother. The street was poor and the paint on the front door was old. A large, fat woman of about sixty answered his knock. This was Mrs Radford, Clara's mother. In a moment Clara appeared. Her face went red: she seemed embarrassed that he had discovered her at home like this. She invited him into the kitchen, where the two women spent all their time making lace. The room was full of the white snowy stuff. Clara gave him a chair, brought him a beer and went on with her work. Her arm moved mechanically as she used the machine, her head was bent over the lace. Her life seemed so narrow, so limited, Paul thought. Her grey eyes at last met his. He recognised that she was deeply unhappy, a kind of prisoner. He felt shaken. It was not what he had expected. She had seemed so high and proud. He left in a kind of dream.

The girl in charge of the stocking department at Jordan's was leaving to get married. He told Clara about the vacant position. So Clara came back to Jordan's. Now they were fellow-workers and saw each other several times a day. When Paul was painting in the afternoon, she often came and stood near him, keeping perfectly still. Although she stood a yard away, he felt as if she was pressed against him and he was full of her warmth. Then he could paint no more. He threw down the brushes and began to talk.

On Paul's birthday he met Clara by chance in the dinner hour. They decided to go together up to the Castle. At the top they leaned over the wall. Away at the foot of the rock, tiny trees stood in their own pools of shadow, and tiny people went rushing about with amusing self-importance. She disliked towns, Clara told him. 'When things are natural, they're beautiful.'

'And what isn't natural?' asked Paul.

'Everything man has made,' she answered, 'including man himself.'

'But his women made him,' he remarked. 'Wasn't Baxter Dawes natural?'

She changed colour and looked away from him.

'We will not discuss it,' she said.

Later that afternoon the postman brought Paul a small packet. It was a book of poems with a note inside. 'Please allow me to send you this. I am sympathetic to your problems and wish you well. C.D.'

Paul felt deeply moved, and warm towards her. After this they often went out together in the dinner hour. Paul asked her about Dawes.

'How old were you when you married?'

'Twenty-two.'

'That was eight years ago?'

'Yes.'

'And when did you leave him?'

'Three years ago.'

'Five years together! Did you love him when you married him?'

'I thought I did – more or less. I didn't think much about it. He wanted me.'

'And why did you leave him finally?'

'Because he was unfaithful to me.'

'I believe he still loves you,' said Paul.

'Probably,' she replied.

She was a married woman and believed in simple friendship. Paul considered that he was behaving quite correctly towards her. It was only a friendship between man and woman such as any sensible people might have. It seemed to him quite plain. Miriam was his old friend and lover: she belonged to Bestwood and home and his growing up. Clara was a newer friend, and she belonged to Nottingham, to life, to the world. Clara rarely saw Miriam now. They were still friends but the friendship was much weakened.

'Will you come to the concert on Sunday?' Clara asked Paul just after Christmas.

'I promised to go up to Willey Farm,' he replied. 'You're not upset, are you?'

'Why should I be?' she answered.

Again Paul found himself telling her about Miriam.

'She wants me so much that I can't give myself. She wants the soul out of my body.'

'And yet you love her?' asked Clara.

'No I don't love her. I never even kiss her.'

'Why not?' Clara asked.

'I don't know.'

'I suppose you're afraid. Anyway, she doesn't want to have your soul. That's your imagination. She wants you.'

He thought about this. Perhaps he was wrong.

'But she seems–' he began.

'You've never tried,' she answered.

Chapter 11   The Test on Miriam

With the spring, the old madness came back to Paul. He did not feel he wanted marriage with Miriam. And yet he wanted to belong to her. It was a powerful need struggling with a still stronger shyness. He had a great tenderness for Miriam. He could not fail her.

Mrs Morel saw him going back to Miriam and was amazed.

He said nothing to his mother. He did not explain or excuse himself. If he came home late and she made a comment, he answered coldly:

'I shall come home when I like. I'm old enough.' And his mother went to bed, leaving the door unlocked for him. But she lay awake listening until he came: often long after. It was a great bitterness to her that he had gone back to Miriam.

♦

That summer the cherry trees at the farm were heavy with fruit. They stood very tall, hung thick with bright red and dark red drops. Paul and Edgar were gathering the fruit one evening. It had been a hot day and now the clouds were rolling in the sky, dark and warm. The wind made the whole tree swing with a thrilling movement that excited Paul. He sat unsteadily among the higher branches, feeling slightly drunk with the tree's movement, and tore off handful after handful of the smooth, cool fruit. Cherries touched his ears and neck as he leaned forward. Red-coloured fruit glowed under the darkness of the leaves. The sun, going down, caught the broken clouds. Enormous piles of gold shone out in the south-east. The world, until now grey, was bathed by the golden glow, making trees and grass and far-off water shine.

Miriam came out to watch.

'Oh,' Paul heard her call, 'isn't it wonderful!' He looked down. There was a pale light on the soft face turned up to him.

'How high you are!' she said.

He threw a handful of cherries at her. She was taken by surprise and was afraid. He laughed and rained more cherries down on her. She ran off to escape them, picking up some cherries on the way. She hung two fine pairs over her ears, then looked up again.

'Haven't you got enough?' she asked.

*He threw a handful of cherries at her. She was taken by surprise
and was afraid.*

'Nearly. It's like being on a ship up here.'

'How long will you stay?'

'Till the sunset ends.'

She watched the gold clouds turn to orange, then rose, then reddish purple, until the passion went out of the sky. Paul climbed down with his basket.

'They're lovely,' said Miriam, feeling the cherries.

'I've torn my sleeve,' said Paul. It was near the shoulder. She put her fingers through the tear.

'How warm,' she said.

He laughed. There was a strange, new sound in his voice.

'Shall we walk a little way?' he said.

They went down the fields as far as a thick wood.

'Shall we go in among the trees?' he asked.

'Do you want to?'

'Yes.'

It was very dark in the wood. She was afraid. Paul was silent and strange. He seemed hardly conscious of her as a person: to him she was only a woman. He stood against a tree and took her in his arms. She gave herself to him, but as a victim, feeling some sort of horror. This thick-voiced man was a stranger to her.

Later it began to rain. Paul lay with his head on the ground, listening to the sharp sound of the raindrops. His heart was heavy. He realised that she had not been with him, that her soul had stood back. His body felt calmer but that was all. She put her hands over him to feel if he was getting wet.

'We must go,' said Miriam.

'Yes,' said Paul but did not move.

'The rain is coming in on us,' said Miriam.

He rose and helped her up. They walked hand in hand. In a while they went indoors.

They made love a number of times after this. Afterwards Paul always had the feeling of failure and death.

'You don't really want me when I come to you,' said Paul gloomily after a week or two.

'No, don't say so,' she said, taking his head in her arms. 'Don't I want your children?'

'Shall we get married then?' said Paul.

'We're too young,' she said, after a pause. 'Not yet.'

With Paul the sense of failure grew stronger. At first it was only a sadness. Then he began to feel he could not go on. He wanted to run, go abroad, anything. Gradually he stopped asking her to have him. He realised consciously that it was no good.

He told his mother that he would break off with Miriam. On Sunday he went up to the farm in the early afternoon. Miriam met him at the end of the farm road. She was wearing a new dress with short sleeves. She had made herself look so beautiful and fresh for him. They sat down. He lay with his head on her breast while she stroked his hair. She knew that he was somehow 'absent'.

'I've been thinking,' he said finally, 'we ought to break it off.'

'What?' she cried in surprise.

'Because it's no good going on. I want us to break off – you to be free of me, I free of you.'

'How many times have you offered to marry me and I wasn't willing?'

'I know – but I want us to break off.'

'You're a child of four!' she said in her anger. 'And what can I tell my mother?' she asked.

'I told my mother that I was breaking it off – cleanly and completely,' he said.

'I shan't tell them at home,' she said. 'It's always been the same: one long battle between us – you fighting me off!'

'Not always – not at first,' he argued.

'Always – from the very beginning – always the same.'

He sat in silence. His heart was hard against her. He left her at the road-end. As she went home alone, in her new dress, having to face her family at the other end, he stood without moving on the high road, filled with pain and shame.

Chapter 12   Passion

After leaving Miriam, Paul turned almost immediately to Clara. One evening they went to the cinema and he took her hand in his. She neither moved nor made any sign. On Saturday evening he invited her to have coffee with him after work. Afterwards they walked for a little in the park and in the darkness he caught her suddenly in his arms and kissed her. For the whole of the next day he only thought of seeing her again.

Monday was his half-day at work. He asked her if she would come out with him. They agreed to meet at half-past two. In the bus she leaned against him and he took her hand. They got out beside the river and crossed the bridge. They walked along the path above the river and came to a locked gate. Paul climbed over first. Then Clara climbed up onto it and he held both her hands. Laughing, she looked down into his face. Then she jumped, her breast came against his, he held her and covered her face with kisses.

They decided to go down to the river's edge below. Slipping and sliding, they made their way to the bottom of the steep wooded bank. Paul found a flat place at the foot of two trees. It was covered with wet leaves but it would do. He threw down his raincoat and waved to her to come. She sank down at his side. He pressed his lips to her throat and felt the beat of her blood under his lips. Everything was perfectly still. There was nothing in the afternoon but themselves.

They had a steep climb to get back to the public path at the top. Then they walked into Clifton and had tea at a guest-house.

He was madly in love with her now. Every movement she made, every fold in her clothes sent a thrill through him.

Mrs Morel was sitting reading when he got home.

'You're late,' she said, looking at him. His eyes were shining, his face seemed to glow.

'Yes, I've been down at Clifton Grove with Clara. She's – she's awfully nice, mother. Would you like to know her?'

'Yes,' said Mrs Morel coolly, 'I should like to know what she's like.'

'You don't expect to like her,' said Paul. 'I'll bring her here on Sunday for tea. Shall I bring her?'

'You please yourself,' said Mrs Morel, laughing.

Paul knew that he had won. He mentioned to Miriam that Clara was coming to tea on Sunday.

'I want my mother to meet her,' he added.

'Ah!' There was a silence.

'I may call in before I go to the church service,' Miriam said. 'It's a long time since I saw Clara.'

'Very well,' said Paul, surprised and unconsciously angry.

On the Sunday afternoon, Paul met Clara at Keston station. Clara followed Paul into the house. Mrs Morel rose. The younger woman was very nervous.

'I hope you don't mind my coming,' she said hesitatingly.

'I was pleased when Paul said he would bring you,' replied Mrs Morel. Looking at Paul, she thought what a man he looked in his dark, well-made clothes. Her heart glowed.

She and Clara started talking about Nottingham, Clara still rather nervous, Mrs Morel still rather proud. But they were getting on well together, Paul saw. Mrs Morel measured herself against the younger woman and found herself easily the stronger. Clara was very respectful. She knew how highly Paul thought of his mother and she had been fearful of this meeting, expecting someone hard and cold. She was

515

surprised to find this little, interested woman, chatting so easily with her.

At tea the atmosphere was cool and clear, where everyone was themselves and in tune with the others. Afterwards Paul cleared the table, then walked into the garden, leaving the two women to talk. Clara offered to help wash the dishes and was allowed to dry the tea-things. It was painful for her not to be able to follow him into the garden but at last she allowed herself to go. She went to Paul, who was watching the bees among the autumn flowers.

At that moment Miriam was entering through the garden gate. She saw Clara go up to Paul, saw him turn and saw them move together. Something in the relationship told her that they were already a couple. They were looking into each other's eyes, laughing. At that moment they became conscious of Miriam, and everything changed.

Miriam shook hands with Clara, saying: 'It seems strange to see you here.'

'Yes,' replied the other, 'it seems strange to be here.' There was a pause.

'It is pretty, isn't it?' said Miriam.

'I like it very much,' said Clara.

Then Miriam realised that Clara was accepted here as she could never be. She asked Paul for a book to read. He ran indoors to find one. When he returned, Clara turned to go indoors, leaving him to walk with Miriam to the gate.

'When will you come to Willey Farm?' Miriam called to her.

'I couldn't say,' replied Clara.

'Mother asked me to say she'd be pleased to see you any time.'

'Thank you, but I can't say when.'

'Oh, very well,' said Miriam with some bitterness, and left.

♦

That evening the lovers went out over the fields. Clara leaned

516

against him as they walked, and he held her closer and closer. Suddenly Paul's blood flamed up in him. He caught her in his arms and kissed her again and again. But she was worried about catching her train. They had only fourteen minutes to get to the station, so they ran madly through the darkness. Away to the right they could see the lit-up train approaching. At last Clara fell into the train, completely out of breath. The whistle blew. She was gone.

Before he knew where he was, he found himself back home in the kitchen.

'Do you like her?' he asked his mother, rather unwillingly.

'Yes, I liked her. But you'll get tired of her, my son, you know you will. You'd better take some hot milk.'

He refused and went to bed, feeling confused and angry.

Chapter 13   Baxter Dawes

Paul wanted to see a play which was at the Theatre Royal in Nottingham that week. He asked Clara to come with him. He took his evening clothes in a suitcase and changed at Jordan's after work. At the theatre Clara took off her coat and he discovered she was in a sort of green evening dress that left her arms and neck and part of her breast bare. He could almost feel the firmness and softness of her body as he looked at her. He sat all the evening beside her beautiful bare arm, watching the strong throat, the breasts under the green stuff, the curve of her body in the tight dress. He somehow hated her because she made him suffer the ache of her nearness. When the lights went down, she sank against him and he stroked her hand and arm with his fingers. The play continued but it seemed like a dream, far away from him. The reality was Clara: the white, heavy arms, her throat, her chest rising and falling.

When all was over, the lights up, the people clapping, he came to himself. He helped her on with her coat.

'I love you. You look beautiful in that dress,' he whispered over her shoulder, among the crowd of people. It seemed to him that he met a pair of brown eyes full of hate as they made their way out of the theatre but he did not know whose eyes they were. He and Clara turned away and walked towards the station.

♦

Two or three evenings later, Paul was drinking in the 'Punch Bowl' pub with some of his friends when Baxter Dawes came in. He looked much thinner and seemed to be on a downhill path. His woman, Louie, had left him and he had recently spent a night in jail for fighting. Paul and he were enemies but, as fellow-workers, there was a familiarity between them. Paul often thought about Dawes and wanted to know him better. This evening he offered Dawes a drink. Dawes refused with a curse and went on making insulting references to Paul's friendship with Clara. Paul tried to pay no attention but one final remark caused him to throw half a glass of beer in Dawes's face. There was nearly an ugly fight but the quick-thinking barman led Dawes to the door and forced him to leave the pub.

Paul told Clara jokingly of the quarrel with her husband. The colour rose in her face, her grey eyes glowed with anger. She advised Paul to carry a gun because, she said, Dawes was dangerous. Paul laughed at the idea; but in fact a violent quarrel at the factory a few days later led Dawes to attack Mr Jordan, and ended with Dawes losing his job.

Clara was indeed passionately in love with Paul, and he with her, as far as passion went. One evening they were walking down by the river and his mind was somewhere else. Clara listened to him whistling a sad, dissatisfied tune. She walked on in silence.

When they came to a bridge, he sat down, looking at the stars in the water. She sat beside him.

'Will you always stay at Jordan's?' she asked.

'No, I shall leave Nottingham soon and go abroad.'

'Go abroad? What for?'

'I don't know. I feel restless. I shall not go for long, while my mother's there.'

'And if you made a nice lot of money, what would you do?' she asked.

'Live in a pretty house near London with my mother.'

'I see.'

There was a long pause.

'Don't ask me anything about the future,' he said gloomily. 'I don't know anything. Just be with me now.'

She caught him passionately to her, pressing his head down on her breast. She could not mistake the suffering in his voice. And soon the struggle within him died away and he forgot Clara was there any more: only a woman, warm and passionate, there in the dark. And she gave herself to him. She knew how alone he was.

When Paul came to his senses, he realised he was lying on the grass. The warmth he felt was Clara's breathing. What was she? A strong, strange, wild life, breathing with him in the darkness. After such an evening they were both very still, having known the enormous power of passion. But Clara was not satisfied. He might leave her. She had not got him. For Paul, the fire of love slowly died away. He felt more and more that his experience had been impersonal and not with Clara. He felt a great tenderness for her but it was not she who could keep his soul steady. He had wanted her to be something she could not be.

Once, when they were by themselves, he asked her: 'Do you ever want to marry me?'

'Do *you* want to marry *me*?' she replied.

'Yes, I should like us to have children,' he answered slowly. 'But you don't really want a divorce from Baxter, do you?'

It was some minutes before she replied.

'No,' she said, 'I don't think I do.'

Gradually their love-making became more mechanical, without the wonderful high points of that first time.

◆

One night he left her to go to the railway station, over the fields. He did not have much time and it was very dark. He was going through a gate when he saw a dark figure leaning beside it.

'Paul Morel?' said the man.

He knew it was Dawes.

'I've got you, haven't I?' said Dawes.

'I'll miss my train,' said Paul.

'All right then,' answered Dawes, and suddenly the younger man was knocked backwards by a blow across the face. The whole night went black. Then he began to see Dawes more clearly and hit him above the mouth. Suddenly from nowhere came a great blow behind the ear. He heard Dawes's heavy breathing, like a wild animal's. He hung on to the bigger man like a wild cat, till at last Dawes fell with a crash, and Paul went down with him. His hands pressed the other man's throat in a blind need to kill him. Then he was thrown to one side. He felt his enemy kicking him as he lay on his back, helpless, then he lost consciousness.

Paul woke gradually. He knew where he was and what had happened but he did not want to move. At last his willpower forced him to get up. He was sick with pain but his brain was clear. He found a pool of water and washed his bloody face and hands. The icy water stung but woke him fully. All he wanted was to get to his mother. On foot, as in a terrible dream, he made the journey home.

His hands pressed the other man's throat in a blind need to kill him.

Everybody was in bed. His face was raw and badly marked, almost like a dead man's face. The night was a long, bad dream. In the morning he woke to find his mother looking at him. Her blue eyes! They were all he wanted to see. She was there, he was in her hands.

'It's not much, mother,' he said. 'It was Baxter Dawes.' He had a displaced shoulder, and the second day his breathing also became very difficult. His mother was as pale as death and very thin. She sat and looked at him, then looked away into space. Clara came to see him, then Miriam came.

'You know I don't care about them, Mother,' he said.

'I'm afraid you don't, my son,' she replied sadly.

People were told it was a bicycle accident and soon he was back at work again.

Chapter 14   Life at an End

In May Paul decided to spend four days in Blackpool with a friend. His mother went to stay for a week in Sheffield with Annie, who now lived there. Perhaps the change would do her good. Paul arranged to join them on the fifth day and stay in Sheffield till his holiday was over.

His four free days passed enjoyably, without a worry or a black thought. On the fifth day, Paul ran up the steps of Annie's house, expecting to find his mother laughing in the front room. But it was Annie who opened the door.

'Is Mother ill?' he said.

'Yes, she's not very well. Don't upset her,' Annie replied.

'Is she in bed?'

'Yes.'

A strange feeling came over him. He dropped his bag and ran upstairs. His mother was sitting up in bed. She looked at him almost as if she were ashamed of herself. He saw her greyish colour.

'Mother!' he said.

'I thought you were never coming,' she answered brightly.

But he only fell on his knees at the bedside and buried his face in the blankets, crying in pain. She stroked his hair slowly with her thin hand.

'What is it, Mother?' he said at last.

She said without looking at him: 'It's only a lump, my boy. It's been there for some time.'

His tears rose up again. His mind was hard and clear but his body was crying.

'Where?'

She put her hand on her side to show him. He sat on the bed and took her hand.

'When did you get ill?' he asked.

'It began yesterday,' she answered.

'You ought not to have travelled alone,' he said.

'As if that had anything to do with it,' she answered quickly. 'Now go and have your dinner. They're waiting for you.'

After dinner he went into the kitchen to help Annie wash the dishes. Annie began to cry again.

'The pain she had yesterday, I never saw anyone suffer like it!' she cried. 'Leonard ran like a madman for Dr Ansell. And when she got to bed, she said to me, "Annie, look at this lump on my side. I wonder what it is." And when I looked, I nearly dropped. It's a lump as big as an apple. I said, "Good heavens, mother, whenever did that come?" "Why, child," she said, "it's been there a long time." She's been having these pains for months at home and nobody looking after her.'

'But she's been seeing the doctor in Nottingham, she says, and she never told me,' he said.

In the afternoon he went to see Dr Ansell, a wise, lovable man.

'Can't you operate?' asked Paul.

'Not there,' said the doctor.

'Might it be cancer?'

'I don't know. I would like an examination by her regular doctor, Dr Jameson, but you must arrange it. He will charge you not less than ten pounds to come all the way from Nottingham.'

Paul agreed to make the arrangement and went to see Dr Jameson in Nottingham two days later. He was friendly, busy, kind. He agreed to come to Sheffield the next day, a Sunday. Paul went home to see his father. They now employed a little serving girl called Minnie, and she was looking after him. Paul had written him a letter to tell him about his wife but his father was afraid to mention her. They ate in silence.

'Well, and how is she?' asked the old miner at last.

'She can sit up − we can carry her down for tea,' said Paul. 'You must go and see her next week, Father.'

'I hope she'll be home by that time,' said Morel.

'If she's not,' said Paul, 'you must come.'

Dr Jameson came on the Sunday, as agreed, together with Dr Ansell. The examination did not take long. Arthur, Paul and Leonard waited nervously for the two doctors to come downstairs. They were told that an operation was impossible: Mrs Morel's heart was too weak; but it might be possible to reduce the lump by using suitable drugs.

Paul had to go back to work. On the Saturday Walter Morel took the train to Sheffield. When he arrived, he looked lost. The old man came into the bedroom rather fearfully.

'How do I find you, my girl?' he said, kissing her hurriedly and shyly.

'Well, I'm half and half,' she replied.

'I can see you are,' he said, looking down on her. Then he

wiped his eyes with his handkerchief and sat looking at her almost as if she was a stranger.

Mrs Morel did not change much. She stayed in Sheffield for two months. At the end of that time she was, if anything, rather worse, but she wanted to go home. So they got a motorcar from Nottingham because she was too ill to go by train. Morel knew she was coming: he had the front door open. Half the neighbours came out to greet her. Mrs Morel, smiling, drove home down the street. They saw her smile and nod. It was a great event in Bestwood.

Morel wanted to carry her inside but he was too old. Arthur picked her up as if she was a child. They put a big, deep chair near the fire, where her old chair used to stand. When she was unwrapped and sitting down and had drunk a little wine, she looked round the room.

'Don't think I didn't like your house, Annie,' she said, 'but it's good to be in my own home again.'

And Morel added in a shaky voice:

'It is, girl, it is.'

While Paul was in Sheffield, he heard from Dr Ansell that a man from Nottingham was in the local fever hospital. He was none other than Baxter Dawes. Paul decided to visit him. It appeared that Dawes had come to take up work in Sheffield but after only a day or two had fallen seriously ill. Paul told him about his mother's illness and offered to visit him again when he returned to Sheffield. Back in Nottingham, he told Clara about Dawes. She seemed very upset by the news.

'Is he very bad?' she asked guiltily.

'He has been. He's improving now.'

There was a distance now between the lovers.

'I've behaved badly to him,' she said, 'and now you're behaving badly to me. It's what I deserve. He loved me a thousand times better than you ever did.'

As soon as she could, she went to Sheffield to see her husband. The meeting was not a success; but she left him roses and fruit and money. She wanted to repay him, even though her heart was not warm with love.

Mrs Morel got gradually worse. Paul knew, and she knew, that she was dying but they kept up a pretence of cheerfulness.

Dawes was now in a rest home near Nottingham and Paul visited him there sometimes. A peculiar friendship developed between the two men. Dawes, still very weak, seemed to rely on Paul.

The days and weeks went by. December came, and some snow. Paul stayed at home all the time now. They could not afford a nurse, so Paul shared the nursing with Annie. Their mother had strong drugs every night to help her sleep and her heart beat irregularly. Annie slept beside her. Paul went in in the early morning when his sister got up. Mrs Morel's eyes grew darker and darker, her body thinner, her skin greyer.

'Can't you give her something to put an end to it?' he asked the doctor at last.

But the doctor shook his head.

Walter Morel was silent and frightened. Sometimes he went into the sickroom to look at her, then left in confusion.

One evening Paul collected all the sleeping pills there were and took them downstairs. Carefully he made them into a powder. He put the powder into the hot milk which he took to his mother at nine o'clock. She drank a little and looked at him with dark, wondering eyes.

'Oh, it *is* bitter, Paul,' she said, making an expression of distaste.

'It's to help you sleep better,' he said.

She drank some more of the milk. 'Oh, it *is* horrible,' she told him.

Paul brought her a little cold milk to take away the taste. Mrs

'Oh, it is bitter, Paul,' she said, making an expression of distaste.

Morel drank it down. She was sighing with tiredness. Her heartbeat was very irregular. Paul and Annie settled her down for the night. As usual, Annie slept with her and Paul slept in the next room. He was woken suddenly by Annie's whispered: 'Paul – Paul! Come and look at her!'

His mother lay with her cheek on her hand, in the same position as before. But her mouth had fallen open and she was breathing with loud, heavy breaths, with long pauses in between. They sat silently listening to the great rough breaths. The night went by breath by breath. Still it was dark. His father got up.

'Had I better stay?' he whispered.

'No – go to work,' answered Paul. In a few minutes he heard his father's heavy footsteps on the snow outside. He watched the snow growing blue. A grey, deathly dawn followed. Annie came in and looked at him questioningly.

'Just the same,' he said calmly.

Soon the neighbours came with their frightened question: 'How is she?'

At ten o'clock the district nurse came.

'Nurse!' cried Paul, 'she'll continue like this for days.'

'She can't, Mr Morel,' said the nurse, 'she can't.'

At about eleven o'clock he went downstairs and sat in the neighbours' house. Suddenly Annie came flying across the garden crying: 'Paul – Paul – She's gone!'

In a second he was back in his own house and upstairs. They all stood back. He kneeled down and put his face to hers and his arms round her: 'My love – my love – oh my love,' he whispered again and again. 'My love – oh my love.'

Their father came home from work about four o'clock. He came silently into the house and sat down. Tired, he laid his black arms on the table. The serving girl hurried to give him his dinner. At last Paul said: 'You noticed the curtains were closed?'

Morel looked up. 'No!' he said, 'Why? Has she gone?'

528

'Yes.'

'When was that?'

'About twelve this morning.'

'Hm.'

He ate his dinner, washed and went upstairs to change. In a little while he went out. Paul went to get the doctor's certificate and to tell the men to come and measure for the coffin. When he got back about eight o'clock, the house was empty, except for her.

Her room was cold that had been warm for so long. She lay high on the bed, the shape of the covering from the upright feet was like a clean curve of snow, so silent. With a candle in his hand, he bent over her. She lay like a girl asleep and dreaming of her love. Only the hair as it curved back from her face was mixed with silver.

After two days the relations came for the funeral and the children had to welcome them. They buried her next to William in a terrible storm of rain and wind. The wet earth and all the white flowers shone with rain. Annie held Paul's arm and leaned forward. Down below, she saw a dark corner of William's coffin. The wooden box sank steadily. She was gone. The rain poured down and the crowd in black with their umbrellas turned away. The burial ground was empty under the pouring rain.

Paul went home and kept himself busy passing round drinks to the guests. His father sat in the kitchen with Mrs Morel's relations and cried, saying what a good woman she'd been and how he'd tried to do everything he could for her. Paul hated his father for his self-pity.

Chapter 15   The Death of Hope

Paul felt lonely and defeated. His mother had really supported his life. He wanted someone to help him, of their own choosing. But Clara was not strong enough for him to hold on to. She wanted him, but did not want to understand him. If no one was willing to help him, he would go on alone.

Baxter Dawes was almost completely recovered from his illness. He had found a job and a place to live in Sheffield. He was going to start work on Monday. Paul knew that his own relationship with Clara was over and that she would go back to Dawes. She did in fact go with her husband to Sheffield and Paul scarcely saw her again.

There was little affectionate feeling between father and son. As there was no one to keep the home together, and as neither of them could accept the emptiness of the house, Paul took a room in Nottingham and Morel went to live with a friendly family in Bestwood.

Paul's life had fallen to pieces. He could not paint. At work there was no Clara. There was nothing left. Everything seemed so different, so unreal. There seemed no reason why people should walk along the street or why houses should stand in their places. The most real thing to him was the thick darkness of night. That seemed whole and meaningful and restful. Sitting alone in his room, he heard two voices in his head.

'What am I doing?'

'Destroying myself.'

'That's wrong.'

'Why wrong?'

'She's dead. What was it all for, her struggle?'

'You're alive. You've got to stay alive for her sake, carry on for her. Go on with your painting.'

'Painting is not living.'

'Marry then, have children.'

'Marry who?'

'Miriam.'

But he did not trust this answer. Always alone, his soul swung first to the side of death, then stubbornly to the side of life. The real disaster was that he had nowhere to go, nothing to do, nothing to say and *was* nothing himself. He felt completely disconnected from other people.

He went by chance to church one Sunday evening, and there was Miriam a few rows in front of him. He found her outside after the service.

'What are you doing in town?' he asked.

'I'm staying at my cousin Anne's – just till tomorrow.'

He invited her to come back to his room for supper. They took the bus and scarcely spoke until they reached his place, on the edge of town. In his room supper was laid. Paul made coffee. Miriam told him shyly that she was going to train as a teacher at Broughton College.

'I suppose you're glad,' said Paul.

'Very glad.'

'Well, you'll find earning your own living isn't everything.'

After supper they sat by the fire facing each other.

'You've broken off with Clara?' Miriam asked.

'Yes.'

'You know,' she said, 'I think we ought to be married.'

'Why?'

'You're wasting yourself like this.'

'I'm not sure,' he said slowly, 'that marriage would be much good. You want to put me in your pocket and I would die there.'

'What will you do instead?' she asked.

'I don't know – go on, I suppose. Perhaps I'll go abroad.'

There was a long silence.

'Will you have me, to marry me?' he said in a very low voice.

'Do you want it?' she asked, deeply serious.

'Not much,' he replied with pain. 'And without marriage we can do nothing?'

'No,' she said, her voice like a deep bell. 'No, I think not.'

He went with her to her cousin's house and left her there. As he turned away, he felt the last foothold for him had gone. The town stretched away to the distance, a flat sea of lights. Behind him lay the country, with little points of light for more towns – the sea – the night – on and on! On every side the enormous dark silence seemed to be pressing him into nothingness; and yet, though so small and unimportant, he was *not* nothing.

'Mother!' he whispered in sharpest pain, 'Mother!' She was the only thing that helped him to remain himself among all this. And she was gone, a part of the earth again.

But no, he would not give in. He straightened himself and closed his lips firmly. He would not take that direction, to the darkness, to follow her. He walked towards the distant noise, the glowing golden lights of the city, quickly.

ACTIVITIES

Chapters 1–3

Before you read

1 In this story the educated daughter of an engineer is married to an uneducated man. What problems will they have in their marriage, do you think? Why?

After you read

2 Choose the correct answer.
   a Paul is Gertrude and Walter's
   (i) second child   (ii) third child   (iii) fourth child
   b Walter is
   (i) dishonest   (ii) unsuccessful   (iii) lazy
   c Life seems empty to Gertrude because
   (i) Walter is unkind to her.
   (ii) Walter is never at home.
   (iii) Walter is so different from her.
   d Gertrude is worried about William because
   (i) he's going to London.
   (ii) he doesn't look after himself.
   (iii) she doesn't like his friends.
3 Who does these things, and why?
   a He cuts it off.
   b He locks her out.
   c He follows her everywhere.
   d She sees it and laughs.
   e He burns them.
4 How do Gertrude's and Walter's feelings for each other change? Why?

Chapters 4–6

Before you read

5 William has gone to London. What effect will this have on Mrs Morel and Paul, do you think? Why?

533

6 Find these words in your dictionary.

appliance   candle   coffin   elastic stocking   engaged

Which of them go in the following spaces?

   a He wore a(n) . . . . . on his leg.

   b A washing machine is a kitchen . . . . . .

   c A(n) . . . . . is made of wax.

   d A(n) . . . . . is made of wood.

   e They are . . . . . to be married.

After you read

  7 Which of these sentences are true? Correct the false ones.

   a Paul doesn't have any friends.

   b Mrs Morel likes shopping.

   c William sends money regularly from London.

   d All the brothers like reading.

   e Gyp reminds William of his mother.

  8 Match the descriptions with the names on the left.

William	generous / sensitive / selfish
Paul	shallow / shy / dark-haired
Arthur	unable to show love / ambitious
Gyp	quick-tempered / pale / quiet
Miriam	fashionable / small

  9 How do these people feel about each other?

   a Paul and William

   b Mr Morel and William

   c Mr Morel and Arthur

   d Mrs Morel and Gyp

Chapters 7–9

Before you read

 10 What effect will William's death have on Mrs Morel and Paul, do you think? Why?

 11 Find these words in your dictionary.

exhibition   passionate   swing

Which of them go with the following words?

   a garden . . . . .   **b** art . . . . .   **c** . . . . . kiss

After you read

12 Do these things describe Miriam or Clara?

unhappily married / religious / passionate mouth

unfriendly / romantic / she isn't interested in her appearance

she doesn't like men / she touches Paul's imagination

she excites Paul / she doesn't find Paul's comments clever

13 Finish these sentences.

a Miriam encourages Paul to . . .

b Paul gets angry with Miriam because . . .

c Paul stops going to Willey Farm because . . .

d Mrs Morel feels proud because . . .

e Paul burns the bread because . . .

f Paul doesn't hit his father because . . .

g Paul grows more and more restless because . . .

14 Work with another student. Act out this conversation between Paul and his mother.

Student A: You are Paul. You want to marry Miriam. Say why.

Student B: You are Paul's mother. You want Paul to marry Clara. Say why.

Chapters 10–12

Before you read

15 Will Paul stay with Miriam, Clara or his mother, do you think? Why?

16 Find these words in your dictionary.

cherry impressed lace

Which of them is

a a material? **b** a fruit? **c** a feeling?

After you read

17 Who are these sentences about, and why?

a He is impressed

b She is embarrassed

c He nearly goes mad

d She's deeply unhappy

    e They work together

    f She sends him a book

    g She wants his soul

    h She is amazed

    i He has a feeling of failure

18 How are these things important to the story?

    a Jordan's **b** cherries **c** river **d** garden

Chapters 13–15

Before you read

19 Will Baxter Dawes be pleased to see Paul, do you think? Why, or why not?

20 Find the words *divorce* and *cancer* in your dictionary. Make sentences. Show the meaning of each word clearly.

After you read

21 How does the relationship between Paul and Dawes change during the last three chapters? Why?

22 'For Paul, the fire of love slowly died away.' (page 519) Why?

23 How does Paul help his mother to die more quickly?

24 Who says or feels these things, and why?

    a 'It's what I deserve.' (page 525)

    b 'You noticed the curtains were closed?' (page 528)

    c There seemed no reason why people should walk along the street. (page 530)

    d He felt the last foothold for him had gone. (page 532)

Writing

25 Just after the end of the story, Miriam and Clara meet. They discuss and compare their opinions of Paul's good and bad points. Write their conversation.

26 You are Paul. Write a letter to Miriam on her twenty-first birthday (page 505). Tell her why you want to finish your relationship with her.

27 At Mrs Morel's funeral, Mr Morel tells her relations what a good woman she was and how he tried to be a good husband. Write what he says.

28 Who do you feel most sorry for at the end of the story? Why?